Praise for *Business Basics for Musici*

"In this day and age, it's irresponsible for an artist to enter the music industry without having a grasp of the business. This book should be required reading for all industry neophytes."

—STEVE VAI, internationally renowned guitarist

"As a veteran of both the creative and business sides of the industry, Bobby has the background necessary to assist artists and explain the changes in the business in a way that is easily understood."

—STEVE WINOGRADSKY, attorney and author, *Music Publishing: The Complete Guide*

"There are many books out there dealing with the music business, but Bobby's book has a special and important perspective—that of the working musician."

—MARK GOLDSTEIN, former senior vice president of business affairs at Warner Bros. Records

"Thoughtful, insightful, sobering and—above all—useful insights and advice for anyone in need of a road map through the tangled jungle that is the new music industry."

—MARK NARDONE, senior editor, *Music Connection* magazine

"If you can read this sentence, you are already more than qualified to be an international rock superstar. If you can read this book, you might even get your music into the marketplace with a price tag on it, and actually make a couple of bucks in the process, too."

—MIKE INEZ, Alice in Chains

"The information in Bobby's book is worth its weight in gold; it can mean the difference between succeeding and failing in the new music business. In his second life, Bobby will be reincarnated as a music attorney. This book is a must-read!"

—DINA LAPOLT, entertainment attorney at LaPolt Law, P.C.

"Bobby's book is an easy read. It gives a synopsis of our business today—a great quick reference guide for anyone interested in the new business of music."

—FRED CROSHAL, CEO of Croshal Entertainment Group and former general manager of Maverick Records

Business Basics for Musicians

Business Basics for Musicians

The Complete Handbook from Start to Success

Bobby Borg

Hal Leonard Books
An Imprint of Hal Leonard Corporation

Published in 2015 by Hal Leonard Books
An Imprint of Hal Leonard Corporation
7777 West Bluemound Road
Milwaukee, WI 53213

Trade Book Division Editorial Offices
33 Plymouth St., Montclair, NJ 07042

Printed in the United States of America

Book design by Kristina Rolander

Library of Congress Cataloging-in-Publication Data

Borg, Bobby, author.
Business basics for musicians : the complete handbook from start to success / Bobby Borg.
pages ; cm -- (Music pro guides)
Includes index.
ISBN 978-1-4950-0776-7
1. Music trade--United States--Vocational guidance. 2. Music trade--United States--Handbooks, manuals, etc. I. Title.
ML3790.B6786 2015
780.23'73--dc23

2015024274

www.halleonardbooks.com

Contents

Preface

Why should you read this book? Most musicians spend years developing their musical talent only to learn about the music business the hard way—one mistake at a time. Focused on their creative passions and the dream of an exciting career, musicians often leave business matters entirely in the hands of others. As a result, they are frequently taken advantage of, or they develop unrealistic expectations which inevitably are not met. But, if you want music to be your livelihood, you must treat it as a business or the business will take advantage of you.

What inspired me to write this book? When setting out to revise *The Musician's Handbook* (my first work, used by top schools and talented artists nationwide), my objective was to carry on the tradition by providing the most up-to-date, accurate, and relevant information in a readable way. But, as I considered the vast changes in the music industry today, and studied the way in which information is consumed in our fast-paced, high-tech world, I identified a need for an extraordinary rendition of a classic—one that breaks down the basics into bite-sized chapters, bullet points, and memorable anecdotes, and that helps musicians navigate fundamental career matters from start to success. *Business Basics for Musicians* is the "layperson's guide to the music industry." It simplifies core essentials and decodes the latest issues, so that artists can focus more confidently on what they do best—create music!

How is this book different? *Business Basics for Musicians* contains invaluable tips for artists pursuing a career that only a musician who's lived through it can reveal. Along with my firsthand experiences and knowledge of the music business, this book includes one-on-one interviews, real-life anecdotes, and invaluable wisdom from a variety of industry professionals so readers can benefit from a broad perspective. And because I'm not affiliated with any one corporate entity, there's no question of bias—I'm able to offer candid views on every aspect of the music business. Fledgling attorneys, personal managers, producers, and anyone else interested in the music business can also benefit from reading this book, which will give them a solid foundation of industry knowledge and an invaluable view from the artist's side.

What does this book offer and how is it organized? *Business Basics for Musicians* is divided into five parts that cover the most important issues facing the business today:

- **Part 1—Career Execution:** This section gets musicians into the right mind-set for pursuing a career in today's music industry with "15 Tips for Career Success." Although the best lessons often come from experience, you can learn a great deal from those who have been down the path before you. Topics include creating your own destiny by being proactive, climbing through back windows when front doors aren't opening, and developing a realistic attitude by ignoring the media hype.
- **Part 2—Business Relationships:** This section covers the primary relationships in which you may find yourself: as a band member, solo artist, and employer; or as a contract employee or self-employed musician. Not only is it important to understand the differences between these relationships; it is equally important to understand the various business issues associated with each one. From the AFM and SAG-AFTRA new scale wages to the latest methods for running an effective team, these chapters give you the basics relevant to your career status.
- **Part 3—Pro Teams:** This section focuses on the many business professionals you may need to help you make the right career decisions. Individual chapters cover the vital roles played by entertainment attorneys, personal managers, business managers, talent agents, and record producers in the new music industry. It is important to understand not only what role each of these important team members plays, but also when in the development of your career their assistance is necessary.

- **Part 4—Deals and Dollars:** This section provides an analysis of new revenue streams, royalty payments, and fee structures for the digital age, including publishing royalties, live performance fees, and merchandising monies. Chapters also include copyright basics as they apply to today's business, the pros and cons of giving up your publishing rights, common misconceptions about touring, and the types of merchandising that may be considered. Overall, this section simplifies complex topics so you can make your way safely through the legal minefield of the music business. And finally . . .
- **Part 5—Future Predictions:** This section looks ahead and offers a realistic view of the music business in 2020, provided by professionals from every facet of the business.

So, who am I? I'm a former major label, independent, and DIY recording/touring artist with over 25 years' experience working alongside the most respected managers, producers, and A&R executives in the music industry. As an adjunct professor of music business, I teach at Musicians Institute and UCLA Extension, where I received the Distinguished Instructor of the Year award, and speak at Berklee College of Music and other prominent schools worldwide. I'm the author of *The Musician's Handbook*, *Music Marketing for the DIY Musician*, and over 1,000 magazine and blog articles. As the founder of Bobby Borg Consulting, I assist rising music professionals globally.

How should this book be used? The best way to read this book is from cover to cover so that you don't miss a single beat. However, *Business Basics for Musicians* is designed so that each section stands alone, and I encourage you to consult the individual chapters that are applicable to your personal career status. That way, you can get exactly what you want, when you need it. And for those of you who are really on the fast track, *Business Basics for Musicians* is full of boxed anecdotes that relate to important aspects of the text, making it easy to flip through these pages and read interesting real-life stories and facts. There are also chapter quizzes and assignments in the back if you want to test your knowledge. Note that every attempt has been made to keep the information current, but understand that the music business is ever changing—especially in the face of new technologies—so be sure to check in for articles at www.bobbyborg.com. Additionally, though *Business Basics for Musicians* is designed to provide you with a thorough understanding of the music business, every business situation you come across will be unique; therefore it's recommended that you also consider the advice of the appropriate professional.

Keep in mind that the music business is not easy to understand, and it will require some patience and work to do so. The information presented here is only as good as your desire to comprehend and use it. And a journey of a thousand miles begins with a single step.

With talent, preparation, and luck, you can have an extremely rewarding career in music, both creatively and financially. I hope you will find this book to be a valuable tool to help you to achieve your professional goals. Let's get to it!

THE FACTS, NOT THE FAIRY TALES

Business Basics for Musicians investigates the "realities" of the music business behind the glamorous fantasy world often portrayed in the media. It is designed to help you to understand the ins and outs of the music industry. At times it will seem harsh. But the more aware you are of the potential obstacles in your path, the better prepared you will be to overcome them. Make no mistake, the purpose of this book is to encourage, and never to discourage. Whether you're out on the road or just getting ready to cut your first record, it pays to be armed with as much ammunition as possible. Perhaps these quotes from a book popular among music industry executives will help illustrate my point:

> Know yourself and know your enemy and you will fight a hundred battles without disaster.
> Know the ground, know the weather; your victory will then be total.
>
> —Sun Tzu, from *The Art of War*

Acknowledgments

Thanks to my dearest Dad; family; closest friends; UCLA and Musicians Institute staff; and John Cerullo, Jessica Burr, Zahra Brown, Wes Seeley, and everyone else at Hal Leonard Performing Arts Publishing Group for understanding my vision and making this book possible.

Thanks to my technical advisors, consultants, focus group members, proofreaders, and close friends, and those directly involved with the development of this book: Michael Eames (president, PEN Music Group, Inc.); Neil J. Gillis (president, Round Hill Music); Kyle Staggs (director, Music Business Affairs at Universal Pictures); Brad Andersen (head of touring, Global Merchandising Services); Bob Fierro (president, Zebra Marketing); Sidney Kibodeaux White (SAG-AFTRA); Stephanie Taub (national director, Sound Recordings, SAG-AFTRA); John Pantle (agent at APA Talent and Literary Agency); Justin Paul (founder, Playloop Records); Karl Louis (Moral Compass Management); Aaron Meza (adjunct professor, Musicians Institute); Dina LaPolt (LaPolt Law P.C.); Burgundy Morgan, Esq.; Steven Winogradsky, Esq.; Shawna Hilleary, Esq. (Artist Law Group); Jeff Cohen, Esq. (Millen, White, Zelano, and Branigan); Marty O'Toole, Esq.; Ben McLane, Esq.; Robert Nathan (law consultant); Ryan D. Kuper (founder, Redemption Records/Balance Entertainment); Britt Draska (consultant and director of royalties, formerly at Lakeshore Entertainment Group); Brian Perera (president, Cleopatra Records); Rob "Blasko" Nicholson (Mercenary Management, bass player for Ozzy Osbourne); Robert Shahnazarian, Jr. (producer of Killers, Incubus, John Legend, and others); Jeff Weber (Weberworks Entertainment Group); Geza X (producer of Black Flag and others); Samm Brown III (award-winning record producer and songwriter); Michael Levine (Levine Communications Office); Jeff Hinkle (Gudvi, Sussman & Oppenheim); George Fernandez (Deloitte Consulting, certified public accountant); Sharon Gilday (Down to Earth Business Management); Ian Copeland (Frontier Booking International); Michael Laskow (CEO of TAXI); Pascale Halm (director, UCLA Extension); Mike Inez (bass, Alice in Chains); Randy Castillo (drummer, Ozzy Osbourne); Chris Arnstein (tour manager); Don Gorder (chair and founder, Music Business / Management Department, Berklee College of Music); Tony van Veen (CEO, AVL Digital Group, CD Baby, Disc Makers); John Hartmann (former manager of Peter, Paul & Mary; Crosby, Stills & Nash; America; Poco; the Eagles; and others); Chaz Austin (Ed.D.; former career development director, Musicians Institute; author of *How to Find Work and Keep Finding Work for the Rest of Your Life*); Dan Kimpel (author of *It All Begins with the Music: Developing Successful Artists and Careers for the New Music Business*); Ira S. Kalb (professor of marketing at the Marshall School of Business at University of Southern California; president, Kalb & Associates); Fred Croshal (Croshal Entertainment Group, LLC); and Mike Gormley (LA Personal Management; former manager of the Bangles, Oingo Boingo, and Danny Elfman).

Thanks to all of the educational institutions that use this book, to my UCLA panelists, and to those from whom I have obtained invaluable advice throughout the years. You know who you are. For a more complete list, see www.bobbyborg.com.

Business Basics for Musicians

Part 1
Career Execution

1

Pursuing a Career in the New Music Industry

15 Tips for Career Success

"The music business is a cruel and shallow money trench; a long plastic hallway where thieves and pimps run free, and good men die like dogs. There's also a negative side."
—Hunter S. Thompson

Let there be no mistake—pursuing a career in the music industry is not easy, nor is it for the thin-skinned. The successful musicians you see today in the media—getting millions of hits on YouTube, performing before large audiences at the coolest music festivals, or getting reviewed on popular music blogs—represent only a minuscule percentage of all the musicians in, or trying to break into, the music business today.

Knowing these odds, why would anyone continue to pursue a career in the music business? The love of playing music, the tools and technology of the digital age, and the success stories of hardworking artists inspire plenty of people to try. After all, why can't you be one of the lucky ones who achieves tremendous success, or at least makes ends meet, doing what you love as an independent musician? You're talented, you're smart, and you're reading this book to better understand the inner workings of the music industry. You've already got a lot going in your favor!

While there are no rules or set guidelines that can guarantee a prosperous and long-lasting career, I've outlined 15 general tips for career success—from visualizing your dreams to being proactive. Whether you are a rapper, DJ, producer, songwriter, solo artist, band, or anyone else wishing for a successful career in music, these useful tips apply to you!

Tip #1: Realize Your Dreams by Visualizing Them First

The first tip for pursuing a successful career in the music business deals with having a clear vision of what you'd like to achieve. You must see, feel, and believe in the potential outcome. If you can clearly hold a picture of success in your mind, your subconscious can bring it to pass.

In the early 1990s, in a small club called the Button South in Fort Lauderdale, Florida, I witnessed Marilyn Manson gaze out into the audience and say, "One day I'm going to be a pop star who shocks the world." He truly believed this. Friends tell me he even kept drawings in a notebook mapping out precisely what his success would look like. With years of hard work, and one successful album and tour after another, Manson made his vision complete.

In his best-selling book *The Power of Your Subconscious Mind*, author Joseph Murphy calls this the "mental-movie method." In his words, "If I act as though I am . . . I will be."

Tip #2: Analyze Your Career Motivations

Dovetailing nicely from tip number 1, another important tip for career success is to consider just why you are pursuing a career in the music business. Is it for the fun and crazy lifestyle it may offer? Is it for the artistic respect it may earn you among your peers? Or is it for the spiritual satisfaction it may bring, and because there is nothing else in life you would rather do? As you know, fun, artistic respect, and spirituality are not always aligned. Thus, your answers to the above questions are crucial!

By understanding your true motivations and what's most important, you'll stand firm about what you are (and are not) willing to give up in order to succeed. You'll surround yourself with people who share your vision and are willing to pay allegiance to that flag. And you'll accept the consequences of your actions and not whine and bitch about the results in the end.

Tour manager/agent/promoter Chris Arnstein calls this approach to self-awareness the "decision-making tree." Your career decisions (or branches) should be based on the core (or root) of who you truly are as a person. Without this level of self-awareness, you can easily go astray in this business. As they say, if you don't stand for something, you can easily fall for everything.

If you haven't thought about your real motivation for pursuing music professionally, now is a good time to do so.

Tip #3: Develop a Realistic Outlook by Ignoring the Media Hype

You'll enter the music business from a much stronger position if you refuse to be blinded by all of the media hype or glamour you see and hear in music videos, magazines, and news shows. The expensive houses and yachts and the carefree attitudes and overnight success stories are often spun to make it look like the music business is an easy path to the good times. The truth is that these "riches" that artists flaunt are often leased, loaned, advanced, or purchased via other businesses and investments just to help a celebrity "look the part."

By developing a realistic outlook, you'll be better prepared for what may lie ahead and more accepting of this wonderful and crazy business of music. You'll understand that it could take a great deal of time and money honing your professional skills, building a fan base, and putting up with a great deal of rejection just to get ahead. But you'll be okay with that. You'll know deep down inside that the true talents of music lived and breathed their art with no thoughts of ever turning back, and that this determination and tenacity in regard to your craft and career is precisely what is required of you.

So get your head together! Focus on the realities of the business, not the fairy tales.

Tip #4: Be Ready to Pay Your Dues, but Use Your Head

One of those unavoidable realities of the music business is that pursuing a career will mean paying your dues.

Paying your dues essentially means paying the price for your lack of professional experience. That price is your time and hard work, which may yield little or no compensation (in other words, you work for free).

However, keep in mind that the more experience you gain, the more valuable a commodity you become. The day will arrive when you're justly compensated—whether you are a vocalist singing background sessions, or a band paying promoters to play local clubs.

Just remember to stay focused on the bigger picture. It's not always what you earn, but what you learn that matters. Of all the tips for career success, this ranks extremely high.

WARNING: KNOW YOUR PERSONAL BOUNDARIES

While on the topic of paying your dues, you should know that there are many people in the business who will take advantage of your inexperience and make you pay more than your usual dues. Welcome to the "school of hard knocks," or, as some call it, "the new kid" treatment.

In the classic movie *Swimming with Sharks*, an intern is embarrassed, harassed, insulted, and even bullied by his boss. The intern bravely tolerates this abuse, all in the name of moving up the ladder to success, but it eventually takes a serious toll on him.

Should you feel that you are being treated unfairly, stay focused on the bigger picture. Think of the situation as only a stepping stone toward achieving your ultimate vision.

However, know your personal boundaries and what you will and will not tolerate. No matter how big the gig may be, draw the line if you feel that the outcome may have a negative impact on your psyche, or if you generally feel that you're being ripped off! Nothing is worth more than your self-respect and dignity. Don't forget it!

Tip #5: Expect the Worst to Happen So That the Worst Won't Seem So Bad

At 1/3 of the way through our 15 tips, I think you're in the right mind-set already to hear one of the toughest tips for pursuing a career in music. Ready for it? Here goes: expect the worst to happen, because it will! The good news, however, is that you can be prepared for it.

Remember the old saying, "Shit happens!" Recordings sell poorly, bloggers write unfavorable reviews, and people will try to rip you off. Such events are an inevitable part of pursuing a career in music and an aspect that's certainly not for the thin-skinned.

Expect to be knocked down, but learn how to get up quickly and see the lesson in every negative experience. Realize you can't control everything that happens in this crazy business, but you can definitely control your attitude. You must focus on the positive. To survive in the biz, you must be resilient and prepared to fight forward.

As Jon Kabat-Zinn says in his book *Wherever You Go, There You Are*, "You can't stop the waves, but you can surely learn to surf."

Tip #6: Let Go of Your Fears and Learn How to Go for It

According to Danny Sugerman and Jerry Hopkins' book *No One Here Gets Out Alive*, Jim Morrison once asked, "If your life was a movie, would anyone want to watch it?" For many artists, the answer is a flat "no." They take a "one-foot-in/one-foot-out" approach to their careers and never dive in fully.

Jared Leto of Thirty Seconds to Mars pursued various opportunities in Washington, D.C.; New York; and Philadelphia before moving out west to pursue his vision as an actor and rocker. He saved a couple hundred dollars, packed a backpack, and bought a one-way ticket to Los Angeles. With an Academy Award for Best Supporting Actor and over 10 million records sold, the rest, as they say, is history.

If you have what it takes—if you're realistic, smart, and talented—then what's holding you back from giving your career your best shot? Is it the fear of moving to the big city, fear of rejection, or fear of going broke? Whatever it is, remember that fear is only a thought that can replaced by more positive thoughts. As boxer Mike Tyson said during his years as the world champion, "Fear is like fire. It can either cook for you, or it can burn you. Let it cook for you."

Look, what's the worst that can happen, anyway? You might fall short of your dreams, but you'll at least know that you gave your career your best shot. You'll have no regrets! And that, my friends, is priceless! So let go of your fears and learn to go for it. You'll be glad you did.

Tip #7: Form Solid Connections in the "Clique of the Future"

Make no mistake that networking is a vital part of establishing a successful career in the music industry. But rather than using all your energy trying to break into established and seemingly impenetrable cliques, be sure to recognize others who are talented, intelligent, and ambitious (like your fellow students or local musicians), and create your own "clique of the future." Get in on the "ground floor" and form solid relationships that will last forever.

I got my first break recording in Jimi Hendrix's Electric Lady Studios in New York City when two of my longtime college buddies from Berklee College of Music looked me up after graduating. As a result of getting that studio gig, I was able to move from Boston to New York City and start my career in the majors. Thanks, Nunzio and Dave!

Look, gang, a lot really does depend on whom you know—and who knows you! The majority of the work you do will be based on word-of-mouth recommendations and personal relationships you form over the years. So be sure to put yourself in situations where you can meet others who are already doing what you want to do, and who are working toward similar goals.

Great places to network and make new connections include college courses, songwriting workshops, networking groups, jam sessions, and music conventions. A few conventions worth checking out include MIDEM (www.midem.com), SXSW (www.sxsw.com), CMJ (www.cmj.com), Durango Songwriters Expo (www.durango-songwriters-expo.com), and West Coast Songwriters (www.westcoastsongwriters.org/conference).

Finally, for a great read that will improve your ability to form solid relationships, check out Dale Carnegie's best-selling book *How to Win Friends and Influence People*.

Tip #8: Nurture New Opportunities While You're Already On the Job

Yet another important tip for career success deals with "connecting the dots" and seeking out opportunity. Be clear that the best time to find work is when you're already working.

If you're currently an employee or a member of a band, use your situation to make new connections. People who see you perform in situations where you feel confident can help you find new opportunities down the road. My friend Mike Inez (now with Alice in Chains and Heart) originally played bass with Ozzy Osbourne when Alice in Chains was Ozzy's opening act. He was able to connect one gig to the next and stay working for years.

Remember that nurturing new career opportunities while you're still on the job is not deceptive or dishonest; it is a must for survival. The music business is very fickle. Tours are canceled, record releases are postponed, bands are suddenly dumped, music supervisors decide not to use your songs, and producers decide not to use your beats. That's the reality! And you must be prepared if you want to stay working.

It's only natural for younger musicians to believe that their current musical relationships will exist indefinitely—and they very well might. However, in the words of Miyamoto Musashi in *The Book of Five Rings*: "The best time to prepare for adversity is when all appears calm."

A BIRD IN THE HAND IS WORTH TWO IN THE BUSH

It's important to take advantage of every opportunity to make connections and find work, but not at the expense of your current situation.

A musician who was working with a very successful singer/songwriter (Billy Joel) was growing tired of his life on the road. When he heard of an audition to be part of the house band for a television talk show, he jumped at the opportunity.

But to make the audition, the musician had to back out of a prior obligation to Joel. As it turns out, the musician not only failed to get the television gig, but he was also fired from Joel's band for being unreliable.

Remember, if you make a commitment to an employer, band, or cowriter, you must honor it first or suffer the consequences. While networking is important, maintaining the highest professional standard should be your top priority.

Tip #9: Climb Through Back Windows When Front Doors Aren't Opening

If doors aren't opening, then climb through back windows. As the old saying goes, the definition of insanity is doing the same thing over and over and expecting different results.

To demonstrate this concept, instead of trying to put your recording directly into the hands of higher-ups who are unapproachable and standoffish, get to know these people personally in more casual settings.

Jeff "Skunk" Baxter of the classic group the Doobie Brothers says, "It doesn't matter whether you're driving an equipment truck or sweeping studio floors; get yourself into the music business any way you can."

You may find that working as an intern for a publishing company or writing for a local music magazine provides great opportunities to make connections. You'll have the opportunity to get to know people more naturally than you will in situations that make you appear desperate and needy.

Look, whatever it is you're trying to accomplish, consider a variety of approaches to achieving your goals. It's important to be tenacious and not to abandon your initial plan of attack, but banging your head against the same stone wall is pointless.

Tip #10: Create Your Own Destiny by Being Proactive

With only 1/3 of our 15 tips left, it's a good idea to talk about proactivity! It's not enough to gain employment or opportunity by simply being good. You need to take control of your career and create your own destiny. Attract attention to those who can help you by first helping yourself.

Consider the following:

- If you're a musician who wants to be known as a dynamic live player or a killer studio cat, then form your band and post videos of you performing covers on YouTube. It worked recently for Arnel Pineda, who bypassed millions and got the gig with Journey.
- If you're a songwriter who wants to get your music placed with successful artists and in television commercials and films, then start composing for student films. It worked for indie artist Jonathan Coulton, who works steadily.
- Finally, if you're a solo artist or band that wants to attract a manager, or record label, or major distributor, cut and release your own record first! It worked for Macklemore and Ryan Lewis. In fact, they won four Grammy Awards.

You'll be surprised by how many people you'll attract in the industry once you set the wheels in motion. This is what the do-it-yourself (DIY) movement is all about. In fact, everyone from band leaders to record company A&R to publishing people expect you to have a buzz before they'll even take a look at you. Simply put, if you don't DIY you die. Check out my book *Music Marketing for the DIY Musician* if you want to learn more about this fascinating subject.

Tip #11: Adapt to Change by Diversifying Yourself Now

Another success tip for pursuing a long-term career in music deals with diversification. It was Charles Darwin who once said, "It is not the strongest of species that tend to survive; it is those that are most adaptable to change." How true! It really does pay to broaden your career opportunities to increase your earning potential and "staying power" in the music business.

Dave Grohl, drummer for the grunge-rock sensation Nirvana, was able to transform his career after Kurt Cobain (Nirvana's lead singer/songwriter) took his own life. Grohl formed a new band, the Foo Fighters, and assumed the role of vocalist, guitarist, and songwriter. The Foo Fighters entered the *Billboard* charts at No. 24 with their first album and have enjoyed a successful career ever since with several studio albums, a string of hits, and numerous Grammy nominations. If Dave hadn't been prepared, he could easily have been at the end of his musical career.

So what's your plan to diversify? Is it like independent rapper J-Riv, who operates his own production studio, entertainment company, and urban clothing retail store (6th Ave Stylez)? Whatever it is, J-Riv said it simply in an interview with *Skewln* magazine, "I had to find a hustle that was legit, but at the same time relevant." Right on, J-Riv. I couldn't have said it better.

Tip #12: Be Practical About Money by Keeping It and Making It Grow

While on the topic of surviving for the long haul, remember that when you make money in the music business, you'll need to learn how to save it and make it grow. There are far too many musicians who "hit the big time" only to end up penniless.

By 2006, producer Scott Storch (Beyoncé, 50 Cent, The Game) had amassed a fortune worth $70 million. As a result of living a lavish lifestyle (he maintained a $10 million home in Miami, a private jet, a 117-foot yacht, 20 luxury cars, and a cocaine habit), Storch was in dire straits by 2007. In 2009, he filed for bankruptcy. Certainly, he wasn't watching and respecting his money, or his life. What a shame!

On the flip side, most super wealthy people, like Donald Trump, swear they are extremely conservative with money despite their conspicuous consumption. In the book *Trump: How to Get Rich*, the Donald says it himself: "I still turn off the lights in every room I leave and I look for deals on shaving cream when shopping at Duane Reade. It's about respecting money."

So get smart and save and invest your money wisely! It doesn't take much to get started, so even if you have very few funds, speak with a successful financial planner. The money you invest today could be the money you depend on tomorrow.

AFTERTHOUGHT: GOT MORE MONEY? To learn more about money, try books like the best-selling *Think and Grow Rich* by Napoleon Hill and *The Wealthy Barber* by David Chilton. Also check out magazines and newspapers like *Business Week*, *Entrepreneur*, and the *Wall Street Journal*.

Tip #13: Maintain Control in the Face of Drugs and Alcohol

Moving on to a point that may be a bit sensitive, I've got to bring up the issue of addiction. Drugs and alcohol are a big part of the music culture and have led to the downfall of many successful artists and bands. What might begin as casual partying can end up spiraling out of control.

Keep yourself and your band members in check before your life turns into a train wreck! If this advice means nothing to you, at least consider your professional responsibilities to the other members of your band, and to the people who have invested a lot of time and money in your career.

Also be aware that the industry is less tolerant of artists who have drug and alcohol problems than it was in the past. With other talent waiting in line to take your place, professionals simply don't have the time to waste on your personal issues.

So, in closing, if you think that you or your bandmates are developing a serious problem with drugs or alcohol, both Alcoholics Anonymous (AA) and Narcotics Anonymous (NA) offer free meetings in a city near you. Conduct a search online today and get to a meeting. This is no joke.

SAD BUT TRUE: DEATH, DRUGS, AND ROCK 'N' ROLL

Finding solutions to drug and alcohol problems is clearly beyond the scope of this book, but one thing's for sure—you're not going to find answers to your problems by indulging in extreme behavior. As illustrated below, the problems only worsen.

Mike McCready of Pearl Jam was nearly fired at the apex of the group's career because of his drinking. Steven Adler of Guns N' Roses was booted out of his band for drug abuse. And Scott Weiland of Stone Temple Pilots jeopardized the continued existence of his band after being jailed on drug possession charges.

Even worse, Layne Staley of Alice in Chains suffered from a heroin addiction that forced his band into a long hiatus, then killed him when he overdosed. Singer/songwriter Amy Winehouse died tragically of alcohol poisoning. And, in a situation that's very close to me, Jani Lane, the lead singer for one of the groups I worked with, died as a result of poor health conditions related to alcohol. Sad but true.

Tip #14: Remember That Finding Your Passion Is a Blessing Within Itself

As we approach the end of our list, it's a good time for a spiritual tip intended to have a profound, long-term effect on your path to success. Allow me to reflect on the gift of love, purpose, and music. I'm totally serious. Read on.

When I was very young, I knew precisely what I wanted to accomplish. I would wake each morning driven by a specific agenda—practicing, writing, promoting, etc. When I went to sleep at night, I reflected on what I had accomplished and always felt fulfilled. There has never been a wasted, sad, or lonely day in my life. I can't imagine things being any other way.

So rejoice and feel blessed! You too have something that moves you and gives your life meaning, something that gets you up in the middle of the night with pad and paper in hand to jot down that song idea. It's not about how much you accomplish, but the fact that you've found your inner self, your true purpose! Because, in the end, there's nothing greater than that!

Tip #15: Hang On to the Basics

Of course, there is not one way to succeed and thrive in the music business. However, with the preceding tips in mind, up-and-coming artists should at least remember these important basics.

Focus on your craft first—put in your time—and be great. Write amazing songs, be amazing on stage, make fans love you and kids want to be like you, and believe in yourself for many, many, many years. Hang out and meet people—support other bands and form powerful alliances. Put your music up on the Internet and let your audience know that you exist. Give fans a reason to care.

If the heavens are all aligned, then perhaps things will happen. Till that big day, learn how to bring in income on your axe so that you at least won't kill yourself at a random day job you hate. Know the business and don't look for handouts (desperation is repulsive). Have a vision and a clear strategy to get there, and stay away from the haters. They are vampires and will drain your spirit. Always stay positive and never whine.

Hopefully, the rest, as they say, will be your amazing history. Peace and good luck!

Q&A with Success Coach and PR Expert Michael Levine

Los Angeles PR firm Levine Communications Office (LCO) has represented many diverse celebrities, such as Michael Jackson, Michael J. Fox, and Kareem Abdul-Jabbar. Michael Levine has also provided media counsel to three U.S. presidents and is the author of 17 books, including the best-selling *Guerrilla P.R.* He lectures at universities and corporations on the topic of success and efficiency, which he discusses here.

Q: What are the most common attributes of the super successful?

M.L.: I've found the super successful possess three qualities I call the "Three Magic O's": 1. Obsession, 2. Optimism, 3. Obligation.

Q: Obsession?

M.L.: Super successful people are obsessed! Obsession is not ambition. Obsession is a burning maniacal rage as if their lives depended on it.

Michael Jordan did not play basketball by telling his teammates, "Guys, look, we have a challenging and important game tonight. If we win, we win; if we lose, we lose. Let's have a good time and just see what happens." On the contrary, Jordan played basketball as if his life depended on it. Barack Obama ran for president as if his life depended on it. You get the idea!

If I were to ask the readers of this book to perform a specific task, like selling a thousand tickets in a week's time, they might tell me that it is impossible given their circumstances—and this might very well be true.

However, if I were to reach into my pocket, stick a Colt .45 revolver down their throats, and tell them to sell the tickets, I guarantee that some way and somehow they'd get the job done. Why? Because now their lives would depend on it! I've found that all super successful people possess a burning maniacal rage to succeed at all costs, as if their lives depended on it.

Q: Optimism?

M.L.: The super successful believe that if you work really, really hard for a long, long period of time, tomorrow could be better than today. They have this paradoxical sense that while the game is not easy and the game is not fair, the game is winnable—as long as you have enough focused intensity.

Make no mistake, optimism, or, more specifically, "perpetual optimism," is a force multiplier. General Colin Powell spoke of perpetual optimism. If you took 10 men and saturated them with optimism, those 10 men could fight with the force of 50. If you took the same 10 men and saturated them with negativity, they couldn't fight with the force of 2.

Remember, the game is absolutely winnable if you truly believe it to be.

Q: Obligation?

M.L.: Super successful people have a sense of responsibility and are never flaky. "Flaky" is another word for "loser."

When they say they are going to do something, they do, and they do it on time. And on the rare occasions when they don't complete an assignment, they blame only themselves—not the weather and not the state of the entertainment industry. They make themselves 100 percent responsible and are never victims.

Super successful people value their time and never maintain relationships with flaky friends, colleagues, and band members. There is nothing worse than inhaling the secondhand fumes of flakiness. So I'd like to suggest to your readers that if they want to be super successful, they fire their flaky friends. Get rid of them all. If you want to be the best, then surround yourself with people who hold high standards.

Q: Your top 10 "must dos" for a successful career?

M.L.: To close this interview, I'll give your readers 10 concise and essential tips:

1. Recognize that if your goals are not written, they are not goals; they are just dreams. Create a solid game plan and keep it in a place where you can refer to it regularly.
2. Realize that your product is important, but not as important as promoting it. If people don't know you exist, it doesn't matter how good you think you are.
3. Remember that it's not what you know; it's whom you know, and who wants to know you.
4. Nurture strong relationships by frequenting specific events (mixers, seminars, and classes) where good, inspired people congregate.
5. Create mastermind alliances or partnerships with friends who truly share the same life aspirations as you.
6. Join an internship program with a successful company and work for free to experience how the industry operates from the inside. You can always volunteer at annual conventions or other events to learn the ropes.
7. Find a mentor, a trusted counselor or guide, who believes in you. Just be equally prepared to give back to the mentor, whether you bake him an apple pie, run his errands, or hang out with him at a ball game.
8. Get out of your own fucking narcissistic self-involvement. Most creative people are suffering from an acute case of narcissism—it's all about their dreams, their careers, and their wealth. Enough! Get interested in others and in the world around you. It will make you a richer, finer, kinder, more interesting artist and human being.
9. Don't be afraid to take chances and go for it! Fear plays an enormous role in the underachievement of human beings.
10. Be good at what you do, and love it! You absolutely have to love it. Because, when the going gets tough, the love for your craft is what gets you through.

Part 2
Business Relationships

2

Band Membership, Part 1

Formation and Self-Management

"Individually we are an ass; but together, we are a genius!" —Rush

Being a member of a band is not much different from being a member of a professional sports team: you're a group of individuals united in the pursuit of a common goal, each person playing a unique and integral part in achieving a vision. The motto—at least in theory—is "All for one and one for all."

But unlike young athletes, who are expected to meet extremely high standards before being drafted by a professional team, young musicians unite merely because they listen to the right music, have the right haircuts, and play the right instruments. While these attributes are all important, they are unfortunately not enough to create and sustain a successful band.

To ensure that your band has a fighting chance, this chapter reveals where and how to look for musicians, criteria for choosing band members, and the day-to-day operating rules for a band. In the next chapter, I'll cover band membership agreements and close with an interview with attorney Jeff Cohen on trademarks and business entities. Now, let's get this show started.

How and Where to Look for Musicians

The first step in creating a solid band is knowing where and how to look for musicians. While you may think the process is an intuitive one, you would be surprised at the number of musicians—even those living in larger cities like Los Angeles and New York—that don't consider all of the possibilities. What follows is a short list to help you get started with your search.

- ***Go to Open Jams:*** Attend local jam sessions and introduce yourself to other musicians. I've run into some serious players hanging out at jam sessions over the years.
- ***Ask Other Bands:*** Attend the shows of established bands in your hometown and ask them for referrals. Great musicians usually know other great musicians.
- ***Steal Musicians:*** Attend the shows of established bands in your hometown and steal their musicians. Just don't create too many enemies in the process.
- ***Ask Local Music Stores:*** Visit your local music stores and put out the word. Needless to say, music stores attract working musicians, and sales reps may be able to recommend some great players.
- ***Contact Local Magazines/Stations:*** Ask local music journalists and radio DJs to make recommendations. They've been covering your scene for years and may know a few available players.
- ***Contact Local Music Teachers:*** Ask local music teachers if they can refer a few eligible candidates. The best teachers usually teach the best musicians.

- ***Call Bookers/Bartenders:*** Call the bookers at local clubs and see if they have any suggestions. You might even speak with the bartenders that work at these clubs as well.
- ***Network at Conventions:*** Network at the NAMM show (www.namm.org) and other highly trafficked music conventions that attract musicians.
- ***Use Message Boards:*** Post a message on online discussion boards. Sometimes services like Craigslist (www.craigslist.com) actually work.
- ***Social Network:*** Stimulate the word of mouth on all of your social networks (Facebook, Twitter, etc.). Get your fans/friends to put out the word to their fans/friends too.
- ***Ask Tastemaker Fans:*** Ask *passionate* fans in your hometown if they know any available musicians. Some fans know your local scene better than anyone.
- ***Poster Rehearsal Rooms:*** Put up posters at local rehearsal complexes where bands are coming in and out. Someone is bound to see them and give you a call. And finally . . .
- ***Hang at Your Local Record Shop:*** Speak to people who work at your local comic and record shops. With all the musicians and music lovers coming through daily, they must know someone.

Don't give up if you don't immediately uncover some leads. And remember that the above list is by no means complete—so be sure to brainstorm your own ideas.

But once you've found some potential candidates, how do you know whether they are truly right for your band? Good question. It starts with having criteria for choosing members. Read on.

Criteria for Choosing Band Members

At first, when everyone in a band is excited and eager to get things rolling, character flaws and differences of opinion are often overlooked; but if problems are ignored, with the intention of dealing with them later, they always come back to bite you in the you-know-what.

For this reason, it is crucial that a band put together a list of requirements (or criteria) for forming. These should take into account the band's vision, the personality of each member, and the band's short-term goals with a breakdown of the work, schedule, and budget. All of these are discussed below.

Discuss the Band's Vision

The first step in assessing whether you have the right members in place is to discuss the band's long-term vision. A vision is where the group would like to see itself being in 5 to 10 years.

A clear vision serves as a group's North Star and guiding light. It is what motivates each member and keeps everyone moving in the same direction.

A vision is usually made up of the following elements:

- ***Style/Direction:*** What style of music does the band ultimately see itself playing?
- ***Revenue Generators:*** What products and services does the band see itself releasing?
- ***Level of Success:*** What strategic alliance is the band shooting for: major label, indie, or a DIY approach with a major-independent distributor?
- ***Values:*** What does the band stand for? And finally . . .
- ***Branding:*** What lasting vibe or attitude does the band see itself projecting onto the marketplace?

Without a general consensus of what everyone wants to one day achieve, a band is already starting off on the wrong foot.

While a vision is often discovered through experimentation and just figuring things out as you make one mistake after another, remember that you only have so many years to pursue a career in music freely before life's responsibilities start getting in the way.

Talking about a vision now helps ensure that everyone shares the same dream and it reduces the possibility of members bailing ship down the line. So talk about your vision today!

Use the Personality Questionnaire

The second step in determining whether the right members are in place is to consider the personalities of the individual members. This can be done with a personality questionnaire—an informal interview to help spot underlying flaws and determine whether you should proceed together in the music business.

Below are some questions you may want to include in your interview (note that I do not recommend presenting these questions to potential band members the moment you meet, but after you've jammed and are considering a long-term relationship):

- ***Tenacity:*** Do you believe in making music your life's career so strongly that, if in three years the group is still unsigned or struggling to "make it," you'll remain on board?
- ***Priority:*** How important are band rehearsals and other tasks in relation to your other commitments and social schedule?
- ***Continual Improvement:*** If the band should decide private lessons and individual practice time are what you need to get to the next level, would you be cool with this, or offended and hurt?
- ***Image:*** How open would you be to experimenting with—and changing—your visual image?
- ***Social Behavior:*** Do you drink, smoke, or do any drugs?
- ***Addiction:*** Do you have a problem with drinking, smoking, or doing any drugs?
- ***Contribution:*** How do you feel about working a regular part-time job so that you can help contribute to band expenses?
- ***Flexibility:*** Could you drop everything to go out on the road for several weeks at a time without being held back by domestic responsibilities?
- ***Ruggedness:*** Could you handle traveling cross-country in a small passenger van and sleeping in a hotel room with three other band members—for little or no money?
- ***Relocation:*** If the band should decide it was necessary and practical, would you relocate to another city?
- ***Relationships:*** If your significant other asked you to choose between staying in the relationship and staying in the band, what decision would you make?
- ***Exclusivity:*** Are you willing to make this band a priority over all of your other projects and work? And finally . . .
- ***Agenda:*** If you could be in the ultimate band, would that band be your own solo project?

Although the above questionnaire might seem rather intense and even scare off potential band members, trust that it will only scare off those musicians with whom you should never partner.

The last thing you want is to fire someone, have someone quit, or have the band break up over something stupid after spending several months, or years, building it from the ground up. Needless to say, this would be a horrible waste of time! Trust me, I'm speaking from experience.

FOUR CAPTAINS ON A SINKING SHIP

The following true story illustrates what can happen when the personalities of a band are not aligned.

A band that formed in California consisted of two members from New York and two members from Florida.

After investing a full year of time in the group, one of its members decided the band should move to New York because this was where his wife needed to be for her career. Another member wanted to stick to what he believed was the original plan of staying in California. The other two members suggested the band should move to their homeland of Florida simply because they hated California.

As it turns out, the entire band moved to Florida, but broke up shortly thereafter when one member reneged on his agreement and moved to New York anyway. What a headache!

If the musicians had considered and shared their priorities at the beginning, they might have realized they had no business being in a band together in the first place. This story is hardly an isolated incident, so don't let it happen to you.

Set Goals, Break Down the Work, and Estimate the Schedule/Costs

Moving on to the last step in assessing whether you have the right members in place, you should now set one-year goals (based on your long-term vision), break down the work required to achieve the goals, and estimate a schedule and costs.

This helps to identify any problems certain members may have with career planning/strategy, work ethic, finances, and time. Without uncovering these issues from the start, a band is quite likely to fail when all of its members begin to metaphorically row the oars of the boat in opposite directions, or decline to row at all.

Here's what a first draft schedule and estimate might look like for one year (divided into 4 quarters), with a grand total of the costs at the bottom:

- ***Overall Goals:*** *Release six-song debut EP, manufacture T-shirts with brand slogan, play eight shows locally in various alternative venues, and build a database of 5,000 fans.*
- ***Months 1–3 (Q1)***
    - Rent a rehearsal studio and meet four times a week.
    - Write 20 songs and hone the band's sound and direction.
    - Demo the best compositions and get feedback.
    - Define the band's image and meet with a fashion consultant.
- ***Months 4–6 (Q2)***
    - Complete an electronic press kit, including a professionally shot photo.
    - Hire a webmaster to build a professional website.
    - Book live performances locally, and start building a database of fans.
    - Assign promotional responsibilities to each member.
- ***Months 7–9 (Q3)***
    - Hire a songwriting coach and/or find a local producer.
    - Pay to record our best songs professionally.
    - Manufacture recordings and band merchandise.
    - Give-away and sell recordings/merchandise at shows and popular websites.
- ***Months 10–12 (Q4)***
    - Attend and showcase at networking conferences and conventions.
    - Enter songwriting competitions.
    - Contact music libraries and pluggers (those who can get music in films or TV).
    - Hire a music business consultant to assess career direction.
- ***Total Projected Budget:*** $15,000 ÷ 4 = $3,750 per member

So there you have it. In addition to serving as a great organizational tool and a forecast of the work and costs yet to come, the above exercise is an excellent method of ensuring that you have serious and like-minded members in place.

Being in a band requires clear goals, smart planning, money, and time. It takes a special breed of musician to make a group come to life. I wish you the best in finding the right team.

The Day-to-Day Operating Rules of the Band

Once you have your band members and schedule in place, you must now take measures to ensure the band will function effectively from day to day.

Thus, to close out this chapter, let's take a look at three very important areas to the functioning of a band: teamsmanship, conducting effective band meetings, and running rehearsals efficiently.

Talk About Teamsmanship

Teamsmanship covers the elements that enable the members of an organization to work effectively as a unit over the long term. Without it, I'm convinced that there is no way a band can complete its tasks and meet its goals on time, on budget, and to the desired standard. A healthy team is everything.

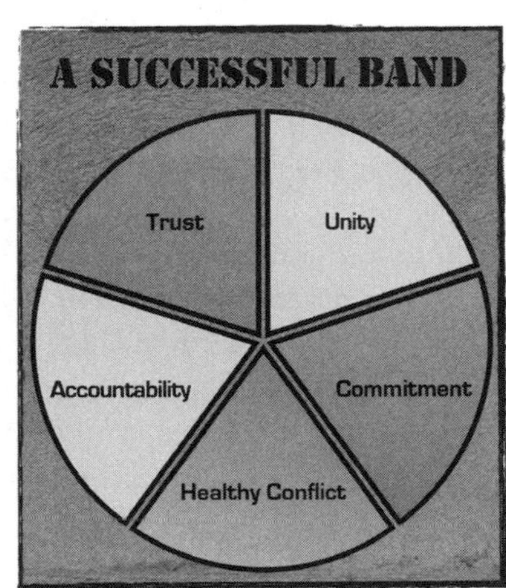

The elements necessary to run an effective team include the following:

- ***Trust:*** The confidence that all members can express themselves freely and be heard without feeling exposed, vulnerable, and as though their ideas are not valued
- ***Healthy Conflict:*** The reassurance that all members can openly debate problems that are important to the band and focus on quick resolutions without letting interpersonal issues get in the way
- ***Commitment:*** A pact that each member of the band will commit to the organization and buy into the long-term vision, even when things might not always be precisely as "you" think they should be
- ***Accountability:*** A vow that all members will hold themselves and each other accountable for screwing up (being late, making mistakes, having a bad attitude, etc.)
- ***Collective Results:*** A pledge that all decisions will be made for the collective good of the band first, and not for the gain of an individual member

The above standards are what help some of the world's most successful organizations come together effectively and succeed—from professional sports teams to multinational companies. And now your band can benefit, too. For more information on running a functional team, check out *The Five Dysfunctions of a Team* by Patrick Lencioni.

Hold Band Meetings That Don't Suck

The next important issue to the functioning of a band is holding effective meetings.

We've all heard of those infamous band meetings where members arrive late—only to talk (and sometimes scream) about important (and sometimes completely unimportant) matters in a disorganized fashion. Just watch the Metallica documentary *Some Kind of Monster* for a shocking dose of dysfunction.

By definition, meetings are formal gatherings of people, or committees, intended to update, debate, and solve various business matters. To ensure that your meetings go smoothly, checkout the following easy-to-execute tips:

- ***Schedule in Advance:*** Schedule your band meeting in advance at a convenient time for all. This can be done by using helpful tools like Doodle (www.doodle.com) or Meeting Wizard (www.meetingwizard.com).
- ***Choose a Convenient Location:*** Be sure the meetings are held in a convenient location, such as your rehearsal room. You can also hold "distant meetings" by using the Internet (www.Skype.com), or conference call (www.freeconferencecall.com).
- ***Distribute an Agenda in Advance:*** Write a clear agenda of specifically what will be discussed in the meeting. Submit the outline to all members in advance so that they can begin to formulate their questions and thoughts and talk with each other.
- ***Set a Limit:*** While the length of a meeting is determined by the agenda, try to keep meetings no longer than one hour, moving efficiently from one item to the next.
- ***Appoint a Representative and Set Ground Rules:*** Appoint one member to oversee the meetings. The leader opens the meetings, addresses each issue one at a time, and offers the members the floor (or right to comment) in an organized, respectful, and efficient manner. Cell phones and other distractions are prohibited from the meetings
- ***Vote on or Table Issues:*** After an issue is discussed, the representative "moves" to vote on it and waits for the members to approve or "second" the proposal. Should people feel an item needs further discussion, it can be "tabled" for the next meeting. The point is to keep the meeting moving forward and not let one issue dominate the discussion.
- ***Adjourn Meetings:*** The representative must officially close all meetings before members begin wandering off. I have been in countless situations where members start playing games of pool or firing up their amplifiers while others are still talking. And finally . . .
- ***Approve Minutes:*** After each meeting, the representative sends out a detailed e-mail of what was discussed and agreed upon to ensure there are no misunderstandings. Each member must approve the meeting minutes by simply responding with "approved."

The above methods may seem rather rigid and so un-rock 'n' roll-like, but remember that a band is a business, just like any other, and cutting through the bullshit that plagues so many bands is not a bad thing at all.

In fact, should you decide to incorporate your band (discussed more later), your group (or your elected "board" of members) is required to hold regularly scheduled meetings and keep detailed notes (or "minutes") of what was discussed. Yup, I bet you didn't know that!

No matter what your business entity, give the tips above a try. I wish that all my bands had! For more information, check out *Robert's Rules of Order* at www.robertsrules.com.

Run Your Rehearsals Effectively

The last issue important to the functioning of a band is running efficient rehearsals. To be sure, rehearsals are where you craft your songs and put together your live performance sets.

To ensure that you get the most out of your sessions (in both time and money), check out the following important tips on topics from finding the space to holding sectionals.

Decide on the Space

When a band, or just one member, is writing songs, it may not be necessary to have a full-size rehearsal space where you can set up a lot of equipment. Your home recording studio may be all you need. But in all other circumstances, there are essentially three rehearsal/writing options:

1. **Lockouts:** A lockout rehearsal room provides you 24-hour access and the luxury of keeping your gear set up, but you'll need to supply your own PA, mixer, and microphones and be able to afford the monthly rent. You can find smaller affordable lockouts ranging from about $500 to $700 monthly.
2. **Hourly Rooms:** An hourly rehearsal room provides convenience to those who don't want to commit to the monthly expense, but you'll have to rehearse on the studio's backline (drums, PA, and mixer) or otherwise drag in (and drag out) your own equipment. Hourly studios can run as cheap as $18 to $24 an hour.
3. **Personal Space:** Your personal rehearsal space (band's rental house, parent's house, etc.) affords many benefits. You have the luxury of keeping your gear set up, being surrounded by certain amenities (your kitchen, shower, backyard, etc.), and keeping a few more bucks in your pocket. However, you'll likely experience noise problems with your neighbors, and you won't have the liberty of rehearsing all night.

AFTERTHOUGHT: SHARING COSTS Rob Danson of the band Death to Anders reminds us that when getting a lockout studio, you can pair up with another band to share the rental costs. You'll probably have to move your gear off to the side on your nights off, but this is a small price to pay.

Make the Call

Once you've decided on the rehearsal room that's best for you, it's time to make a list of available places in your area and make the call. Consider the following:

- **Ask for Referrals:** Ask fellow artists you trust to recommend the most affordable and secure rehearsal spots in your town.
- **Conduct an Internet Search:** Use Google (www.google.com) to conduct a keyword search using something like "[your city] + rehearsal rooms."
- **Check Local Music Mags:** Flip to the back pages of your local music magazine or entertainment paper and you'll find plenty of ads for rehearsal rooms. In Los Angeles you'll discover services like Sound Arena, Downtown Rehearsal, and Swing House Studios.
- **Call a Realtor:** If you're interested in renting a band house where you can all live and rehearse, check the yellow pages online to find a realtor near you who can help.

With phone number in hand, contact these companies and specifically ask about their services (hourly or lockout), security measures, and costs. Ask them whether their fees include air conditioning/heating in their rooms and adequate parking.

When speaking with a realtor about renting a house, ask her to focus on more secluded residential areas of your town so that you can get away with playing louder and for longer.

Schedule Rehearsals and Meetings

Now that you have your rehearsal space in order, you need a regular practice schedule. Examine the personal schedules of all involved to consider the most convenient times and days, and then schedule three to four sessions a week, leaving a day or two off in between to avoid burnout.

If you schedule a rehearsal on a weekend night, consider ending it early so that members have time to catch other bands' performances, to network, to promote upcoming shows, and to simply have some free time for fun (after all, you are human).

Rehearse Before the Rehearsal

Whatever the objective for your next rehearsal session, remember this priority rehearsal tip: do your homework! It can save time and money, and prevent unnecessary tension.

Nothing is more unproductive than sitting around for an hour while a member figures out the chord changes to a song that could have been figured out at home. It's disrespectful to the fellow band members who came prepared, and it's a waste of your rent money, too.

Don't Show Up Late

Time is valuable—especially when you're shelling out precious rehearsal fees—so be sure to show up early for scheduled rehearsals.

If you have pedal boards, double bass pedals, or keyboard stands to set up (as you may when renting a studio by the hour), don't spend the first 30 minutes of rehearsal doing so. Set up your gear in pieces outside of the room in the hallway or parking lot, and then move it all into place upon your allocated time. This way you can immediately get started with your rehearsal.

No Noodling Around In Between Songs

Here's another time saver, courtesy of Rick King of Wall of Voodoo: "There's nothing more distracting, unproductive, and annoying than a member noodling around in between songs when others are trying to work out parts. Everyone must remain focused on the same agenda at all times."

I agree totally! There's a time to practice rudiments and scales, and there's a time to sit still and keep quiet.

Rehearse with a Click

Perhaps the best rehearsal tip I can offer is to use a click track. Whether you're rehearsing for a live performance or for a recording session, rehearsing with a click can train you to "hold back" during live performances when you're all pumped up from the crowd. It can also prepare you for recording sessions, where consistency of tempo from the beginning to the end of a song is crucial.

Your drummer can play along to a click by using a set of headphones and a Boss Dr. Beat metronome (www.bossus.com) plugged into a stereo amplifier. This will also give your drummer a chance to get used to using headphones, just like in the recording studio. Or if you prefer, your whole band can play along with a click by running it through a channel on your PA mixer (most rehearsal rooms that charge by the hour have a PA system). In any case, use a click!

Record Your Rehearsals

Rehearsals should be recorded to help uncover where tempos are pushing or pulling, where song arrangements are working or not working, and where set orders are flowing or not flowing.

A portable digital recorder is really all you need to get the job done. Just place it in a section of the room where you can capture the best sound, hit record, and verbally title the recording (e.g., *New Song #1, Set List A*, etc.).

Appoint a band member to review the recording, take notes, and report back to the band at the next rehearsal with needed improvements and suggestions. If you want to feel like you're really making progress, this tip is one of the most important to remember.

Hold Sectionals

Breaking up your rehearsals into different groups can help to isolate certain areas of concern and to remedy problems. For instance, the drummer and bassist can work on sections where the meter may be pushing and pulling, and the lead vocalist and background singer can tighten up harmonies.

Stephen Perkins, drummer for Jane's Addiction, notes that his band often holds sectionals without vocalist Perry Farrell. Says Perkins, "Without vocal cues to rely on, you really learn to communicate well as a rhythm section. Furthermore, it gives Perry an opportunity to rest his voice. Be sure to add sectionals to your rehearsal schedule. You'll be so much more productive."

AFTERTHOUGHT: PRACTICE LIKE IT'S LIVE Andrew Trout of Abandon Ship! reminds us to also rehearse the live performance aspect (choreography, what the singer is going to say between songs, etc.), and to get it on video for further study. It will really improve your live gigs.

Bring Spare Supplies

As we approach the end of our discussion on rehearsal tips, let's discuss spare parts.

To avoid ending your next rehearsal long before due, drummers and percussionists should carry extra snare heads and sticks, guitarists and bass players should carry extra strings and amp chords, and vocalists should bring a spare mic.

The last thing you want to do is spend your valuable rehearsal time racing around to find the nearest music store. Enough said!

Determine Your Guest Policy

A band must determine whether it wants its rehearsal sessions to be open to friends and family or kept private.

In the company of friends, you can run new sets and get immediate feedback. In private settings, you can work up new songs and arrangements without feeling pressured to entertain.

A possible solution: go for the best of both worlds. Schedule one evening of the week where friends can drop by at a specified time, and leave the other days of the week closed to your friends. But, whatever you do, determine a policy! Simply allowing friends to drop by as they wish will lead to unproductive sessions.

To Party or Not to Party?

And finally, for my last rehearsal tip, I suggest you create a party policy. Seriously! Hey, I'm not advocating this stuff, but beer and pot are nearly synonymous with a rock 'n' roll lifestyle.

Says producer/singer/songwriter Raphael Saadiq, "If passing around a joint before rehearsal gets everyone in the vibe to create like it does for me, than do as you will. But if certain members are known to lose focus and to get goofy, save the partying for later. There is a time for play, and a time for work. Keep your priorities straight."

Now that we've talked about forming and functioning as a band, in the next chapter I tackle the legal stuff: band memberships, trademarks, and business entities. Whenever you're ready to get started, just turn the page.

3

Band Membership, Part 2

Partnerships, Trademarks, and Business Entities

"Band agreements are like prenuptials. No one really wants one till the divorce."
—Burgundy Morgan, attorney

After reading chapter 2, you already know how important it is for bands to find the right members and set ground rules for operating like a functional team.

Now let's pick up where we left off and talk about band memberships, trademarks, and business entities. While most bands feel uncomfortable talking about this stuff, this chapter is one that can save you a mountain of frustration and millions of dollars. Read on!

Band Membership Agreements

Now that all of your members are in place and everyone is working together effectively as a team, it's time to define the terms of your business and legal relationship in a written agreement.

This document, called a "band membership agreement," compels a band to deal with important legal issues before they become problems.

Let's take a look at legal partnerships, key members and minority partners, hiring an attorney, and the basic elements of band membership agreements.

Your Band Is a Legal Partnership

The first step in understanding the importance of band membership agreements is to understand partnerships. Partnerships are formed when two or more people (like a band) come together and share willingly in the profits and losses of their business.

State partnership laws vary, but if a group does not have a written band agreement that stipulates anything to the contrary, all members may be presumed to have the following:

1. An equal right to the profits and financial losses of the band.
2. An equal say in making decisions.
3. The right to use the band name should they decide to leave the group, and . . .
4. Liability for the other members' negligence while conducting business.

Though most bands are usually fine with wanting everyone to have equal power and an equal share in the profits, sometimes members will want to break up the relationship based on their individual feelings (i.e., sometimes the founder, lead singer, or main songwriter may feel more entitled to a bigger share of the publishing or want to own the rights to the band name).

For the aforementioned reasons, the sooner a band can create a written band agreement that fleshes out important issues, the less likely the group will get held up in costly legal disputes that might occur down the road. So schedule a meeting and draft your band agreement today.

HIRE AN ATTORNEY OR DIY?

How should a band proceed with creating a band membership agreement? Good question! You can DIY or hire an attorney.

- ***Do It Yourself (DIY):*** In the early stages of a band's career, it may barely have enough money to pay for a rehearsal room, let alone an experienced music entertainment attorney. Fortunately, a number of resources, like Nolo (www.nolo.com) and LegalZoom (www.legalzoom.com), provide adequate form agreements. A helpful book that you may also want to check out is *Music Law: How to Run Your Band's Business*, by attorney Richard Stim.
- ***Hire an Attorney:*** As a band becomes more established and can save up a few hundred dollars (approximately $200 to $400), the members can now afford to hire an experienced entertainment attorney to draft a more customized band membership agreement. Just keep in mind that if the group is dividing up income and control disproportionately, each member may want to hire his or her own attorney to look at the agreement before signing it. You can get inexpensive legal advice by contacting your local office of the Volunteer Lawyers for the Arts.

Elements of Band Agreements: What to Include

Now that you have an understanding of partnerships and how various band members may want to divide the rights and controls, you can finally take a more detailed look at the elements of a band membership agreement.

According to attorney Jeff Cohen, band membership agreements should include the following 14 points at minimum:

1. ***Voting:*** How will the members vote on key issues—by unanimous vote (all of the members agree) or majority vote (more than half of the members agree)? Majority votes work fine for less serious matters. For deadlocks, one person can be appointed as the tiebreaker.
2. ***Division of Income:*** How will profits from merchandising, live performance fees, artist royalties, master recording licenses, and music publishing incomes be split? Although most bands usually split income equally to avoid dissension (at least in the beginning), sometimes the main songwriters or founders of the band are allotted a larger share, and/or they will even maintain the rights in certain assets (like copyrights and masters).
3. ***Purchases:*** What vote will permit the band to make equipment purchases? As an example, an investment under $250 may require a majority vote, while a purchase of over $500 may require a unanimous vote.
4. ***Investments:*** What happens to the assets acquired as a group when one member departs or is terminated? For equipment already owned, the band may buy out the departed member's share that he or she initially invested (less depreciation) by paying in full or making several smaller payments over a predetermined number of weeks or months.
5. ***Band Name:*** Who has the right to use the band name? A band will usually own the name as an asset and agree that departing or terminated members have no right to use the name on their own. When the band breaks up completely, all members must agree when any one member wants to continue using it.

6. ***Hiring and Firing:*** How will people be hired and fired? When hiring a manager, a unanimous vote may be required. When firing a member, a majority vote may be required. A band may also want to stipulate the conditions under which a band member may be terminated (for instance, not fulfilling his or her obligations to the band) and spell out the terms of a "cure provision," which gives the offending member a chance to fix a problem within a specified number of days (say, 35 to 45 days).
7. ***Obligations:*** How much will each member be required to give to the organization? Usually, a band may want to list what is expected of each member in the band, such as "first priority" over outside work and showing up to rehearsals.
8. ***Quitting:*** Will members be able to pick up and leave whenever they want? A member may be able to leave if he or she is unhappy, as long as it is not in the middle of a tour or in other situations in which the band may incur a loss as a result.
9. ***Departed Members' Rights to Profits:*** Will a member continue to earn income after departing? Usually, a departed member will continue to earn his or her share of income on work in which he or she was "involved" and/or has ownership, but not on new work by the band.
10. ***Amendment of the Agreement:*** What kind of vote can change the terms of the agreement? To change more significant terms, a unanimous vote might apply. To change less significant terms, a majority vote might be sufficient.
11. ***Arbitration or Mediation:*** How will disputes be settled? Rather than incurring excessive fees in the courts, a band may choose mediation or arbitration as a more practical alternative. In mediation, a third party, a "professional mediator," assists the parties to negotiate a settlement. In arbitration, a third party, a "professional arbitrator," decides on the outcome of the dispute.
12. ***Indemnification Clause:*** Will the band be liable for the misconduct of each member? In a partnership, where there is no liability protection, the answer is yes! But should the band be sued successfully and all members are responsible for paying a settlement, a band can stipulate that it can go after the offending member for repayment of such fees.
13. ***Term:*** How long will the band membership agreement be in effect? Most bands choose a term of one to two years. And finally . . .
14. ***Signature and Date:*** All members must sign and date the agreement.

While an agreement won't stop a band from breaking up or running into conflicts, it will help define the individual beliefs, desires, and perspectives of the members from the start. Remember that without a written agreement, should a serious argument ensue regarding control or profits, state partnership laws may dictate the outcome for you. So schedule a meeting with your band and get that agreement drafted today. You'll thank me later.

Now, let's see what attorney Jeff Cohen has to say in his interview below about other important issues such as trademarks, DBAs, and business entities. Get ready to learn a lot!

Q&A with Attorney Jeff Cohen

Jeff Cohen is a partner in the law firm Millen, White, Zelano, and Branigan, where he heads the firm's trademark, copyright, and entertainment practice. In this interview, Jeff discusses band names and federal trademark registration, the basics of setting up shop as a band, fictitious name statements (a.k.a. DBAs), and business entities (partnerships, corporations, and LLCs). The interview has been expanded and edited slightly by the author.

CREATE A BAND NAME THAT'S COOL AND LEGAL

This chapter discusses how to protect your band name with federal registration and other means—but before doing all that, you'd better make sure to create a very cool name. Here are some tips:

- ***Reflect the Right Mood and Imagery:*** Marilyn Manson took part of Marilyn Monroe's name (to reflect his glam appeal) and Charles Manson's name (to reflect his shock appeal) and created one of the coolest names in the business.
- ***Change Your Personal Name:*** Will.I.Am of the Black Eyed Peas shortened his name from William James Adams, Jr., by separating the syllables in his first name.
- ***Make It Adaptable to Your Products:*** Trent Reznor of Nine Inch Nails denies any deep meaning to the name other than that he wanted one that looked cool as an abbreviation.
- ***Make It Easy to Spell:*** I still can't spell the band Lynyrd Skynyrd correctly, and couldn't find them on the Internet for this reason. Don't confuse your fans.
- ***Connect to a Geographic Region:*** Cypress Hill named themselves after a gang-infested area near their home base in South Gate, California, which helped brand the band's vibe and attitude.
- ***Appeal to Your Fans' Lifestyles:*** Green Day named themselves after a phrase used by San Francisco kids for smoking pot all day.
- ***Invent a Name:*** Metallica's name was invented when Lars Ulrich helped a friend brainstorm names for a metal magazine.
- ***Find a Name That Converts into a Cool Acronym:*** The band Life, Sex, and Death used the acronym LSD interchangeably to help brand the vibe of the band.
- ***Describe Your Company:*** The late Ian Copeland named his international and innovative talent agency Frontier Booking International. By the way, this also made a cool acronym: FBI.
- ***Choose a Name That's Legally Available:*** No matter what name you choose, conduct a search to see if others are using a name first. Use your favorite search engine and www.uspto.gov. And finally . . .
- ***Be Unique:*** Be different and descriptive, but never generic. This goes not only for your name, but also for your logo, fonts, and colors. Don't create the perception of confusion with other products.

Q: Jeff, let's get right into it. Define "trademark" and "service mark."

J.C.: A service mark is a word, logo, or design used to identify an entertainment "service" (such as a band's live performance).

A trademark is a word, logo, or design used to identify a physical "product" (such as a recording).

Despite the above-noted distinction, the term "trademark" is simply used to describe both marks.

Q: Federal registration—why do it?

J.C.: First let me say that as soon as an artist performs in public, sells recordings at his or her shows or on the Internet, or commercially exploits his or her name by some other means, he or she already has a trademark. The rights, however, are limited to the "geographical areas in which the name is being used."

That being said, the purpose of registering with the federal government is to:

- ***Make a Public Record:*** Make a public record that you secured the rights to use the name nationwide (including the states where you have not yet exploited your name).
- ***Provide the Legal Presumption:*** Provide you with the legal presumption that you own the name nationally (meaning others have to prove you wrong).

- ***Give Notice:*** Help ensure that professionals searching for the availability of your name will find you and realize that you have already claimed it.
- ***Use the Registered Symbols:*** Gives you the right to use the "registration symbol" (®) next to your name, rather than just the "registration pending" symbol (the abbreviation TM).

Q: Federal registration—when should one do it?

J.C.: If a band is still in its infancy and deciding on whether its members really want to pursue a career in music, I suggest they spend the money on other things.

However, as soon as they begin to exploit the name at the national level by promoting themselves or selling product on the Internet, playing locally and across state lines, or preparing to sign a recording deal, the band must file for registration.

Q: Please explain "intent to use."

J.C.: When a musician wants to secure a name before ever using it, he or she can file an intent-to-use application (This is the one exception to the "when to file" rule above.) Of course there are fees and specific requirements associated with this practice, such as using the name within a specific period of time.

Q: How can a band find out whether its name has already been trademarked?

J.C.: As soon as a band comes up with its name, the members should all conduct a limited search to make sure that no one else is using it. Otherwise, they could find themselves building value in a name only to realize later that it has to be changed. As a band becomes more established, an even more extensive professional search should be conducted. Below are a few search methods:

- ***Google:*** Use a popular search engine like Google to search community sites and blogs.
- ***Band Lists:*** Look through local music publications that provide lists of unsigned groups. (*Music Connection* magazine publishes a "Hot 100" list of top unsigned bands each year.)
- ***Record Stores:*** Search stores that still sell records, including lifestyle businesses.
- ***Trade Mags:*** Use handy resources like the *Billboard International Touring Directory*, which lists hundreds of touring bands.
- ***USPTO.gov:*** Utilize the United States Patent and Trademark Office's website (www.uspto.gov) to search for bands already registered at the federal level.
- ***Professional Services:*** Use a professional trademark searching company such as Thomson Compumark (http://trademarks.thomsonreuters.com) or an attorney who is well versed in the area of trademarks. This, of course, can be extremely costly.

Q: What forms must be filed, and what will it cost?

J.C.: After making sure your name is free to use, you'll need to fill out and sign a trademark application form.

Furthermore, you'll need to submit a drawing of your logo, send advertisements and other proof (or "specimens") that you are exploiting the name in interstate commerce (across state lines), and pay a fee of several hundred dollars (fees are subject to change but are approximately $350).

The patent office will first check the availability of the name and post your mark in the U.S. *Official Gazette*, offering anyone the opportunity to challenge your registration. Assuming there are no problems, expect the entire registration period to take up to one year.

Forms and further information are available at the United States Patent and Trademark Office's (USPTO) website (www.uspto.gov) or by calling 800-786-9199.

Q: What does it mean for a name to be "active?"

J.C.: To keep a band name active you must continue to use it. In the fifth year from registration, you should file an "affidavit of use" and an "affidavit of incontestability."

An "affidavit of use" maintains a valid federal registration and ensures your trademark has not been "abandoned" (i.e., inactive for three years).

An "affidavit of incontestability" ensures that if anyone were to come out of the woodwork and claim they'd been using the name before you, they'd have a real difficult time winning in a court of law (if it even went that far).

Q: When must a name be renewed?

J.C.: In the 10th year from registering, you must renew your trademark by contacting the Commissioner of Trademarks.

An "affidavit of continuing use" and a renewal application must be filed. Failure to file both forms will result in cancellation of your registration.

Q: When is foreign registration required?

J.C.: Foreign trademark laws differ from those in the United States.

A "first to file" system is used rather than a "first to use" system. This essentially means that if someone in another country decides to be sneaky after hearing about your band's success in the U.S., and beats you to registering your name in that country, he or she could stop you from using the name in that territory.

So when your band is having some success in the U.S. and it appears that things are really moving forward, be sure to talk to your attorney about foreign registration.

A "Madrid Protocol" registration process will allow you to register with key countries in one shot (saving you time and money), rather than registering on a country-by-country basis.

Q: Tell us about classifications.

J.C.: Several classifications of marks might apply to a band's career as it advances in its career position and financial resources. Here are a few of the most relevant:

- ***Class 41:*** This is for entertainment services, such as a band's live performance in clubs, theaters, and stadiums—anywhere it's performing.
- ***Class 9:*** This is for selling products, specifically records and the like.
- ***Class 2:*** This is for selling merchandise such as T-shirts, hats, etc. And finally . . .
- ***Class 35:*** This is for online retail services.

Filing each classification costs an additional fee, but doing this when you have the funds is recommended to provide full protection nationwide. Be sure to speak with an attorney experienced in trademarks to determine what type of registration is necessary for you.

Trademarks are a complex and confusing area of the music business, and you want to make sure you handle your band name with care.

Q: Please explain domain registration versus trademark registration.

J.C.: Domain registration is not the same as registering your band name with the Patent and Trademark Office in Washington, D.C. (i.e., it does not give you the presumption of ownership and make a public notice that you have secured the rights nationwide).

Domain registration is specifically the process of reserving your band name as a "virtual address" (e.g., yourbandname.com) on the Internet. Domains are like telephone numbers and are given out based on who registers them first.

Registering a domain name is cheap (as little as $10 for a year). Thus, domain registration is something you can, and should, do right now, before someone else gets the name.

NAME DISPUTES: GREEN JELLO VERSUS JELL-O

To avoid disputes over band names, remember to create a name and logo that are different from those of other music companies, as well as those of non-music companies. This is legally important.

Attorney Donald Passman shares a story about the punk band Green Jello (now Green Jelly), who received a notice from the owners of Jell-O (a dessert brand) asking it to change its name and logo typeset. The issue was not whether a "likelihood of confusion" existed between the two parties—a factor that would typically prohibit one from using a certain name—but whether there was "dilution" (the idea that using an already famous name and logo in another field dilutes or "tarnishes the reputation" of the original name). Pretty tricky stuff. So, first, be original. And, second, contact an attorney if you need more help.

Q: Are DBAs mandatory?

J.C.: It depends. The most important time to file a DBA ("doing business as"), also called an FBN (fictional business name), is when you're receiving payment under a fictitious name. In other words, if a club owner is writing checks to a name other than your own (or your corporation's name), you need to file a DBA.

A DBA shows proof that you're an authorized representative of the band. Without proof, you cannot walk into a bank and cash the check.

Q: Moving on to business entities, which is best?

J.C.: There's no absolute answer to which business entity works best, but a band essentially has four choices: partnership, classic C corporation, S corporation, and LLC.

Q: What constitutes a partnership (number 1 of 4)?

J.C.: When two or more people come together to conduct business and they share in the profits and losses of that business, a partnership is essentially formed. So, for many of your readers, their band is already a partnership.

Setting up and running a partnership is easy and requires no more than creating an oral agreement (though a written agreement is advised).

For tax purposes, the partnership's profits and losses flow through to the individual members in a prorated share and are filed on the partner's individual returns.

The down side, however, is unlimited personal liability. This means that if one partner is sued by another party, each partner's personal assets can be at risk. If the band is in the genre of music where there's a lot of energy and there's a high possibility for serious injuries in the mosh pit, then a partnership can be a potential disaster.

Q: What is a classic C corporation (number 2 of 4)?

J.C.: The benefit of forming a classic C corporation is that it is treated as a separate legal entity. This means that your personal assets are not at risk. Corporations are also entitled to certain tax fringe benefits for expenses that partnerships are not.

Setting up a classic C corporation requires you to file articles of incorporation (also called articles of association) as well as SS-4 forms to get a taxpayer ID number. This is the number that allows you to open a bank account. Then you need to put together bylaws or "rules" for how your company will be run. Bylaws might address issues like who owns the band name, what happens if a member leaves, and what shares each individual has in the company. The day-to-day business matters are handled by officers who are appointed by a board of directors, who are elected by the shareholders (all of whom can be the same persons).

Running a classic C corporation requires a number of formalities and some paperwork (such as keeping minutes for company meetings and annual meeting filings) and it is therefore far more difficult to run than a partnership.

For tax purposes, a classic C corporation is subject to double taxation, whereby both the corporation and shareholders are taxed separately.

The fees for setting up a classic C corporation are different in every state. In California, it costs approximately $100 for the initial paperwork with an annual payment of $800. Keep in mind that you also have fees for your attorney and/or accountant, whom you will likely hire to assist you at this stage. There may also be fees for local business licenses and permits.

Q: What is an S corporation (number 3 of 4)?

J.C.: An S corporation provides similar benefits to those of a classic C corporation in that it affords the shareholders a shield from personal liability and offers certain tax fringe benefits for expenses (though these are more restrictive than those of the C corporation—talk to your accountant).

Setting up an S corporation is similar to setting up a C corporation. It requires filing articles of incorporation, getting taxpayer ID numbers, and putting together bylaws for how your company will be run. The day-to-day business matters are also handled by officers who are appointed by a board of directors who are elected by the shareholders.

Running an S corporation, just like running a C corporation, requires a lot of formalities and paperwork and can therefore be difficult. There are also restrictions on the maximum number of shareholders an S corporation can have; but, as these are in the tens, this probably won't be an issue for most of those reading this book.

For tax purposes, the profit or loss of the business can either be handled like a classic C corporation, where the corporation and shareholders are taxed separately, or it can pass through to the shareholders' personal tax returns and be taxed only once—based on that shareholder's pro rata share ownership percentage. This is definitely a huge advantage and attraction for smaller businesses.

The fees are similar to what was discussed above for classic C corporations, but you should check with your local accountant or business manager.

Q: What is an LLC (number 4 of 4)?

J.C.: Last but not least, an LLC (limited liability company) is rather a new concept in comparison with the other business entities we've discussed. Like both the C and S corporations, an LLC limits the liabilities that someone suing you can grab; however, the down side is that it may not afford you the same tax fringe benefits.

Setting up an LLC is similar to setting up a C or S corporation in that you must file articles of organization and get taxpayer ID numbers. However, the good news is that you can establish a simple operating agreement to run it. The day-to-day business matters can also be conducted by the member/owners or by officers who are appointed to manage.

Unlike the S or C corporation, an LLC requires far fewer formalities and less paperwork and therefore is easier to operate. This is the real good news about LLCs.

For tax purposes, just like an S corp, the profit and loss of an LLC can be handled two ways: either double taxed, whereby the LLC and the members are taxed, or passed through to the individual members and filed on their personal tax returns. Again, this is definitely an advantage for smaller businesses.

Check with your local accountant or business manager for the costs.

So that's about it. I know this was a lot to digest, but this should give your readers a good place to start.

BUSINESS ENTITIES AT A GLANCE

What follows is an easy-to-read breakdown of business entities provided by attorney Burgundy Morgan, Esq.

Sole Proprietor

- ***What:*** Business owned by one person
- ***Formation:*** No formalities required
- ***Liability:*** Unlimited (your personal assets at risk)
- ***Ownership:*** By sole proprietor
- ***Management:*** By sole proprietor
- ***Taxation:*** Filed on personal tax returns
- ***Governed by:*** Business plan

Partnership

- ***What:*** When two or more persons engage in business, a partnership is presumed by law in many states
- ***Formation:*** No requirement (written partnership agreement recommended)
- ***Liability:*** Unlimited (personal assets at risk)
- ***Ownership:*** By the partners as the partners decide
- ***Management:*** By the partners
- ***Taxation:*** Filed on personal tax returns via IRS forms
- ***Governed by:*** Understanding of the partners (partnership agreement recommended)

Classic C Corporation

- ***What:*** A separate legal entity (which could consist of one or more people)
- ***Formation:*** Filing articles of incorporation with the state
- ***Liability:*** Limited liability up to the value of assets of the corporation
- ***Ownership:*** By shareholders
- ***Management:*** Shareholders elect directors who appoint officers to manage
- ***Taxation:*** Two levels: corporate taxes and shareholder taxes
- ***Governed by:*** Bylaws between shareholders, and an employment agreement with the corporation

LLC (Limited Liability Company)

- ***What:*** An entity with limited liability but fewer formalities than a corporation
- ***Formation:*** Filing articles of organization with the secretary of state
- ***Liability:*** Limited liability protection in the amount you personally invested
- ***Ownership:*** By members
- ***Management:*** By members, unless officers are appointed
- ***Taxation:*** On personal returns, or on two levels: LLC and personal
- ***Governed by:*** An operating agreement between members, and an employment agreement with the limited liability company

S Corporation

- ***What:*** A separate legal entity provided that the number of shareholders is limited (see your state's laws for limits)
- ***Formation:*** Filing articles of incorporation with state
- ***Liability:*** Limited liability protection in amount you personally invested
- ***Ownership:*** By shareholders
- ***Management:*** Shareholders elect directors who appoint officers to manage
- ***Taxation:*** On personal returns, or on two levels: corporate and personal
- ***Governed by:*** Bylaws between shareholders, and an employment agreement with the corporation

Note: Attorney Burgundy Morgan notes that the good news about forming a business entity is that you can always change; so you are not limited. You can move, for instance, from an LLC or S corp to a C corp. Be sure to speak with an attorney or accountant to determine what entity is best for your needs.

4

Contract Employment or Self-Employment, Part 1

Gigs and Unions

"As a working musician, you are in the business of you."
—Tony DeNicola, professional drummer, professor of music at Trenton State College

Being in a band is not easy! It requires years of hard work and sacrifice, and even then there is no guarantee of success. This is one reason many musicians resort to hiring out their services as a contract employee or self-employed performer, in return for a sure and immediate paycheck.

The term "contract employee" refers to anyone who agrees to work on a long-term, continuing relationship under a set of conditions usually specified by a contract. This might include touring regularly as the music director with an established act or performing daily with a house band for a television show, such as *Jimmy Kimmel Live* or *The Late Show*.

On the other hand, a self-employed performer, or independent contractor, is essentially anyone who makes his or her services available for hire for shorter-term relationships. This might include a day of overdubbing a solo on another musician's record, transcribing a chart for a publisher, and then spinning a set at a local nightclub.

In both cases, you're in the business of you! You have no claim in the organizations for which you work, no share in the band's future royalties (except in some relationships), and no real job security. For this reason, it's your responsibility to understand your rights as a working musician and to make sure you're compensated fairly for each and every gig you perform.

This chapter offers tips on getting that gig as well as career support from the unions. In chapters 5 and 6, I'll cover negotiating your employment agreement and taxes and insurance. Let's get started.

Getting the Gig: How to Be a "Working" Musician

So how does one go about getting that gig—and gigs for years, even decades, to come? In short: you'd better have some skills to pay the bills.

Let's take a look at 25 helpful tips spanning every period of your career—from the preliminary necessities, to breaking into the scene, to lasting over the long haul.

The Preliminary Necessities

First things first: to get that happening gig, you must hone your skills as a musician and become a force to be reckoned with. Consider the following:

- ***Be Amazing:*** Invest thousands of hours of practice first and foremost and be a great musician, because nothing else in this chapter or book will otherwise matter.
- ***Be Versatile, but Have a Focus:*** Learn to play several styles of music so that you can survive and pay the bills, but have one style that you play better than the rest and that forms the essence of "your brand."
- ***Be Unique:*** Don't be afraid to develop your own style and break some rules. Jimi Hendrix played a right-handed guitar upside down, and Stanley Jordan developed the "touch technique" and played chords and soloed at the same time.
- ***Sound Awesome:*** Find the right combo of amps, effects, strings, cymbals, snare drum heads, turntables, or whatever gadgets you play. In the crowded marketplace, your distinctive sound can mean everything.
- ***Look Interesting:*** Become visually appealing—whether by exercising, dressing a certain way, or wearing your hair in a certain style. Just create your own brand.
- ***Know How to Hang:*** Develop a happy, warm, and outgoing personality. Be fun to hang with. Learn to make people laugh, even if that means memorizing a few jokes or famous lines from a great movie. And finally . . .
- ***Learn How to Read Music:*** Learn how to read and write music. Many gigs won't require reading charts, but understanding what you're playing helps you to play it better and prepare for rehearsals.

Breaking into the Scene

Once you've developed some serious skills as a musician, you need to let people know you exist. Consider the following tips:

- ***Know How to Promote Yourself:*** Inform people about your special skills and, most importantly, how these skills can save them time and money in the studio, on the gig, and on the road. Communicate this message via personal websites, social networks, message boards, your local branch of the union (AFM or SAG-AFTRA), and more.
- ***Record with Everyone:*** Volunteer to play on as many indie artists' demos and recordings as possible. A seasoned producer or engineer on the session may call you for another session down the line, and/or the artist may rehire you when he or she hits it big.
- ***Jam at Open Mics:*** Sit in frequently at open mics and jams.
- ***Play at Church:*** If you belong to a church, get involved with performing there (not only will it make you feel good, you never know who is a member of your parish).
- ***Study with Working Pros:*** Take lessons with actively gigging teachers and impress the hell out of them. Who knows, one day they may need a sub and recommend you.
- ***Form Your Own Band:*** Form your own band that features the style of music you play best, and get out there and be heard.
- ***Learn from the Old-Timers:*** Consider working with an older artist, one who may not be currently in the spotlight, but with whom you can gain valuable experience. Many artists seek out musicians to form regional bands across the United States to be their touring act for a specified region. Perhaps you can put one of these bands together.
- ***Become a Roadie for a Minute:*** Consider becoming a road technician for your favorite artist, learn all of his or her songs, and cross your fingers that a spot will open up in the band. At the very least, you'll learn a great deal about life on the road, and make some really good friends as well.
- ***Get Great at Auditioning:*** Learn to transcribe songs note for note, get your musician friends to rehearse the songs with you, and visit the audition hall long before the actual audition—all of this will help you to reduce your nerves on that "big day."

- ***Get Great at Interviewing:*** Know everything about your potential employers—from what they are looking for in an employee, to what their favorite sports teams are, to what their needs are. It's not just what you play, it's what you say. And finally . . .
- ***Befriend Everyone in the Business:*** Make friends with other musicians, bands, roadies, club promoters, producers, managers, talent agents, attorneys, equipment manufacturers, photographers, journalists, actors, models, and others in the business. You never know who may hear of the perfect working situation and recommend you.

Lasting for the Long Haul

The last group of tips deals with going the distance. Remember that it's not enough just to find work today; you have to keep on working over the long term. The following tips can help:

- ***Keep in Touch:*** Maintain a relationship with all past employers. Reach out to them with holiday greeting cards at the end of the year, or take them out to lunch now and again. Not only is it good karma to say thanks, but their referrals are invaluable.
- ***Act Like a Pro, Always:*** Never be late for a gig, play your ass off every night, and never cancel on anyone at the last minute and leave them hanging. Maintaining your good reputation is everything.
- ***Maintain Your Gear:*** Make sure your equipment is always up-to-date and in great shape for both the road and the studio. This includes road cases, electronics, and more.
- ***Maintain Your Passport:*** Be prepared to travel abroad. As a professional working musician, you must always be ready to leave today. Renew those travel documents. Now!
- ***Change with the Times:*** Be prepared to adjust your look, playing style, and attitude. That said, you must always be true to yourself. Find a balance.
- ***Stay Healthy:*** Eat well and stay away from all unhealthy habits.
- ***Love Music:*** Always remember why you started performing—for the fun and the love of it—no matter how challenging your career gets. Don't fall out of love.
- ***Stay Happy:*** Finally, keep smiling inside and out. Remember, no one likes a "downer."

Now that you know how to get the gig, you must know how to get justly treated. But how's that possible when the business of music can seem like the Wild West—a place with no apparent payment guidelines, regulations, or support for musicians?

Never fear, the unions are here: the American Federation of Musicians (representing instrumentalists) and SAG-AFTRA (representing vocalists and actors) can help. Read on.

Seeking Fair Treatment and Guidance via the AFM

The American Federation of Musicians (AFM) is a labor union based on the idea that through "strength in numbers" or, as they put it, "collective empowerment," musicians will have a stronger voice in the workplace.

The AFM is 100,000 members strong and includes artists from every field of musical endeavor—such as Bruce Springsteen, Bon Jovi, Metallica, Aerosmith, the Red Hot Chili Peppers, Hans Zimmer, Maroon 5, and Paul Shaffer and the CBS Orchestra.

The AFM has 240 branch offices, called "locals," in cities throughout the United States and Canada. Each local is run autonomously, and thus the benefits they offer may fluctuate slightly from branch to branch.

What follows is a brief overview of the benefits and member requirements. Whether or not joining makes sense to you right now, you'll still get a sense of how professional musicians are treated. Read everything, but feel free to skim the main headers if you must.

AFM Major Benefits: Payment Regulation and Enforcement

The AFM has the ability to get thousands of employers (record companies, motion picture studios, theme parks, circuses, broadcasting and cable companies) to enter into collective bargaining agreements and establish good working conditions for instrumentalists. The union enforces these rules and collects payment defaults by the employer when necessary.

Some of the areas the unions regulate include the following:

- ***Live Performances:*** *Rehearsals: for the time it takes to prepare for performances. *Cartage: for the costs associated with transporting your equipment. *Travel expenses: for airfare, hotels, and shuttle services. *Travel time: for the time it takes to get to and from each gig. *Personal mileage: for the miles you travel in your vehicle to and from gigs. *Per diems: for daily food expenses. *Holiday payment scales: for the extra pay you deserve for working on major holidays.
- ***Recording Sessions:*** *Studio albums: for major label recording sessions and some smaller label sessions. *Live concerts: for when that mobile truck pulls up to record the "live album." *Television and radio performances: for commercial advertisements.
- ***Motion Picture Performances:*** *On-camera appearances: for the filming of a bar or concert scene in a movie. *Off-camera appearances: for the studio recording of a movie soundtrack.
- ***Video Game Sessions:*** *Small group sessions: for small recording sessions including one to five musicians. *Orchestral sessions: for large orchestral sessions including hundreds of musicians.
- ***Videotaping:*** *Live concert taping: for broadcast over the Internet, cable, and television. *Promotional video shoots: for MTV-styled promo videos to be broadcast over the Internet, cable, and television.
- ***Live Television Taping:*** *Talk and award shows: for taped performances like *The Tonight Show* and the Grammys to be broadcast on television, cable, and the Internet.

UNION TO THE RESCUE

A group of ska musicians from Los Angeles (who had only been in the union for three months) drove to Florida to play a New Year's Eve gig. The group received a bad check for the show, and their van broke down in Texas on the way home. They contacted the AFM, who was able to pursue their claim via Local 23 in San Antonio, Texas, help them get their van fixed, and get the promoter to settle up on the bad check. Although the band had to endure a lecture from the union about their poor business practices, they welcomed it—after all, they were no longer stranded thousands of miles from home. The AFM pursues claims less dramatic than this all over the country every day.

In another instance, an artist who performed with her band on *Late Night with David Letterman* believed that since her musicians were being paid by Letterman's television production company via the union, she wasn't responsible for paying them for the job as well. She was wrong; under the Collective Bargaining Agreement for Video Taping, the AFM stipulates that musicians shall receive payment when taped for television appearances. This fee is *in addition to* the standard wage musicians should receive from their employer for a live performance. As it turned out, all of the musicians in the artist's band were paid.

Special AFM Benefits: Funds, New Use Fees, and More

In addition to the wage regulation and enforcement benefits discussed above, the AFM also helps you to collect a number of different payments as outlined below:

- ***New Use Fees:*** The AFM SRMP/TV department closely monitors all of the sound recordings (e.g., singles, albums, etc.) on which its union members perform. Should these recordings be used in a way other than originally intended (e.g., if they are used in a film or TV show), the union collects residuals called "new use" fees and pays you.
- ***Sound Recording Special Payments Fund:*** The AFM encourages members to sign up for the sound recording special payments fund—an additional payment collected from record labels and issued to you based on a percentage (ranging from 20 to 80 percent) of the scale dollars you earned on AFM-covered recording sessions on which you performed in the prior year; this payment will continue for the next five years.
- ***Sound Recording Intellectual Property Rights Distribution Fund:*** Finally, thanks to the Digital Performance Right in Sound Recordings Act of 1995, and the Digital Millennium Copyright Act of 1998, if you are a "non-featured" performer on sound recordings (i.e., a session musician), you may be entitled to "digital performance royalties" (for webcasts on stations like Pandora, SiriusXM, etc.)—distributed to you via the fund, and in partnership with SoundExchange. Additionally, you may be entitled to "private copy royalties" (pursuant to the U.S. Audio Home Recording Act), as well as "record rental remuneration" royalties or "foreign royalties" from Japan (where CDs are rented and copied).

AFM Health and Retirement Benefits

Moving right along to the next group of AFM benefits, the union provides a number of health options and a pension for qualifying members—this is a life-saver for those with serious medical bills, or for those who are no longer working. Here's a summary of the benefits you may receive:

- ***Health Insurance:*** Medical insurance to help you cover hospital bills and dental insurance to reduce dental costs and brighten that star smile of yours.
- ***Retirement:*** To provide regular payments when you retire early at age 55, or retire later at age 65 (note that the payout for retirement at age 65 is typically higher). Retirement may seem like a long way off for you, but it's nice to know you'll have money waiting. Right?

Other AFM Benefits

And now let's take a look at some of the other goodies in store for you through the union—from job referrals to studio discounts. Here's the complete list:

- ***Insurance:*** The AFM offers various discount insurance options, including disability (for when you're unable to work and earn an income due to sickness or injury), auto (for your vehicles), liability (for protection from others who claim bodily injury or damage to their property), and equipment (for theft/damage to instruments).
- ***Prescriptions:*** You'll get reduced prices on most pharmaceutical drugs.
- ***Job Referral Services:*** The AFM registers your name (band, instruction company, etc.) in their job referral database (called GoPro), which could lead to future work.
- ***Booking Service:*** You'll get your name, picture, and music posted on a special site and assistance with getting booked at weddings, parties, and other events.
- ***Legal Advice:*** The AFM provides limited legal supervision and career development.
- ***Twenty-Four-Hour Telephone Assistance:*** You'll get 24-hour telephone assistance for problems on the road or questions about contracts.
- ***Discounted Rehearsal and Recording Studios:*** The AFM offers discount rehearsal and recording rooms. In fact, there's a studio just five minutes away from my home.

- ***General Discounts:*** You'll receive travel discounts, health club discounts, credit card options, loan programs, mortgage programs, deals on electronics, and more.
- ***Subscriptions:*** The AFM offers you a subscription to their monthly magazine, *International Musician*, which keeps you up-to-date on all the industry happenings.
- ***Young Musician Member Rates:*** The AFM provides discounted rates for musicians who register as a band, an enrolled student, or a "youth" (a musician under 21).
- ***Venue Alert:*** The AFM provides a website where musicians are kept informed about venues who treat musicians poorly, so that they know where not to play.
- ***Opportunities to Make a Change:*** The affiliated organization Friends of the AFM helps you to directly contact members of Congress regarding important issues for musicians (such as Internet piracy, payments for your recorded performances that get broadcasted on terrestrial radio, and funding for arts education). Visit http://www.afm.org/departments/legislative-office/friends-of-afm.

AFM Membership and Benefit Requirements

Now that we've discussed what unions do and all the benefits they offer, let's take a quick look at the requirements you'll need to fulfill in order to receive these benefits. Note that the rates discussed are subject to change and vary from one local to another. Check the following with your local branch:

- ***Pay an Initiation/Membership Fee:*** Applicants must pay a one-time initiation fee of about $90, and members are charged a yearly fee of approximately $210. Note that certain reductions apply to those under 21 or those who have been longtime members.
- ***Perform Enough Covered Gigs:*** Members are required to work "union covered gigs" only. A union covered gig means that the person or organization for which you work has entered into a collective bargaining agreement acceptable to the union. Your employer is then required to pay you at least the minimum-scale wages. Your employer must also report all of the gigs in which you work to the union and make an additional contribution toward your pension and health-care fund.
- ***Earn Pension Vesting:*** To be fully "vested," members must earn a minimum of $750 in "covered employment" for five consecutive years (with some exceptions; see www.afm-epf.org). This means that you can begin collecting retirement benefits at age 55, or wait and collect higher benefits at the full retirement age of 65.
- ***Reach Health-Care Contribution Limits:*** Members must reach a minimum dollar amount from their employers' health contribution payments, usually within six-month periods (from January to June and July to December), to qualify for health care.
- ***Pay Work Dues:*** Members must pay work dues of approximately 3.5 percent of the suggested minimum scale for live performances, and 4.5 percent of the suggested minimum wage for recording sessions. This fee is deducted by your employer.
- ***Attend Local Meetings:*** Finally, members must try to attend monthly local meetings to discuss current union events, meet other union members, and offer input for future policy development.

Is Joining the AFM Right for You?

After everything you've learned about wages, funds, and pensions, I bet you're wondering if joining the union is right for you. Consider the following:

- ***Covered Gig Requirement:*** The union's strengths lie mostly in major venue performances; major label recordings; and television, theater, orchestral, Broadway, and motion picture work. Playing these types of gigs regularly is the only way that you will qualify for the major benefits, such as the health-care and pension funds.

- ***Good Standing Rule:*** It is not considered "good standing" to accept any nonunion gig as an "active member." Although the union is known occasionally to turn a blind eye and allow you to perform nonunion gigs, they may still require you to pay dues for the job performed. In other words, if you're a musician who plays small jazz clubs, than perhaps the union is not the perfect choice for you right now.

Whether you feel it's the right time to become a member of the AFM or not, I encourage you to talk to an AFM representative at 800-762-3444 or at www.afm.org. In the words of Mark Heter, a former local 808 division head, "The union is ready to serve you."

MEMBER OR NOT, HERE THEY COME!

A contract musician touring with a rock group found himself in a serious dispute.

The musician felt he should be compensated for a live album the group had recorded while he performed with them on the road. On the other hand, the group felt that the meager salary they had paid the musician covered an unlimited number of services to be determined at their discretion.

Neither the musician, the band, nor the independent record company to which the group was signed were union signatories. However, the record label that handled the distribution of the recording (Universal) was a union signatory, thus entitling the contract musician to payments.

With the assistance of a union representative, the musician finally received compensation. Bam! Needless to say, the musician thereafter became a union member.

Seeking Fair Treatment and Guidance via SAG-AFTRA

Now that you have a better sense of what the AFM does for instrumentalists, let's take a look at what SAG-AFTRA does for vocalists. I promise I'll keep this brief.

SAG-AFTRA is the result of a 2012 merger between the Screen Actors Guild (representing actors and singers in scripted television, film, videos, and commercials) and the American Federation of Radio and Television Artists (representing singers, actors, and news broadcasters in sound recordings, commercials, and radio and television programs).

SAG-AFTRA has over 160,000 members. They are headquartered in Los Angeles, with 35 branch offices located in major cities throughout the United States. As with the AFM, benefits vary slightly from local to local, so be sure to contact a local branch near you.

General Differences: SAG-AFTRA Versus the AFM

Since I already gave you the full rundown on the American Federation of Musicians (AFM), I'm providing the general differences between SAG-AFTRA and the AFM in a nutshell.

SAG-AFTRA differs from the AFM in the following ways:

- ***Vocalists, Not Instrumentalists:*** SAG-AFTRA covers vocalists, not instrumentalists. Vocalists who are instrumentalists must also join the AFM (and vice versa).
- ***Sessions, Not Live:*** SAG-AFTRA focuses primarily on recording sessions, not live performances (unless they are recorded).
- ***Already Working Union Gigs:*** SAG-AFTRA applicants must have already worked a SAG-AFTRA "union-covered" gig to be eligible for membership.
- ***Higher Costs:*** Initiation fees and dues at SAG-AFTRA are far more costly than the AFM. The initiation fee is currently $3,000 (in some states, it may be lower). Minimum dues for the first period

are $99. Dues for the following periods are payable every six months (May and November) and are usually based on gross earnings combined from all SAG-AFTRA work done in the previous year.

- ***Health Coverage Guaranteed to Recording Artists:*** Individual health coverage is guaranteed to vocalists who are signed recording artists thanks to contribution payments made by the label on your behalf. This is a huge benefit.
- ***Health/Pension Contributions Based on Royalty Credits:*** Health/pension contributions are made on behalf of vocalists who are signed recording artists based on sales and royalties credited (whether your label has recouped its expenses to you or not). This makes it easier to meet the health/pension benefit requirements and to qualify for services.
- ***Voice-Over and Acting Workshops:*** Finally, workshops for voice-over and acting are available to those who want to expand their skills and increase their earning potential.

So that's really the bottom line, folks. Surely you get the general gist of unions and SAG-AFTRA. However, for more information, contact SAG-AFTRA at 855-724-2387 or at www.sagaftra.org. Also see www.bobbyborg.com and search for SAG-AFTRA. Okay? Now let's move on.

5

Contract Employment or Self-Employment, Part 2

Employment Agreements and Negotiations

"In business, you don't always get what you want; you get what you negotiate."
—Chester Karrass, negotiations expert

Now that you've gotten through all of the information on unions in chapter 4—and I know that it was a lot—it is important to discuss written employment agreements.

At the beginning of your career, no matter what the AFM and SAG-AFTRA have to say about fair treatment and minimum-scale wages for musicians, the fees and treatment you'll be able to negotiate for will vary greatly from one employer to the next.

This depends partly on your working relationships and whether you are providing services for 1) employers with limited budgets, 2) employers with larger budgets, or 3) employers that offer a salary and percentages. All of these scenarios are covered below. Let's take a look.

Working for Employers with Limited Budgets

When working as a contract employee or a self-employed musician early in your career, you'll be regularly offered work that pays substandard wages—far below the union's suggested minimum scales. This may be due to your inexperience, an employer's greed, the employer's non-signatory status with the union, and/or the employer's financial restrictions (a limited budget).

When working for employers with limited budgets, there really are no fairness guidelines, but you should at least negotiate for pay increases on a sliding scale in proportion to your employer's growth in earnings. This is especially important if you're a contract employee working with one employer on a regular basis. Otherwise, you may continue to be paid the same substandard wage in spite of the group's newfound success and ability to pay fairly. This is an extremely important safeguard, as you'll see in the following story.

SINGING THE BLUES!

A group of musicians agreed to work with an up-and-coming blues guitarist for a minimal fee of $275 per week, due to the guitarist's limited budget. As the tour progressed, the guitarist's new record began to do extremely well. In no time, the group was performing in larger venues with the Rolling Stones and Aerosmith and appearing on national television shows such as *The Tonight Show*. The guitarist was now earning substantially more and could afford to pay his musicians comparable union-scale wages (and more).

When the group requested a raise (which was only fair), they were replaced on the following tour with musicians who, in the employer's words, "are hungry and looking for a break." (So much for loyalty!) If only the musicians had anticipated this "burn and churn" philosophy used by a lot of employers in the music business, they would have been in a far better position to negotiate a more favorable deal.

Working for Employers with Larger Budgets

Moving on to greener pastures, the day will eventually come when you're asked to work with successful and reputable employers who are willing to pay fairly and offer special perks—far greater, in some cases, than the minimum scales and fairness guidelines suggested by the unions.

But after adapting an "anything goes" approach to business for so long in your formative years, you may end up undercutting yourself in these new and potentially advantageous situations. To avoid that, you need to understand just what you may be entitled to.

The following discussion sheds light on your wages, retainers, per diems, buyouts, and much more. Keep in mind that the agreement you're able to negotiate, whether as either a contract employee or as an independent contractor, is substantially influenced by your reputation and experience, and/or how badly a potential employer wants to work with you. Be sure to hire an attorney before signing anything that you do not understand.

Wages

The wages you can expect from employers that have larger budgets will naturally be much greater than the compensation offered from employers with limited budgets.

On tour, Justin Timberlake paid a relatively unknown horn player a weekly salary of $4,000 to tour—which is a far cry from the $275 salary our blues musicians received in the story "Singing the Blues." Rod Stewart paid his musical director around $7,000 a week. And KISS paid their drummer, Eric Singer, a flat fee of $100,000 to cover all of his obligations in a year.

In the recording studio, employers often pay their musicians double or triple the union minimum scale for recording an album or overdubbing a solo (instrumentalists receive minimums of about $400 for three hours or less. Thus, double and triple scale fees are $800 and $1,200).

While employers with larger budgets can afford to pay handsomely to keep their musicians happy, there may be some who still prefer to lowball. Should this happen to you, never be afraid to negotiate politely for more money if you feel you have the clout to back it up.

Retainers

Moving on to another area related to wages, you should know that in times of temporary unemployment, such as during a break in a tour schedule, employers with larger budgets may provide you with additional benefits such as a "retainer." A retainer enables you to maintain an income while your services are on hold. You are expected to be, more or less, on call and are thus limited or excluded from taking on other work. A retainer is usually 50 percent of your weekly salary. Retainers are most common when you're working regularly for one artist.

Rehearsals

Rehearsals are yet another issue to consider when negotiating your employment agreement. However, if you are getting paid a really excellent wage, you may not want to rock the boat by asking for more. In any case, employers with larger budgets will often provide payment in preparation for phonograph recording sessions, single live performances, and extended tours. The amount will vary between employers, but minimum compensation of around $100 for a two-and-a-half-hour rehearsal is typical.

Per Diems

Moving on, per diems are the next matter to consider when negotiating your agreement. These are standard daily allowances for food and are not at all difficult to get written into your employment agreement. The amount varies greatly depending on the employer's budget, but ranges from around $50 to $250 per day and more. If you're performing a gig out of the country, remember that your per diem should be adjusted to reasonably accommodate the exchange rate.

Buyouts

In addition to providing a per diem, employers with larger budgets may offer you money in something called a buyout. A buyout occurs when the concert promoter does not fulfill his or her contractual obligation to provide food and drink backstage. This obligation is stipulated in a band "rider" (i.e., a contractual addendum in live performance contracts that also includes lighting and sound requirements for the group, dressing room accommodations, and security needs).

When the promoter fails to provide the requested food for backstage, he "buys" the band "out." Since buyouts are based on the number of people traveling with the band, a group may provide you with additional funds ranging from around $20 to $60 per buyout, and even more—but this is completely negotiable. There are cases where musicians receive hundreds of dollars in buyouts over the course of a concert tour. The amount is subject to the individual situation.

Special Travel and Lodging Accommodations

Travel costs (such as airline tickets and hotels) are always covered by employers, and are not a serious point of negotiation.

However, the quality of these services may be negotiable depending on how badly the employer wants you. It's not uncommon for employers with larger budgets to provide first-class airline tickets, single hotel room accommodations, and more.

Note, however, that hotel "incidentals" (phone calls, room service, and minibar) are typically your responsibility. So be careful! Incidentals can add up quickly—especially telephone calls and online services.

AFTERTHOUGHT: FREQUENT FLYERS Remember that employers pay for airline tickets and even purchase the seats for you. Just be sure that "you" get the frequent flyer credit. Register your name with every available airline frequent flyer program, give your ID numbers to your employer, and ask him or her to register your numbers when booking your tickets.

Special Clothing

Moving on to yet another point of negotiation that's really not too big a deal, let's discuss special clothing. If specific clothing that is not "standard" or "ordinary" is required for a promotional video shoot, stage show, or tour, the employer will usually reimburse you for the costs.

For instance, one musician was allotted $750 to buy studded black leather pants for a video shoot. Keep in mind that the amount of money you're offered depends on the specifics of each individual situation, but your total expenses should at least be covered in your agreement.

Instruments and Travel Cases

Musical equipment is another important factor to consider when arranging your deal with an employer. Instruments and protective travel cases may be provided via your employer's recording and/or deficit tour budgets.

One drummer I know needed heavy-duty travel cases for an upcoming European tour. After a brief discussion, the employer paid $4,000 to have the cases custom built. Better yet, when the tour was over, the employer offered the drummer the option of purchasing the gear at a tremendously low price.

Equipment Parts and Repairs

Getting close to the end of our discussion, you should know that employers with larger budgets may also cover minor equipment expenses for maintenance or usage of items, such as guitar picks, guitar strings, amplifier tubes, drumsticks, and drum skins.

When I was out on the road for one successful group that was earning large nightly guarantees, the techs regularly charged back sticks and skins to the employers. Pretty standard.

Equipment Endorsements

When your employer does not cover instrument and travel cases, and/or parts and repairs, he or she will usually be willing to help you leverage an equipment endorsement (by writing a letter of recommendation, making a call, etc.). This is not something that is written into an employment agreement, of course, but something that you definitely can discuss after hashing out other terms.

Most equipment manufacturers will begin your relationship by offering you a reduced price on equipment (usually 60 to 70 percent off the retail price). If you're currently working regularly for a very large and successful organization, some companies may offer you free equipment and advertise your name and likeness with their product. Sweet! Can't beat that! Note that endorsements are discussed more at the end of this chapter.

Equipment Techs

Moving on to the next point of negotiation, employers with larger budgets will typically hire equipment techs to tune, maintain, and set up / break down your equipment when recording or touring. A tech adds to the professionalism of a tour or recording session by allowing you to concentrate on your principal job—performing.

Should an employer refuse to guarantee you an equipment tech, you should at least ask that he or she increase your fee accordingly so that you can afford to hire one yourself. It's worth asking. Remember that a good tech is really worth his or her weight in gold.

Equipment Insurance

No matter whether you or your employer hires the equipment tech, you should know that if your musical equipment is lost or damaged on the road (e.g., if an amplifier is dropped from a truck or a guitar is left at the last gig), your employer or, in some cases, the venue in which you are performing should cover the repair or replacement costs under their own insurance coverage. Be sure that insurance is discussed with your employer and that it is noted in your agreement.

So now let's check out yet another type of employment situation that can offer even more money and perks—working for employers under a salary/percentage involvement.

HOW TO GET, AND KEEP, AN EQUIPMENT ENDORSEMENT

While the topic of endorsements and equipment is still fresh, and since endorsements are so important to any working musician, I should probably expand on this topic for a moment. Just keep in mind that until you're getting the type of "attention" that can help manufacturers sell product, a deal may be a long way off. In any case, here are a few tips for when you are ready:

- ***Build Some Accomplishments:*** Pay your dues and build your list of professional accomplishments (i.e., the artists you've played with, number of students you have, and top producers you've recorded for).
- ***Create a Slamming Press Kit:*** Put together a press kit, including pictures of your current setup, upcoming/past tour dates, samples of your playing, management and record label contact info, and proof you're generating "attention" in your community.
- ***Solicit Manufacturers You Truly Love:*** Don't send your press package to every equipment manufacturer on the planet. Only solicit to those manufacturers whose equipment you love and know well.
- ***Be Patiently Persistent:*** Be very polite, courteous, and humble when making follow-up calls. Never get mad if you don't get past the receptionist.
- ***Know Your Local Music Store Reps:*** Get to know the salespeople at local music stores—these folks are regularly in touch with major manufacturers, and knowing them could be an "in" to getting a first-level discount endorsement.
- ***Attend NAMM:*** Get out and network in the industry—attend the NAMM convention and introduce yourself directly to product reps.
- ***Pitch Newer Companies:*** Keep an eye open for new and developing companies—they are often more interested in working with less established artists.
- ***Invent Something:*** Conceive new product ideas of your own and then pitch them to various companies. Manufacturers are usually very receptive to useful ideas.
- ***Honor Your Contract:*** If you get an endorsement, be sure to expose the brand name whenever possible, don't attempt to hook up friends with free gear, and always give your product rep VIP treatment at the shows he attends.
- ***Keep in Touch:*** Don't just call your rep when you need something. Make friends and take him or her out to lunch now and again. And finally . . .
- ***Get a Big Gig:*** Score a gig with a major artists and ask his or her management to assist you in a letter of recommendation. That's almost an automatic endorsement.

Working for Employers Who Offer a Salary and Percentages

Last but not least, let's look at another employment situation that can affect the way you negotiate your employment agreement. I like to call these situations "salary/percentage involvements."

Salary/percentage involvements exist when an established artist desires your contributions to the writing, recording, and touring of an album, and therefore may hire you and offer you both a salary and a percentage of the future profits. Here's what you need to know:

- ***Salary:*** As an employee, you should always be compensated fairly for your services, plain and simple. If, however, you are offered percentages, you may be expected to make some of the same sacrifices that the members of the band have to make, such as attending "promotional events" (i.e., group photo shoots, video shoots, press interviews, radio interviews, and record store promotions). Just keep in mind, though, that if you're ever asked to work for free, it shouldn't cost you a dime to do so; you should always receive a per diem and have all your expenses paid.

- ***Artist (Record) Royalties:*** Artist royalties are percentages the record company pays the artist for the sale of his/her record. While owning a percentage or two sounds tempting, it could amount to zero pay when factoring in all of the advances that must first be "recouped" (earned back) by the record company. Your objective is to negotiate record royalties in your agreement with the band. But don't be deceived by the apparent significance of these royalties when negotiating other aspects of your deal.
- ***Merchandising Monies:*** If your image is used on T-shirts, or if merchandise generally reflects work in which you were involved (e.g., a T-shirt including a lyric from a song you helped to write), you may receive some percentage of the merchandising revenue. When negotiating your agreement, ask for sales statements to track your fair share.
- ***Music Publishing Royalties:*** Finally, if you're asked to participate in the songwriting process, ask for guaranteed compensation. Since no one can foresee whether the songs to which you contribute will make the final cut on the album (everyone but you will have the final say), you could end up investing weeks or months demoing the group's ideas for free without gaining much, if anything, in music publishing royalties. If you think I'm kidding, see the story below, "Read the (Song) Writing on the Wall."

In closing, salary/percentage involvements can be misleading. You may feel as if you're occupying the gray area between employee and band member. But be clear—you're simply an employee in the business of you. So be smart. Be professional. And handle your business well.

READ THE (SONG) WRITING ON THE WALL

Preliminary employment agreements that outline clearly the terms of your compensation are a must.

According to former employees of a well-known guitarist, after a tour of Japan, they were all asked by the guitarist to begin "throwing around song ideas" for a new album. They met with the guitarist for five days a week, over more than two and a half months, and worked primarily on the guitar player's ideas.

When it came time to record the album, the guitarist not only chose to replace his band with a new group of musicians, he also didn't use any of the compositions to which his original musicians had contributed musically or lyrically. The old band had donated approximately 250 hours of their time arranging and demoing the guitarist's material, received zero compensation, and were all out of work! Could they have found a way to sue? They didn't have the time or money!

So, is this all just "tough luck" on the part of the musicians or just bad business? It's bad business! As I said before, it is extremely important to pay your dues and be grateful for work, but you are in the business of "you" and you must cover your ass with a clear understanding of your compensation. If you think you have the clout, never be afraid to negotiate your employment agreement before taking the gig.

6

Contract Employment or Self-Employment, Part 3

Taxes and Insurance

"Did you ever notice that when you put the words 'the' and 'IRS' together it spells 'theirs'?"
—Anonymous

I saved the most exciting material in this three-part section for last—taxes and insurance.

But, with all sarcasm aside, one must never underestimate the importance of this stuff! IRS audits are not just reserved for the super wealthy anymore. And considering the dangers of traveling from city to city, night after night while working for an employer out on the road, your chances of injury are increased significantly and you want be insured and protected.

Let's check out some of the basics.

Understanding Your Taxes: Uncle Sam's Cut

Taxes are mandatory payments imposed on individuals and businesses by the federal and state governments. They are used for everything from supporting our military and law enforcement, to maintaining our parks and roads.

While taxes are boring, they cannot be ignored, even by musicians. Failure to file your taxes correctly can lead to strict penalties and an examination (or audit) by the Internal Revenue Service (IRS).

Taxes are where the distinction between contract employees and self-employed performers becomes really relevant. Why? Each worker is treated differently under law, and the difference in taxes can be substantial. So pay close attention! [Note: All rates are subject to change.]

Contract Employment (Why Is My Check So Small?)

If you're a contract employee in an ongoing working relationship, your paycheck is going to be significantly lower than the amount that was promised by your employer thanks to mandatory taxes.

Income Taxes

The largest portion of your total annual tax bill as a contract employee is the money you pay on your income at the federal, state, and/or local levels. The more money you make, the higher the "tax bracket" you fall in, and the higher the percentage in taxes you may have to pay.

- **Employer Withholdings:** Your employer is responsible for withholding income taxes from all of your pay, including wages and per diems. This is a system referred to as "pay-as-you-go" (pay on the money you earn, as you earn it). If you look closely at one of your paycheck stubs, this is indicated as "FITW," "SITW," and/or "local tax withholdings."

- **W-4 Forms:** The amount withheld from your paycheck represents an estimate of the taxes you owe. This amount is based in part on personal information you provide on federal tax form W-4 (and the state equivalent) as to whether you are single or married, have children, own a home, etc. You should turn in a W-4 form to your employer at the time your employment begins.

Social Security and Medicare

The next significant portion of your tax bill as a contract employee is Social Security and Medicare taxes. These provide retirement and health insurance for people over 62 years of age.

- **Employer Withholdings:** Your employer is required to withhold Social Security and Medicare taxes from your pay. This is indicated on your paycheck as "FICA-OASDI" and "FICA-HI," respectively.
- **Social Security—6.2 Percent:** The Social Security tax required to be withheld is 6.2 percent of your income (up to a yearly income of $117,000). And finally . . .
- **Medicare—1.45 Percent:** The Medicare tax required to be withheld is 1.45 percent of your income (with no limit on your yearly income).

State Unemployment Tax/Insurance

Yet an additional tax that must be paid in most states as a contract employee is state unemployment tax/insurance. This provides benefits to employees who are laid off or are between cycles of seasonal work.

- **Employer Withholdings:** Your employer must withhold state unemployment taxes and insurance (in all states other than Alaska, Florida, Nevada, Texas, South Dakota, Washington, and Wyoming). This is indicated on your paycheck as "SUI."
- **Eligibility:** When you are laid off or between seasonal jobs (like touring), you should contact your state agency immediately to see if you are eligible for benefits. (A little extra cash can come in handy until you resume work.) Eligibility for state unemployment benefits varies from state to state, but generally it is based on a specific minimum amount of dollars withheld by your employer for taxes during a specified period of time.

State Disability Insurance

Finally, another tax that must also be withheld from your paychecks as a contract employee in certain states is state disability insurance. This provides benefits if you're injured off the job, or become sick or pregnant.

- **Employer Withholdings:** Employers who reside in California, Hawaii, New Jersey, New York, and Rhode Island must withhold state disability insurance. Looking closely at your paycheck stub, this is indicated as "SDI."
- **Eligibility:** Your employer is required to provide you with information about state disability insurance at the time of your employment. If you're unable to work for several months due to an injury, disability insurance can be a lifesaver. Note: Workers' compensation insurance, which covers you for job related injuries, is discussed later.

Year-End Reporting: W-2s, Deducting or Itemizing, and More

As the end of the year approaches, all contract employees (this means you) must make sure that their business and tax affairs are in order and that they are prepared to file their returns.

- **W-2 Forms:** Your employer will issue you form W-2, which indicates both your total income and the total amount of taxes withheld from your paycheck during the calendar year. This form must be issued by your employer no later than January 31 (following the tax year). Remember that the amount withheld from your paychecks throughout the year only represents an estimate of the taxes you must pay to the IRS and/or state tax authorities by April 15 (or the extended due date). Thus, be sure to contact a certified public accountant (CPA) who specializes in entertainment business taxes to help you minimize your ultimate tax liability.

- **Schedule-A "Itemized" Deductions:** One way to minimize your liability might be to "itemize" (i.e., list) various allowed tax deductible expenses. These expenses (reported on tax form Schedule A) can add up substantially and reduce your tax bill. They include miscellaneous expenses related to your home office, magazine subscriptions, union dues, stage clothes, education, travel, and tax preparation. You'd be surprised at what you can write off, so be sure to hold on to all of your receipts and paycheck stubs and keep detailed records of all of your business activities in an Excel spreadsheet. (Now see the box that follows for a comprehensive list of deductions to which you may be entitled.)

TWENTY TAX DEDUCTIONS THAT COULD KEEP MONEY IN YOUR BANK

Below are a few examples of the deductions that you *may* be able to claim on your tax returns—either miscellaneous itemized deductions if you're a contract employee (Schedule A deductions), or trade/business deductions if you're an independent contractor (Schedule C deductions).

- ***Union Dues:*** The cost of joining the AFM or SAG-AFTRA.
- ***Service Fees:*** For joining professional services like Taxi, ASCAP, and TuneCore.
- ***Mailing:*** Mail costs for résumés and promotional kits.
- ***Dry Cleaning:*** Dry cleaning costs for stage clothes, etc.
- ***Conventions:*** Music conferences such as NAMM and SXSW
- ***Business Gifts:*** Greeting cards, alcohol, etc.
- ***Attorney Fees:*** The cost of hiring an attorney to review a contract, etc.
- ***Accountant Costs:*** Tax preparation costs.
- ***Education:*** Educational expenses for music lessons and seminars.
- ***Telephone Calls for Business:*** The portion of your bill that was specifically used for business calls. For practical purposes, this might require making an estimate.
- ***Promotion:*** Website hosting, Internet service providers, and business cards.
- ***Stage Clothing:*** For stage clothing that would not normally be worn on the street, like your winged bat costume or your DeadMau5 mouse head costume.
- ***Entertainment Meal Expenses:*** Lunch meetings, business dinners, and cocktails with a colleague to discuss business.
- ***Research Tools:*** The cost of CDs, streaming subscriptions, and movie tickets.
- ***Related Work Tools:*** Instrument fees, repairs, and maintenance.
- ***Depreciation of Work Tools:*** You can deduct a portion of your equipment's cost over several years as it depreciates in value.
- ***Subscriptions:*** Magazines such as *Billboard*, *Guitar Player*, and *Rolling Stone*.
- ***Home Office Expenses:*** The cost of office space in your home or apartment used exclusively for business, such as home studios and rehearsal rooms. Deductions may include a portion of your rent, utilities, cable, phone, and the like.
- ***Travel Expenses:*** The cost of airline tickets, lodging, taxis, limousines, food, personal grooming related to work (shampoos and conditioners, etc.), tips (for meals, baggage handlers, etc.), travel costs for an associate (if for a bona fide business reason), passport photo, and application fees. And finally . . .

- ***Car Expenses or Standard Mileage:*** The cost of leasing fees, insurance, gas, tolls, parking, car washes, depreciation of your vehicle, and trailers to haul extra gear. Or you can deduct the miles you put on your car for commuting to a temporary, but not a regular, place of business.

Self-Employment / Independent Contractor Status

Now let's discuss taxes as they apply to self-employed musicians. As you'll see, freelance musicians have a lot more responsibilities.

Income Taxes

If you're a self-employed musician working in shorter-term relationships, you are also subject to income taxes, including federal, state, and/or local taxes, but these are handled differently than they are for contract employees.

- **Withholding Is on You:** You are responsible for estimating and paying your own taxes. These payments are usually due throughout the tax year on a quarterly basis—April 15, June 15, September 15, and January 15. However, there are some exceptions, for instance, for those who are also doing contract work and getting a significant portion of their pay from this work withheld from their employers. Be sure to talk to your accountant.
- **W-9:** The people with whom you work will usually issue you form W-9, which obligates you to provide important information, such as your name, address, and social security number (or tax ID number). A W-9 is usually used by employers to track the amount of money that they pay you throughout the year.

Self-Employment Taxes (Social Security and Medicare)

In addition to paying income taxes, you may have to pay a "self-employment tax."

- **Self-Employment Tax—15.3 Percent:** Self-employment taxes are approximately 15.3 percent on your net earnings. This consists of 12.4 percent for Social Security and 2.9 percent for Medicare. Note that this is double the percentage of income that you pay in Social Security and Medicare taxes as a contract employee.

Year-End Reporting: 1099s, Schedule C Deductions, and More

Now, as the end of the year approaches, all self-employed musicians must make sure that their business and tax affairs are in order and that they are prepared to file their final tax returns.

- **1099 Forms:** No later than January 31, the bands or organizations you have worked for should provide you with tax form 1099-MISC, which indicates the total income that you received from them for the calendar year. You must then report this income and related expenses on your federal and state tax returns.
- **"Schedule C" Deductions:** You may be able to reduce the amount of money you owe in taxes by deducting what the IRS considers "ordinary" and "necessary" expenses related to your trade/business. These expenses, called "Schedule C" deductions (filed on IRS tax form Schedule C), are for office supplies, business travel expenses, car expenses, legal expenses, union dues, etc. Just be sure to hang on to all of your business expense receipts throughout the year. And finally . . .

- **Self-Employed Tax Deduction:** You can deduct the employer-equivalent portion of your self-employment tax (i.e., 7.65 percent) in figuring your adjusted gross income. Adds accountant George Fernandez, "Note that this deduction only affects your income tax. It does not affect either your net earnings from self-employment or your self-employment tax." Right on, George! We'll take your word for it.

In closing, the rules regarding tax deductions for independent contractors, as well as for contract employees, are tricky and subject to interpretation. Therefore, it's always a good idea to contact an experienced certified public accountant specializing in entertainment for assistance.

HOW TO KEEP BETTER BUSINESS AND TAX RECORDS

A key part of handling your business and taxes correctly is staying organized and keeping good records. Below are 14 tips to help you get started:

- ***File Important Documents:*** Buy a two-drawer filing cabinet from your local office supply store and keep important documents in clearly marked envelopes.
- ***Keep Paycheck Stubs:*** Be sure to keep all of your paycheck stubs. At the end of the year, when you receive your 1099 and/or W-2 forms, be sure that all of these amounts match up.
- ***Create and Store Invoices:*** Any time that you provide a service for a fee, it may not be a bad idea to create an invoice for the event. When you are paid, file it. Invoices can be easily created in any word processing program.
- ***Keep Copies of Your Bills:*** Be sure to save all copies of your utility bills, including electricity and phone bills, since these can sometimes be included as write-offs.
- ***File Your Contracts:*** Always keep employment agreements (and music licensing contracts or record deals, too) in clearly marked files.
- ***Keep a Notebook in Your Car:*** Be sure to keep a small notebook in the glove compartment of your car and log all of your business mileage, since this can be written off in some cases. Admittedly, this is kind of pain to do, but it can save you money.
- ***File Receipts:*** Create specific folders for your expenses (gas, entertainment meals, etc.) and be sure to neatly store all of your receipts in these folders. If you can keep a running total of each category you'll save yourself a lot of time at the end of the year.
- ***Digitize Receipts:*** There are a number of hardware devices and software programs that allow you to scan, digitize, organize, and total your receipts. This is a much more efficient system than keeping paper receipts. Check out NeatReceipts (www.neat.com).
- ***Consider Do-It-Yourself Accounting Services:*** Companies like Intuit have created services that allow you to organize your financial life and keep track of bank deposits and withdrawals, account balances, and expenses. Classes are offered in how to use these programs, or you can check out online tutorials. Software programs and online subscription services are available. Check out QuickBooks (www.quickbooks.com).
- ***Log Correspondences:*** Keep business e-mails stored in digital folders and keep letters (if you still get those) in files where you can refer to them later.
- ***Consult with a Professional:*** A professional organizer and/or business consultant can really help set you straight in regard to keeping an efficient office environment. Why not consider hiring one today? Conduct an online search or ask for referrals.

- ***Learn Excel:*** Excel, a program that is part of Microsoft Office Suite, is an excellent tool for creating databases and spreadsheets containing your important information. You can also find free online spreadsheet services that you can create and store "in the cloud." Google offers great options with Google Docs (https://www.google.com/docs/about/).
- ***Buy Books on Decluttering:*** There are a number of books that offer suggestions on organizing your office space, including decluttering, storage techniques, and more. And finally . . .
- ***File All Your Tax Forms:*** File all of your W-2 and 1099 forms in one place when they are sent to you at the end of the year. You will need these forms when filing your taxes.

Workers' Compensation Insurance

Now that you've got the basics of taxes down, let's jump into the important subject of workers' compensation insurance. This will be brief, I promise.

Workers' compensation covers your medical expenses if you are hurt on the job, pays you an income while you are disabled, and offers "vocational rehabilitation" if you are permanently unable to return to work. It can make the difference between thriving and going bankrupt (as you'll see below in the story "Shit Happens").

Contract employees and independent contractors are treated differently when it comes to insurance, and you must understand what your employment status offers you. Take a quick look at this breakdown of the rules.

Contract Employees: Covered

Employers are required by state law to provide contract employees with workers' compensation insurance issued by a licensed carrier. There are exceptions, however.

In some states, an employer with two or fewer employees may not have to purchase workers' compensation insurance. Be sure to ask your employer about coverage at the time of your employment.

Self-Employment / Independent Contractor Status: Not Covered

The people for whom you provide freelance work are not responsible for providing workers' compensation insurance. This means you're responsible for getting your own insurance to cover medical costs for injuries that occur on and off the job. Additionally, you'll need to be covered if you become sick, pregnant, or disabled, and unable to work for several months or years.

If Not Covered, Where Can I Find Insurance?

Securing insurance is expensive, but you might consider the following alternatives:

- ***Shop Around:*** You can use the Marketplace to find affordable health coverage that works for you. Check out www.healthcare.gov for more information.
- ***Join the Unions:*** You may qualify for health insurance coverage by joining the music unions, especially after working several union-covered gigs.
- ***Get on a Spouse's Plan:*** If you have a spouse who works a steady job, you may be able to receive coverage on his or her policy.
- ***Find Steady Employment:*** Seek full-time employment (like drummer Kenwood Dennard does at Berklee College of Music) in addition to all of your sideman work. And finally . . .
- ***Consider Special Assistance Programs:*** Contact the MusiCares Foundation (www.grammy.com) and the Actors Fund's Musicians' Assistance Program (www.actorsfund.org).

Whatever you decisions you make for insurance, just make sure that you are covered. With the passing of the Affordable Care Act by President Obama, there is no excuse in this day and age not to be covered with some form of insurance. It could come in handy. Just read the story below.

SHIT HAPPENS!

For touring musicians in particular, your risk of injury is increased when traveling from city to city, night after night, and it should not be underestimated.

Eminem's tour bus crashed while swerving to avoid an 18-wheeler. Eminem's rapper "The Alchemist" and several crew members were hospitalized.

Metallica's guitarist/vocalist James Hetfield suffered first- and third-degree burns after a stage prop exploded during a show in Montreal, Canada.

And, in a near-fatal incident, one anonymous musician was hit by a truck while on the way back to his hotel after a performance in New York City. He suffered a pulmonary embolism and was very grateful to be covered by his employer's insurance, even though it took two frustrating years before the insurance company paid a total of $73,000 in hospital bills and compensated him for the many months he was not able to work. Without the aid of insurance, he would have been wiped out. Can you guess who this musician was?

The IRS: Qualifications for Employment

Coming to the close of this chapter, it should be apparent that there are major differences between contract employees and independent contractors when it comes to tax issues and workers' compensation insurance. So, can you choose between one status and the other?

- ***What an Employee Might Naively Think—Bigger Checks:*** An employee may prefer to be treated as an independent contractor to avoid having taxes taken out of his or her paycheck and receive more money up front. But you can't run from Uncle Sam, and eventually you'll need to report your income to the IRS and pay taxes on what you earned. Also keep in mind that if you're treated as an independent contractor, you won't be eligible for state unemployment benefits.
- ***What an Employer Might Think—Less Responsibility:*** An employer may prefer to treat you as an independent contractor rather than as a contract employee because it limits his or her responsibility to you. By treating you as an independent contractor, employers avoid withholding certain taxes and matching payments, as well as payments toward workers' compensation insurance. This means that you either have to purchase your own insurance or risk not being covered.
- ***What the Government Says:*** While employers may tend to bend the rules from time to time, the IRS has very specific guidelines for employers about how they should treat their musicians. Failure to follow these rules can result in penalties. So, legally speaking, no matter what musicians or employers think, they'd better abide by the law, because Uncle Sam is watching and will find them.

So that's all I have for contract employees or self-employed musicians. The next type of business relationship in the following chapter will examine solo artists. Enjoy!

EMPLOYEE OR NOT—THAT IS THE QUESTION

Suppose you've been hired by a band to go out on the road for three months with the promise of a weekly salary as compensation for your services. Before the tour starts, you're required to show up for rehearsals from Monday through Friday from 8 p.m. to 12 midnight to learn the band's material with the group's musical director.

The day before the first performance, you're flown out on a commercial airliner (at the band's expense) to the city where the tour is to begin. From that point forward, you travel on a tour bus under the direction of a tour manager, who makes sure that you get on stage on time and that you're on the bus every morning when traveling to the next city. Additionally, all of your hotel accommodations are paid for.

In this scenario, you would be considered an employee by the IRS and your employer should treat you accordingly or suffer the consequences.

7

Solo Artist and Employer

Pros, Cons, and Responsibilities

"With great risk comes great reward." —Thomas Jefferson

The solo artist is a rare and special breed of musician. He or she might be an exceptional writer or instrumentalist who plays a melodic instrument, a producer/DJ who creates and "spins" records, a skilled vocalist who's blessed with undeniable looks and image, a highly motivated individual who possesses the desire to lead, or any combination of the above.

Although your name and likeness may be individually displayed on venue marquees and merchandising, you'll rarely be working alone. You might lead a group of studio and gigging musicians, or may even collaborate with skilled songwriters and producers.

As your career develops, it's also likely that you'll have a team of advisors consisting of an attorney, a personal manager, a business manager, and a talent agent. The solo artist sits at the helm, steering this musical battleship into the turbulent waters of the music business.

This chapter takes a look at the advantages and disadvantages of going solo, "leaving member clauses" found in recording agreements, the business and legal responsibilities of solo artists, and an interview with DJ solo artist/entrepreneur Justin Paul.

The Advantages of Going Solo

While being a solo artist, or the "captain of your own ship," may not be for everyone, it has its advantages. These include fewer hassles over making decisions, increased earning potential, greater job security, and more freedom to "sail" alone.

Fewer Hassles over Making Decisions

Perhaps the greatest advantage of being a solo artist is that the decision-making process is far simpler than for that of a band. Bottom line: you don't need approval from the other band members on every creative, personal, and business matter that comes up.

It's no surprise that many bands break up due to difference of opinion (the Who, the Beatles, the Police, Oasis, NWA, Bone Thugs-N-Harmony, Smashing Pumpkins, My Chemical Romance, and Evanescence come to mind, for a start). While it is often the creative polarity between band members that helps shape the best music of our time, many solo musicians prefer the autonomy of going solo.

Increased Earning Potential

The "love of your music" should be your number one motivator, but money is an important part of life.

That said, another advantage of going solo over being in a band is that you will earn a greater share of the profits (artist royalties, music publishing incomes, merchandising monies, concert monies, and sponsorships funds) as your career develops into a fruitful endeavor.

After all, you're the boss and essentially call the shots in regard to how you'll split profits and pay your musicians—that is, considering you even hire musicians at all. As you'll hear in the interview at the end of this chapter, many electronic DJs show up to their gigs totally solo with no more than a thumb drive containing their music.

Greater Job Security

Job security may be another advantage to going solo as opposed to being in a band. One thing's for certain: You'll never have to worry about getting kicked out of your own solo project due to something like creative differences—unless, of course, your dual personality begins to hate you. And if this happens, job security is the least of your problems. [Grin.]

More Freedom to "Sail" Alone

Going solo can also mean that there's more freedom to come and go as you please—there's simply no "dead weight" (a.k.a. other band members) holding you back.

It's the indie artist at the beginning of her career who can hit the road armed with no more than her voice and guitar if she should so choose (no vans and trailers hauling drum kits and amps needed here). In fact, I've even seen some do-it-yourself artists brave enough to hitchhike from state to state on their "bare bones" tours—something four band members certainly would have trouble pulling off.

As a solo artist you make your own schedules and timelines and essentially do as you please. As indie artist Gilli Moon eloquently states, "There's more freedom to sailing solo."

The Disadvantages of Going Solo

Although being a solo artist may exempt you from the democracy required in a band, offer more job security, and increase your earning potential, there are several disadvantages to going solo. These include greater financial burdens, increased workload, greater leadership and business demands, fewer people to blame or hide behind, and more pressure to succeed.

Greater Financial Burdens

Being a solo artist means that all financial burdens rest entirely on you, including all expenses, investments, debts, and loans.

For the indie artist just starting out on a limited to zero-dollar budget, money usually presents a serious challenge. There are costs for rehearsing, recording music, manufacturing albums, building websites, shooting professional photos, putting together press kits, and copying postcards—expenses that are all far easier to split between band members.

Going solo can be a costly proposition. On this note, have you ever noticed the number of artists that were part of self-contained bands and established a name before they went solo? One must wonder if there's a correlation.

Nonetheless, never opt for being what I call a "solo artist in disguise": someone who forms a "band" only with the intention of going solo once his or her finances are strong. That's just bad karma and unfair to the other members. Enough said!

Increased Workload

Being a solo artist also means that the brunt of the work falls on you. Unlike being in a band, where each member shares sacrifices on the road to success, you're essentially working 24/7. Whether it be responding to e-mail, updating your social media sites, creating and posting videos on video sharing sites, promoting your live performances, or composing all of the songs, you're essentially on your own!

Even when your career progresses into the big leagues when you're signed and you can afford to hire a professional team to help, your job is really never done—you're the one whom people want to interview, and you're the one who'd better show up. Make no mistake: bands may break up, but solo artists break down.

Greater Leadership and Business Demands

Solo artists must also endure the pressures of finding their musicians and keeping them happy. Remember that the best method for finding musicians is through recommendations from people you trust: musicians, producers, managers, and club promoters. You can also call your local musician's union, attend local jam sessions and open mics, check out the hottest bands in your area, place ads in your local music paper, ask reps at local music stores, attend music seminars, and post announcements on message boards and blogs on the Web.

Once you find those talented and experienced players, you must eventually offer them good pay, good gigs, and career growth—it's only so long that your musicians are going to play at the corner bar while being compensated with Subway sandwiches or free drink tickets.

Finally, you need to always make your musicians feel appreciated, while at the same time reminding them who's in control. This can be one of the more difficult aspects of your job. It's important to recognize the fine line between being your employees' friend and their leader.

BE A LEADER, BUT NEVER A DICTATOR!

Although most solo artists understand the importance of treating their musicians with respect and fair compensation, and they strive to abide by this rule (as, one day, you will), many superstar performers are known to dangle the proverbial carrot of fame before their musicians' eyes and treat them like crap. However, this attitude usually prevents bandleaders from keeping great players over the long term.

According to infamous published stories, big band leader Buddy Rich actually made his band get off the tour bus in the middle of the Nevada desert because he didn't like the way they had played that night. The musicians (24 in total) had to literally hitchhike all the way back to Los Angeles. That's just wrong!

In another story (according to the hired keyboardist), a very famous singer (who I'll keep anonymous) prohibited all of his musicians while out on tour from talking to all females within 50 feet of his presence. In fact, the keyboardist was fired on the spot when he was found talking to a female fan in the hotel lobby as the singer passed through to go to the restaurant. Even worse, the keyboardist wasn't allowed to go back up to his room to pack his bags. The road crew did it for him.

Fewer Members to Blame or Hide Behind

Moving on with more disadvantages of going solo, you must also deal with all the heat, the criticism, and the stress. From record critiques to press reviews to concert performances, you sink or swim on your own. Simply put, there's no band to blame or hide behind if your creative and business choices fail. As Jerry Cantrell of Alice in Chains puts it, "It's my shit. My name is on the marquee, as well as on the paychecks, so it all comes down to me."

More Pressure to Succeed

Last but not least, many musicians feel the pressure of living up to the title "solo artist." The term "solo artist" essentially implies that you don't need anyone but yourself. Then there's the added pressure for some solo artists of living up to the successes of their former bands. Although many artists have gone on to succeed in their own right (Beyoncé Knowles of Destiny's Child, and Justin Timberlake of *NSYNC), there are just as many solo artists who have failed (U-God of Wu-Tang Clan and MC Ren of N.W.A.). You have to be tough to go solo.

Leaving Member Clauses: The Record Company's Rights to Solo Artists

As mentioned above, many solo artists are first part of self-contained bands that progress forward to signing recording agreements and releasing albums. Thus, it's a good idea to briefly look at something called a "leaving member clause" found in recording contracts.

What Is a Leaving Member Clause?

Understand that when a band signs a recording agreement with a record company, the label usually wants the rights to all members as a band, as well as the rights of any leaving member who becomes a solo artist or member of another band.

In case that didn't mean anything to you, if you're an artist who was once a member of a signed group (successful or not), the record company may own the rights to your new solo career! Their rationale is that if the company is going to invest a lot of money into developing your career and making you a star, then it has the right to reap the long-term benefits as well.

How Does a Leaving Member Clause Work?

Let's say you decided to leave your group because of creative differences. Coincidentally, suppose their record was also a flop and they had an outstanding balance to the record company of $400,000. If you record a new album and spend another $150,000 in the studio, you'll now be $550,000 in debt to the record company.

In other words, before you receive a dime in artist royalties from sales, all monies will be credited toward paying your former band's unrecouped balance as well as your new debt to the record company. Yikes! But before you decide to throw the idea of your solo career away, let's close out this section with some good news.

Leaving Member Clauses and Prorating Expenses

In most instances, you can negotiate an agreement with the record company that stipulates that only your share of your band's unrecouped balance carries over to your new account as a solo artist. This means that if there were four members in your former band, only a quarter of the unrecouped balance can be charged against your royalty account. Staying with the above example of the band with the $400,000 debt to their label, only $100,000 can be carried over to your new account. Hey, it's better than $400,000!

Oh, and in case you're wondering, if your former band stays together and records a new album that also flops, typically no new debts to the record company will affect you. You had nothing to do with these records and are not responsible for any debt associated with them.

PEARL JAMMED

Because of the leaving member clause, Pearl Jam already owed $500,000 to their label before ever recording an album. This debt carried over from Stone Gossard and Jeff Ament's first band, Mother Love Bone. Mother Love Bone's singer died of an overdose before their debut record, *Apple*, was ever released. Mother Love Bone broke up, but their label had the rights to Stone and Jeff as individual artists. When Stone and Jeff went on to form Pearl Jam, their debt followed, as per their contract.

The Business and Legal Responsibilities of Solo Artists

Now let's briefly discuss the business and legal responsibilities you'll have as a solo artist to your musicians.

In the early stages of your career, when you're making little or no money, your business responsibilities to your musicians might simply consist of supplying lunch after rehearsals or buying a round of drinks after gigs. As long as these musicians aren't misled into believing the relationship is something more substantial, like that of a partnership (i.e., a band), this may be an acceptable course of action for right now.

However, as your career starts evolving as a solo artist and employer, you will need to start treating your business affairs more professionally. You may be responsible for paying your musicians minimum-scale wages, deducting payroll taxes, and providing workers' compensation insurance. While I highly recommend you seek the advice of an experienced entertainment accountant, business manager, or attorney on these often complex and tedious issues, the following sections will provide a brief overview of what's needed.

Treat It Like a True "Work Made for Hire"

The first step in handling your business and legal responsibilities as an employer is to have your musicians fill out an agreement that stipulates they are being hired under a "work made for hire" arrangement, and that any rights in your songs or master recordings that might be otherwise granted to them by law, are irrevocably quitclaimed and assigned to you.

What this agreement essentially states is that your musicians' involvement in no way entitles them to ownership in your musical compositions, recorded masters or performances, or any other aspect of your solo career (unless, of course, you intend to offer them a share in the future profits, and you explicitly note this in a written employment agreement from the start).

So take this step seriously. Make sure your employees know where you and they stand.

Pay Wages and Commissions

As solo artists advance to the pros, employers must pay their musicians an hourly wage, flat salary, or a salary plus a percentage of the future profits. These are discussed below.

Minimum Hourly Wage

Employers typically pay their musicians—who are working on a shorter-term basis—a minimum wage imposed by state and federal laws. Information regarding minimum wages, hours, and working conditions can be obtained by contacting a local state department of labor.

The American Federation of Musicians (AFM) and SAG-AFTRA also provide information regarding "fairness" guidelines and recommended compensation for musicians. The unions are discussed in detail in chapter 4.

Flat Salary

When musicians are hired for tours or other situations that will extend over several weeks or months, employers often pay their them a flat salary that covers all of their services.

Solo artist Henry Rollins says, "My musicians are out on the road doing the same job as me, so I show them respect. I pay them the same salary I pay myself. This is sound advice!"

Salary Plus a Percentage

Finally, employers pay their "more permanent" employees a salary plus additional perks such as a predetermined percentage of merchandising sales, record sales, music publishing monies, and more. This usually happens when an employer desires a musician's presence on recordings, merchandise, and tours, and wants to sweeten the deal to keep that musician happy and focused on the music.

Just remember that the happier your musicians are, the better they're going to make you look and sound. So pay them well! "If all you pay is peanuts, all you'll get is monkeys." So true!

Handle Income, Social Security, and Payroll Taxes

Another business and legal responsibility of employers to their contract musicians involves withholding taxes for musicians working on a long-term basis. Don't worry, I'll be short.

All employers are responsible for withholding federal, state, and/or local income taxes, as well as Social Security taxes, from their employees' paychecks. Keep in mind that the IRS has severe penalties for employers who don't comply with federal and state withholding and other payroll tax requirements.

Note: Remember that employers are not responsible for deducting income, Social Security, and payroll taxes from the earnings of individuals working on a freelance short-term basis (also called "independent contractor status").

Although it's likely you'll have an experienced accountant or business manager assisting you in these matters, it's important to have a basic understanding of the mechanics of taxation—no matter how dry and boring tax laws may seem. Please refer to chapter 6 for a brief overview.

Provide Workers' Compensation Insurance

As if the above responsibilities were not enough, employers may also be required by state law to purchase workers' compensation insurance for their contract musicians working on a long-term basis.

Workers' compensation insurance covers injuries that occur on the job, pays your employees' medical expenses and income while they are disabled, and provides vocational rehabilitation should an employee be permanently unable to return to work. Once again, please refer to chapter 6 for an overview of this subject.

Note: As with deducting taxes, employers are not responsible for providing workers' compensation insurance to freelance musicians or independent contractors.

Know the Difference: Contract Employee or Independent Contractor Status

Finally, remember that it is the employer's responsibility to know whether to treat his or her musicians like employees or independent contractors. This is crucial for both tax and workers' compensation purposes. Mishandling of these matters can lead to serious fines by the IRS.

The solo artist must treat the musician as an employee when these factors exist:

- ***Instructions:*** When the solo artist requires a musician to comply with rules about when, where, and how he or she is to work, and the solo artist has the rights and control to enforce these rules.
- ***Continuing Relationship:*** When the solo artist hires a musician to perform services in a continuing relationship, and the solo artist provides directions as to where the work is to be performed at frequently recurring although irregular intervals.
- ***Set Hours of the Week:*** When the solo artist establishes set hours of work and enforces this as a condition of employment.
- ***Payment by Hour, Week, Month:*** When the solo artist pays by the hour, week, or month of regular amounts at stated intervals.
- ***Full-Time Required:*** When the solo artist requires a musician to devote his or her full time to the business, and the solo artist has control over the amount of time the musician spends working and implicitly restricts the worker from doing other gainful work.
- ***Training:*** When the solo artist has another musician or musical director training or overseeing the work of a musician, requires a musician to attend meetings, and wants a musician to conduct work in a particular manner.
- ***Payment of Business and/or Traveling Expenses:*** When the solo artist regulates a musician's business activities and pays his or her business and/or traveling expenses. And finally . . .
- ***Right to Discharge:*** When the solo artist has the right to discharge a musician, and exercises his or her control over the musician through the threat of dismissal.

RELEASE FORMS AND INDEMNITY PROVISIONS ALSO SUGGESTED

Attorney Burgundy Morgan cautions that there is yet another business matter that solo artists must take seriously: "release forms" and "indemnity provisions." You see, solo artists can be held responsible for the acts of their employees occurring within "the course and scope" of their employment. That's right! Here are a few examples.

Solo artists can be held responsible when the drummer gets into a brawl at a gig, and as a result, a fan gets injured and seeks medical expenses and further compensation.

Solo artists can also be held responsible when an overzealous fan knocks the entire drum kit off the riser after charging the stage, and the drummer wants to be compensated.

Finally, solo artists can also be held responsible when the bus driver dumps approximately 800 pounds of human waste from the bus's septic tank while driving over a bridge, and the waste lands onto a boat filled with tourists.

With these stories in mind, it's always a good idea for employers to have their employees (session players, roadies, etc.) sign a release stating that employees are responsible for their own actions, including any injuries to people or damage to property, with an indemnity provision requiring them to reimburse you for any money or loss you incur as a result of those same actions.

When you can afford it, a solid insurance policy is also a wise move.

For additional information on the business and legal responsibilities of employers and solo artists, check out *Small Business for Dummies* by Eric Tyson and Jim Schell.

Q&A with DJ Entrepreneur Justin Paul

Justin Paul is an acclaimed DJ, producer, and founder of Playloop Records. He has played at some of the nation's most elite clubs, festivals, and shows alongside Deadmau5, Bassnectar, Orbital, The Prodigy, Rusko, Thievery Corporation, LCD Soundsystem, and The Crystal Method. In this interview Paul sums up the varied role of the artist DJ/entrepreneur, the advantages and disadvantages of being a solo artist, and the skills needed to survive as a true professional.

Q: What's an artist DJ/entrepreneur?

J.P.: Artist DJ/entrepreneurs are solo musicians, composers, producers, engineers, merchandisers, promoters, or any combination of the above. They play music from other artists, as well as music they create, produce, and even self-release on their own labels.

Artist DJ/entrepreneurs have their own sound, style, look, and attitude that combine to form one consistent brand that the fans can depend on. While they often have a team of people working with them, the artist DJ/entrepreneur is essentially a one-man show.

Some of the more popular artist DJ/entrepreneurs on the scene include Calvin Harris, Deadmau5, Skrillex, Tiësto, Avicii, Afrojack, Kaskade, Pretty Lights, Diplo, and Armin van Buuren. Some of the guys on the underground scene that deserve major props in my opinion include Marques Wyatt, Lee Burridge, DJ Everyday, and Lee Mayjahs.

Q: What are your revenue streams?

J.P.: Live performances are definitely a key revenue generator for the artist DJ/entrepreneur. Even with a struggling economy, people crave interaction with other human beings, whether that be in clubs, museums, warehouses, casinos, or top festivals around the world like Ultra Miami, Mysteryland, and EDC (Electric Daisy Carnival). I played about 50 gigs last year. Some superstar artist DJs, like Steve Aoki, perform up to 250 shows in a year.

Production is definitely another major revenue stream for the skilled artist DJ/entrepreneur. Besides producing music on my own label, I often get calls from artists who need assistance with their records or want remixes done of their singles.

Q: Do you work totally solo or with a helping hand?

J.P.: I perform live by myself. However, I partner occasionally with a DJ/drummer to add a visual and dynamic appeal, and to help me promote certain events. Together we find and rent the venue, book the other DJs, and supply the sound systems. We split the net profits 50/50.

My record label, Playloop, is generally run by me (but it was founded with a few other artist/DJs). I A&R talent, produce product, mix songs, oversee manufacturing and distribution, execute the promotion, and overall manage the brand. It's definitely hard work, but it's rewarding to see my own brand take shape over the years exactly as I envisioned it.

Q: Do you have an agent and manager or DIY?

J.P.: Artist DJ/entrepreneurs have to build awareness, create an interesting brand, and start generating income before most agents or managers with clout will take notice.

I had an agent, but lately I have been booking myself by utilizing the personal relationships I've developed over the years. As a solo artist, you really have to get out on the scene and expand your network. Who you know is really everything.

For your readers, I suggest that they network with local club and festival promoters, DJs and bands, and event coordinators who book house parties, weddings, fashion shows, cruise ships, and more. Additionally, they can connect with folks they meet via sites like www.gigfinder.com, www.gigturn.com, www.craigslist.com, and www.wedj.com.

Q: What are the advantages of doing it solo?

J.P.: Greater earning potential! At first you work for free, but as you advance up the food chain and start getting paid, you don't have to split anything with four other band members.

For live performances, you can show up with as little as your CDs, laptop computer, and thumb drives and can earn a flat guarantee of $500, plus a percentage of the door or bar sales (that translates to about $3,000 on a good night). At the highest level, star DJs like Skrillex can get guarantees of up to $200,000 a night for a residency in a Vegas hotel.

For studio projects, you might get $500 to $3,000 a track. Superstars can get as much as $25,000 and more. If you write, you may also get a percentage of the publishing subject to negotiations with the artist.

Q: What are the disadvantages of doing it solo?

J.P.: A major disadvantage is that it requires a great deal of work when just starting out working without a team. Promoting oneself as an artist DJ/entrepreneur can be particularly daunting, because, unlike with a band, you can't delegate to three other band members.

Q: What's the promotion workload like?

J.P.: Artist DJ/entrepreneurs can promote themselves by creating and posting podcasts on iTunes (www.itunes.com), posting mixes on Mixcloud (www.mixcloud.com) and SoundCloud (www.soundcloud.com), and participating in mix competitions via sites like indabamusic (www.indabamusic.com), Wavo (www.wavo.com) and Remix Comps (www.remixcomps.com).

Artist DJ/entrepreneurs can also maintain quality websites, build a strong social media presence, get played on Internet radio stations, utilize e-mail lists, post live videos, establish street teams to hand out postcards and posters, and network and form alliances with like-minded artists and promoters who can help spread the word of mouth.

Once again, this requires a lot of work, and the artist DJ/entrepreneur must do it all.

Q: Do you use DJ pools, websites, or other sources for material?

J.P.: Pools apply mostly to club DJs who play primarily other people's music. Pools are organizations that charge you fees of about $50 per month, send you high-quality and legal new music they think you'll want to play, and ask for feedback. Pools help you save the time it takes to discover new music for your DJ sets. The most popular pools are DJcity (www.djcity.com), Digital DJ Pool (www.digitaldjpool.com), and MassPool (www.masspoolmp3.com).

Major websites like Beatport, Juno, Stompy, Traxsource, Ministry of Sound, and SoundCloud are where most artist/DJs get music. These sites provide the full-length versions and remixes of every dance song. Beatport and Juno offer the highest-quality music in WAV format so that when mixed with intros and outros in clubs/festivals, the sound quality is totally clear.

Q: What are the opportunities for the solo artist/DJ today?

J.P.: Right now, the marketplace is overflowing with DJs—including artist DJs who primarily create their own music, tastemaker DJs who play underground music that no one has ever heard, and mobile service and celebrity DJs who spin popular hit music in clubs.

Despite the competition, the marketplace always presents opportunities for those who study what's going on closely. Electronic music has been around for a long time and will likely stay—even if it falls back into the underground. The smart solo artist always watches trends, studies new technology, and looks for market voids. One must figure out where things are going and get there first, while always maintaining a sense of integrity and what you stand for.

Q: How can readers learn more about what you do?

J.P.: To learn more about the art and business of DJs, the issues that affect the DJ world, and the business of solo artists, you can take classes at Dubspot (the world's electronic music school) or the Art Institute in Hollywood, California, where I teach my recording/business class.

You can also check out blogs like Wired, Hypebot, MacRumors, Resident Advisor, Digital Music News, DJ Tech Tools, Boilerroom.tv, Magnetic, and Beatport News.

Books on running a small business and being an entrepreneur are also very useful for any solo artist. Check out *The Intelligent Entrepreneur* by Bill Murphy, *The Entrepreneur Mind* by Kevin Johnson, MD—and, of course, *Music Marketing for the DIY Musician* written by Bobby Borg. (Ha ha, I got to plug the interviewer.) That's pretty much it. Thanks for having me!

Part 3
Pro Teams

8

Entertainment Attorneys

What They Do and What They Cost You

"A man who is his own lawyer has a fool for a client." —Proverb

Just mentioning the word "attorney" sends most new artists into a state of panic. After all, how can one pay an attorney's fees when one can barely afford to pay for rehearsal space?

Even when money isn't an issue, most people don't like the formalities associated with attorneys and the law. I once heard a musician joke that he needed an attorney just to explain to him what his other attorney was talking about, and a secretary to get either of them on the phone.

Despite these concerns and bad jokes, attorneys are necessary to the business of music—and to your career. If you're going to survive in the music business, you're going to need a lawyer you can trust.

In this chapter I will discuss the role of an attorney, hiring an attorney, attorney fee structures, conflicts of interests, and changing your legal representation.

The Role of an Attorney in Your Career

Not everyone understands what an attorney does, so let's begin with a brief rundown.

A great attorney does most, or all, of the following:

- ***Specializes in Music-Related Issues:*** Serves clients exclusively in music-related deals and issues, and practices law exclusively as it applies to music.
- ***Provides Limited Legal Services:*** Helps with limited legal services early on in your career, like drafting a band membership agreement, registering your band name (i.e., trademark), or reviewing a synchronization license.
- ***Shops Deals:*** Provides "shopping services" to record labels (i.e., utilizes contacts to get you a record or publishing deal).
- ***Stays Connected:*** Maintains relationships with industry professionals, including record label personnel, publishers, TV people, merchandisers, and personal managers, all of whom can potentially help shape your career.
- ***Looks Out for Your Best Interests:*** Reviews contracts you receive with your best interests in mind.
- ***Deciphers Legalese:*** Translates contract clauses and complicated writing (popularly called "legalese") into terms you can understand.
- ***Negotiates for What's Really Important:*** Knows what issues are most important to negotiate for in recording, publishing, and merchandising agreements (e.g., understands controlled composition clauses, options, and guaranteed release clauses).
- ***Understands Your Wants:*** Strives to ascertain what issues are important to you, such as creative controls or advances, and then negotiates within reason for these issues.

- ***Helps You Make Informed Decisions:*** Provides all the information you need to make the right business decisions, but never tells you what to do.
- ***Stays Current:*** Stays current with changing business models in the music industry, especially with what's happening with new technologies.
- ***Litigates:*** Represents you in lawsuits with other musicians and music companies, or, when he or she doesn't litigate, refers you to colleagues who do. And finally . . .
- ***Gets You Out of the Messes You Make:*** Helps you get out of the bad deals you signed long before you were inclined to read this book.

In short, attorneys see the "big picture"; they handle all the business and legal matters that come up in the course of your career.

Hiring Your Attorney

Now that you understand what an attorney does, let's talk about how to find one with the qualities you'll need.

Finding an Attorney

Personal referrals, lawyer referral services, and music publications are just a few of the methods you can use to find an attorney. Let's break them down.

Personal Referrals

The first and best approach to finding a good attorney who specializes in the music business is to ask for referrals from other musicians and industry professionals you trust.

Check out your local scene and observe those artists who appear to be successful and have a great reputation. Perhaps they will be willing to refer their attorney to you.

You might also try asking your private instrument teacher in your local town. Usually these folks know someone in the business and they'd be more than happy to provide a contact number.

And finally, after reading this book and becoming more than my close friend, feel free to contact me. Fortunately, I know a number of wonderful attorneys who are also my friends.

Lawyer Referral Services

Another way to find an attorney is through a lawyer referral service.

For a small fee, operators listen to your legal concerns and then direct you to a few lawyers on their panel who best fit your situation. Be clear that big-league attorneys aren't typically available through referral services, so you're not going to connect with Dr. Dre's lawyer. Sorry!

Referral services do not guarantee the quality of the lawyers they recommend or tell you which one you should choose. Instead, it's up to you to set up short phone consultations (typically 15 to 20 minutes each) and assess the attorneys for yourself.

If you decide to meet with an attorney face to face, remember that there may be an additional fee for the initial consultation; fees for continued services are discussed between attorneys and clients on an individual basis.

To find a referral service available in your area, get in touch with your state or local bar association. In Los Angeles, you can call the Lawyer Referral Service of the Los Angeles County Bar Association. In Beverly Hills, there's the Beverly Hills Bar Association Lawyer Referral Service. In New York City, you can call the Association of the Bar of the City of New York. And in Nashville, there's the Lawyer Referral Service for the Nashville Bar Association.

Music Publications

Music publications may also be helpful in your search for an attorney. *The Music Attorney, Legal and Business Affairs Guide* (published by Music Business Registry) lists hundreds of attorneys. This resource can be found online and is regularly updated.

Weekly trade magazines such as *Billboard* and *Music Connection* are also good sources of information; they'll tell you which attorneys are signing the coolest bands.

Music Conferences

Music conferences such as the National Association of Music Merchants (www.namm.org), South by Southwest Music and Media Conference (www.sxsw.com), and the Music Business Association, formerly NARM (www.musicbiz.org), may provide a number of opportunities to find an attorney.

Attorneys usually sit on industry panels where they demonstrate their wisdom, answer challenging questions, and hang out afterward to chat with folks one-on-one.

Should you like what a particular lawyer had to say, approach him or her and ask for a business card. Just be realistic. The big shots may be too busy to work with you.

College and Adult Education Courses

Another way to find and meet a good attorney is to get your butt back in school. Seriously! Attorneys active in the business often teach entertainment courses like those offered (on campus and online) by UCLA Extension (www.uclaextension.edu) and Berklee College of Music (www.berklee.edu).

Taking an extension class—or any adult education course, really—not only will teach you a great deal about the music business, but also can provide you the opportunity to form new working relationships as well.

I had the pleasure of studying with Mark Goldstein (senior vice president of Warner Bros. Records), among many other instructors, who became very helpful when I started writing this book. Hey, if it worked for me, it can also work for you!

Album Artwork and Band Websites

Finally, be sure to check the website and album artwork of your favorite national or local artist. Who knows—they just may have listed their trusted attorney in the contacts section or liner notes for good measure. Okay? Cool!

AFTERTHOUGHT: SHORT LEGAL CONSULTS Is it necessary to hire an attorney when all you need is a few short business questions answered, or a short-form agreement to download? The answer varies by case, but many attorneys are fine with speaking with you for a few minutes on the phone for free—with the hope that you may become a client down the road. Websites like Nolo's self-help legal center (www.nolo.com), in addition to the many books about the music business available today, are also helpful.

Qualities to Look For in an Attorney

Once you've compiled a realistic list of potential attorneys, you can begin the process of contacting them, talking about your legal issues, and deciding whether they are *right for you.*

Getting in touch and chatting is the easy part. You can pick up your phone, set up an appointment, and meet in person to discuss your legal matters and his or her fee structures.

The challenging part, however, is determining whether an attorney is right for you. While there are many qualities to consider, I suggest two that are very important: attitude and clout.

Attitude

When you meet with an attorney, it's important to assess his attitude toward you and to others. Consider these points:

- **How He Treats You:** When you're sitting in the same room or talking on the phone with him, does he make you feel comfortable and respected? Does he take time to explain things to you, or does he rush through the conversation or talk down to you? Does he take a genuine interest in your career and music, or do you feel that he's meeting with you because you were referred by "so and so"? Bottom line: you want someone cool.
- **How He Treats Others:** Also of concern is your attorney's attitude toward other business professionals. Does he have a reputation for being a hothead who can potentially blow business deals for you? Or, conversely, does he carry himself like a soft-spoken wimp who won't make deals happen at all? You want someone in between.

Trust me on this one: take your attorney's attitude seriously before hiring him! Okay?

Clout

An attorney with clout can open doors at the best companies and help you get the best deals. Clout equates to the successful number of clients an attorney has represented, the number of powerful relationships she maintains, and the level of experience and respect that she has earned. Consider this:

- **Who She's Represented:** When meeting with an attorney, don't be afraid to ask about the various artists that she has represented and then to check out these references. When first starting out in the music business, I hired an attorney in my home town of Princeton, New Jersey, who had never represented anyone notable in the music industry. The New York heavyweights he went up against had a field day with him. They waited several weeks between correspondences and essentially paid him zero in respect. We accomplished absolutely nothing. It was a frustrating experience.
- **Who She Knows:** Also be sure to consider the various business relationships your attorney maintains. It really does matter who your attorney knows, and who knows her. People prefer doing business with people they know and like. One attorney got my friend's small record label a great distribution deal based largely on his personal friendship with the distributor. Surely there were other factors involved, but you get the point.
- **Years She's Been Practicing:** And finally, be sure to consider the number of years your potential attorney has been practicing, and the level of experience she has earned. In this day and age, attorneys are a dime a dozen—current stats say there are more attorneys graduating from law schools than ever before, fewer of these attorneys are finding work, and many stay in the music business for no more than a few years. So the longer an attorney has practiced in your town or city, the more regarded they often are by other professionals and the more quickly their phone calls are returned. This isn't to say that a young, smart attorney can't do the job, but rather that nothing trumps experience.

AFTERTHOUGHT: CANON OF ETHICS Attorneys should be open with you about the people they have represented. But don't expect to get detailed information about the deals they've negotiated. As part of the rules (or "canon of ethics") an attorney must abide by, personal information between clients is privileged.

Attorney Fee Structures

After assessing the qualities of your attorney, be sure to ask about the fee structures he or she uses and for an estimate of what it may take to resolve your matters.

In California, if an attorney estimates that your bill will total more than $1,000, you have the right to ask for a "fee agreement" in writing. A good attorney will suggest that you have your fee agreement reviewed by another professional to make sure his or her charges are reasonable.

What follows is a brief rundown of the various fee structures music attorneys use.

Hourly Rate

Attorneys will often bill by the hour. Just be sure to consider this:

- ***Range:*** Hourly rates might begin at $100 for a young attorney and jump to $600 for a high-powered attorney. (One attorney I know charges $1,250 hourly. Yikes.)
- ***Increments of the Hour:*** Your account may be charged incrementally. In other words, when your attorney makes a three-minute call on your behalf, you'll be charged for 10 or 15 minutes instead of the 3 minutes. My attorney (now fired) charged me $35 when I called for directions to his office from my car, and another $35 when he sent me an e-mail announcing that he had received my check. I'm serious! Most attorneys have your phone number and e-mail address attached to certain billing software that immediately charges your account every time it is activated.
- ***Caps:*** A maximum cap can sometimes be arranged with your attorney. In other words, you may agree that you will be charged an hourly rate of $250 per hour, but no more than $10,000 total. A cap can protect you in the event that your case unexpectedly drags on for an extended period of time. The last thing you want to do is tell your attorney you can no longer afford him or her before your issues are resolved.
- ***Expenses:*** Certain costs for postage, messenger services, or even administrative work are often charged to you in addition to your hourly fee. Yup, that's right, just one scanned document can cost you a case of Top Ramen noodles. In any case, be sure to ask about these expenses with your attorney when discussing the hourly rate, so that you don't have any surprises when you see your bill.
- ***Billing Policies:*** Finally, fees are usually billed on a monthly cycle. Find out whether you can use a credit card to make payments, and ask if you'll be charged interest for any late payments you make. When you get your bill, it should be easy to understand and clearly outline exactly what you're paying for. If there's a line item charge that concerns you, don't be afraid to ask about it. But that being said, you better make sure that the attorney doesn't charge you for the time it takes to review your bill! No joke!

Flat Fees

Sometimes attorneys charge a flat fee for their services. In actuality, this is their hourly rate multiplied by the number of hours they expect it will "reasonably" take to complete a job.

To draft a short band membership agreement, for instance, you might be charged $500 (for a few hours' work), plus out-of-pocket expenses, such as mailing and phone calls.

To negotiate a recording agreement, you might be charged $2,000 to $20,000, and sometimes more (for several hours of work).

As long as your attorney does not overestimate the time it will take to complete the job, this method of payment often works out best. I prefer it. Bottom line, there are no surprises!

YOU MAY GET WHAT YOU PAY FOR

Many young musicians on a shoestring budget must resort to hiring attorneys who are willing to represent them for a discounted flat fee. If you're lucky, you'll get all the attention you need and your issues will be resolved to your satisfaction. But this isn't always the way things work out!

One musician I know hired an attorney who was a friend of a friend to review a short, eight-page contract. As a favor, the attorney quoted the musician a flat fee of $250, but the job ultimately required much more time than the attorney had initially estimated.

The attorney was obviously frustrated with the matter and began rushing the musician through phone conversations and taking a long time to review second and third drafts of the contract. It was clear the job wasn't a priority to him—and perhaps rightfully so!

Moral of the story: business and legal matters can be very complex and take many twists and turns. If you're about to sign a deal and stand to make a couple thousand dollars, then expect to spend a little bit on getting the proper representation. If you're not willing to invest in yourself, then you just might get what you pay for (or don't pay for).

Percentage of the Deals (5 Percent)

In lieu of the hourly rates and flat fee payments discussed above, many attorneys work for a percentage of the deals they negotiate.

For example, an attorney may agree to negotiate a recording deal for you in return for 5 percent of the recording fund you receive (which, by the way, is the industry standard).

Out-of-pocket expenses for postage, messenger services, or even administrative work are separate.

Be clear that in this arrangement, the band has contract offers in place. In other words, the lawyer does not shop the band for various deals, as he or she does in the next arrangement.

Label Shopping Percentage Deals (10 to 20 Percent)

Similar to the percentage method above, some attorneys will provide "label shopping services" and work for a percentage of the deal "for the entire term," or a capped payment. Consider this:

- ***The Amount:*** Since shopping your band and finding deals takes more time and work than simply negotiating a deal that you or your manager initiated, the percentage is usually 10 to 20 percent. Note that this percentage usually applies for the full length of the deal. For instance, for every album your band records—long after your attorney's job is done—he or she may earn a 10 to 20 percent fee for initially shopping your band.
- ***A Cap:*** A cap or maximum can be negotiated that determines the total amount the attorney's percentage will yield (e.g., $100,000 over the life of the recording deal). In some cases, a de-escalating percentage can be established (e.g., 10 percent on the first recording, 7.5 percent on the second, and 5 percent on the third, etc.). Just be sure to discuss these terms with your attorney in detail from the very beginning.

Attorney Stan Findelle sums things up: "Shopping a deal is worth as much as 20 percent. Why? Because this lawyer has turned water into wine: He or she got the artist plucked out of the unwashed mob and into the ballpark. And in this day and age, my good friends, that's a miracle."

AFTERTHOUGHT: NO UP-FRONT FEES Watch out for that rare attorney who charges "up-front fees" to shop your act. This is a red flag and usually signals a scumbag attorney on the prowl. A lawyer who really believes he or she can get you a deal will gladly take you on for a percentage of the deal you're hiring him or her to negotiate.

A Flat Retainer

Finally, some attorneys ask for a retainer, which is really a flat sum of money paid up front to cover legal services you haven't received yet. It's like paying a bill up front.

To illustrate, if you pay a retainer of $500, and your attorney provides you with his or her equivalent of $1,000 in hourly-billed legal services, the $500 retainer will be deducted from your bill. At this time, you may be asked to pay the $500 balance as well as another retainer to be held in trust for further services rendered.

In the event that your attorney never earns the amount of the initial retainer and you decide to discontinue your business relationship with him or her, the remaining retainer should be paid back; if you pay a retainer of $500 and your attorney's charges for the month are only $300, the attorney should return the extra $200.

So that's about it for fee structures. Let's move on to the next section.

GETTING THE MOST OUT OF YOUR ATTORNEY

Once you've found an attorney, assessed his or her qualities, and agreed on the fee structure, you want to make sure that the relationship runs smoothly and affordably. The following tips will help:

- ***Prepare Questions and Take Good Notes:*** Before calling your attorney or showing up for a meeting, create a detailed list of questions. Research the answers yourself so that you are not completely in the dark about certain issues that will be discussed.
- ***Take Great Notes:*** When speaking with your attorney, always take great notes (or record each session on your phone's voice memo) so that you can review the information later.
- ***Be on Time and Carpool:*** If you're part of a band, take one car to your meetings with your attorney and arrive a few minutes early. This is especially important when you are being charged hourly.
- ***Appoint a Band Representative:*** Appoint one band member to serve as your liaison between the attorney and the rest of the band. This will make the meetings run more smoothly and will save you money in the long run, too.
- ***Provide Good Records:*** Get and keep clear records of all business correspondence you have with people in the industry, and be prepared to e-mail important documents to your attorney for review. Should you discuss a potential business deal orally, ask the other party to summarize the discussion in an e-mail, and forward that to your attorney.
- ***Do Not Accept Delays:*** Give your attorney a time frame in which you would like to bring a legal matter to close. While he or she does not always have control of this, avoid letting your issue drag on for months while your attorney's receptionist tells you he or she is "out of town" or "unavailable." These may be clues you're a low man on a roster of more successful clients and that it is time to move on.
- ***Never Sign Anything Without Your Attorney:*** Never sign anything without having your attorney review it first. After all, that's why you hired him or her in the first place. Right? Right!
- ***Pay Your Bills, but Check Your Statements:*** Pay your bills on time. But always remember to check your statements first. I hate to say this, but it is not uncommon for attorneys to overcharge you and then adjust your bill after you complain.
- ***Make Sure Your Best Interests Are Looked After:*** Finally, ask your attorney whether he or she thinks any potential conflicts of interest may exist. This may be a sensitive question, since it is the attorney's responsibility to disclose such conflicts, but I'd ask anyway. For more information on conflicts, please see the text below.

A Conflict of Interest

In working with an attorney, it is important to consider the potential for something called a conflict of interest.

In situations in which your attorney represents another party with whom you are conducting business, a conflict of interest may occur, since the attorney cannot represent the best interests of each party fairly.

An ethical attorney should disclose when a conflict of interest exists, or could exist, and advise you to seek representation elsewhere. The exception to this rule is a situation in which both parties consent to the representation of the same attorney. The attorney must show that both parties can be represented fairly and then ask both parties to sign something called a "conflict waiver." A conflict waiver protects the attorney in case either party later claims it was represented unfairly.

Let's take a look at a few examples where a conflict of interest may exist.

Conflicts with Record Companies

Suppose you're on the verge of signing a record agreement and have hired an attorney who is known to represent the record company in other deals. You want the biggest advance without giving up rights to multiple revenue streams, while the record company wants to get away with giving you the smallest advance and take all of your revenue streams. Will the attorney really look out for your best interests fully in this case, or is he or she concerned about going too hard on the label in fear it might interfere with future work? A conflict of interest might exist here.

Conflicts with Band Members

A conflict of interest may also exist when an attorney is representing the members of a band who are putting together an internal band membership agreement. If the members decide not to divide the profits equally, how can the attorney represent the best interests of each individual member? He or she can't. Unless of course, the band agrees on the terms as a whole, and the attorney simply drafts the agreement.

Conflicts with Personal Managers

Another instance where a conflict of interest may exist is when a band hires its manager's lawyer to review its management agreement. How can the attorney possibly represent both sides fairly? Who will he or she favor? You get the idea!

Conflicts with Your Own Attorney

Finally, a conflict of interest might exist when your attorney is shopping your music and he or she is working for a percentage of the deals he negotiates. If your attorney appears exceptionally aggressive in negotiating for large, and perhaps unreasonable advances (remember, the larger the advance, the larger the commission), and is letting business deals and opportunities slip by as a result, this is a situation that may be perceived as a conflict of your best interests. Hey, I'm not making these scenarios up; they're known to happen occasionally.

Wrapping this all up, just remember, when hiring an attorney, or even after hiring one, it's always advisable to keep your eyes open for potential conflicts of interest. If you think a conflict exists, it's probably fair to assume that neither side can be represented fairly and that you should therefore immediately seek representation elsewhere.

Changing Your Legal Representation

Finally, let's take a look at what happens when you want to fire your attorney. In his play *Henry VI, Part II*, William Shakespeare wrote, "The first thing we do, let's kill all the lawyers." Don't take that literally, of course. Instead, I suggest you talk about it first and sever the relationship.

Talk About It First

The best way to resolve any problem is to bring it out in the open. Even when dealing with a friend who is also your attorney, remember that business is business and immediate steps must be taken to amend any situation gone awry. If a situation can't be resolved, you should know that it's your legal right to change representation at any time by severing the relationship.

Sever the Relationship

You can sever the relationship with your first attorney via a written letter, e-mail correspondence, or certified letter. At your request, your first attorney must allow your new attorney to review and photocopy all confidential records regarding your case, even if you have an outstanding bill. If your bill is all paid up and there's still unused money in your retainer, your former attorney must return it to you at the time you terminate your relationship.

Firing your attorney (or anyone else, for that matter) is never an easy thing to do. But your career comes first. If you're not getting the legal representation you need, then make a change.

SOME CRAZY CONTRACT LANGUAGE DEFINED

To end on a different note, be sure to check out a few definitions that will get you up to speed on some common contract language. Just don't get too excited and try to negotiate your own agreements. An entertainment attorney is always advised.

- ***Licensor:*** The person who grants the license.
- ***Licensee:*** The person who is given the license.
- ***Agent:*** A person authorized to represent another.
- ***Fiduciary:*** A professional responsibility or duty to another (e.g., an attorney's fiduciary duty to his client).
- ***In Perpetuity:*** Forever.
- ***The Universe:*** The world and the entire celestial cosmos. Commonly used with "perpetuity" in regard to a grant of rights (e.g., in perpetuity throughout the universe).
- ***Intellectual Property:*** A process, creation, or idea derived from the mind or intellect, and a right or application relating to this (e.g., artwork, compositions, books).
- ***Pecuniary:*** Money, or relating to money.
- ***Herewith:*** Contained within; in this writing or contract.
- ***Hereinabove:*** In some earlier part of a writing or contract.
- ***Hereinafter:*** In the following part of a writing or contract.
- ***Heretofore:*** Up to this point in time, until now.
- ***Henceforth:*** From this point in time onward.
- ***Notwithstanding:*** Despite; however; regardless (e.g., "Notwithstanding anything contained herein to the contrary") (i.e., whatever was just stated, the following now prevails).
- ***Indemnity:*** To secure against hurt, loss, or damage.

- ***Warranties and Representations:*** A promise that a statement or fact (e.g., you own your compositions, or masters) is true.
- ***Exclusive:*** To the exclusion of anyone else.
- ***Nonexclusive:*** That which does not limit the rights of another.
- ***Boilerplate:*** Common; standard; the same (e.g., boilerplate clauses like warranties and representations found in contracts).

Note: For a similar but complete and expanded list of terms, be sure to check out *The Business Affairs Glossary* by Robert J. Nathan.

9

Personal Managers

Roles, Options, and Agreements

"Inspiring the right things, and ensuring that things get done right."
—Peter Drucker, management consultant, educator, and author

Personal managers are at the top of most developing artists' minds. Managers help chart the course toward an artist's vision and help ensure that day-to-day business matters are handled efficiently. They help uncover business deals, assist with touring, and make sure that everyone is doing their job.

But personal managers are not a right; they are a privilege. And before you've generated a little traction on your own, most personal managers with clout and experience may not be interested in working with you. If you sit around waiting to be rescued without rolling up your sleeves and getting some work done on your own first, your career may go nowhere.

It's the general misunderstanding of personal managers that makes this chapter so important to your success. From understanding the role of a personal manager, to knowing when to hire one, to learning how to self-manage, the following sections contain information that you certainly do not want to miss.

The Role of a Personal Manager in Your Career

By strict definition, a personal manager advises and counsels artists in all aspects of the music business. This may include artist development, project management, touring, contracts and income streams, and so much more.

Artist Development

The manager may assist with the development of an artist's career via the following activities:

- ***Encouraging You to Get Your Brand Together:*** Inspiring you to polish up your brand—from your artist name and logo, to what you wear and say in public, to the charities and other organizations and brands with whom you associate.
- ***Assisting with Your Sound and Songs:*** Inspiring you to polish up your compositions and musical sound. If needed, the manager may even help set you up with songwriting consultants and cowriters, and help you find complete songs to record and perform.
- ***Helping You to Improve Performances and Merch:*** Inspiring you to perfect the quality of your live performances (set list flow, presence, etc.) and merchandising designs (T-shirts, hats, stickers, etc.). And finally . . .

- ***Helping You Build Your Fan Base:*** Encouraging you to strengthen your connections with fans, including building a database, improving upon your Internet presence, and finding ways to get fans' assistance with promoting your career.

Contracts and Income Streams

Your manager may also help initiate various business deals by doing the following:

- ***Setting Up Meetings:*** Setting up showcases and meetings with potential record companies, publishing people, merchandisers, sponsors, and more.
- ***Researching the Right Deals:*** Researching what companies and representatives are best suited to your talents and musical style, based not only on a company's past signings or successes, but also on its financial stability and understanding of your vision.
- ***Recommending You Find Legal Counsel:*** Providing recommendations for legal counsel to help shop your music to various companies and review important contract terms. And finally . . .
- ***Working Collaboratively with Your Attorney:*** Communicating with your attorney about important contract deal points, but knowing when to step aside and let the attorney do his or her job.

Project Management

When, and if, an artist signs a recording agreement, your manager may also assist by doing this:

- ***Getting Everyone at the Label Excited About Your Career:*** Lighting the fire under the label's ass and trying to make sure that you will be a top priority.
- ***Monitoring Pre-Release and Post-Release Activities:*** Providing marketing ideas regarding the branding, price, place, and promotion of your record, and fighting tactfully for what is best for your career. And finally . . .
- ***Meeting with Departments:*** Meeting with the various departments at the record label, (radio promotion, new media, licensing, press, sales, and marketing) to make sure that everyone is talking and working in concert to further your professional career.

Hybrid Services: Merch, Publishing, and More

As if the above tasks were not enough, some management companies operating under newer business models may even assist your career by doing the following:

- ***Providing Label Services:*** Handling all matters concerning the funding, recording, manufacturing, distributing, and monitoring of a record, in addition to all other management services. Said another way, the management company is a label, or the label is a management company—however you see it.
- ***Providing Publishing Services:*** Seeking creative uses of your songs in film, TV, and games, issuing licenses to music users for the use of your songs, and collecting all income generated by these uses. And finally . . .
- ***Merchandising:*** Helping design and manufacture effective merch that sells, helping the group sell merch on the road and via retail outlets, and seeking sublicenses to expand the product line.

AFTERTHOUGHT: HYBRID EXAMPLES Silverback Management, Crush Management, Sumerian Records, and Nettwerk are just a few examples of these hybrid manager services mentioned above. There are many more.

Live Engagements and Touring

Moving on to another role, a personal manager may also assist with the following:

- ***Securing a Talent Agent:*** Helping you to find a licensed talent agent who specifically works on procuring live performances. Your manager will work together with this agent to determine what tours are best for you, to make sure that you're getting the best offers from concert promoters, and even to help direct your performances from city to city.
- ***Working with Your Business Manager:*** Helping you find a business manager who specializes in the music business, and working together with him or her to ensure that your tours are properly budgeted. Hotel accommodations, transportation, stage crews, and other expenses will be closely examined in effort to minimize expenses and ensure that you turn a profit (or at least cover expenses). And finally . . .
- ***Hiring a Tour Manager:*** Hiring a "tour manager" who is responsible for keeping a watchful eye on all business matters from city to city, night after night. This could mean checking you in to hotels, "advancing" the shows (making sure that each venue has the proper accommodations in place for you), "settling" money with promoters at the end of each night, babysitting, and bailing you out of jail—seriously!

Physical and Mental Health Issues

Finally, once an artist is successful, a great manager can assist the artist in the following ways:

- ***Monitoring Physical and Mental Health:*** Looking out for the artist's health and well-being, and knowing when to say no to that extra morning radio show, public appearance, or leg of the tour.
- ***Checking In with the Artist:*** Checking in with the artist and simply asking him or her, "How are you doing?" Said another way, the manager checks the goose that is hatching the golden eggs, rather than just focusing on the golden eggs. This is important. Artists are known to break down when they're pushed too hard. Elvis Presley is one example.

TURNING BAD INTO GOOD

To illustrate yet another role of a personal manager, manager Bud Prager (Foreigner, Bad Company, and Megadeth) shares a legendary road story concerning one of his classic bands, Foreigner.

Tickets were not selling well for a specific date on the Foreigner tour, so Prager and the concert promoter put their heads together and decided to charge a "one car, one price" admission to the show. This meant that regardless of how many people could squeeze into a car, the car would only be charged for the price of one.

To everyone's disbelief, the plan backfired when a tractor-trailer truck showed up with over 130 people crammed into the cargo space. Rather than turning the truck away, Prager quickly phoned up the local news media, and in minutes helicopters were buzzing above with cameras rolling. The exposure the band received on television that night was priceless.

Prager took a potentially bad situation and made it good. In Prager's words, "That's the true essence of management." Pretty awesome.

Sadly, Prager has since passed away. He will be remembered as a legend in the business.

Management Options

Now that you understand what a manager does, we can discuss the various management options available to you. The most common choices, depending on how far along you are in your career, are self-management, start-up management, and established professional management.

Self-Management

In the early stages of your career, good management must always begin with the artist. Unless one of your relatives happens to be a record label or publishing company president, no one is going to help you until you first help yourself!

As your self-manager, consider the self-assessment checklist below to determine whether or not you are doing all the right things.

- Have you given serious thought to your long-term career vision?
- Have your written a large repertoire of songs or even cowritten with professionals?
- Have you developed a consistent and unique brand (name, logo, look, attitude)?
- Have you professionally recorded, mastered, mixed, and packaged your music?
- Are you selling music online in download and streaming format?
- Are you drawing people to your live shows and selling a lot of records and merch?
- Are you involving fans in promoting your music and creating street teams?
- Are you making money with your music or will you soon be?

Musicians often believe that the solution to their problems is finding someone to whisk them up from rehearsal room to superstardom. An experienced manager can make good things happen fast, but he or she is not a solution for your laziness. This is the digital age, where doing it yourself is far easier than ever before. Bottom line: you must generate some action yourself in order to give managers a valid reason to want to work with you.

Start-Up Management

After you've reached a point in your career when you've done all the things mentioned in the list above, and you just can't go any further without a helping hand, then perhaps you're ready for a start-up manager. This might include one of the following:

- ***A Friend:*** A close friend who's willing to make phone calls and help promote shows without getting paid for the first few months or years. In fact, he may not even be called a "manager" at all, working with the understanding that as soon as your career progresses, he will be replaced by an established professional manager and offered some other position with the band.
- ***A Retired Musician:*** An experienced musician who wants to "right all the wrongs" she encountered in her professional career, and has got all the passion and drive needed to set you on course.
- ***A Businessperson:*** An educated businessperson who's always dreamed of being in a band and has the desire to live those dreams through you.
- ***A Club Owner:*** A club owner in your hometown who sees hundreds of bands perform each year. This individual has a good idea of what works and what doesn't and is willing to offer you an objective point of view and career guidance. And finally . . .
- ***An Intern:*** An intern or junior assistant of a professional manager by day who's looking to cut his teeth on managing his own band on his downtime at night. He's got the advantage of having his boss's ear for guidance and observing how a professional office is run all day.

While start-up managers may not be the most experienced folks, don't underestimate their value. They can be some of the most loyal and hardworking people around, and they'll stick with you through the tough times. And who knows, they may even grow into being legends. Look at Andrew Oldham. He started out with the Rolling Stones when he was just 17, and he became one of the most successful managers of all time. Bravo, Andrew Oldham!

Established Professional Management

Finally, if you're able to create serious momentum in your career (get thousands of streams, start generating some income, and/or attract labels and publishers), then established professional managers will be more interested in working with you. You might be referred to these folks via your record label, or they might seek you out. Let's look at mid-level and big-league managers.

Mid-Level Managers

Mid-level managers are those who have a great deal of experience in the industry but have not quite broken a band into superstardom. Maybe they have one client on their roster who was able to sell a respectable hundred thousand records, but still don't have a gold or platinum record hanging on the walls—and that's what they're shooting for! They are typically well liked in the industry and have a big enough network to open some doors for you.

However, the problem with mid-level managers is that they are not as powerful as big-league managers, and therefore it may take them longer to get things done.

Big-League Managers

Big-league managers have been around for years and have lots of gold and platinum records hanging on their walls. The relationships they've formed, the respect they've earned, and the favors they can trade give them the power to make things happen with just a few phone calls.

However, the problem is that you could easily get lost in the sauce. This means that you get overshadowed by their more profitable clients. I was with a group that had one of the most successful rock management companies in the word (one that handles Metallica), and we never even did one date with the band or really much of anything. We soon left the management.

QUALITIES OF THE MANAGER

There are dozens of experienced, professional, established managers out there, any one of whom is capable of doing the job. The important thing is picking the one who really wants to work with you.

Don't just pick a manager who has the biggest stars on his or her roster, takes you out to the most expensive restaurant, or makes the biggest promises.

Above all, your manager must possess a genuine enthusiasm for your music and a commitment to going the long haul. And truthfully, even then your dreams may not come true.

Be sure to read the biographies of some of the most interesting managers of all time and make note of some of the other character traits that you admire. One I'd like to recommend is the story of the Rolling Stones manager titled *Stoned: Andrew Loog Oldham*. Oldham understood branding and how to create the Stones' "bad boy" image; he was an innovative thinker and helped the Stones retain ownership in their masters; and he knew how to form the right alliances for the band (he connected them with the Beatles).

So, what traits are important to you? Be sure to give this some thought.

Management Agreements

Now that you understand your management options, it's time to discuss management agreements. Key elements include exclusivity, a key person clause, the agreement term, the manager's commission, expenses, power of attorney, a talent agent disclaimer, and post-term provisions.

Exclusivity

The first thing you must understand about the management agreement, is that it is an exclusive management agreement. This means that during the full term of your agreement, you cannot be managed by anyone else.

Thus, before entering into a relationship with a personal manager, be sure you're absolutely confident in that individual's ability to represent you. Remember, you're going to be working with the manager for a very long time.

Key Person Clause

An important clause to insert in management agreements is a key person clause. A key person clause states that the manager with whom you initially signed is your key person, and under certain conditions explicitly stated in your agreement, you can void your contract.

- ***When It Matters:*** If your manager is part of a larger firm and decides to leave, is terminated, or becomes disabled or ill, you may be able to terminate the agreement rather than get stuck with the company and assigned to a representative you don't like.
- ***When You Shouldn't Care:*** Managers should not be expected to be present for every gig and activity. A representative of the firm (i.e., a non-key person) is just as capable of doing day-to-day work. Adds manager Gary Borman: "Don't worry about whether your manager comes to your rehearsals; worry about whether he's working your tour."

The Agreement Term

A common section found in management contracts deals with the agreement term (i.e., the length of the management agreement).

Typically, managers want a longer term, which gives them more time to recoup their investment, and artists want the shortest term so they can walk if the manager is a dud.

Terms are usually based on years, album/tour cycles, and performance guarantees.

Terms Based on Years

Agreements based on years are simple enough. They usually last from one to five years, with three years being the norm.

Terms Based on "Album/Tour Cycles"

Agreements based on "album/tour cycles" are a little more complex. An album/tour cycle starts from the day the recording of an album begins to the last day of promoting it. Deals usually last from two to three album/tour cycles.

Terms That Have Performance Guarantees

Finally, agreements based on performance guarantees last for as long as the manager lives up to his or her end of the bargain. Performance guarantees are like benchmarks that if not met within a certain time, the artist can void the agreement. Performance guarantees are usually based on deals and/or income.

Here are some examples:

- ***Guaranteed Record Deal:*** An artist may want the manager to guarantee him or her a recording deal within the first year.
- ***Guaranteed Publishing Deal:*** An artist may want the manager to guarantee him or her a publishing deal within a year.
- ***Guaranteed Tour Income:*** Or, an artist performing in larger venues may expect to earn up to *x* dollars over the first album cycle, up to 2*x* dollars in the second album cycle, and up to 4*x* dollars in the third album cycle.

Whatever the arrangement, a reputable manager will only agree to performance guarantees that he or she has a reasonable chance of achieving. Remember, managers aren't magicians. Even if you have a lot of talent, the best manager may not always be able to make things happen so quickly. So be fair.

The Manager's Commission (15 to 30 Percent)

Yet another important section of management contracts deals with the manager's commission. Personal managers commission their "artist's earnings" at anywhere from 15 to 30 percent, with the norm being 20 percent.

This amount can be based on gross earnings or net earnings, and it can be subject to certain limitations and exclusions. These matters are all discussed further below.

Gross Earnings and Customary Deductions

A manager's commissions are based on your gross earnings. But note that the word "gross," which typically means total earnings, must be defined here as all monies other than recording funds, deficit tour support, video expenses, and other specifically defined expenses). Without a clear definition of these expenses, the manager may be taking a bigger commission than he or she deserves. Consider the following example.

Suppose you're advanced a healthy recording fund of $250,000; $200,000 of that is budgeted as a recording cost, and $50,000 is left over as income. The manager commissions the $50,000 income ($50,000 × 20 percent = $10,000), not the full $250,000 fund ($250,000 × 20 percent = $50,000). Once again, this is because the fund is an expense, and not income.

Gross or Net Commissions for Tours

In special cases, such as touring, personal managers will not take a commission of the gross monies (frequently referred to as "off the top"). If they did, they would make a lot more money than the artists after every tour, and that doesn't make artists very happy.

Instead, personal managers often take a commission of the net tour income (the amount remaining after expenses are paid out). But note that these expenses must be reasonable. In other words, managers are not going to allow expenses such as hotel parties and smashed TV sets to determine their compensation. And as an additional precaution to ensure they get paid, managers who commission the net will take as much as 50 percent. Got it? Good. Let's move on.

NINE INCH NAILS COME SCRATCHING

NIN front man Trent Reznor was shocked to discover that though he had earned millions over 15 years of touring, he only had around $400,000.

Reznor's claim was that his manager, John Malm, Jr., had tricked him into signing a management contract that permitted Malm to collect 20 percent of the gross earnings, without factoring in customary deductions or offering a deal based on the net for touring income.

Malm defended himself by stating that he had never hidden any of his dealings from Trent and that Reznor simply had not paid attention to his finances at all.

When the jury found Malm guilty for breach of contract and fraudulent action, Reznor was awarded $2.95 million by the court. After adding interest, the damages rose to $4 million.

Escalating, De-escalating, and Deferred Commissions

Personal managers sometimes work on an escalating, de-escalating, or deferred commission scale, depending on their artist's success. Consider this:

- **Escalating:** When you're first starting out and not making much money, a manager may agree to a 15 percent commission based on the premise that when you begin to earn more money, the commission will escalate to 20 percent.
- **De-escalating:** Alternatively, when you're first starting out and not making much money, a manager may ask for a 20 percent commission based on the premise that when you begin to earn more money, the commission will de-escalate to 15 percent. If this seems to make little or no sense, do the quick math: $100,000 multiplied by 20 percent equals $20,000. However, $500,000 multiplied by 15 percent equals $75,000. You get the idea.
- **Deferred:** Finally, in the very early stages of your career, when you're barely making enough money to pay your rent, most managers will defer their commissions altogether on what little money you have coming in. This is typical.

Limitations and Exclusions

And finally, your personal manager may agree to charge you a lower commission, or no commission, on alternative revenue streams established before the manager was hired, on recording funds advanced before the manager was hired, and on alternative revenue streams established after the manager was hired. Consider this:

- **Alternative Revenue Pre-Manager:** If you were already a successful songwriter or an accomplished musician prior to hiring the manager, your manager may agree to charge you a reduced 10 percent commission on these incomes during his or her term, as opposed to the standard 20 percent commission on everything else. It's also possible that if the manager is not going to be involved in furthering your career in these areas (because of lack of time, expertise, or interest), he or she will agree not to charge you a commission at all.
- **Recording Funds Pre-Manager:** If you get signed to a record deal before hiring the manager, many managers will still want a commission of the deal. Major-league managers may want their usual percentage, mid-level managers may accept a reduced percentage, and some managers may take no commission at all. Keep in mind that the initial advance can be the determining factor of whether a manager chooses to work with a band.
- **Alternative Revenue After Hiring:** Finally, if you find opportunities (as a result of your own hard work) to write a cookbook or start your own clothing line (activities outside the typical work of your personal manager), your manager may take a reduced commission or no commission at all. In any case, this should all be discussed far in advance at the time of hiring the manager.

Business Expenses

It's important to specify what the manager can (and cannot) treat as an expense, set a limit on what the manager can spend, and indicate who monitors expenses and makes certain payments.

What's Included (or Not Included)

First, you should know what costs a manager should and should not include as reimbursable expenses.

- **What's Not Included:** Expenses that are necessary for the manager to run his or her business, such as rent, office machines, and personnel, should not be reimbursed.
- **What's Included:** All business expenses relating to your career, including flights to New York, packages mailed to other countries, and expensive lunch meetings, are reimbursable—and can add up quickly.

Limiting and Prorating Expenses

To regulate the expenses that are reimbursed to your manager, a limit is usually set on what the manager can spend. Some expenses can also be prorated.

- **Limit Expenses:** An artist can ask that a single expense above $200, for example, or total monthly expenses that exceed $1,000, must be approved by you first.
- **Prorate Expenses:** An artist can also ask that expenses be prorated when a manager handles more than one client. To show why this can be important, I once knew a manager who flew out to an industry convention in Cannes, France, and charged the entire trip as an expense to one of his primary bands. He justified the expense by setting up a meeting or two for that primary band, but he mostly spent time shopping his other artists to record labels. The manager should have prorated his expenses and charged each band accordingly. If he was representing three bands, and each band was given equal attention, expenses should have been split three ways.

Who Monitors and Makes Payments? The Business Manager Does

And finally, although most managers may initially insist that all monies flow through them, they will accept an outside accountant or business manager to collect monies, pay expenses and issue commissions. Business managers are discussed in chapter 10.

Limited Power of Attorney

Yet another important issue in management agreements is power of attorney. This could give your manager the legal right to act for you in making major career decisions, cashing checks, and signing contracts. But never agree to any more than a "limited power of attorney." Here are some examples:

- ***Example 1:*** In a limited power of attorney, you might stipulate that your manager, in the event that you're out of town, can sign an agreement on your behalf, but only after you approve the deal. The paperwork can then be scanned and e-mailed to you.
- ***Example 2:*** You might also stipulate that your manager, in the event that a timely offer comes in from your agent, can approve live performance engagements on your behalf, as long as the shows do not exceed a certain number (e.g., 10) and they fall within a certain calendar period (e.g., March to November).

Remember, there's a reason you hired your manager in the first place. When you're on the road or in the studio trying to be creative, you don't want to be bothered with business issues. On the other hand, you don't want to get screwed, either. It's not that you should distrust your manager, but putting limitations on how your manager can act on your behalf helps ensure that you'll always know what's going on. It's never good for a manager to have too much power.

Talent Agency Disclaimer

Be aware that under California state laws (as well as many other states, notably New York and Massachusetts), anyone who engages in the occupation of procuring employment for artists must apply for an agency license with the state labor commissioner and become a licensed agent.

In plain language, this means that managers cannot book gigs! It's not like agency police are driving up and down Sunset Boulevard ready to arrest violating managers, but should it ever be determined in arbitration or courtroom proceedings that the manager has acted as an unlicensed agent (such as when the artist and manager are at odds and the artist hires a smart attorney), the manager could end up in a heap of trouble.

Thus, for the sake of clarity, some management agreements (especially those in California) will explicitly state that the manager will not act as your agent to procure employment, and that you will at all times have a "licensed agent." But, as music industry consultant Robert Nathan states, now the manager has to be sure to abide by his own contract.

ARSENIO HALL DOES THE TALKING!

As noted in Richard Schulenberg's book *Legal Aspects of the Music Industry*, the ex-managers of entertainer and former talk show host Arsenio Hall (known as X-Management) were ordered by the labor commissioner to repay $2,148,445.78 in commissions earned over one year (you read right!). The labor commissioner found that the managers had engaged in the occupation of a "talent agency" without being licensed. Ouch!

For further information on the above-noted case, be sure to check Schulenberg's book. For further information on talent agency laws in general, search online for the case brief for *Marathon Entertainment v. Blasi*. Interesting stuff!

Dispute Resolution: Arbitration and Mediation

On the topic of disputes, there will always be a clause in management agreements that stipulates how disputes will be handled: by arbitration (binding or non-binding) or mediation.

- ***Binding Arbitration:*** Binding arbitration involves an impartial third-party arbitrator who "imposes" a resolution on the parties.
- ***Non-Binding Arbitration:*** Non-binding arbitration involves an impartial third-party arbitrator that only "determines" the liability.
- ***Mediation:*** Mediation involves a third party who tries to help both parties work through their issues and find a resolution that both parties can "choose" to act on.

Note that all of these methods are faster and less costly than courtroom proceedings.

Post-Term Provisions (Sunset Clauses)

And finally, be sure to insert a post-term provision into your contract with a manager, specifying what will happen after the term of the manager's agreement ends. Because this can be very important, I'll break it down in three parts: commissions to which your manager may be entitled, negotiation of sunset clauses, and the manager's view of sunset clauses.

Commissions to Which Your Manager May Be Legally Entitled

You should know that when the term of your manager's agreement expires, he or she is still entitled to earn a commission on royalties from contracts entered into, or substantially negotiated, during that contract term.

For instance, suppose you sign a whopping five-record deal with a label a few months before the manager's term expires. Legally, your manager is entitled to commission royalties from all five records—even without being involved with your career anymore.

To make matters worse, if you hire a new manager, you'll be required to pay that manager a commission on your earnings as well. If both your former manager and your new manager are charging a 20 percent commission, you're now paying out 40 percent in commissions. Let me repeat this: 40 percent!

Negotiation of Sunset Clauses

To limit the amount your manager can commission after the contract term expires, he or she may be willing to agree to something called a "sunset clause."

A sunset clause "ends the day" on the commissions to which the manager is entitled.

In our above example, the manager would continue earning a commission after the term of the agreement on all five of the recordings. However, with a sunset clause, your manager may be willing to accept the following:

- **Sudden Death After a Defined Period:** Full commission for albums recorded and released during the term only. This would last for a contractually defined period (e.g., 7 years after the term), and then end.
- **Gradual Reduction over Time:** Full commission for albums recorded and released during the term only. This would last for 3.5 years after the term, decrease by half for the next 1.5 years, and then end (see the graphic below).

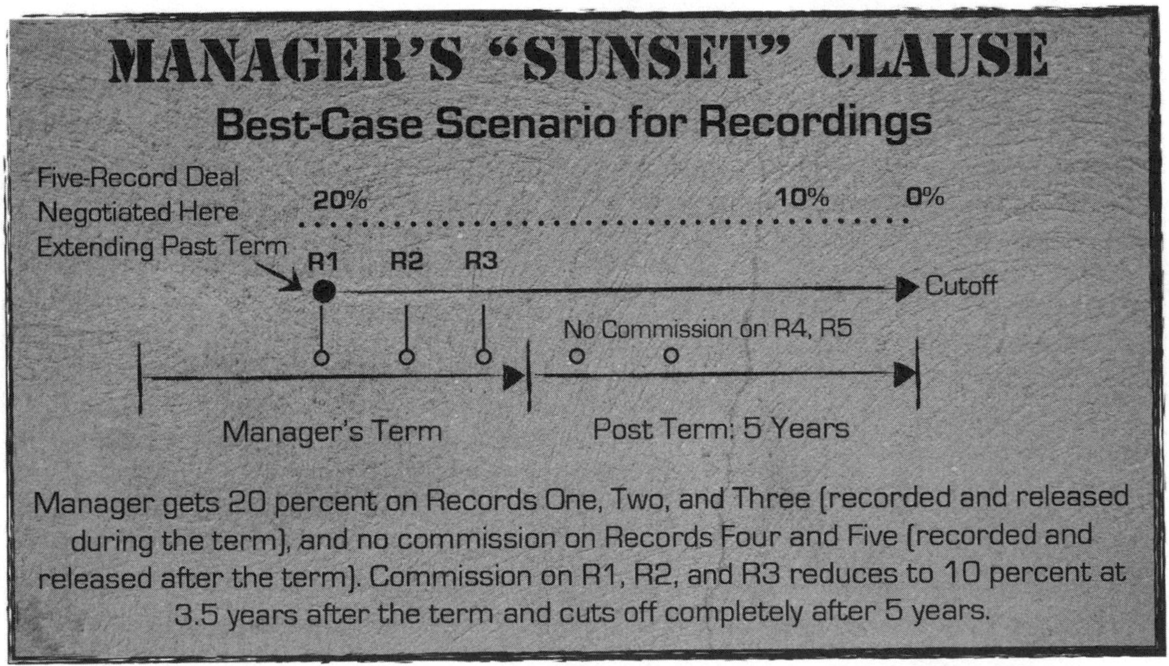

Many different options are possible here, depending on your personal manager, your bargaining strength, and the type of money (recordings, publishing) on which a sunset clause is being negotiated.

The Manager's View of Sunset Clauses

Not all managers are going to be happy with a sunset clause. In a UCLA lecture, veteran managers Bud Prager (Foreigner, Bad Company, and Megadeth) and Mike Gormley (Bangles, Oingo Boingo, and Danny Elfman) revealed that they don't believe in sunset clauses. Says Gormley, "It's the manager who helps take the artist from obscurity to popularity. If the artist continues to make money from deals that were negotiated, or substantially negotiated, during the term of the manager's agreement, then shouldn't the manager do likewise?"

Although the personal manager's side of the argument may be valid, your attorney will be able to advise you as to what is appropriate in your individual situation. An attorney who is skillful at negotiating should be able to reach terms that are acceptable to both sides.

Good luck.

10

Business Managers

Bills and Investments

"Money is better than poverty, if only for financial reasons." —Woody Allen

We've all heard about musicians who hit it big, then ended up penniless. In one such infamous story, rapper MC Hammer, who was once reported in *Forbes* magazine as being worth $40 million, actually had to file for bankruptcy. If you don't want this to happen to you, the assistance of a good business manager is crucial.

In the early stages of your career, when you're trying to get noticed and you're making no money or just making ends meet, you're probably not ready for a business manager. In fact, all you may need is a certified public accountant experienced in music to help with taxes and to provide general business advice.

But if you plan to hit it big one day, learning about what a good business manager can do now is worth millions to your career and to your future. This chapter covers the role of a business manager, hiring a business manager, important terms of your agreement, and tips on handling finances yourself.

Those who say money isn't everything are usually those who never had to worry about it. Read on.

The Role of a Business Manager in Your Career

The role of a business manager is not to be confused with that of a personal manager.

A personal manager is more like the chief executive officer (CEO) of your company, who helps generate income by helping you attract recording deals, publishing deals, and tours.

A business manager, on the other hand, is more like the chief financial officer (CFO) of your company, who helps manage the income from these deals once they're in place.

A business manager handles all financial issues, such as investments, financial planning, bookkeeping, tour account services, asset administration, tax services, insurance monitoring, and royalty examination. These are all discussed below.

Investment Strategies and Financial Planning

One of the most important roles that a business manager can play in your career is to help you plan for your future. It's not enough to bank on hitting it big.

Planning for the Long Term

A good business manager helps his or her clients plan ahead by first determining what investment strategy is best suited for their needs.

For instance, is a high-risk, short-term strategy (such as stock investments in emerging technologies) a wise plan, or is a long-term, low-risk strategy (such as investing in pension plans, mutual funds, and municipal bonds) a more appropriate scheme?

Jeff Hinkle of the Los Angeles–based business management firm Gudvi, Sussman & Oppenheim (www.gsogroup.com) says,

> We like to think in the long term for our clients. One of the first things that we would do, especially for our younger clients, is to set up a pension plan and start saving for their retirement. Depending on how much they can afford to put aside, we'll probably use the assistance of a professional money manager.

Managing the Portfolio and Minimizing Risk

The money manager opens the investment accounts and recommends appropriate investments such as stocks, mutual funds, treasury bills, and high-quality bonds. Once the investment choices have been made, the money manager then oversees the portfolio on a day-to-day basis; he makes ongoing recommendations as to the mix of investments to maximize clients' return on their money and also minimize their downside risk. The business manager is always involved in these decisions, but the business manager is not a stock picker. That's the money manager's job.

Bookkeeping and Accounting

Business managers not only look out for your future by helping with investments and financial planning, but they also help manage your money on a daily basis by reviewing invoices, paying monthly bills, collecting royalty earnings, depositing money, and monitoring your bank accounts. All of these issues fall under a service known as bookkeeping and accounting.

Opening Accounts

Business managers have long-established relationships with local banks that are familiar with the business management firm and its clients. Your business manager will usually open a checking account (to pay all of your bills) and what's called a pocket account (for whatever personal expenses you may have, ATM withdrawals you may make, etc.). Of course, these accounts are open under your name, and you have to provide your signature to the bank.

Paying Bills

Your business manager then collects all of your income, which can range from touring and merchandising monies to publishing and artist royalties, and deposits it into these accounts. He or she monitors your bank accounts to make sure there's enough money to meet your expenses, reviews your bills (car payments, credit card bills, home mortgages, gardener, personal trainer, etc.) to ensure that all charges are justified, requests your approval and signature (unless you authorize him or her to sign on your behalf), and then pays your bills.

Jeff Hinkle notes:

> We really encourage our clients to be involved in the bill-paying process. Not paying your own bills can be a dangerous thing; it's the old "out of sight, out of mind" problem. We prefer for clients to sign their own checks, although this isn't always possible due to their generally busy schedules. I've had clients who seemed to have a phobia when it came to bills and discussing their spending. Sometimes, as long as they know they can meet all of their expenses, they would rather not deal with any of it at all.

Tour Services

Another important role played by your business manager is the handling of all financial matters pertaining to touring. Business managers are involved with a tour from its inception and planning to the very last show a band performs.

Handling Pre-Tour Activities: Budgeting and More

Your business manager, along with your personal manager, is responsible for putting together tour budgets when you're planning to hit the road. He or she will review all of the performance deals offered by concert promoters around the country to determine the total gross earnings of the tour. A projection of expenses is then made to determine what the potential net profit or loss of the tour may be. Expenses may include the following:

- Tour bus
- Airfare
- Hotels
- Insurance (for personal injury, theft, if you miss a show—called "nonappearance")
- Rehearsal fees
- Per diems (daily allowances paid to the band and crew for food)
- Salaries for the band
- Salaries for the crew
- Production costs (for the sound and lighting equipment)
- Trucking cost (to carry the sound and lights)
- Contingency (an additional percentage [usually 5 percent]) calculated into the budget in case expenses are estimated low or there are unexpected emergencies
- Your agent's fees
- Your manager's commission
- Your business manager's fees

The expenses listed above are an oversimplification of what is usually incurred by a band on the road; the list can easily be a page long. Nevertheless, after determining the total expenses of a tour and then deducting them from the projected gross income, the business manager works at making adjustments in areas where he or she feels money could be saved. Careful planning is required. Any miscalculation of expenses can lead to serious problems at the end of a tour, and instead of making money, you can find yourself thousands of dollars in the red.

Monitoring the Tour During and After: Taxes, Insurance, and More

Once you're on the road, your business manager's work does not end by any means. He or she collects monies taken from each performance and makes sure that the concert promoter paid the appropriate sum. Your business manager then pays all bills owed to the tour bus companies and trucking companies and pays salaries to the band and its crew.

He or she also makes sure a tax return is filed in every state in which a tour is planned. By submitting a budget to the appropriate authorities in each state, your business manager can limit the band's tax obligations by making sure the band is taxed on the net profits of a performance rather than on the total gross earnings taken.

Lastly, your business manager makes sure your band is properly insured while out on the road, especially with something called "non-appearance insurance." This means that if a concert is canceled because your lead singer gets sick or your tour bus breaks down, the insurance company will pay the band the amount it was expecting to earn from that performance. As you can imagine, non-appearance insurance is extremely important. One or two live performance cancellations can cause a band to lose incredible sums of money.

Asset Administration

Moving away from making money, now let's talk about spending it. This brings us to your business manager's next important role, known as asset administration. Let's take a look at common purchases like a home and automobile.

Shopping for a Home

When you're shopping for a home, your business manager will advise you as to what price range you can afford and explain deal points such as loan fees, title insurance, and credit reports.

Unless you're exceptionally fortunate and can pay cash for a home, your business manager will rely on relationships with mortgage brokers to arrange loans.

Shopping for an Automobile

Shopping for a car is not unlike shopping for a home. Your business manager will advise you of the price range you can afford and explain the finer points of deals such as buying versus leasing. After you decide what you want to do, the business manager contacts an automobile broker.

Jeff Hinkle remembers one instance in which a client wanted a particular Mercedes model that was especially hard to find. An automobile broker located the car, down to the exact specifications, in Texas and delivered it to Jeff's client in California in a few short days; how's that for service?

Financial Reporting

While on the topic of spending money, let's discuss financial reporting.

Every month, your business manager must send out a detailed statement to his or her clients that includes every deposit made, every transfer of funds made in and out of investment accounts, and every check written. Rather than these reports looking like something a bank would send out, your business manager may categorize items under certain headings, such as recording expenses, housing expenses, and business expenses. This makes it much easier for you to read and understand your statements.

Your business managers will also meet periodically with you to review financial statements and to make projections as to where they see your finances in six months to a year. Jeff Hinkle adds that this is one of the most challenging parts of his job:

> Communication with the client about their money is the key. Most artists would rather think about mixing their new album or an upcoming tour than their finances. That's why we make it a point to have regular financial meetings with all of our clients. Since most of our clients are touring artists, finding the time and place to meet can be difficult. So several times a year, we will get on an airplane and fly out to meet with a client who is on tour. I've had plenty of business meetings on tour buses and backstage in dressing rooms. Sometimes that's the only way to get in front of the client.

Tax Planning

Another important function undertaken by your business manager involves tax planning. This crucial responsibility can be divided into three categories: determination of an appropriate business entity, handling of payroll and income taxes, and estate planning.

Determining a Business Entity

One of your business manager's major responsibilities is helping you determine what business entity best suits your needs. Should you be a partnership, a corporation, or an LLC (limited liability company)? The choice can significantly affect the taxes you pay. Your business manager, together with expert lawyers, will help you set up the business entity best suited to your needs.

Handling Payroll and Income Taxes

Your business manager also handles payroll and income taxes. He or she writes checks and pays all personnel, from the crew to the side musicians to the band itself, and deducts all applicable taxes. He or she also prepares all W-2 and 1099 forms for the purpose of filing tax returns. Having a working knowledge of the special deductions that entertainers are allowed to take, your business manager also prepares your tax returns (or, in some cases, business managers hire an outside firm to do this).

Should you ever be audited by the Internal Revenue Service, your business manager will have the authority (granted by you under contract—discussed later in this chapter) to meet with the IRS field agent and show all proper documentation of receipts and deductions taken on your returns. If your business manager is doing his or her job correctly, this is usually not too difficult. But without a business manager working for you, an audit by the IRS can be a nightmare unless you have been extraordinarily organized and careful with your record keeping.

Helping with Estate Planning

Lastly, your business manager helps you with estate planning. In plain English, this means that he or she will assist you in preparing for what will happen to your assets when you die. It may not be something you want to think about while you're young and healthy, but if you've worked hard all your life and are finally successful, you want to be sure your assets are left with the people you love.

Estate planning includes such important issues as setting up wills, trust funds, life insurance, and gifting (the process of giving equitable gifts such as cash or property in order to reduce estate tax liability on inheritance). Your business manager will work with expert attorneys specializing in estate planning to make certain that you and your family members are protected.

Insurance: Liability, Auto, Home, and More

Your business manager also makes sure that you have all of the appropriate insurance coverage in place, including general liability, workers' compensation, auto insurance, home insurance, and non-appearance insurance.

When taking on a new client, a business manager typically contacts that client's current insurance broker to determine what insurance is already in place. If the broker is not experienced in entertainment, the business manager will recommend someone who is.

Although business managers typically have established relationships with experienced entertainment insurance brokers, they will not take their advice at face value. The business manager makes sure that his or her client is getting all the best rates, premiums, and deductibles. Jeff Hinkle notes that insurance is a very important responsibility for business managers. If their clients are sued and don't have adequate coverage, or the right kind of coverage, or have no coverage at all, it can lead to substantial losses and even bankruptcy.

Royalty Examination

Last but not least, let's discuss royalty examination as the responsibility of the business manager.

Most music business management firms have royalty-examination departments that understand the detailed aspects of royalty earnings. Your business manager monitors royalties from record, merchandising, and publishing deals and makes sure you're paid appropriately when these monies are due.

If your business manager finds discrepancies in accounting statements, he or she will contact the appropriate company with a series of detailed questions concerning the matter. If the problem at hand cannot be reasonably resolved, the business manager will contact a royalty-auditing service and conduct a field audit on your behalf. Jeff Hinkle says that these audits usually result in sizable settlements for the artist. (Disturbing, isn't it?)

ONE-CENT ROYALTY AND A $19 MILLION AUDIT

Most of the horror stories you hear in the music business pale in comparison to what took place in the early days of rock 'n' roll. Take the Beatles, for example. If anyone should have been able to get a good deal, it's the "Fab Four," right? Wrong!

In 1962, music attorneys didn't even exist. The Beatles' first recording contract with EMI called for a paltry one-cent-per-album royalty. Not 1 percent—one cent! And due to several one-year options contained in their contract, it wasn't until 1967 that personal manager Brian Epstein was able to renegotiate the band's record deal.

To make this story even juicier, business manager Jeff Hinkle adds that in 1980, 10 years after the Beatles broke up, an accounting firm was hired to audit EMI for back royalty payments on the Beatles' behalf. The audit resulted in a settlement in the Beatles' favor of around $19 million. (You can double that amount to get an idea of the money's value in today's dollars.)

If you made a list of all the rock stars who signed one-sided contracts early in their careers and got ripped off by the industry, your list would read like a "who's who" of the music world. So, first and foremost, be extremely careful what you sign and what you agree to when you're nobody, and as you start to make money, be sure to get yourself a great business manager, too.

Hiring Your Business Manager

Now that you have a pretty good idea about the role a business manager plays in your career, it's time to discuss when to hire a business manager, how to find one, and what qualities you should look for.

When to Hire a Business Manager

The best time to hire a business manager is when there's a substantial amount of money passing through your hands (such as at the time when you are about to sign a recording deal and receive a recording fund).

Jeff Hinkle warns:

> Just don't wait till the last minute before hiring a business manager. Usually this is done to avoid paying the business manager a commission on their first round of advances. However, this can end up costing the artist more than they save in fees. The problem with waiting is that their money is often wasted or mismanaged, and more times than not, they forget to file their tax returns. By the time the artist decides to hire a business manager, they may have already blown through the

advance, but no taxes have been paid. Remember, advances are almost always taxable income in the year received. Once the delinquent tax returns are filed, the IRS adds penalties and interest to the tax bill, compounding the problem.

Finding a Reputable Business Manager

Once you've decided you're ready for a business manager, now you have to find one. The best way to do this is usually through personal referrals from people on your professional team, such as your manager and attorney, or from artists who are more successful than you are.

Jeff Hinkle suggests that you get more than just a single recommendation and that you meet with all of the business managers before making your final decision. This is really important. Remember that your business manager is the one person to whom you're usually giving significant control of your money!

And if that's not scary enough, you should know that in the state of California (check other states), a business manager needs no credentials, licensing, or educational qualifications. That's right. So be sure to choose your business manager wisely!

Qualities to Look For in a Business Manager

After you've received a few referrals for business managers and made a few appointments, there are a few things you need to consider before deciding whom to hire:

- ***Is the Business Manager a Certified Public Accountant?*** Being a CPA doesn't necessarily provide someone with the skills to be a business manager (many great business managers aren't CPAs), but it does give you some assurance that your business manager is at least a college graduate, is board certified, and has some organizational and accounting skills. Remember, there are no qualifications needed to be a business manager, so essentially anyone can be one.
- ***Is the Business Manager Part of a Larger Firm or a Smaller Firm?*** Some smaller business management firms (with a staff of 1 to 20 people) simply don't have the same resources larger firms do. For instance, they may not have the capability to undertake a royalty examination, which is often the province of a dedicated department of experts. You don't want to be with a firm that you're going to quickly outgrow. On the other hand, if you start out at a larger firm (50 to 100 people on staff), you risk being overshadowed by their larger, more successful clients.
- ***Who Are Some of the Business Manager's Other Clients?*** If you haven't heard of any of the clients the business manager represents, it may not be a good idea to go with him or her.
- ***How Long Has the Business Manager Been in Business?*** An established business management firm is one that has been in business for about 10 years. That's not to imply that firms that have been in business for less than 10 years are not any good; it just means that they haven't handled as many clients and are not as experienced.
- ***Does the Business Manager Specialize in Music?*** This is perhaps one of the most important questions to consider. If the business manager handles clients in film and television but doesn't work with musicians, he or she may not be right for you. Your business manager must understand the complexities of touring (in both the United States and foreign territories) and royalty issues (publishing, recording, merchandising, and more).
- ***Does the Business Manager Handle New and Developing Artists?*** This is also important! You want to know that this business manager has the patience and know-how to make your pennies grow into nickels and your nickels grow into dollars.
- ***Is the Business Manager Approachable and Pleasant?*** If you can't communicate with your business manager, or if you feel uncomfortable or stupid discussing money in his or her presence, then no matter whom he or she represents, you should look for someone else to hire.

- ***Does the Business Manager Welcome Your Questions?*** You want someone who's going to be helpful enough to take your calls on weekends or at home if you have an important question or concern.
- ***Can You Trust Your Business Manager?*** This is an obvious concern, but extremely important. You want a business manager who projects a genuine feeling of concern for the security of your future.
- ***What Investment Strategies Does the Business Manager Have in Mind for You?*** As previously discussed, does the business manager have a long-term, low-risk plan, or a high-risk, short-term plan in mind for you? You probably want to look for someone who is thinking about the long term.
- ***Is the Business Manager Independent of the Deals and Investments He or She Is Putting Your Money Into?*** If the business manager owns a share in a shopping center and wants you to invest in it as well, you should be wary of his or her advice. Or, if your business manager aggressively pushes you in the direction of investing in a particular stock, he or she may be getting a commission from the stock broker for making the referral.
- ***What Kind of Financial Reports Will the Business Manager Give You?*** Will the financial reports be issued monthly? Will they be categorized in a way that is easy to read and that you can understand?
- ***Will the Business Manager Handle Your Tax Returns?*** Some business management firms hire outside CPAs to handle tax returns, and as a result they charge you extra. You want to know this in advance.
- ***Is the Business Manager an Expert in Handling Royalties?*** Royalties from publishing, merch, and record sales can be a great source of income for you. A business manager needs to understand this very complex and detailed area to ensure that no money is lost or uncollected.
- ***Does the Business Manager Have Insurance?*** Many business managers are insured against errors and omissions they may make while providing accounting and investment services to you. And finally . . .
- ***Has the Business Manager Ever Been Sued?*** "Never be intimidated to ask this question of both the smaller and larger firms," says Sharon Chambers of Down to Earth Business Management. "It's often the smaller firms that get the bad rap for unscrupulous activity, but the big firms are just as likely to rip you off. The reason why you rarely hear about these cases is that they settle out of the courts. You should never subscribe to the 'the larger the firm, the safer you are' way of thinking."

As you can see from this list of questions, there is a great deal to consider before hiring a business manager. Just don't forget to use your good old gut instinct. If things don't feel right from the start, they're probably not!

That's about it for hiring a business manager. Now let's move on to the last part of this chapter and discuss business management agreements.

Important Terms of Your Agreement

For many years, formal contracts between business managers and their clients were not standard, but this is no longer the case—at least for many firms. The basic terms of an agreement might include the payment structure, audit rights, power of attorney, and termination rights.

Payment Structure

There are three methods by which business managers are typically paid. These are discussed below.

Flat Retainer

A flat retainer is a fixed monthly sum that is based on the success of the client. Obviously, the more successful a client is, the more attention he or she will need. On average, a monthly retainer can range from $500 to $3,000 for new artists, and far more for successful clients.

Hourly Fees

A straight hourly fee is just that: you're charged by the hour for your business manager's services. The hourly fee is based on the professional level of the person working with you.

For instance, a file clerk can get around $30 per hour, while a partner of the firm can get $300 per hour or more. It's usually not possible to pay one hourly rate for everyone involved with your career, so your bill will reflect various rates and charges. For instance, during the tax season (January 15–April 15), you may see higher charges on your bill, since the higher-level CPAs may be preparing your returns.

The "by the hour" system of paying a business manager usually works best for artists making substantial sums of money. As you'll see in a minute, when you choose to pay your business manager a percentage of the deals you enter into, he or she can end up with substantially more money—especially if you're earning large sums from concert performances or publishing deals.

Percentage of the Deal (5 Percent)

The last method of payment is for your business manager to take a percentage, typically 5 percent, of your gross income (excluding investment income, tour support, and recording "costs").

Jeff Hinkle tells me that for tour services, that 5 percent can either be a percentage of the tour's gross (artist guarantees plus overages, but not production reimbursements) or a percentage of the net (total gross minus all tour expenses).

This can add up. Thus, your business manager may sometimes agree to set a cap on the amount of income he or she can earn per year. For instance, a business manager may agree to take in no more than $100,000 in commissions, and no less than $30,000.

But business manager Sharon Chambers cautions you to be sure to check on the firm's cancellation policy regarding minimums. Some firms will dump you in a year after they've commissioned your initial advances and monies from touring have slowed down.

Audit Rights

Another point that you may want to stipulate is your right to audit your business manager's books. Business managers will always allow their clients to review all financial records.

That said, Jeff Hinkle adds:

> An audit can actually be a healthy exercise for artists. If anything, they'll get a greater appreciation for what the business manager does by seeing that everything is in order. And in the worst-case scenario, if the business manager is up to no good, an audit may help reveal whose pockets the artist's money has been going into. The stories you often hear of unscrupulous business managers, personal managers, attorneys, or whoever else ripping off unsuspecting artists occur when artists allow one person to have too much control over their career and finances without having any checks and balances. The artist must always pay attention to what's going on around him or her, and not get caught up in the whole fantasy of being a star.

Power of Attorney (or "Limited" Power of Attorney)

The term "power of attorney" simply grants another person "the right to act for you."

Jeff Hinkle says:

> Generally, all we ask for is what is called a limited power of attorney for handling certain IRS matters (like representing you in tax audits) and signing bills on your behalf (when you're out on

the road and too busy to deal with this matter). Always think twice about what rights you grant under a power of attorney, and think three times—no, four—about granting someone full power of attorney—or you might find someone buying a home or financing new automobiles using your money without you knowing about it. Remember, your business manager should only have a limited power of attorney, with the rights you're giving him or her clearly stipulated in writing.

The Right to Terminate

Last but not least, in all relationships between a business manager and client, the client must have the right to terminate at will. Said another way, if you are unhappy with your business manager for any reason, you can fire him or her on the spot.

Just be fair! If you suddenly snap out of rock stardom and realize that you're running out of money due to excess spending or neglect of your finances, despite your business manager's warnings, the only person to blame is yourself. No one should care more about your future than you!

HOW TO SELF-MANAGE YOUR PERSONAL FINANCES AND LIFE

The time will one day come when you are making great money and hiring business managers. But until then, here are a few tips on managing your own financial life:

- ***Trim Your Expenses:*** Determine your exact monthly expenses (rent, car insurance, phone, food, health insurance, Internet) and decide which expenditures you can really do without.
- ***Set Your Sights on Earning Twice as Much as Your Expenses:*** You may not succeed, but you can at least push for this!
- ***Don't "Fake It Till You Make It":*** In other words, don't live above your means. You can find ways to make a good impression by shopping around for great deals, buying secondhand, etc., without putting yourself in debt.
- ***Keep Track of Your Bills:*** Pay your bills on time to avoid paying late fees, and always check your bills for accuracy—even major corporations make mistakes!
- ***Watch Your Money Daily:*** Keep track of what you're spending your money on and what's in your checking account. You can balance your checkbook the old-fashioned way (using the register your bank gives you) or by learning to use financial software programs like Quicken.
- ***Find Ways to Limit "Necessary" Expenses:*** You can reduce monthly banking fees by limiting ATM use, finding a bank that offers free checking, raising your car insurance deductible, shopping around for long distance and cell phone rates, moving into a smaller apartment or getting a roommate, packing a lunch, and drinking at home instead of drinking in a bar (that is, if drinking is really necessary).
- ***Pay Off Credit Cards:*** Pay off your credit cards in full each month to avoid paying interest charges, and consider using convenient secure cards (i.e., cards in which your limits are pre-deposited into an account so that you'll never find yourself in debt).
- ***Get Out of Debt Now:*** If you're in debt, make it a priority to start getting out now. There is nothing that weighs on your mental well-being more than worrying about money. Check out the Internet for advice, or speak with your local bank or personal accountant.
- ***Don't Borrow Money Unless You Absolutely Have To:*** If you're trying to fund your next recording project, get creative. Set up a barter deal with a local producer in which he or she records you in return for playing on his or her other sessions. Or get the fans to invest in you.
- ***Save Some Amount of Money Each Month:*** No matter how little it is, save something!

- ***Invest:*** Speak with a financial planner about your future goals (e.g., when you'd like to retire, how much money you'd like to save for your retirement, etc.) and discuss investments (stocks, bonds, real estate, etc.) that will help you reach your goals.
- ***Look Into Creating a Retirement Fund:*** Sometimes your "day job" (if you have one) will offer a plan. Just be sure to speak with a financial planner or CPA about this.
- ***Reduce Your Tax Liability:*** Save all of your business-related receipts, and file them in separate envelopes by the month (or scan them and save them on your computer). If you're really good, also separate them in various categories like gas, auto repairs, entertainment and meal receipts, business phone charges, subscriptions, and union dues. These may help you save money when doing your taxes.
- ***Get Financially Fit:*** Read motivational and business books like *Think and Grow Rich* by Napoleon Hill, *The Money Book for the Young, Fabulous, and Broke* by Suze Orman, *Get a Financial Life* by Beth Kobliner, and *The Wealthy Barber* by David Chilton. Or take a class on bookkeeping or money management at a local college.
- ***Find an Accountant:*** Find a good CPA experienced in the music business by using referrals from people you trust.

11

Talent Agents

Work, Scope, and Contracts

"Ten percent of zero is zero." —Ian Copeland, founder, Frontier Booking International

Many young artists still believe that there are magical talent agents in the world just waiting to send them off on the road to major success. But until you've built up a buzz on your own and inked a deal with a record label, or a label deal seems imminent, you're probably a long way from getting an agent with serious clout.

As John Pantle of APA puts it, "Remember that an agent's business model is based on receiving a percentage of clients' winnings, and thus his or her motivation is slated towards artists who are bringing in the most money."

While your best plan as an emerging artist is to book your own gigs first and stimulate demand, the day will eventually come when you're ready for a talent agent's services. Thus, you need to know what a talent agent does, when to hire one, what qualities to look for, what agreement terms are standard, and how to be your own booking agent.

Note: A significant portion of this chapter includes excerpts from a candid one-on-one interview I conducted with Ian Copeland, founder of Frontier Booking International. Sadly, Copeland recently passed away. His contributions to the world of touring and the music business will always be valued.

The Role of an Agent in Your Career

The role of a talent agent is to procure employment in a variety of areas—from modeling to acting to writing books. However, a talent agent's primary role is to help you get live gigs. Let's take a closer look.

Formulating Your Tour Strategy

According to Ian Copeland (whose agency has represented Sting, No Doubt, the Red Hot Chili Peppers, and more), the first thing an agent must do for his or her client is get on the phone with concert promoters around the country and test the waters. Your agent must first determine whether there's a real interest in your band, and develop a number of different strategies for how he or she can move your career forward.

As Copeland put it:

> It's like an army strategizing its plan before going into battle. You have to survey the terrain and figure out the opportunities and potential risks.

Packaging the Artist

Another important role of your agent is packaging—the process of grouping your act with other artists on a concert tour. Packaging requires careful, creative consideration, especially for the new artist who is still trying to establish his or her "brand image" in the marketplace.

While there may seem to be a basic logic that goes along with packaging (e.g., don't put speed metal with country, and country with speed metal), individual bands and agents are going to have significantly different ideas about how to package a tour. The truth is that no one really knows what will and won't work, but it is the creative agent who pushes the boundaries.

Determining Whether to Open or Headline

An agent must also help decide whether it would be more advantageous to open for a successful artist on a major tour, or to go out on the road as a headliner playing in smaller venues.

While going out with a larger act may put you in front of many more people (assuming that the perfect opening slot is waiting for you), the headlining act may impose limits on your sound, lights, stage, and set time—thus preventing you from showing off what you've really got.

On the other hand, headlining small clubs may provide you more opportunity to shine. Says Copeland:

> You essentially own the show when headlining in smaller clubs and there's significant potential for career growth. If the shows start selling out, you can work your way up to playing larger rooms, to performing in theaters, and, eventually, to playing in stadiums.

Routing the Tour

The talent agent's role also consists of routing (or mapping out) the tour's direction.

When you're the support act for a major artist, you won't have much say in the routing—you're told when to show up, and you're extra careful to show up on time "with bells on."

However, when you're the headliner for the night, you can make special requests about the number of consecutive dates you'll perform, and the days you want off (e.g., between Christmas and New Year's Eve).

The agent then strives to connect one city to the next, leaving the fewest number of miles in between so as to conserve time and reduce expenses. This information, together with the venue names, dates, and times, is gathered up in an "itinerary" and sent to the manager to review with the artist. If needed, all parties will go back and forth on the plans until everything is just right.

Pricing the Artist

When you're the headlining act of a tour, your agent is also responsible for determining the ticket price for your show. Determining the ticket price for a live performance begins with your agent contacting concert promoters to get a sense of what other acts are doing, and also considering the demographics of the audience.

As Copeland put it:

> If you're a jazz artist whose music caters primarily to an adult audience with strong disposable income, you can get away with charging a higher ticket price, assuming of course, that you also have a preexisting fan base and are in high demand.

If you're a metal act whose music appeals primarily to a much younger audience with low or no disposable income, you'd better charge a much lower ticket price, or no one will be able to attend the show—and, even worse, no one will want to put on the show in their venue. Knowing your audience is paramount.

THE MOST EXPENSIVE TICKET PRICES EVER

- ***Paul McCartney:*** Average price $241
- ***Fleetwood Mac:*** Average price $282
- ***Beyoncé:*** Average price $294
- ***The Who:*** Average price $314
- ***Justin Timberlake:*** Average price $339
- ***The Eagles:*** Average price $354
- ***Maroon 5 with Neon Trees & Owl City:*** Average price $364
- ***One Direction:*** Average price $460
- ***The Rolling Stones:*** Average price $624

[Source: www.forbes.com. Based on secondary ticket sellers (those who purchase all of the tickets from primary markets—i.e. Ticketmaster, the box office, official team/artist website, etc.—and then resell them to the public at a huge markup.)]

Determining When to Put Tickets on Sale

Your talent agent must also determine the best time to put your concert tickets on sale. Copeland's overall strategy was: "Not too soon, not too late, and not on someone else's date."

Explains Copeland:

> If you put tickets on sale "too soon," you'll incur higher costs in advertising. If you put tickets on sale "too late," you won't have enough time to add a show if the night sells out. If you put tickets on sale on "someone else's date," such as on the date that another big artist is releasing tickets, then you'll have two titans competing head to head, and you don't want that.

Negotiating Fees for Live Performance Deals

Another major role of the talent agent is negotiating live performance deals. The methods he or she uses will vary depending on where you are in your career.

In the early stages of your career, when you're the support act for other artists, your compensation in dollars may consist of whatever the headlining act wants to offer—which may not amount to very much at all. Even when going out on your own and headlining small clubs, there will usually be little room for negotiating a fee at first, but the benefit comes from building fans and market demand.

As your demand starts to build in the marketplace, live performance fees are usually negotiated by your agent using the "gross potential" of the venue. The gross potential can be found by taking the ticket price for the venue and multiplying it by the number of seats in the venue. (Keep in mind that there are usually several ticket prices within a venue depending on the proximity of the seats to the stage. So, x seats at $A each, plus y seats at $B each, equals the gross potential.) The agent and the promoter then negotiate backward from this price until it makes sense for all parties involved to put on the show.

(Note: The various methods by which you're paid for a live performance, as well as the negotiations involved, are covered in detail in chapter 22.)

Collecting Deposits

Besides negotiating a fee for live performance deals with promoters, your agent is also responsible for negotiating and collecting deposits to ensure you're not screwed out of what the promoters promise you. According to agent John Pantle of APA, the amount of the deposit varies, but is typically one of the following:

- ***10 Percent of the Fee:*** When dealing with national promoters (like Live Nation and AEG) representing larger venues.
- ***50 Percent of the Fee:*** When dealing with regional promoters representing smaller venues.
- ***100 Percent of the Fee:*** When dealing with promoters who know that your band is a winning act. When negotiating for Sting, Copeland collected 100 percent of the live performance fee in advance—with no questions asked!

Whatever the amount, deposits are usually collected 30 days in advance of the show. They are held by your agent until after you perform the gig.

After the show, the agent subtracts his or her commission and forwards the rest to your business manager. The other part of the performance fee is collected by your tour manager when he or she "closes out" the show at the venue while you're still on stage performing.

Handling Hall Fees

The last role of your talent agent deals with handling hall fees. Hall fees are discussed in more detail in chapter 24, but generally they are a commission (or fee) the venue (or hall) sometimes charges an act for selling T-shirts, hats, posters, and other goods.

When a hall fee exists, it can range from 25 to 30 percent of the gross sales. Note that talent agents do not share in a percentage of your merchandising incomes, so it does no good for them to negotiate one way or another. However, agents will help to reduce, and in some cases even eliminate, merchandising hall charges when their help is requested by the band's manager.

Hiring Your Agent

Now that you know what an agent does, we can talk about when to hire one, how to hook up with one, and the qualities he or she should possess.

When to Hire an Agent

As stated at the beginning of this chapter, the best time to begin looking for a talent agent is after you've generated extensive buzz around your career and you've signed a deal with a record label (or are close to signing one).

When you get signed to a label, whether it be a major, an independent, or your own label with a major distributor contract, there is an increased perception of legitimacy about your career among promoters around the country. The greater the perception, the greater the offers, and the more likely a talent agent will come aboard.

Hooking Up with a Talent Agency

There are typically three methods by which an artist and a professional talent agency come together: the record company makes referrals, the booking agency initiates contact, and the band or manager takes action. Let's take a look.

The Record Company Makes Referrals

Your record company may recommend you to a variety of agencies and even make the introductions. Sometimes, when the record company has a booking division, it will act as your agent under the terms of the initial recording agreement.

The Booking Agencies Initiate Meetings

The booking agencies may reach out to your record label (or your management company) and arrange meetings to discuss representation. Sometimes, in cases when you're creating a huge buzz, the agencies will scout you out in clubs before you ink a label deal.

The Band or Personal Manager Takes the Initiative

Lastly, you or your manager may make the first move and reach out to agencies by doing the following:

- ***Making the Rounds at the Majors:*** Your manager may follow a more obvious path by setting up appointments and meeting with all the majors, like ICM Partners (formerly International Creative Management), CAA (Creative Artists Agency), APA (Agency for the Performing Arts), WMA (William Morris Agency), and the Agency Group.
- ***Seeking Referrals from Other Managers:*** Your manager may conduct a more thorough search of the various agencies that exist by contacting other personal managers in the business and asking for recommendations.
- ***Utilizing Resource Guides:*** And finally, your manager may refer to one of the many resource guides available on the market today, such as the *Booking Agency Directory*—a magazine that lists practically every agency, its roster of artists, and the names of the agents who work for the agency.

But with so many agencies to choose from, how do you really know who's going to be the best one to represent you? Read on.

Qualities to Look For in an Agent and Agency

While the personal manager typically spends the most time working with the booking agent, it's still important for you to understand what qualities to look for in a potential agent and agency. After all, it's your career we're discussing. So here are a just a few questions to consider.

- ***Is the Agent Part of a Specialized Agency?*** Music-only agencies such as Windish or the Agency Group can do a fantastic job at booking live performances and helping you grow your audience. The downside, however, is that they are limited in the services they can offer you.
- ***Is the Agent Part of a Full-Service Agency?*** Full-service agencies offer a broader range of services, including television and motion picture work, sponsorships, and literary jobs. This can be useful for multitalented musicians. However, you should never choose one agency over another because they promise to make you a movie star. More often than not, this is only a sales pitch to get you to sign with their company.
- ***Is the Agent Part of a Boutique Agency?*** A boutique agency (one that represents no more than, say, 75 bands) might be exactly what you need in the early stages of your career. There won't be many bands to compete with on the roster, and you'll probably get more individualized treatment. However, a boutique agency may not have the expertise, staff, and experience necessary to get you into larger venues or on bigger tours.
- ***Is the Agent Part of a Major Agency?*** Major agencies typically have the skill set and experience needed to take your career to a higher level. They represent a number of money-making clients and thus have more pull with promoters around the country to put young and developing artists like you on a

quality tour. The downside is that you run the risk of being overshadowed by more successful artists on the agency's roster.

- ***Are You One of the First Artists on an Agency's Roster?*** While it might appear you'll get more attention (when a jazz agency opens up a rock department, for instance, and you're the first rock band it wants to sign), you never want to be the guinea pig at any agency. Adds Ian Copeland, "No matter how hard it may try to sell you on the idea, don't do it!"
- ***Is the Agent Enthusiastic About Your Career?*** The agent's enthusiasm for your career will greatly affect how hard he or she will fight for you. No matter how reputable the agent may be, if you don't get a sense that he or she will kill for you, think twice about signing. Says Ian Copeland, "An agent who has real passion for an artist can make a huge difference."
- ***Will the Agent Be Your "Responsible" Agent?*** If you're impressed with the agent with whom you initially meet, make sure that he or she is going to serve as your "responsible agent," and not the person who wines and dines you and gets you to sign with the firm, and then passes you off to someone else you're not as impressed with. For the sake of clarity, a "responsible agent" is the "key person" who will serve as the liaison between you and the agency and who will do the bulk of the work. Bottom line: it's your right to know who that person is going to be, and to meet with that person from the outset.
- ***How Long Has Your Agent Been with the Firm?*** Is your agent known for jumping from one agency to the next? Does the agency itself have a high turnover rate? If so, you might be concerned with whether your agent's days with a particular agency are numbered. Once you establish a good working relationship with a certain person, the last thing you want is to lose continuity by having to reestablish what you've already worked hard to build, or, in the worst case, get stuck with someone at the agency who's not as enthusiastic about working with you. And finally . . .
- ***Do You Like Your Agent's Personality?*** Your agent is the person who sells you to potential buyers. He or she is your calling card. That being said, you want to know that he or she is going to be aggressive enough to get you the best deals and tours, and tactful enough to handle business in a way that won't be damaging to your career. As the saying goes, you can get more bees with honey than you can with vinegar.

Terms of the Agreement

Lastly, let's discuss your agreement with an agent. While there are many terms found in talent agency agreements, let's focus on some of the more important issues. These include the agent's fee, the scope of the agreement, exclusivity, the territory, duration, and termination.

The Agent's Fee (10 Percent)

Agents typically earn 10 percent of the monies they generate for you via live performances, sponsorships, television and motion picture work, and literary projects.

Just watch out for the agent who also wants a percentage of monies from other work you do (such as writing and recording songs)—this is not an industry standard. Also watch out for the agent who wants you to cover expenses for mailing packages and making calls—this too is not standard.

So, just remember, agents earn 10 percent of the money they generate via live performances, bookings, sponsorships, television and motion picture work, and literary projects. That's it. Okay? Cool.

AGENTS' FEES ARE REGULATED

While laws vary from state to state, talent agents are bound by specific laws that require them to get a license and charge certain fees. In California (arguably the entertainment capital of the United States), an agent must file detailed applications, submit affidavits from two reputable persons asserting the agent's good moral character, post a bond, and have all contract forms between the agent and client approved by the California state labor commissioner (these "approved" contract forms typically stipulate a 10 percent commission).

Agents are also regulated by unions—the American Federation of Musicians (for musicians) and SAG-AFTRA (for vocalists and actors). Under union rules, an agent must not charge union members more than a 10 percent commission (unless under certain approved conditions) and must abide by other contractual "dos and don'ts." So, while agents are very hardworking, honest folks, they are highly regulated and typically get 10 percent, tops.

Oh, and just in case you're wondering and hear the terms thrown around at parties, the union's regulation of agents is called franchising, and an agent who abides by union rules is known as a "franchised agent."

The Scope of the Agreement

Moving on with our discussion on agency agreements, let's discuss the agreement scope. While the bulk of your agent's job is to book you for live performances and tours, major agencies may also want the rights to procure employment in a variety of other areas, including the following:

- Product sponsorships with branded companies
- Acting gigs in film and TV
- Literary deals for books about your life story, etc.

While granting these rights to one agency might sound like a sensible convenience, Ian Copeland suggests that you think twice.

At large agencies, it's not like the booking guys are playing tennis with the acting guys and strategizing the next 10 years of your career. The departments can be entirely separate.

So according to Copeland, assuming you actually have acting or modeling skills, it might be far better to limit the rights you give up to one agency, and to seek representation from other agencies that can focus on the other talents that you possess.

Exclusivity

Agreements with agents are exclusive. This means that you cannot be booked in a particular area (e.g., live performances) by other agents working in that same area. It also means that all offers that are made personally to you must be forwarded to the agent so that he or she can handle it.

This all makes good sense, right? It would be unfair to expect your agent to spend all day trying to get you work when another agent is doing the same thing—it could also create a lot of confusion in the marketplace and cause a lot of people to step on each other's toes. The one exception to the exclusivity clause deals with territory, as you will see in a moment.

The Territory

Agents typically want the worldwide rights to represent you. While this is standard, Ian Copeland advised that you should try to hold on to your rights outside of the States. Although your agency may have affiliations in foreign markets, they may not be the best people to represent you.

It's likely that you'll start touring in the United States first, and by the time you get to playing overseas, you'll have had the chance to see how your agent performs. If you've held on to your rights, then you can decide whether you feel confident in your agent's connections abroad, or you can make the rounds of the various agencies yourself and find someone you want to represent you there.

Duration of the Contract

The typical term of an agreement between an agent and client is usually three to five years. However, it's not uncommon to negotiate for a shorter term, such as one year. You can even build provisions into the contract for situations that will trigger your immediate right to terminate. These issues are discussed below.

Rights to Terminate

There are a few issues to discuss that could trigger termination of your agreement as follows:

- **Labor and Union Terms:** Note that in the contract forms approved by the state labor commissioner, as well as the contract forms used by the unions, there is a clause that states that if your agent does not get you work (or an offer of work) within a specified period of time (90 days in the state of California), you may have the right to terminate your agreement.
- **Key Person:** A "key person clause," when inserted in your agreement, gives you the right to terminate your agreement with an agency should your responsible agent be fired or leave the agency. This prevents the possibility of your being passed around the agency from one agent to the next or being stuck with an agent who is not enthusiastic about working with you.

Are Contracts Even Needed?

Finally, to close out this section on agency agreements, Ian Copeland summed up his overall view on agreements this way:

> Most agencies will tell you that you must sign a written agreement with them at the beginning of your relationship. But if you have any bargaining power at all, you may want to consider not signing anything. Think about it. There's no reason why an agency should ask you to sign a contract with them, because the truth is, the agency works for you. Tell them that you'll be loyal to them till the end of the earth as long as they're delivering "the goods," but if they're not delivering, you don't want some loophole in a contract that prevents you from moving on.

Furthermore, Copeland stated,

> From the artist's perspective, I can't see one benefit to signing an agreement with an agency. You already know that by law an agent can't take any more than a 10 percent commission. You also know that a key person clause is just a means to terminate your contract if your responsible agent leaves or is fired—but if you have no contract, you don't need a key person clause at all. If an agent adamantly insists you sign an agreement with them, could it suggest they're not confident you're going to stay with them? Assuming it does, then you'd better consider looking for an agent elsewhere.

HOW TO BE YOUR OWN BOOKING AGENT

Until you can successfully build a buzz and command "healthy" fees for your live performances, getting a talent agent is unlikely. Therefore, here are a few tips on how to do it yourself:

- ***Create a List of Venues:*** Put together a list of venues you intend to target in your town and surrounding territories and include the bookers' names, addresses, e-mail addresses, and phone numbers. Start with resources like Musician's Atlas (www.musiciansatlas.com) or a subscription to PollstarPro (www.pollstarpro.com).
- ***Contact Promoters and Be Professional:*** Call or e-mail the booker with a clear idea of your style and the dates you'd like to perform. Present bookers with exact facts as to your band's history in their market as well as your radio play and any pertinent social media numbers. Use as many facts and as few fluffy adjectives as possible.
- ***Be Patient and Don't Give Up:*** Don't get frustrated or angry if you cannot get in touch with a particular booker. These folks are super busy and there are a lot of other acts that are trying to get in touch, too.
- ***Keep Good Records:*** Keep good records of all correspondence. You don't want to call back a booker in a week when he or she advised you to call back in a month.
- ***Maintain Your Website and Public Image:*** Make sure that you are constantly updating your website and social media sites. Both areas should have your biography (updated weekly to include your successes) as well as advertising for upcoming shows—these areas show the local booker that you have initiative, that you understand the concert experience from their perspective as well as yours, and that you are a true professional.
- ***Be Available and Flexible:*** Let the booker know you're available to fill in for cancellations. It may also help to have two sets' worth of material prepared in case you're asked to perform for longer.
- ***Understand Deal Structures:*** Understand the deal structures of clubs in your area: you'll be asked either to play for free, to receive a percentage of the door, or to buy and then "pre-sell" tickets. Whatever your deal structure, get all terms in writing and understand everything you sign.
- ***Don't Oversaturate One Market:*** Limit the frequency of your performances to no more than two gigs per month within a 30-mile area. You don't want to oversaturate the marketplace.
- ***Consider Alternate Venues, Like Colleges:*** Organizations like the National Association for Campus Activities (NACA) (www.naca.org) can really help. Also, consider playing youth centers, house concerts, bookstores, art galleries, military bases, and convention halls.
- ***Promote Your Ass Off:*** Finally, promote your gigs well and make every show a huge event. Remember that moving up in the club circuit is not just about how good you are but about how many people you can draw. Be sure to check out *Music Marketing for the DIY Musician* for more information on marketing your music.

12

Record Producers

Creativity, Budgets, and Fee Structures

"You're going in to represent what the artist is doing, while at the same time keeping the marketplace in mind—hopefully making something where business and commerce and art meet at the same intersection."
—Ed Cherney, producer for the Rolling Stones and Bob Dylan

While the proliferation of home recording tools has enabled many talented artist/producers to record quality masters right out of their own bedrooms, there are still just as many talented songwriter/performers like you who need help from an experienced record producer.

An experienced record producer understands the technical and creative aspects of bringing your recording to life, as well as the business and legal issues of clearing samples, hiring union musicians, and even balancing your record company budget (should you ever get signed). In short, record producers are expert project managers who know how to deliver a commercially viable record on time, on budget, and at the desired level of quality.

The right collaboration with a producer can take you to places you never imagined, but the wrong one can be a nightmare whose implications are far-reaching. Thus, what producers do, when their involvement may begin, and how they're hired and paid is information you can't afford to miss.

The Role of a Record Producer in Your Career

If the role of a record producer could be summed up to one phrase, it would be "guardian of the recording process" or simply "project manager." Depending on your career level, this could mean any or all of the following:

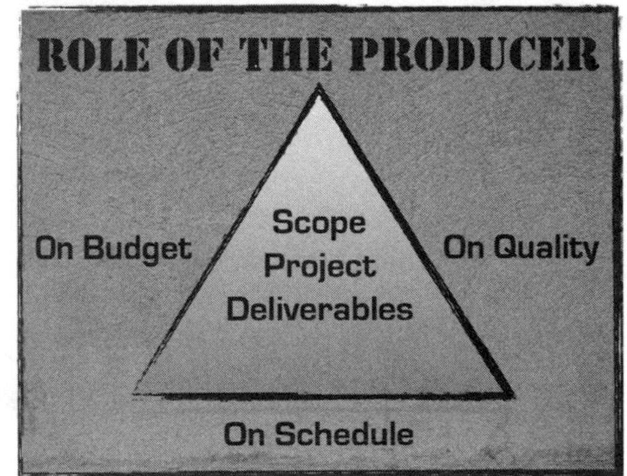

- *Getting the Songs Together:* Helping the artist select the best songs to record, arranging these compositions, and even cowriting and composing complete songs with the artists, whether that means contributing lyrics, music, and/or well-structured beats.
- *Deciding on the Best Recording Approach:* Determining the best recording approach by gathering specific considerations about the artist and musicians (like whether they're comfortable recording with a click reference or in isolated and more restrictive conditions).

- ***Capturing Exceptional Performances:*** Helping the artist get the most out of each studio performance . . . "Even to the point of frustration if necessary," adds Geoff Emerick, producer/engineer for the Beatles, Paul McCartney, and Elvis Costello.
- ***Balancing Egos:*** Dealing strategically with the various personalities within a band to keep the environment in the studio productive and creative. Geza X, producer for Black Flag, says, "Playing the role of a record producer means being part psychologist, part babysitter, and part social engineer."
- ***Creating a Timeless Sound Recording:*** Making sure that artist's work sounds current in the marketplace—now, and several years after its release. Stevie Wonder's record *Songs in the Key of Life*, for instance, still sounds fresh and original 40 years later.
- ***Fulfilling the Artist's Vision:*** Helping the artist bring his or her vision to life and knowing when to stay out of the way. Steve Churchyard, producer for the Pretenders and INXS, says, "As a producer, it's my job to make the artist's dream a reality and actually make it better than the dream."
- ***Creating a Commercially Viable Recording:*** Delivering a product that can be commercially successful in the marketplace. Ed Cherney, producer for the Rolling Stones and Bob Dylan, says, "You're going in to represent what the artist is doing, while at the same time keeping the marketplace in mind—hopefully making something where business and commerce and art meet at the same intersection."
- ***Engineering the Project:*** Handling technical aspects of the project or working together with an associate engineer.
- ***Making Magic:*** Experimenting with and inventing new sounds and production techniques that can uniquely position the artists and producer as being first in the marketplace.
- ***Balancing the Budget and Schedule:*** Putting together a recording budget and making sure the recording project stays within its budget and schedule.
- ***Taking Care of Paperwork:*** Handling administrative duties associated with recording an album, such as making sure samples are cleared and filing union contracts.

PULLING RABBITS OUT OF HATS

To illustrate one of the many roles a producer must play, in his book *Free at Last* (SAF Publishing), Steven Rosen spoke with legendary producer Eddie Kramer about his magical work with the classic rock band Bad Company.

Kramer said: "We didn't have many recording effects in the studio at our disposal, so when the band wanted a swirling or tremolo effect for one of their recordings, I tied a couple of microphones together and spun them around in the air. It actually worked great! Sometimes you just have to try anything to get the right sound on tape."

Another Kramer experience involved the late, great Jimi Hendrix. For the intro to the song "Crosstown Traffic," the artist imagined a sound he couldn't quite explain. Musician and producer put their heads together and finally came up with something simple—Hendrix blowing through a comb covered in tissue paper (creating a kazoo sound). To hear this effect, check out Hendrix's classic record *Electric Ladyland.*

When and How a Producer May First Get Involved

A record producer's involvement in your career may begin at a number of different junctures and be handled in a number of different ways. While the possibilities are endless, let's take a look at some of the more common scenarios. These include the barter system deal, the on-spec deal, the do-it-yourself deal, the production deal, and the record label deal.

A Barter System Arrangement

When you are just starting out and have little or no money to pay for a recording studio and record producer, your first involvement with a producer might exist under a barter system arrangement with a local producer.

A barter system deal is a straightforward arrangement where the goods or services of the artist are "exchanged" (i.e., used as currency) for the goods and services of the producer. Just be sure that the terms of the arrangement are clear and there are no misunderstandings about additional ownership of songs, recordings, and/or hourly fees owed.

In a barter arrangement, a young artist who also builds websites might offer to maintain a recording studio's online presence in exchange for letting him record tracks. Or a talented artist who also teaches might offer to give acoustic guitar lessons to the producer's daughter in exchange for production assistance.

As long as both parties see the goods and services being exchanged as equal trades, a barter arrangement is win-win. Just figure out what you can offer to others and pitch the exchange to them. You just might be surprised at the number of helpful producers who are willing to accept.

The On-Spec Agreement

Another scenario for struggling artists at the beginning of their careers is the on-spec deal.

The on-spec deal is a situation in which the artist makes contact with a local producer or studio owner (perhaps one who is a friend, fan, or close relative of the band), and arranges to record at no cost under the terms of an informal agreement. Such an agreement may state that if the band gets a record deal, they will pay the producer a predetermined flat fee for services rendered and consider him or her as a candidate to record the final product for the label. If the band never gets signed to a recording agreement, it never owes the producer any money.

Another agreement could state that the artist gives up ownership in the master recordings or shares in certain songs for a specific term. This way, when the artist makes money down the line, the record producer also gets paid. (Remember: be sure that you understand the terms of any agreement before signing, and speak with an attorney or consultant if unsure about anything.)

The Do-It-Yourself / Work Made for Hire Approach

When a young artist is resourceful enough (or lucky enough) to have the funds necessary to pay a producer at the full going rate, his or her involvement with a producer might exist under a do-it-yourself / work made for hire approach.

In this scenario, the artist makes contact with the producer or studio owner via referrals from other local indie artists or adverts in local music magazines. After discussing recording philosophies, listening to recorded tracks, and examining the facilities, the artist hires the producer for a flat fee to record tracks and even to mix and master the recording.

Just be clear that the producer is hired by you via a contract that explicitly states that he or she is to perform a job for a fee, and that he or she does not retain any rights in the sound recording or own any shares in your compositions. Speak with an attorney if needed. Okay?

The Production Company Deal

Now let's take a look at production deals. These are situations that exist when talented young artists can show that they have the potential to be a worthy business investment (i.e., they have exceptional looks, songwriting or performing skills, and a unique sound).

In a typical production company deal, the production company discovers, grooms, and records the artist, and then enters into a recording agreement with a label on the artist's behalf. The production company receives a royalty rate for sales from the label, which it usually splits with the artist 50/50. The production company also typically receives a recording advance, and if anything is left over after it covers its recording expenses, it will normally be split 50/50 as well.

The Record Label Deal

Finally, when artists can prove that they are self-sufficient (i.e., they can record and distribute their own albums, build a strong fan base, and make sales), they may be offered a record label deal to help take their career to the next level.

In a typical label deal, the artist is obligated by contract to hire an experienced record producer to help guide him or her through the recording process and to deliver a product that has the commercial sales potential to meet the company's expectations. The artist receives an advance, typically known as the "recording fund," from which all recording costs (including the producer) must be paid. Additionally, the artist receives an artist royalty rate (typically structured as an "all-in" royalty), of which the producer gets a percentage share.

Since the record label deal is still held as a coveted accomplishment for young artists who dream of worldwide success, and since the business issues can be far more involved than at any other level discussed, I'll expand upon the record label deal scenario for the rest of this chapter.

Additional Responsibilities of the Record Producer

I already discussed the role a record producer plays in your career from a creative and business perspective. However, a few areas that are worth expanding upon, as they are far more involved in a record label deal scenario, are creating a recording budget, maintaining a recording budget, and handling administrative duties.

Creating a Recording Budget

In the typical record label scenario, the artist receives a recording fund from which a recording cost budget must be established. Typically, the artist, the A&R representative, and the producer (or producers) discuss and create a recording budget before it is submitted to the record company for final approval. What follows are the costs that are commonly included:

- The producer's advance
- The engineer's and mixer's fee
- Studio rental costs (which may fluctuate greatly, depending on whether you are charged the advertised rate or the discounted rate)
- Editing costs
- Mastering costs
- Equipment rentals
- Sticks, skins, strings, picks, and amplifier tubes
- Union minimum-scale wages for the band
- Union-scale wages for hired musicians (for overdubs, guest appearances, etc.)
- Cartage (to transport your equipment to and from the studio)
- Lodging (depending on your needs and budget, this could consist of either extravagant or conservative accommodations)
- Transportation costs to and from the studio (including airfare, rental cars, etc.)

Maintaining a Recording Budget

As if creating the recording budget were not enough, the record producer is also responsible for maintaining it. This isn't always easy—producers often have trouble getting the right sounds, capturing magical performances, and bringing the compositions to life as initially imagined.

When a project goes over budget, the record company will typically advance the extra cash needed. However, the deeper the record company has to dig into its pockets, the quicker it may pull the plug should the record not have immediate success. Furthermore, the overages may come out of monies deemed as your artist advance, your next recording fund, or even mechanical royalty payments (discussed in chapter 17). The bottom line is that when a recording project goes over budget, it does not reflect well on the producer, and it ultimately affects your pockets.

WHEN THE BUDGET GOES HAYWIRE

While it is the record producer's job to maintain the recording budget, the artist can make the producer's job extremely difficult. According to one musician working with the classic punk rocker Billy Idol, Billy Idol's days in the recording studio consisted of showing up three hours late, leaving the studio for the nearest strip club to get loaded on beer and whisky, and then returning after midnight to do a few lines of blow—with Idol being billed for the studio time all the while.

The band Korn reportedly charged $20,000 of Coors Light and Jack Daniels as a food and beverage expense while recording their album *Follow the Leader*.

Obviously, once a band is successful, record labels are more tolerant of this type of behavior and may even eat the costs. The truth is that if you're a hit and the money is rolling in, no one really cares. This brings to mind Axl Rose's 15-year project recording *Chinese Democracy*. The album was said to cost over $13 million. Wow!

Handling Other Administrative Responsibilities

Besides creating and maintaining a recording budget, the producer (or his or her production coordinator) is also responsible for a number of administrative duties.

These include submitting bills to the record company, filing union contracts, and alerting the label to the use of samples, the need for guest permissions, and the inclusion of cover songs (all of which will be discussed below).

Submitting Bills

The first administrative responsibility of the producer is to submit all invoices to the record label (usually the A&R administration department) to be processed and paid.

Producer Jeff Weber says he usually pays a visit to the administration department at a label to ask how he can help them help him get bills processed efficiently. Weber also says, "Different departments want different things. Some may want a copy of the original invoice and even want prior approval before most expenses are incurred."

In a typical scenario, bills are submitted to the label as they come up and may include cartage of instruments, food bills, studio musicians, drum tuners and techs, the engineer's fee (sometimes paid in two installments—50 percent before starting and 50 percent upon completion), and studio costs (sometimes paid up-front as a way of reserving the facilities).

Filing Union Contracts

Another administrative responsibility of the producer deals with union issues. The producer ensures that all union forms are filed with the various musicians' unions and that bills are submitted to the label so that musicians can get paid.

You see, major record labels and many smaller independent labels are signatories to agreements with the musicians' unions: the American Federation of Musicians and SAG-AFTRA. Under these agreements, labels are required to pay their artists, and all other hired musicians on a recording project, a union minimum-scale wage. The label must also make contributions to pension and health and welfare funds on behalf of their artists.

If union forms are not filed properly, the unions may enforce penalties. Unions are covered in more detail in chapter 4.

Alerting the Label to the Use of Samples

As if the above responsibilities were not enough, the producer also ensures that all "samples" used on a recording are cleared in a timely manner by the record label's legal department (or sample clearance specialists) by pointing out where the sample is used, on what song it is used, and from what artist the sample is taken.

Samples are bits and pieces of other artists' songs and/or recordings (for example, a bass line from a David Bowie song, or a scream from a James Brown record) overdubbed or mixed into the recording of a new song to enhance its overall feel.

If your album is released before you've cleared the sample rights, the owner could insist you pay substantial sums for its use or refuse to grant you permission. Even worse, if you fail to clear samples altogether, the owner could sue you for copyright infringement (see chapters 15 and 16).

Alerting the Label to the Need for Guest Permissions

Moving on to another administrative responsibility of the producer, let's briefly examine permissions.

When you want another artist to make a guest appearance on your record, the producer informs your label's legal department so that they may obtain permission from the guest artist's record label.

Just look at the liner notes of your favorite recording and you'll see these permissions. For instance, on Carlos Santana's Grammy Award–winning record *Supernatural*, Dave Matthews appears courtesy of RCA Records.

Since there's no guarantee a record company will give the proper authorization, the earlier your request gets in to your label's legal department, the better chance you'll have to make the collaboration you desire a reality.

Alerting the Label to the Inclusion of Cover Songs and Filing Mechanical Licenses

Finally, when you decide to cover another artist's song, the producer helps ensure that a compulsory mechanical license (or a simpler version called a mechanical license) gets filed.

For example, when Gnarls Barkley covered "Gone Daddy Gone" by the Violent Femmes, the group had to file a mechanical license.

But again, keep in mind that a license must be filed in a timely manner (before the record is released) to avoid copyright infringement charges from the owner. (The compulsory licensing provision is covered in more detail in chapters 15 and 16.)

HIDDEN AGENDAS

Even as he or she helps to create and oversee the recording budget, a producer may be working from a hidden agenda.

As illustrated in Moses Avalon's book *Confessions of a Record Producer*, the producer may be able to arrange deals with side musicians, recording studios, and others, bill the expense at a higher cost, and then receive a payment in the form of a kickback. In other words, besides receiving an advance payment for his or her services, your record producer may be able to scam additional money from your recording budget under the table.

If you don't think this type of activity takes place, here's another example. A colleague who wishes to remain anonymous recorded an album for a major label under the direction of two world-class producers. Unbeknownst to this young musician, he was entitled to earn a minimum-scale wage for his work as enforced in the union's collective bargaining agreements with the record labels. Instead, the producers kept the musician's payment off the books and kept the artist's entire compensation for themselves. Nice!

There are bad apples in every profession.

Hiring a Record Producer

You already know how important a record producer is to your career, but how should you go about selecting the record producer? And once you select a producer, who negotiates the deal?

Selecting a Record Producer

When a record company signs a new artist to a recording agreement, it will initially insist on having the final say in choosing an experienced record producer. After all, the record company wants to ensure that it is getting the best possible product for its investment, which can run into the hundreds of thousands of dollars.

But since it makes no sense to have you locked up in the studio with a producer with whom you're unhappy, your attorney can negotiate for mutual consent (meaning that both the record company and the artist must agree on the record producer). What follows is a more detailed breakdown of how the record producer may actually be selected.

AFTERTHOUGHT: DIY AND PRODUCERS Are you an unsigned DIY artist looking for a producer? If so, your choices may be limited to local producers and word-of-mouth recommendations. Ask some of the best independent artists in your area where their albums were recorded, and then listen to the production to see what you think for yourself.

Interpret Your Needs

Before even thinking about selecting a record producer, you and your A&R representative should give some consideration to the type of record you're going to make.

Will it be a slick, well-produced album with a lot of sequencers and samplings, or will it be raw and in-your-face?

"These factors," comments producer David Brownstein of Fish Hook Productions, "are going to help you narrow down your choices for finding the best producer for your needs. Every producer has their unique gifts and specialties to bring to the table, but you have to have some idea of the results you want."

Make a Wish List

As another method for selecting the producer, many artists will spend hours streaming their favorite tracks and reading the liner notes of *Billboard* Top 100 albums to compile a "wish list" of potential producers.

Adds producer/musician Jay Gordon of Orgy, "Artists will also speak with their A&R person to get some definite ideas about who should produce the album given the budget and vibe, and then create a master list of the best candidates."

Get in Contact

Once your list of prospective record producers has been compiled and then approved by the record company, it's usually the artist (or artist's A&R person) who first makes contact with the producers, sends out recordings, and provides a sense of the overall buzz about the band.

Bottom line: It is not only the band that selects the producer, but the producer that selects the band. Don't be surprised if your number one choice is simply not into your vibe and style.

Spend Time

Once you receive confirmation that a producer is interested in working with you, a meeting is scheduled to review songs and get a vibe for whether you can work together.

Mikal Reid, producer for Ben Harper, says, "It's important that the artist gets a feeling of trust with a producer before ever choosing to work with him or her. Take the time to get to know your producer first so that there won't be any surprises or conflicting situations in the studio later."

Select Right Before Might

It is important to stress at this point that the selection of the record producer should not be based entirely on what he or she has done, but rather on what he or she can do for you.

In an interview I conducted before his passing, Arif Mardin, who produced numerous artists including Aretha Franklin, the Bee Gees, and Norah Jones, explained, "Surely, a producer with platinum records on his walls proves he has talent, but you don't want to sound like his other hit artists; you want your record to be unique to you. What thoughts does the producer have about your record? How creative is he or she?"

Know Expectations

When selecting a record producer, be sure to also discuss what your producer expects to get out of you.

Producer Dave Darling says that one of the major expectations he has for his artists once they make a commitment to working with him is that they maintain the highest level of trust.

Says Dave, "I like to push my artists to reach new creative heights and to get recorded performances they never thought possible. It's hard work, but it has to stay fun at all times. A positive working attitude is a must."

Arif Mardin said, "Artists must always be on time, make sure that their musical gear is well maintained, and refrain from excessive amounts of drugs and alcohol—otherwise I'm out of there!"

Consider Multiple Producers

As if selecting one record producer weren't difficult enough, sometimes the process involves the selection of several producers. This is often because producers are in high demand and do not have the time to work on one project for an extended period of time. It's also simply par for the course in many genres of music (hip-hop and pop records are typically made using more than one producer).

Self-Produce or Coproduce?

Some talented artists may feel that they can self-produce their record or at least coproduce it. Prince produced his records and was successful at it, as was Paula Cole.

But unless you have had some prior success as a producer and the record company believes strongly that you're capable of delivering a commercially viable product on time and on budget, the label will most likely not approve the request.

If you feel you can coproduce your own record and have someone in mind whom you'd like to work with, the record company may approve the request as long as they feel confident in your abilities and as long as the coproducer you have in mind is experienced professionally at making creative decisions—and not just at engineering records or mixing and mastering projects.

Strive to Keep Everyone Happy

Finally, when selecting a record producer, you must be absolutely confident that the person you ultimately choose has the ability to deliver a final product that makes both you and the record label happy.

Bottom line: Should the album not meet the label's expectations, it can mean the end of your career with that label. Choosing the right producer is not just an important creative decision, it's also an important career decision.

TOP PRODUCERS BEHIND THE ARTISTS

While there have been hundreds of amazing producers throughout the years, the following producers were mentioned the most when I recently surveyed my Musicians Institute and UCLA Extension business classes:

- ***Rick Rubin:*** Chili Peppers, Johnny Cash, Beastie Boys, Slipknot
- ***Bob Rock:*** Metallica, Aerosmith
- ***Pharrell Williams & Chad Hugo:*** Snoop Dogg, Justin Timberlake, Kelis
- ***Timbaland:*** Missy Elliott, Justin Timberlake, Jay Z
- ***The Matrix:*** Hilary Duff, Britney Spears, Avril Lavigne
- ***The Neptunes:*** Snoop Dogg, Clipse, Busta Rhymes
- ***RZA:*** Wu-Tang Clan, The Notorious B.I.G.
- ***Swizz Beatz:*** Britney Spears, Gwen Stefani, The Game, Jennifer Lopez
- ***Just Blaze:*** Kanye West, Jay Z, The Game
- ***DJ Premier:*** Nas, Gang Starr, Termanology
- ***David Foster:*** Mariah Carey, Madonna, Beyoncé Knowles
- ***Quincy Jones:*** Michael Jackson, Frank Sinatra
- ***Dr. Dre:*** Snoop Dogg, Eminem, Kendrick Lamar
- ***Max Martin:*** Britney Spears, *NSYNC, Katy Perry
- ***Scott Storch:*** Chris Brown, Nas, 50 Cent
- ***RedOne:*** Lady Gaga, Nicki Minaj, Jennifer Lopez
- ***Diplo:*** Justin Bieber, Usher, Snoop Lion, No Doubt
- ***Calvin Harris:*** Kylie Minogue, Rihanna, Dizzee Rascal

Negotiating the Producer's Deal

Now that you've found a record producer, your contract with the record company will typically hold you responsible for hiring the producer and negotiating the deal.

How much of an advance against royalties will the producer want? How many points will he or she want in producer royalties? How will the credits be listed on the album cover?

Of course, this means that your attorney has to draw up contracts and negotiate the deal on your behalf, which means even more money out of your pocket at the end of the day.

Attorney Dina LaPolt says,

> I usually build the costs of negotiating the producer's fee right into the record deal. If I have a rock band that I'm signing to Warner's and the deal is for $150,000, I know I have to negotiate the band deal, the producer's contract, and maybe a couple of remixer agreements. Therefore, I might try to build in another $20,000 above and beyond the $150,000, of which a portion goes to me. If it's a rap band I'm working with, I might shoot for an extra $100,000 above the offer because I'll have 20 producer agreements to negotiate and 15 remix agreements to do, and I'll have to hire a production coordinator or sample clearance person.

Attorney Don Passman notes that traditionally it was the record label that negotiated the producer's agreement on behalf of the artist. But since having multiple producers on recording projects has become common and business affairs departments at labels have become tied up negotiating these deals, negotiating the producer's deal is now the artist's responsibility. The label may get involved with the deal to approve it, but the artist pays for it.

The Record Producer's Compensation Structure

Moving on to the final section of this chapter, let's discuss the producer's compensation structure. This includes the producer's advance, the producer's royalty payment, and master monies in the context of a record label deal. Finally, let's take a stab at a question frequently asked by musicians: When does the producer get a share in the music publishing royalties?

AFTERTHOUGHT: PAYMENT AT THE DIY LEVEL Producing fees at the DIY level are quite different from those in the major leagues. Typically, producers are paid a flat fee for the job (without a producer royalty). Should they offer their services below their going rate because the artist is broke, they may request that they earn a share of ownership in the master recording or even the music publishing to make up for their losses. Just be clear on what you're signing.

Producer Advances

As mentioned briefly in the "record label deal" scenario earlier in this chapter, most record label contracts today are structured as recording funds. This means that out of the advances that you negotiate in your recording agreement, all recording costs (including a producer's advance) must be considered.

For example, if you're a rock band signed to a major label recording deal with a very healthy fund of $200,000, $150,000 may be budgeted toward the recording cost budget, and the other $50,000 may be used as your advance.

Of that $150,000, a rock producer at the top level can require an advance of as much as $50,000 for recording a full-length album, and $15,000 or more for a single master. So that could bring your budget from $150,000 down to $100,000 before you've even started.

AFTERTHOUGHT: POP AND HIP-HOP PRODUCERS Attorney Dina LaPolt says that hip-hop and pop artists (even newer artists) may be able to negotiate for recording advances and recording costs that total as much as $500,000 to $1 million per album. Why? There are typically several producers on hip-hop and pop albums (sometimes as many as 20) and they all want to get paid. Top-level hip-hop or pop producers, who are often considered as important as the artist, can get $50,000 or more for just one track.

Producer Royalties

In addition to the advances discussed above, record producers in a record label deal scenario receive a royalty for the sale of your record. In fact, the record producer's advance is really just a prepayment of his or her producer royalties from future record sales.

To understand how this really works, let's take a look at what the industry calls "all-in" and "record one" royalties.

The Artist/Producer All-In Royalty

Most record royalty provisions in recording contracts are structured as an "all-in royalty." This means that out of the artist royalty rate you negotiate with your record company, the producer's royalty must also be considered.

For example, if the record company offers you an artist royalty rate of 16 percent, and the desired producer for a project requires a producer royalty of 4 percent (a typical amount for a mid-level producer), you're now left with a net royalty rate of 12 percent (16 – 4 = 12).

So how much is the net rate worth? To simplify things for our discussion below, let's say one dollar.

When the Record Producer Gets Paid

Record producers typically get paid their royalty after the recoupment of all recording costs at the artist's net rate. So, for the sake of simplicity, if the recording budget for an album is a high $150,000, and 150,000 one-dollar bills get thrown into a pot, the producer will start getting paid.

In contrast, an artist might not get paid until as many as 400,000 one-dollar bills get thrown into the pot. Why? Because artists must recoup so much more than the record producer has to, including the entire recording fund and all other monies deemed as an advance—touring monies, video monies, and radio promotion monies.

Yup! Producers get a better deal. And no, you can't produce your own records and get paid in the same way that producers do. But nice try.

How the Producer Gets Paid: Record One Royalties

Also significant to our discussion is "how" the record producer gets paid. Using our above example, after 150,000 records are sold and 150,000 one-dollar bills are thrown into a big pot to "recoup" (pay back) the costs of recording your album, the producer starts getting paid a royalty back to the very first record sold, a system called "record one royalties."

This means that the producer gets a 4 percent royalty on sales for all 150,000 units (less the advance monies that he or she already received) and then continues to get paid for every unit that's sold after that.

Regardless of how the producer gets paid, once again it is a far better system than it is for the artist: you only get paid for sales from the point after recoupment. In other words, if it takes up to 400,000 units sold for you to recoup the advances paid by the record company, you would get paid a royalty only after the 400,000th record sold (i.e., 400,001, 400,002, 400,003, etc.).

Who Pays the Producer? The Artist Does!

As you've already learned, once the recording costs are recouped, the producer is entitled to be paid a royalty back to the very first record sold. And now comes the good part. Guess who is responsible for paying the producer. That's right, you are! But don't panic just yet!

What typically happens, with the help of your lovely attorney, is that the record company will agree to pay the producer's royalties on your behalf. How nice of them!

But note that every penny paid to the producer by the record company is charged back to the amount of money you must recoup before you ever get paid a royalty. If you haven't figured it out yet, this means that the more records you sell and the more the producer collects, the deeper in debt you can become.

The good news, though, is that if the gods of rock (or pop, rap, or whatever) are on your side and you go on to sell shitloads of recordings (vinyl, downloads, streams, or whatever), eventually everything will balance out and you'll start getting paid.

You'll learn more about artist record royalties and advances in chapters 13 and 14.

Master Monies

Moving on to another form of compensation to the producer, let's briefly discuss master monies. In the record label deal scenario, the label is typically the owner in the copyright of the master recording. Nonetheless, since the master embodies the artist's performance, it is customary for the artist to receive a 50 percent split of any monies that the record label may receive from the exploitation of the masters in other areas such as film and TV.

Of that 50 percent, the producer will receive a prorated split based on the same ratio he or she gets in royalties at the all-in rate. So if the producer gets 1/4 of your rate, he or she will get 1/4 of the 50 percent (i.e., 12.5 percent).

Music Publishing: When Should the Producer Get a Share?

Finally, let's tackle the difficult issue of your songs and whether the producer gets a share.

Under copyright law, a music or lyric "contribution" to a song, no matter how big or small that contribution may be, could entitle the contributor to a "pro rata" (equal) share of ownership, unless there is a written agreement between the parties that stipulates otherwise.

Bottom line: before going into the studio, an artist or band should sit down with the producer and discuss matters of music publishing, to the point of putting something in writing. The issue really comes down to how involved you want the producer to be in the songwriting process. Is he or she going to sit down with you for several weeks and pen a batch of songs with you one-on-one? Or is he or she just going to make minor changes? Read on.

When Writing Songs One-on-One from Scratch—Yes!

When a producer contributes significantly in the songwriting process, then he or she should get a percentage of the publishing.

To illustrate, Alanis Morissette joined forces with producer Glen Ballard to cowrite songs. The collaboration not only helped Morissette to land a major recording deal but also allowed her album *Jagged Little Pill* to sell over 30 million copies worldwide. In this instance, the record producer is clearly involved in the songwriting process and entitled to a share. I'm certain that there was a clear understanding about business matters before the two writers joined to pen the album.

When Making Slight Modifications During the Recording Process—No!

When a producer simply does what a producer is supposed to do (i.e., make minor modifications), then he or she may not share in the publishing.

Said producer Arif Mardin:

> All producers will make modifications to the arrangements of your songs by adding or dropping four bars here and there, rewriting a pre-chorus, etc., but they're hired and offered a handsome advance and royalty of future sales to do so and should not ask for publishing. I suggest all artists/writers should be leery of producers who are overly insistent on taking a piece of the [music] publishing or getting involved in the songwriting process. Your music publishing income can be the very money you live on long after your career is over.

Producer Robert Shahnazarian, Jr., says:

> I'll always make sure to discuss publishing matters with any band for which I work before going into the recording studio. I want the artist to feel free to create music around me, without being afraid that this will somehow involve me in the songwriting and entitle me to a share. This is simply for the best of all parties involved.

Note that music publishing is covered in more detail in chapters 15–20.

Part 4

Deals and Dollars

13

Making and Selling Records, Part 1

Types of Record Deals and Companies

"Whether CDs, downloads, or streams, people will always need music."
—Don Grierson, music business consultant and coauthor of It All Begins with the Music

Making and selling records is the process of transferring music onto a variety of formats (CDs, vinyl, USB flash drives, downloads, and streaming) to build awareness and make profits.

As a do-it-yourself artist (running your own record label), you'll typically own the rights to these recordings. However, when you are a signed recording artist (contracted with an independent, major, or production company), the label will typically own these recordings. What's more, the label will want to own your songs, merchandising, and touring (or at least they'll want to share in these income streams by signing you to something called a 360 deal—sounds ominous, right?).

In this chapter, I'll briefly review the various types of recording companies and deals that exist today. These include DIY companies, independent labels, production companies, and major labels. In part 2, the next chapter, I'll uncover important terms found in recording agreements and provide tips for starting and operating your own DIY record company.

This is all extremely important stuff. So be sure to grab that yellow highlighter pen and get ready to rock! Let's start with DIY recording companies by examining their general philosophy, funding budgets, profits, advances, royalties, and distribution. Sound cool? Good!

Do-It-Yourself Recording Companies

A do-it-yourself record company is one where you fund, distribute, and promote your own recordings to your target audience. No, you don't need a big sign in your front yard and a receptionist to be a label. By virtue of recording your own music, you essentially are a "label."

Ani DiFranco is a poster child for the DIY movement and for starting her own label, Righteous Babe. Master P, who started No Limit, even went on to sign other artists. Pink Martini started the Heinz label and have a tremendous live following. Macklemore and Ryan Lewis started Macklemore LLC and are one of the most impressive DIY examples. The list goes on.

General Philosophy

The philosophy of most do-it-yourself record labels can be summed up in any one of these four bullet points:

- ***Attract Attention:*** I'm an artist who understands that to attract the attention of those who can help me (i.e., managers, labels, etc.), I must first help myself by getting my music out to the public and starting a buzz.

- ***Do It My Way:*** I'm an artist whose work is not going to be contingent upon some corporate businessperson's view of when and how I can do it, so I'll do it myself.
- ***Keep the Money:*** I'm an artist who wants to keep all of the profits from my record sales instead of getting a small royalty that only pays back numerous expenses. And finally . . .
- ***I Can Do It Too:*** I'm not an artist, but I just want to release a record like everyone else I see on *American Idol*, *The Voice*, and YouTube. If they can do it, so can I.

What Makes the DIY Label Possible?

Whatever scenario depicted above describes you, the availability of home recording equipment, affordable disc manufacturing, and the abundance of Internet sites to promote new musicians make it possible nowadays to bypass the record labels altogether. Essentially, you can be your own record label—giving you absolute creative freedom without the worries of fitting into a perfect "box" (look, age group, sound, style) dictated by some executive in a tie and jacket.

Funding

Now that you're convinced the DIY method is a viable and worthy approach, let's discuss funding.

The method by which you generate funds to record your own music, promote it, and perhaps turn a profit, is totally left up to your creativity. However, many artists do the following:

- ***Borrow:*** Borrow money from family members.
- ***Barter:*** Exchange services (i.e., I'll play on your record if you record my song).
- ***Crowdfund:*** Ask fans to pre-purchase records or donate funds utilizing services like Kickstarter (www.kickstarter.com), PledgeMusic (www.pledgemusic.com), and Indiegogo (www.indiegogo.com).
- ***Get a Loan:*** Take out loans from banks or ask a parent or relative to cosign the loan (cosigning means that if you default, Uncle Joey agrees to make payments).
- ***Find an Investor/Sponsor:*** Find investors or sponsors willing to risk their money to help you become the star you really are, while also promoting their own products and services via your brand. Another word for these folks is co-branding partners.
- ***Use Credit Cards:*** Open a credit card account and withdraw a cash advance (although this approach is certainly not recommended due to the high interest rates associated with credit cards). And finally . . .
- ***Use Personal Income:*** Use the money you've saved by working your ass off.

Budgets

Okay, so now you know how to get the money, but how much will you need? While many producers may feel that it takes a minimum budget of $11,000 to record and manufacture a really competitive record, the average budget I've seen the young do-it-yourselfer get by on to produce and manufacture a record is about $7,000.

According to producer Dave Banta, you can set up a home studio with as little as a laptop computer, music production software, a keyboard with sound cards, recording software, and an external microphone. Oh, and don't forget some recording chops and patience as well.

Profits

It doesn't take much to start turning a profit for your DIY label. Keeping things simple and going along with the $7,000 budget mentioned above, and pressing 1,000 records (CDs, flash drives, vinyl) and selling them at your live shows, let's take a look at what you might earn when using a few different price points:

- ***$7:*** If you sell each record for $7, you'll break even and be on the way to making a profit.
- ***$10:*** If you sell each record for $10, you'll not only break even, you'll also have $3,000 in profit that you can use for marketing expenses, or even toward buying more recording equipment.
- ***$5:*** If you charge $5, you'll make back everything but $2,000, and have a lot of happy fans that appreciate the discount.
- ***Free:*** If you give away your records for free, you'll make nothing, but you'll have 1,000 new fans (hopefully)—and fans can be priceless. You get the idea!

Of course, you may not want to print records and only choose to release digitally online.

You also may not want to record a whole album but prefer to release just one song at a designated time each month for several months.

Or you may not intend to release your own records at all, but rather to record a high-quality album and try to get a label to buy the masters for three times as much. The point is, as a do-it-yourself label, you are in more control than ever and you keep all the profit! That's the benefit of being your own boss. Right? Right!

Distribution

Distribution is the process of placing music where your target audience can conveniently find and buy it. Since most of the larger independent distributors (like Alternative Distribution Alliance, owned by Warner Music Group) work exclusively with artists in high demand, the do-it-yourselfer must rely on these more alternative forms of distribution (some, of course, which will require a small percentage or fee):

- ***The Streets:*** Promenades, boulevards, flea markets, and anywhere else you can open up your guitar case and make a sad pouty face as people walk by.
- ***Local Retailers:*** Music and non-music stores where consignment deals are possible. Consignment means you'll get paid when your record sells.
- ***Live Performance Venues:*** Clubs, military bases, rodeos, and wherever else you can set up a table and display your records.
- ***Personal Websites:*** Your own URL where you can accept orders using various e-commerce tools like PayPal (www.paypal.com) and web widgets by services mentioned immediately below.
- ***Online Platforms and Services:*** Sites like Bandcamp (www.bandcamp.com) and Topspin (www.topspinmedia.com), where you can use their websites and software to sell your music. And finally . . .
- ***DIY-Friendly Distributors:*** CD Baby (www.cdbaby.com), TuneCore (www.tunecore.com), the Orchard (www.theorchard.com), Ditto Music (www.dittomusic.com), and MondoTunes (www.mondotunes.com), where you can get your music on download sites, streaming sites, and into the databases of retail stores. Some companies can even help you with certain business responsibilities like promotion, licensing music in film and television, and royalty administration. Reasonable charges apply. See each site for updates and fees and percentage shares.

DIY Ain't Easy, But . . .

In closing, it ain't easy doing it yourself, but when you love what you do, hard work is fun. With talent, patience, and luck, you just might hit big.

DIY MIDDLE-CLASS SUCCESS STORIES

Doing it yourself is no easy proposition, but the artists below are living proof that hard work can pay off. Most of the examples below fit into what has been called the musician's middle class (not rich, but surviving quite well).

- ***Jonathan Coulton:*** Never signed to a record label. He sells his albums at shows, on his website, and on iTunes. He also plays live and sells merch. In one year, he made $500,000. He promotes himself on NPR radio stations, in science magazines, and on Internet blogs. www.jonathancoulton.com
- ***Rebecca De La Torre:*** Never signed to a record label. She sells her CDs at her shows and plays corporate parties, weddings, church services, casinos, resorts, and clubs. She also teaches privately and records other artists in her studio. She makes about $100,000 a year. She promotes herself on social media and at networking events. www.rebeccadelatorremusic.com
- ***Gabriel Douglas:*** Never signed to a record label. He plays lots of shows and sells lots of merch. Some income comes in from synch licensing, but not steadily enough to call it anything other than a bonus when it happens. He makes in the range of $50,000 to $75,000 a year purely on music. He spends a lot of time networking in his scene (going out to see other bands, going to conventions, etc.), blogging, and staying positive. www.4otf.com
- ***Ron Pope:*** Finally, Ron Pope was signed to Universal Republic with no success at all. He now makes money independently from iTunes downloads, streaming music, digital broadcasts of his master recordings (SoundExchange royalties), live performances, and synchronization licenses (placing music in film and television). Money also comes in from selling sheet music on sites like Musicnotes.com, selling handwritten lyrics on his website, and much more. He makes about $100,000 a year. He promotes primarily by connecting with people online. www.RonPopeMusic.com

Independent Labels

The second type of record company I'd like to discuss is the independent label.

Independent record labels (also called indies) are labels formed by passionate music lovers (former musicians, business executives, etc.) who want to create a roster of successful musicians who fit into a specific niche.

Indie labels use their resources and expert staff to fund, distribute, and promote your recordings. Sometimes they may offer additional services, such as management, merchandising, publishing, and touring services, depending on your agreement.

Ownership

Indie labels are called indie because many of them are not owned or controlled by the major labels, nor do they have any business dealings with the majors. I usually call these "true indies." Interestingly, "larger indies" may be owned by the major labels, they are often distributed by the majors, and/or they have upstream agreements with majors where they'll upgrade an artist if certain sales figures are met. Point being, the term "indie" can get a bit blurry.

A few examples of my favorite indie labels are Sub Pop, Victory Records, 4AD, Epitaph Records, Ultra Records, Toolroom Records, Kompakt, Defected, and Hot Creations.

Philosophy

Unlike major labels, which are typically driven by shareholder expectations or artists who are most likely to turn a quick profit, independent labels are more willing to sign undeveloped musicians and bands whose music is outside the mainstream.

Indies were once the breeding ground and lifeline for the punk rock and grunge revolutions in the music industry. Today, they continue their legacy and nourish underground hip-hop, true punk, hardcore, EDM, and metal genres—to name a few.

Advantages

Independent labels are smaller in size than major labels, and thus there is a possibility that you will get more attention from your record company if you sign with one.

I'll tell you one thing: when I was signed to a major, I never once met the president of the record label. However, when I was signed to a smaller independent labels, the owner was buying us shots backstage and watching the show from the mosh pit. I love that shit.

At indies, there is a feeling of real family and that people in your camp really care. The hope is that the attention will help you to build a brand that can generate income for you in a variety of areas far beyond your record deal, or even lead to a bigger deal for you.

For instance, manager Karl Louis tells me that the band In This Moment recorded four records on the independent label Century Media records, and at the end of their deal—due to the traction they gained at their indie—signed to the major label Atlantic Records. Sounds cool to me.

Disadvantages

Indies might give you more attention, but they usually don't have the same marketing muscle or financial resources that the major labels have.

Therefore, they have to rely on a grassroots philosophy.

The bottom line: you're not going to see $500,000 videos, billboards on Sunset Boulevard, or 45-foot Prevost XLII Entertainer tour buses. But you can live without all that, right?

Advances/Royalties/Splits

Now that you understand some of the basics about indie labels, let's talk about the deals. There are a variety of arrangements by which artists are funded and paid under the independent label deal, including traditional deal structures (for lack of a better title), net profit deals, 360 deals, and digital-only deals. Here are the stripped-down basics:

Traditional Deal

Traditional deals are so named because they ruled the music industry for years. Advances and royalties work generally like this:

- **Advance:** The label provides a recording fund ranging typically from as little as $1,500 to $75,000, depending on the size of the indie label and the buzz you've built over the months or years. The recording fund is used to make your record, and only when there's money left over (don't hold your breath) will you pocket some dough. Note: Sometimes an advance (i.e., guaranteed monies up front) can be negotiated separate from an agreed-upon amount to make your record. But this happens more for pop artists at the major labels. More on that later.
- **Royalty:** The label provides an artist royalty for sales of your record that ranges from 11 to 16 percent. But don't get too hung up on what precisely this percentage is based on, or what this calculation amounts to. Why? It's very possible you won't earn a cent of this money. The label reduces your royalty by making a number of fancy calculations, and then credits all of your sales toward the advances and

expenses they pay you (a concept called recouping). For the sake of clarity, it could take hundreds of thousands of record sales before you recoup. Most artists survive on monies from touring, merch, and publishing, not on artist royalties from record sales.

Net Profit Deal

The net profit split deal is appropriately named because the net is split. Here are the basics:

- **Advance:** As with a traditional deal, the label offers a recording fund ranging typically from $1,500 to $75,000, depending on the size of the indie label and the clout of the artist.
- **Splits:** Unlike the traditional deal, the net profit split deal divides the profits from all sales (after deducting all expenses) 50/50 between the label and the artist. Just remember to discuss exactly what expenses the label deducts before arriving at the net. You see, in addition to the customary expenses (the recording fund, video, etc.), other expenses can include advertising and promotion costs, distribution fees, and third-party marketing costs (for publicists, street team marketing firms, and independent radio promoters). These can add up, and you may find yourself with nothing left to split. However, attorney Joe Sofio says more optimistically, "If your record is successful, this situation can really work out nicely for both parties."

360 Deal

Now for the new kid on the block: the 360 deal (appropriately named because it provides for a revenue share in the total revenue pie of the artist). Take a closer look:

- **Advance:** As with the traditional and net profit deals, the label provides a recording fund ranging typically from $1,500 to $75,000, depending on the size of the indie label and the clout of the artist. In some cases, since they share in other revenue streams (as you will see below), the label might front other monies for music publishing or merchandising, but not if they can help it.
- **Royalty or Split:** The record company offers either a royalty on record sales at the rates discussed above (11 to 16 percent) or a split of the net profits.
- **Other Splits:** In addition to record sales (drum roll, please), the record company shares in your other earnings, including touring, merchandising, and music publishing. The amount they'll take can range from 15 to 35 percent of your net (i.e., your gross receipts, less customary expenses) and 8 to 15 percent for tours (based on the gross before expenses, since touring has many questionable costs, like wild parties). These monies may be treated passively, meaning your business manager writes the label a check, or actively, meaning they actually own these rights via a contract that obligates you to their parent or some third-party company. Attorney Joe Sofio says: "Illegal digital downloading killed the record business, and the only way labels can stay profitable and engaged in your career is to share in—and help you grow—other revenue streams." Whatever the reasoning, these deals are here to stay for now.

Digital-Only Deal

Finally, Ryan Kuper, CEO of Redemption Records, notes that there's an increasing number of smaller labels structuring deals that only allow for master exploitation in digital format, generally leaving the rights and profits for physical record sales to the band. Let's take a look:

- **Advance:** Deals vary considerably, but in many cases the artist supplies the finished masters with no advance.
- **Royalty or Split:** The label either pays a royalty for digital sales similar to the traditional deal we looked at already; or the label splits net profits from digital sales 50/50 with the artist after certain expenses have been covered.

That's pretty much all for independent deals. Now let's close out with a brief chat about independent distribution and making sure that your records are conveniently placed where your target fans can find them.

Distribution

Independent labels generally rely on regional or national independent distributors, ranging from successful independent distributors to larger distributors owned by the majors.

Distributors do the following:

- ***Handle General Duties:*** Warehouse physical records, prepare music for digital encoding and release, handle orders, and collect payments.
- ***Serve Various Networks:*** Supply physical stores, digital and streaming sites, and telecommunications providers of ringtones.
- ***Provide Marketing:*** Arrange retail promotions that labels can buy into, including listening booths (which allow customers to try before they buy), end-cap positioning (which provides opportune placement of records on store shelves), and co-op advertising (which helps labels cut costs via collective advertising). Further, they help with online advertising, search engine optimization, online contests, social networking campaigns, listening parties, and more.
- ***Offer New Services (Film, TV, and More):*** There is a new trend in distribution that has distributors pitching recordings for use in synchronization (film, TV, and games); preparing, distributing, and monetizing audiovisual content for video streaming sites (like YouTube) that earn advertising monies; and so much more.
- ***Publishing Administration:*** Some distributors can also assist with the collection of royalties around the world. And finally . . .
- ***Client Support:*** Distributors assist their label clients with customer service.

Examples of successful independent distributors include Redeye Music Distribution (www.redeyeworldwide.com) and Nail Distribution (www.naildistribution.com).

Larger independent distributors owned by major labels include RED (www.redmusic.com), owned by Sony Music Entertainment; and Alternative Distribution Alliance (ADA) (www.ada-music.com), owned by Warner Music Group.

Examples of companies that specialize in working with independent labels to digitally prepare music and to push it out to e-tailers (and so much more) include the Orchard (www.theorchard.com) and INgrooves (www.ingrooves.com).

FROM MAJOR LABEL BACK TO INDIE

I'll discuss major labels later in this chapter, but while on the topic of the independents, allow me to say that many artists seem perfectly happy to leave the majors and come home to the indies. Below are a few examples.

- ***Nipsey Hussle:*** Nipsey Hussle ended his ties to Epic and started his own label, All Money In, releasing his own mix tapes with an impressive list of guests and support from the rap community. Says Nipsey, "Major labels are middlemen to the people. But, with on-demand streaming services, cell phones, and blogs, I can take my strategy straight to the people on my own label and be part of the global underground."

- ***AZ (Anthony Cruz):*** Well-respected rapper AZ started off on Motown/Universal Records, went to EMI, and then formed his imprint, Quiet Money Records. Says AZ, "The strategy is to let the major label build up your rep and credibility, and then get out of the deal with a good attorney." Probably easier said than done, but AZ is still in the game and doing it his way.
- ***50 Cent:*** 50 Cent left Interscope Records to release his own records, as well as those recorded by the artists on his G-Unit label, via the distributor Caroline (which is owned by a major). 50 Cent said in *Rolling Stone* that he is grateful for what Eminem and Dr. Dre did for his career at Shady/Aftermath/Interscope, but that he is also excited to enter this new era of music where he can carry out his own creative vision.
- ***Garbage:*** Finally, the successful alternative rock band Garbage, featuring producer legend Butch Vig, got out of their major-label corporate responsibilities from the past and felt "pleasantly liberated." They formed their own label to maintain all the creative and business control over their records. Their first record on their label, Stunvolume Records, reached number 13 on the *Billboard* Top 200 chart.

Production Companies

Now let's move on to the third type of recording company and deal you should know about. Ladies and gentlemen, introducing production companies and the production company deal.

Production companies consist of record producers who develop artists and then enter into recording agreements on behalf of these artists. Said another way, the production company essentially acts as a middleman between you and the record company.

Production deals are often viewed in the industry as being either a godsend or a pact with the devil. The producer's clout, the royalties/advances/splits, and the distribution associated with these deals should reveal why.

Types of Production Companies (From Start-up to Pro)

Production companies consist of record producers of all levels of skill and clout.

The companies consisting of well-respected and seasoned pros may be those with multimillion-dollar studios in beautiful homes or buildings. These folks have a track record for developing some big names in the music industry.

The companies consisting of less reputable producers may be those with no more than a ProTools rig in a garage. They don't have much of a track record beyond working with a few local artists. Of course, sometimes a less reputable producer could also have an incredible studio, but you get the idea.

How They Operate

In a typical production company deal, the production company finds and signs talent ranging from the obscure artist who needs grooming (much like those the independent record companies sign) to the commercially viable pop artists.

The production company then develops, produces, and records the artist and in turn enters into a recording agreement with a record company on behalf of the artist. In other words, the production company signs to the record label and you sign to the production company. A side letter may then be signed with the label confirming your deal with the production company.

General Deal Structure

The production company receives a royalty rate for record sales (and a percentage for various other incomes), which is typically split 50/50 between you and the production company.

Advance monies left over (if any) after the production company has covered its recording expenses are also split 50/50.

So, in case it hasn't sunk in, the deal the production company enters into with the label is structured, in concept, the same way it would be if you entered into the deal with the label yourself, but only now your deal is essentially cut in half by the production company.

They Are a Godsend

As mentioned in my opening paragraph, production deals can be viewed as either a "godsend" or a "pact with the devil," depending on the finer details of the deal, your stature, and the clout of the producer. Here's what attorney Shawna Hilleary had to say:

> It's a godsend when an artist [who has no connections] gets picked up and developed by a reputable producer who by virtue of his or her clout gets signed to a major on behalf of the artist. While I still have a problem with the artist's royalty being cut in half, it's possible—with a good attorney—to negotiate a more favorable percentage of 70/30 [artist/production company]. Or, at the very least, it's not unheard of to have the percentage increase in favor of the artist on subsequent recordings. That is, a 60/40 split of the income on the first record, and 70/30 on the second record.

They Are a Pact with the Devil

Production deals can be viewed as a "pact with the devil." Here's what Ryan Kuper of Redemption Records had to say:

> It's a pact with the devil when you carelessly sign a deal with some small-town producer who locks you into an agreement you can never get out of. That being said, it's important to ask any production company with which you sign to guarantee that it will enter into an agreement with a reputable label on your behalf (a "major," not a "Joe Blow" distributor) within a set period of time—say six to nine months—after your album is recorded, or the deal is off.

Attorney Stan Findelle adds:

> I see production deals as a pact with the devil as well. The majority of work I do today is getting artists out of unfavorable production agreements. So be leery of production deals and always hire a seasoned professional before signing anything.

Advances/Royalties/Splits

Now here's a basic breakdown of the record royalties and advances in a production deal.

- ***Advances:*** The production company receives a recording fund from the record label ranging typically from $75,000 to $200,000, depending on the stature of the record producer and the artist. If there are any monies left after the recording expenses have been paid, the production company will usually split the remainder 50/50 with the artist.

- ***Royalties:*** As previously stated, record labels pay a production company a royalty rate for record sales. The amount can range from 14 to 18 percent, which the production company typically splits with the artist 50/50. This means that if the label credits the production company for record sales at 18 percent per record, you will receive an artist royalty credit of 9 percent. If there are any other incomes in which the label contractually shares, like merch, publishing, tours, etc., that money flows through the production company, who takes a cut and pays the remainder to you.

I'm aware that I'm only touching the surface of these deals, but don't forget I'll be hitting on a few more key deal points later in this chapter. Sound cool?

Now let's finish up this section with distribution.

Distribution

Finally, the label for which the production company is contracted handles distribution and placing your music before your target audience. The functions are the same as previously discussed under independent labels, but to refresh your memory, here are the basics:

- ***Supplying:*** The distributor supplies your music to physical stores, digital and streaming sites, and telecommunications providers of ringtones.
- ***Accounting:*** The distributor handles orders of your music and collects payments. And finally . . .
- ***Marketing:*** The distributor assists with marketing your recordings in stores and online.

Examples of distributors include RED (www.redmusic.com), Alternative Distribution Alliance (ADA) (www.ada-music.com), Sony Music Entertainment (www.sonymusic.com), Warner Music Group (www.wmg.com), and Universal Music Group (www.universalmusicgroup.com).

Major Labels

Now, as we're getting close to the end of this chapter, it's time to discuss the granddaddy of all record label types: the major record label.

Major labels are large corporations responsible for the majority of commercial recordings sold in the United States. In addition to funding, distributing, and promoting records, they also provide management, merchandising, touring, fan clubs, VIP ticketing, sponsorships, brand endorsements, and so much more.

The ownership, general philosophy, royalties/advances/splits, and distribution methods of the major label deal are all discussed below.

Ownership/Structure

As of this writing, there are three major label groups: Sony Music Entertainment, Warner Music Group, and Universal Music Group. Each of these groups functions as a "parent" corporation for its multiple businesses. For instance, Warner Music Group is the home of Atlantic, Asylum, Warner Bros., East West, Elektra, Fueled by Ramen, and Roadrunner Records (to name a few).

In addition to record labels, major-label groups also own other income-generating businesses, including publishing companies, merchandising companies, touring services, and more. As you can see, it really is no surprise why major labels are called major. They're huge!

Departments/Staff

Each record label keeps a large staff that performs a variety of functions, including A&R, publicity, radio promotion, sales, advertising, new media, business and legal, and finance. This can amount to hundreds of employees. In contrast, smaller indies may have just a few people on staff.

General Philosophy

Major labels are large publicly traded corporations that have one huge responsibility to their shareholders: quarterly profits. Thus, the general philosophy of a major label is to seek artists who have the greatest potential for a return on investment and who have the following characteristics:

- ***A Story:*** The artist has traction (is already cowriting with successful songwriters, has a relationship with an excellent producer or personal manager, and has millions of hits on his or her online videos).
- ***Hit Songs:*** The artist is a great songwriter (or can perform other people's songs incredibly well and look amazing while doing it).
- ***Style:*** The artist's sound is commercially viable (it appeals to the masses, it is current, and it is largely radio friendly).
- ***Look:*** The artist has a very attractive look on camera and is the perfect spokesperson for his or her generation. And finally . . .
- ***Performance:*** The artist is an incredible performer who will be able to deliver the goods on stage.

Advantages

A big advantage of signing with a major label is the company's resources: from multiple employees, to multiple departments, to multiple dollars. Collectively these resources are called the "major label machine." When the machine is focused on your career, it can help build a brand for you that continues living far beyond the term of your deal.

Disadvantages

The disadvantage of signing with a major is that it is very easy to get "lost in the sauce." In other words, you become a small fish in a big pond and attention is placed elsewhere. When this happens, the major label machine goes cold and you're dropped like a hot potato. I know this all too well from first-hand experience, ladies and gentlemen, and it sucks.

Royalty Rates/Advances/Splits/Deal Points

Now that you've got some of the basics about major labels down pat, let's talk briefly about a few key points in record deals, including demo deals, traditional deals, 360 deals, and singles deals.

Demo Deal

Demo deals give the label a chance to see how an artist sounds before shelling out a lot of cash. A few deal points include:

- **Recording Expenses:** The record label offers a small amount of money ($3,000 to $10,000) to the band to record a few tracks.
- **First Right:** If the label likes what it hears, it has the first right to negotiate a deal.

- **Matching Rights:** If a satisfactory deal cannot be reached between the artist and label, it then has the first right to match any deal the band may make with another label.
- **Pay Back:** If another label ends up signing the band, the band has to pay back the demo money.

Demo deals have been around for a long time and are not as common as they used to be, but you still need to know about them. Now let's check out the traditional deal.

Traditional Deal

Traditional deals fueled the record business for years. We already discussed traditional deals under independent labels, but the numbers are a little higher at the majors. I'll keep this brief:

- **Advances or Funds:** The label provides a fund of $75,000 to $200,000—higher for pop and R&B bands, since these genres typically use multiple producers per album and the records can get expensive. Remember, the fund must be used to record your record, and only if anything is left over will you pocket some dough. Sometimes an advance, separate from recording expenses, is offered to artists in the pop genres. The amounts range from $10,000 to $75,000.
- **Royalty:** The label offers an artist royalty from 13 to 16 percent for sales of the record. After they've made a number of fancy calculations that reduce your royalty, and credited whatever is left over to pay back all advanced expenses they've incurred (videos, radio promotion, etc.), you'll probably get nothing (unless you sell hundreds of thousands of records). Seriously! Thank God for touring, publishing, and merchandising!

360 Deal

Next up is a quick review of the 360 deal. The 360 business model is primarily structured on declining CD sales in the digital age. Like it or not, this business model is really the new standard at major labels. Here's an overview:

- **Advance:** The label provides a recording fund ranging from $75,000 to upwards of $300,000—and higher for pop and R&B artists. Sometimes a guaranteed advance up front (anywhere from $10,000 to $75,000) is offered to pop artists, separate from an agreed-upon amount to make the record.
- **Royalty:** The label offers an artist royalty from 13 to 16 percent for sales of your record. Just in case this point didn't get through to you earlier, don't expect to see anything from artist record royalties unless you sell hundreds of thousands of records.
- **Other Splits:** For publishing and merch, the label takes 15 to 35 percent of your net (the gross less customary expenses), and for tours, 8 to 15 percent on the gross (before expenses). Remember that these monies may be treated passively, meaning your business manager writes the label a check, or actively, meaning they actually own these rights via a contract they make you enter into with their parent or third-party company.

Singles Deal

Finally, singles deals are structured on the label's need to maximize its budgets and to determine the potential success of an artist before it spends millions.

In the singles deal, the record company signs the artist to release one or two singles (sometimes called "clusters") with an option to record a full album should certain sales criteria be met. Here's the breakdown:

- **Advance:** The label provides the artist with a small fund (depending on the buzz of the artist) to record the single.
- **Royalty:** The label allocates an artist royalty rate for sales similar to the terms of the other deals discussed above.

- **Other Splits:** The record company often acquires additional income streams, like publishing, merchandising, touring, and sponsorships similar to the terms of a 360 deal.

Note that singles deals are really not that different from the record industry of the past, when the Beatles would release singles and then the album. Candy Hill, a band who signed a single deal on Universal Republic Records, says, "Literally, it's a one-time shot at success."

Now let's talk about distribution and getting your record out to your target customer.

Distribution

As the final section in our discussion about major labels, let's take a quick look at major label distribution. A key distinction is that the majors own their own distributors, which provide services for their labels and for the independents as well. General services summarized include:

- ***Supplying:*** Soliciting and supplying various outlets (stores, streaming websites, telecommunication providers of ringtones, and more)
- ***Accounting:*** Sending invoices and collecting monies
- ***Marketing:*** Working with the sales (and other) departments at the label to arrange marketing

The major distributors include Sony (who distributes Columbia, RCA, Epic, and more), Universal (who distributes Interscope, A&M, Geffen, and more), and Warner (who distributes Atlantic, Warner Bros., Reprise, and more). For more information and the latest happenings, be sure to check out the websites of all of these labels/distributors.

So that's about all for this chapter and types of recording companies and deals. Now be sure to check out part 2 in the next chapter: Key Deal Issues in Recording Contracts.

MAJOR LABEL MARKETING MUSCLE

When one thinks of the advantages of signing with a major label, certainly one of the things that comes to mind is their marketing capabilities. Fred Croshal, former general manager of Maverick Records, and now the new CEO of Croshal Entertainment Group, offers descriptions of the various marketing departments:

- ***New Media:*** Develops the websites for artists and bands, and provides marketing via online promotions (e.g., pre-releases through Amazon, and prominent positioning and exclusive tracks through iTunes). New media also pushes out the message on all social networks (Instagram, Vevo, YouTube, Facebook, and more).
- ***Press:*** Writes the artist biography and sends advance copies of the artist's music to gain exposure in blogs, magazines, newspapers, TV, and radio, and at special events and premieres. The press department also stimulates publicity across the United States for an artist when he or she is out on the road.
- ***Promotion:*** Focuses on getting songs played on radio stations and garnering airplay. This can mean getting a band or artist to play at a special radio station event, organizing contests such as ticket giveaways, and other promotions.
- ***Sales:*** Works with distribution and various retailers to get records online and in stores, and to get them positioned prominently in conjunction with the marketing campaign.
- ***Marketing:*** Works with all the departments above to develop a timeline, budget, and marketing plan for an artist or band. Marketing also plays the role of traffic cop for all departments under its umbrella and makes sure that everyone is doing his or her job.

- ***A&R:*** Works closely with the artist and with all departments within the label to make sure that the artist's music and vision are executed.

Note: Nearly all the services that the departments offer are sometimes farmed out to indies or consultants either to take the workload off staff or to provide specific specialties in targeting a market segment.

14

Making and Selling Records, Part 2

Key Deal Issues in Recording Contracts

"When negotiating contracts, focus on what really matters first." —Dina LaPolt, attorney

Congratulations! You've come a very long way. In part 1, chapter 13, you learned about the different types of recording companies and deals that exist. Now, in this chapter, you'll learn a few more details about recording agreements so that you can better understand what you're signing.

While there are numerous points that can be discussed, and a tremendous amount of detail that could be covered, I surveyed hundreds of musicians and came up with 13 key deal issues in recording contracts that musicians want to know about: Who is the label? How much will I get to record? Can I make the record I want? Will my album ever get released? Will I get guaranteed marketing support? Will I ever make any money? And so much more.

Let's jump right into this chapter with featured issue number one: Who is the label?

Issue #1: Who Is the Label?

One of the biggest concerns artists have about recording agreements revolves around the clout the company offering the contract. Just who am I getting involved with?

Here are a few things that you should consider:

- Is it an indie label, a production company, or a major label?
- Who are the owners/staff/executives involved?
- Who distributes the label?
- What level of professionalism does the label's website exude?
- Who are the other artists on the roster?
- How well has the label done for other artists in your genre?
- How visible is the label in the marketplace?
- How long has the label been in business?
- And finally, what is the label going to do that you cannot do for yourself?

In this day and age, it shouldn't be too hard to get the information you need on Google. And if conducting your own online research isn't enough, you can always reach out to other artists on the label, check out the label's customer rating via the Better Business Bureau, or speak with a well-connected music business professional (an attorney, manager, or consultant) who knows a thing or two about the label.

Just keep in mind that a bigger label is not always better, and a smaller label is not always bad. But research is always smart. Never jump at the first deal that is thrown your way without doing due diligence.

Issue #2: How Much Will I Get to Make My Record?

The second biggest issue for musicians gets right into money matters and the amount of dough one gets to make a record.

I've already discussed advances in general, but let's do a really quick review of recording funds and the advance plus expenses.

Recording Funds

Labels typically offer a recording fund that covers all your recording costs (including the record producer, studio costs, equipment rentals, and fees to pay you a little something while making the record). The amounts vary depending on the label and your buzz.

If there is any money left over after recording, you can usually pocket the dough. But before getting too excited, just keep in mind that you must first pay your professional team their commissions (this includes your manager, business manager, and attorney).

Advance Plus Expenses

Sometimes deals are structured so that the artist gets a small advance, in addition to an agreed-upon amount for recording expenses. This is particularly true in the pop genres and at the majors, where there can be multiple producers and high expenses. The advance ensures that there is a little something extra for the artist for entering into the deal.

AFTERTHOUGHT: GOT ESCALATIONS? Note that sometimes advances are structured to escalate (get bigger) on subsequent releases. In other words, on album one, you might get a fund of $100,000; on album two, $125,000; and so on. But remember, as briefly discussed, that the advance is an expense that is recoupable against any future royalties that might be due to you. So use the advance well!

Issue #3: Can I Make the Record I Want to Make?

The third biggest issue for musicians is whether they will be able to make the record they want to make. Music may be a business, but it an art form first and foremost. Right? Let's take a look at mutual consent of the record producer and approval of artwork and other media.

Mutual Consent of the Record Producer

In order to make the right record, you need the right producer. But in the first draft of your recording agreement, the label will sometimes request the right to select the record producer. Labels fork over a significant amount of cash for your project, and they want to be sure that all goes smoothly.

As we discussed in the producer chapter, some labels will agree on mutual consent at the request of your attorney. This means that both you and the label must agree on the record producer—this a far better proposition for you, don't you think? After all, it makes no sense to have you locked up in the studio with a producer with whom you're unhappy.

Approval of Artwork and Other Materials

Finally, another creative concern for musicians is the right of approval on artwork, photographs, biographical information, and any other promotional materials that are directly and indirectly associated with the record. God forbid you are portrayed as anything other than a god!

First, let me say that the word "approving" is pretty important here. In many first draft agreements, the word is "consulting," which really means that you have the right to voice your opinion. I recently got stuck in a contract with a "consulting" clause where the response to my suggestions about artwork was "Thanks, but we're keeping what we have." That was worthless!

Issue #4: How Do I Know They'll Release My Record?

Moving away from the creation of your record, the fourth biggest concern for artists is the release of their record and whether it will ever see the light of day. Can you think of anything worse than getting your family hyped up on your potential success, and then having to tell poor ol' Grandma that the label decided to shelve your record? Yikes. But there is hope! Read on.

Guaranteed Release Clause

Your attorney can negotiate for a guaranteed release of your record (in both physical and digital format) in the United States, after a specified period of time (e.g., four months) from the date it was delivered to the label. In some cases, your attorney can also get a guaranteed release for specific territories outside the United States.

For instance, one independent label agreement on my desk right now states: "We will release each record in the United States, as well as in Australia, Austria, Belgium, Canada, Denmark, Finland, France, Germany, Greece, Ireland, Italy, Japan, Netherlands, New Zealand, Norway, Portugal, Spain, Sweden, Switzerland, and the United Kingdom."

If this all sounds like good news, don't celebrate just yet. A big surprise awaits!

Free to Leave or Buy Back Your Masters

While a guaranteed release clause states that the label must release your record, it does not actually guarantee the release of your record! Rather, it guarantees the termination of your contract should the label fail to meet its obligations, and in some cases, it provides you the opportunity to buy your masters and shop them to another label.

I know that this doesn't beat having your record released, and Grandma may still be a little upset for you, but it's better than nothing. Well, maybe just a little bit better than nothing!

Issue #5: Will I Get Guaranteed Marketing Support?

The fifth biggest issue that concerns artists about recording deals is marketing support! Let's examine deficit tour support, promotional videos, radio promotion, websites, and publicity—which, by the way, are all recoupable in one way or another by the record company.

Deficit Tour Support?

Touring and connecting with fans around the country is crucial to a band's success. However, without some financial support, you won't be able to do it comfortably for very long.

That being said, attorney Ben McLane told me that with a good lawyer, a band should be able to get something called deficit tour support. This means that after reviewing your tour budget, the label may agree to make up for the expenses that put a band into the red. As McLane puts it, "The label makes sure that your tours at least break even."

Guaranteed Promotional Videos (YouTube, Vimeo)?

Posting high-quality videos on YouTube, Vimeo, and other sites is super important right now. However, the production quality of these videos keeps getting better and more expensive.

With this in mind, you should be able to get the label to agree to making, and releasing at least one video per album. Ben McLane confirms, "This isn't usually too difficult to do. In fact, depending on the buzz of the band, the label may agree to many more videos."

Independent Radio Promotion?

Moving on to yet another important form of promotion for artists, radio is still one of the most expensive forms of promotion that there is. While it's difficult to nail down precisely what the record label will guarantee (or what they can afford), a band with a little negotiation power may be able to get the label to guarantee some sort of radio campaign—for at least one single per album. Any radio support to promote a record and touring is far better than none.

Websites?

Getting close to the end of our discussion on guaranteed marketing support, one cannot forget about the power of websites in this digital age of ours. While the label will usually have no problem with guaranteeing and maintaining a beautiful site for you, they'll want to own the rights to your official website, and even all of your social media sites and fan club sites as well.

Therefore, McLane states that a band's attorney should get the following into the contract:

- The right to mutually approve the "look and feel" of the sites. This is important, since you want to protect your brand.
- The rights to the passwords associated with each site so you can continue to communicate with, and update, your fans (in case the label is not on top of this).
- The rights to fan data (e.g., e-mails, cell phone numbers, etc.) that the label captures.
- And, lastly, the full rights of control to the sites after the contract term.

Independent Publicity

And finally, for the last promotional item in our discussion about guaranteed marketing support, let's examine publicity.

Publicity in magazines, fanzines, and blogs is an extremely important part of any promotional campaign. However, many labels do not have an in-house PR person, and when they do, that person is busy handling dozens of artists at once.

All things considered, a band with some negotiation power should ask for the funds to hire their own independent publicist. Says McLane, "This is not always easy to get, but it's super important to try!"

Issue #6: Do I Have a Say in How the Masters Will Be Exploited?

On a similar topic to promotion, discussed above, the sixth biggest concern for artists deals with the exploitation of the master recordings. After all, integrity is everything to artists, right?

Attorney Ben McLane says that the biggest issue here is to make sure that your music is not exploited in a way that makes you look bad or goes against your beliefs. In his words, "While any exposure is usually good, you can demand that your music cannot be used in connection with porn, religion, politics, or a product endorsement without your mutual approval. Enough said!"

AFTERTHOUGHT: SPECIAL MONIES FROM THE MASTERS Keep in mind that when the label licenses the masters for film, TV, and other uses, you are credited 50 percent of the fees negotiated by the label (subject to recoupment). On a slightly different note, when the masters are broadcast on "non-interactive" stations (like Pandora, satellite radio like SiriusXM, etc.), you receive monies directly from SoundExchange. For more information on this, visit SoundExchange (www.soundexchange.com).

Issue #7: Artist Royalties: Will I Ever Make Money from the Label?

About halfway through our top 13 artist concerns about record deals, let's talk about money and artist royalties. More specifically, artists want to know if they'll ever see a dime from record sales, digital downloads, streaming, and more. Let's take a look.

Artist Royalties and CDs, Vinyl, and More

You already know that artist's royalties can range from 11 to 16 percent for sales of your record, but this amount can be reduced significantly in a number of different ways.

First, you must subtract the producer's royalty, as much as 4 to 6 percent, from your share.

Then, after considering a number of different factors (the price for which records are sold, how they are sold [in retail outlets, mail order, etc.], in what country they are sold, and the physical configuration in which they are sold), your royalty can be further reduced from 85 percent of your standard royalty rate to as much as 50 percent of your rate.

If that weren't enough, your royalty can be further lowered by other crazy calculations such as free goods (a 15 percent "purchasing incentive" to retailers to stock your record)—which means that you may only get credited for 85 percent of all records sold.

Finally, all sales are credited toward recoupable expenses.

After all is said and done, and you recoup (which is next to a miracle), the label will take a reserve of as much as 50 percent (and more) and hold on to your payments for as long as a few years.

So, in short, don't plan your retirement on record royalties!

Electronic Transmissions (Downloads, Ringtones, Audio and Video Streaming)

Electronic transmissions (downloads, ringtones, streaming, and whatever new invention is out right now) are generally calculated by taking your standard royalty rate multiplied by the money received by the label.

The amount your label receives can actually be quite confusing. So if you are really interested in the finer details, I suggest that you check out Donald Passman's *All You Need to Know About the Music Business.*

But any way you slice it, just remember that monies from electronic transmissions amount to pennies (if not fractions of pennies), and it all goes toward recoupment before you ever see one dime.

AFTERTHOUGHT: SALES VERSUS A LICENSE In a hot battle with his label, rapper Eminem claimed that digital downloads constitute a license, in which case the artist is paid as much as 50 percent instead of his standard royalty rate of 11 to 16 percent. Well, the courts agreed with Eminem and he won this battle. Stay tuned for what this might mean for you.

Issue #8: Controlled Composition Clauses

Moving away from the royalties you get as an artist, the number eight fear musicians have about record label deals involves their music publishing rights and controlled composition clauses.

Controlled composition clauses limit the amount the record company has to pay you for the reproduction of your songs on record.

Generally speaking, while Congress says that record labels must pay a statutory (mandatory) rate, the record company makes you agree in your recording contract to a reduction of the rate, and to receiving only a 10-song equivalent (or cap) of that reduced rate.

With some leverage, your attorney can negotiate for a higher rate and a larger cap, which overall means you get more money.

In any case, remember that these monies should not be recoupable against the label's expenses. While independent labels will try to do this, fight with all your might if you can.

Issue #9: 360 Rights in Deals

No surprise to me, the number nine concern for artists dovetails nicely from publishing issues to 360 deals. More specifically, artists are concerned about how much the label will take from their publishing, touring, and merchandising incomes. Let's take a look at everything from active and passive incomes, to the label's cut, to what 360 percentages are based on.

Active Versus Passive Income

Record labels will try to treat 360 incomes as either passive or active income.

Active income means that the label (or one of its own sister companies that it makes you sign to) owns and controls the rights to certain income streams.

Passive income means that the record company does not own the rights, and it is merely taking a cut of your work.

It's a no-brainer when it comes to knowing which one is best, but attorney Ben McLane clearly states, "Shoot for a passive income deal with the label. This is obviously the better scenario for the artist."

The Label's Cut (What They Take for Merch, Publishing, Tours)

The percentages the label takes in 360 deals is all over the map depending on the buzz of the band, the label, and the attorney negotiating the deal. But, that being said, percentages typically range from 8 to 35 percent (but can go as high as 50 percent) during the term of the deal (and sometimes for a period after the deal is done). Adds McLane, "Clearly, the artist wants the label to take the lowest rates possible for the shortest periods of time. Be sure your attorney is on this."

On What Are the 360 Percentages Based?

Finally, 360 rights can be based on either the net or the gross income.

If on the net, net is defined as the gross receipts, less customary arm's-length expenses, but of these expenses, the label may want to cap the commissions payable to your team (manager, agent, etc.) at around 35 percent (but this varies).

If on the gross, which might happen for tour incomes, the label may take a lower cut (8 to 15 percent). Also note that sometimes the label won't even take its share when you are a new band and are making less than $5,000 a night in guarantees.

Says McLane, "However the monies are calculated, be sure that this language is specifically laid out in your contract with the label. All of this, of course, is so important."

HE WHO HAS THE GOLD WINS

Attorney Dina LaPolt of LaPolt Law tells me that when a band has a home run, many attorneys are going to want to go back and renegotiate many of the terms for subsequent albums. Of course, if a band can go into negotiations with a huge buzz from the outset, they are more likely to get the deal that they want.

Black Veil Brides had quite a monster buzz before they signed their deal with Universal Republic. Their first record, on the independent label Standby, sold over 10,000 copies in its first week, ranking at No. 36 on the *Billboard* Top 200 chart. What's more, the band had the top selling T-shirt in the country at the Hot Topic store.

Building their buzz on a DIY work ethic (making their own videos and engaging with fans on social networks) and having great songs and a larger-than-life image similar to KISS, the band attracted the attention of Universal Republic. When the contract offer came in, the band and its attorney were able to essentially call the shots. They signed a 360-type deal where the label shared in other revenues, but the label's interest in these incomes would not kick in until they had helped the band sell upwards of 200,000 units. What's more, they got a larger advance than most rock bands would in this day to do their records. Kick ass!

As the saying goes, he who has the gold wins.

Issue #10: How Many Records and for How Long Is the Deal?

Reaching number 10 of the 13 biggest concerns that artists have about record deals is the topic of commitment: How long will the record deal last, and just how many records does the label commit to making?

Firm Records and Option Periods

Most record deals are based on a firm number of records and options for more records.

An artist will want the label to commit to the highest number of firm-guaranteed albums (or singles), while the label will want to commit to the highest number of optional albums (or singles). The word "optional" means that the label can exercise its right (or option) to record you or to drop you. Sounds like the makings of a beautiful relationship, doesn't it?

In any case, depending on the buzz about your band and your attorney's negotiating skills, you may be able to get the label to commit to two firm records up front with a successive period of options (which might also include an option for two more records). So it will look like this: 2 + 1 + 2 (i.e., a guarantee of two records, an option for one record, and an option for two more records). The label will likely fight back for more like this: 1 + 1 + 1 + 1 + 1 (i.e., a guarantee of one record, and several one-record options). But once again, where the negotiation settles all depends on how badly the label wants you and how strong your buzz is.

Term of the Agreement

Lastly, the term of the agreement relates to how long the record company keeps you bound to an exclusive agreement with them. The term commences upon signing the deal, and, if they do not extend the term into the next option, it continues until the expiration of the period in effect.

Keep in mind that your term is also linked to a delivery requirement on your part. If you do not deliver your record within a certain period of time (3 to 15 months) from the commencement of the deal, or within 12 to 15 months from the delivery of your last record, the label can dump you.

AFTERTHOUGHT: SO WHAT'S DELIVERY, ANYWAY? Delivery means that the label has received and accepted your record, and that the record meets specific commercially satisfactory standards (e.g., it was recorded in a professional studio, all samples have been cleared, all recordings were newly recorded, etc.).

Issue #11: Can I Record Other Projects?

At number 11 of the 13 biggest concerns that artists have about record deals is freedom. Will I ever be able to record my songs again? And can I still do other projects with my musician friends? Let's look at rerecording restrictions and sideman performances.

Rerecording Restrictions

In all recording agreements you will find a rerecording restriction. In simple terms, this means that all compositions you record under contract with the label cannot be rerecorded with any other person for the purpose of making and distributing these records.

This restriction lasts typically for five years from the date of delivery of any record, or two years after the expiration of your deal. But note that you will usually not be able to record a competing "soundalike" version of your song ever again (this means that you cannot record the song to sound precisely as the original did, as if it were the original, and thus you must create a slightly different arrangement, mix, vibe, etc.; you get the idea).

Sideman Performances

Also, during the term of your exclusive record agreement, you cannot be a "featured" artist on any other record recorded by any other label.

And should you want to record a "background" performance, you must first get permission from your label, and the new label must state in any liner notes or promotional materials that you appear courtesy of your record label.

Finally, if you are a band, not more than two members at one time can participate as sidemen during the term.

Issue #12: Everything Else Artists Should Be Concerned About

Coming close to the end of our discussion on record deals and the important concerns of musicians, attorney Ben McLane tackles "everything else that artists should be concerned with."

What follows is a brief look at key person clauses, distribution clauses, and reversion clauses.

Key Person Clause

Says McLane, "A key person clause states that when your primary person leaves the label, the artist can terminate the deal. Otherwise, you could easily get stuck at a label with a new A&R representative who does not give you the same attention. Labels rarely grant key person clauses, but they are worth a shot."

Guaranteed Third-Party Distribution Clause

Says McLane, "Try to build in language that the label must secure and maintain a bona fide third-party distributor, or else the band can terminate. This is really more important at smaller indie labels and production companies than it is at the majors, who have their own distribution."

Reversion of Rights Clause

Lastly, McLane says, "Ask for some sort of reversion, buyout, or lease-back clause that grants you access to master recordings that the label never releases (tracks that don't make the album, etc.). Labels generally don't like to part with their catalog, but it never hurts to ask."

Issue #13: What Does the Label of the Future Look Like?

Finally—drum roll, please—the last concern that artists have about record deals focuses on how deals will look in the future.

Ben McLane says that it's hard to say for sure where the business is heading, but it's very possible that physical sales will become a thing of the past. Most contract clauses will focus on streaming income, and the rates for artists will have settled down and gotten a little bit better.

Deals of the future (at least the near future) will be primarily based on the 360 model. This means that, while artists have always relied on touring, merch, and publishing to make money, it will be more important than ever to fight for as much control and share of these monies as you can get.

Overall, label deals will still be about one thing: leveraging the company to build a strong brand that continues to generate income for you for years to come, even after the deal is over.

HOW TO SET UP A DIY RECORD COMPANY

While the last two chapters focused on record companies and deals, the truth is that many artists are going to release their own recordings DIY style. This is not only because there are a number of useful tools available to help artists start their own labels, but also because many artists have no choice (i.e., if they don't DIY, they simply DIE). With this in mind, Ryan Kuper, CEO of Redemption Records / Boundless Entertainment, offers this list of tips about starting a label. Here goes:

- ***Have a Vision That's Viable:*** It's important to have a clear long-term vision of where you want to go, but temper it with realistic expectations.
- ***Create Short-Term Goals:*** Overnight success is highly unlikely. Set specific, measurable, and realistic short-term goals that are in line with your long-term vision.
- ***Write a Realistic Business/Marketing Plan:*** Examine what's happening in the real world around you. Consider both the opportunities and the threats.
- ***Create Amazing Products:*** Always strive to be unique and to deliver the highest-quality products and services.
- ***Have a Specific Sound:*** Be consistent and clear about who you are and what you represent.
- ***Create a Budget:*** Calculate your break-even point and always know where your finances stand.
- ***Pull Together the Needed Funds:*** Whether you crowdfund or get a loan, be sure to have the money in hand before starting the project. So many labels run out of gas.
- ***Delegate the Workload:*** Employ your band members, fans, and friends to help you with your efforts. You have at least one friend or fan who will kill for you; everyone does.
- ***Create a Label Name and Logo:*** Be creative and make sure it's legally available. Register it at www.uspto.gov.
- ***Get a DBA (Doing Business As):*** If doing business under a fictitious name, get a "DBA." Contact your local county clerk's office.

- ***Start an LLC or Corporation (or Not):*** It's not immediately necessary to start an LLC, S-corporation, or C-corporation, but doing so provides tax and liability benefits and helps brand your company as legit.
- ***Get a Credit Card for Expenses and Record Keeping:*** This can help you keep your business expenses for your label in order and distinct from your personal life.
- ***Get an Office:*** Don't worry about impressing people. Work out of your garage.
- ***Establish the Face of a Company:*** Free resources like Facebook, Instagram, Pinterest, and Tumblr are fine at first, but having a strong central web presence is valuable.
- ***Choose a DIY-Friendly Distributor:*** CD Baby, TuneCore, the Orchard, Ditto Music, and MondoTunes can all help.
- ***Exploit the Master Recordings and Songs in Film and TV:*** Many DIY distributors offer pitching and administrative services.
- ***Promote, Promote, and Promote:*** Use everything that's free, network like mad, and capitalize on social media. Form alliances with other artists and be part of your scene.
- ***Monitor Your Results:*** Recognize what works and what doesn't work. Never make the same mistake twice! Good luck.

15

Music Publishing, Part 1

Copyright Basics

"Music publishing is the business of songs." —*Ed Pierson, former executive vice president and general counsel, Warner/Chappell Music*

Music publishing is the business of songs. It deals with everything from exploiting your music, to collecting incomes that are generated from your songs worldwide, to making sure that no one is ripping you off. Music publishing can be handled by you, or by an experienced music publishing company that represents you. If all this sounds rather involved, it is—and we're just touching the surface of it all.

Music publishing is based on a detailed form of protection called copyrights. These rights evolve, differ from one country to the next, and apply to many forms of creative expression. Analyzing every nuance might make an interesting read for the left-brained veteran, but it would only confuse the hell out of the rest of us creative folks.

So, for the sake of simplicity, I'll take a straightforward introductory approach to this subject, discussing the "ifs," "ands," or "buts" only when necessary. I'll emphasize U.S. laws, centered around the 1976 Copyright Act and all of its latest amendments, and keep the focus on the copyrights in your words and music.

Additionally, over the next few chapters, I'll discuss publishing incomes, publishing deals, starting your own publishing company, and DIY tips on pitching your own music for film, TV, games, and other uses. What's more, I'll include interviews with attorney Steve Winogradsky (on international protection and sampling) and Neil Gillis, president of Round Hill Music (on publishing deals and contract terms). Overall, my objective is to provide you with a strong foundation upon which to build your publishing knowledge base.

Don't be frustrated if it takes a few rereadings before this information sinks in. Your patience and effort will be rewarded significantly. Music publishing is the most important aspect of your music business career. It's an area in which fortunes have been both lost and found. So take everything you're about to read very seriously. Okay? Now let's get started.

Copyright: Definition, Formation, and Benefit

To understand music publishing you must first understand a few basics about copyright. Let's examine what a copyright is, how one is formed, and the benefits you'll get.

What Is Copyright?

Copyright is a form of legal protection that applies to the original compositions you create. It makes it illegal for anyone to use your songs without your permission, knowledge, or compensation.

How Do You Get a Copyright?

A copyright exists as soon as an original idea is created and embodied in a tangible form.

In other words, as soon as an original melody is recorded on your laptop computer or smartphone voice memo, or as soon as an original lyric is written on a pad of paper or a cocktail napkin, you automatically have a copyright. Yup. It's true!

Contrary to popular myth, you create a song, you create a copyright. It's that simple!

What Benefit Does a Copyright Provide?

As the proud new owner of a copyright, you get an exclusive bundle of rights to go with it. These rights, as stated in section 106 of the 1976 United States Copyright Act (effective January 1, 1978), give you the authority to do, or authorize others to do, the following (the most significant rights for songwriters are listed):

- ***Reproduce:*** Copy, duplicate, or print your works in sheet music, CDs, vinyl, digital phonograph delivery (downloads), films, TV, etc.
- ***Distribute:*** Circulate, deliver, or issue your works for sale (or other transfer of ownership), or by rental, lease, or lending.
- ***Perform:*** Perform your work publicly (live, or via the broadcast of a recording or audiovisual recording)
- ***Prepare a Derivative:*** Use your works to create other works (e.g., use samples or parts of your songs to create new songs).

In the following sections, you'll see how all these rights play out, especially when considering some of the legal exceptions to these rights, and when discussing publishing incomes that you are entitled to when people want to use your songs.

Remember that the purpose of copyright protection is to promote the progress of useful arts by giving creators exclusive rights to their works for a period of time. So rejoice! You get a lot of mileage out of owning a copyright, and all for simply being the creative person you are.

SO WHAT THE HELL IS A DERIVATIVE WORK, ANYWAY?

You already know that section 106 of the United States Copyright Act grants the authors of an original work an exclusive bundle of rights. While most of these rights are fairly straightforward, many musicians need clarification when it comes to derivative rights (i.e., the right to decide who can create a work based on your work). Perhaps a few examples will help.

Before rapper Puff Daddy could legally sample the chorus of the Police classic "Every Breath You Take" to create a new song, "I'll Be Missing You," he had to first get permission from Sting (and Sting's record label) and negotiate a deal. Due to the significant portion of the song that Puffy wanted to use, Sting ended up owning a good chunk of the song.

Before comedian Cheech Marin (of Cheech and Chong fame) recorded a version of Bruce Springsteen's "Born in the USA" and changed the lyrics and chorus hook to "Born in East LA," he had to ask the Boss for permission and negotiate a deal. Marin commented on the approval process by saying he would have had an easier time "giving birth."

And in the electronic genre, before DJs can legally record and distribute remixes or mash-ups of other people's songs, they, too, must obtain permission from the owners and make a deal. While an enormous quantity of unauthorized remixes and mash-ups can be found online (likely because owners let the infringement slide in the name of art and for fear of being seen only as a shrewd profiteer), don't be mistaken—you must first get permission to be in compliance with the law.

As you can see, without copyright law, there would really be no point in creating anything new at all businesswise, since anyone could conceivably use any piece of work for any purpose for free. "Free" might be a good thing in the early stages of your career when you're building awareness, but it could also suck when you're trying to maintain a career and pay your bills.

But How Can I Prove I Own a Copyright?

A major concern on the minds of many musicians is proving they are the original authors and owners of a copyright, especially at a time when someone else may claim they hold those rights.

Registration: Sooner Than Later Can Help

As a general rule, establishing a valid public notice with the Copyright Office in Washington, D.C., sooner rather than later is the most prudent course of business for authors of original works.

However, there is a time and place for everything—and if you're still writing duds, unsure you have a chance in hell in music, or just flat broke and living on Top Ramen noodles, your most important concerns now are honing your craft and taking care of life's necessities.

Act Responsibly Until the Time Is Right

All things above considered, until your skills, career, and finances warrant copyright registration, just be sure to at least take these few simple precautions: get everyone with whom you create music to agree in writing to ownership splits, record your writing sessions and keep these recordings on a hard drive, think twice about where you post your music on the Internet (and whether you should even post the entire track at all), and work with credible people (i.e., producers, mixers, etc.) you can trust. This is what I did, and fortunately I never got ripped off. Note: Copyright registration will be discussed in more detail later in this chapter.

WAIT! WHAT ABOUT A POOR MAN'S COPYRIGHT?

Your fellow musicians have been telling you for years that there's a practical and cheap substitution for registering your copyrights in Washington, D.C., called a "poor man's copyright." Is this fact or just fiction? It's fiction!

A poor man's copyright is the process of establishing some proof of the date a copyright was created. This is done by recording a version of the song, stuffing it into an envelope, stamping the date on the seal of the package, and sending it to yourself by certified mail. As long as you don't get too excited and open the package, you have a song sealed in an envelope that *might* make someone say, "How did that song get into that envelope on that date?" While this may help you to sleep better at night, sorry, folks, a poor man's copyright does not provide an alternative to official registration.

Here's what the Copyright Office says: "Please be advised that there is no provision in the copyright law or the practices of the Copyright Office regarding any type of protection known as the 'poor man's copyright.' The mere act of placing a copy in the mail addressed to oneself does not secure statutory copyright protection for the work, nor will it serve as a substitute for registration of a claim to copyright in this Office in terms of legal and evidentiary value."

Okay, gang? So just don't believe any of the hype!

Copyright and Work Made for Hire

Moving away from the basics of copyright and getting into a few more complex areas, let's discuss something called work made for hire.

You've already learned a general principle underscoring copyright law: *if you write it, then you own it.* However, there are situations in which you could relinquish your rights to your own work. Yup, you heard right. So be sure to pay attention.

When It Exists

As defined in section 101 of the United States Copyright Act, a work made for hire exists when:

1. An employee creates a work under the scope of his or her employment, or
2. When one is commissioned to create a work for a specific use (such as a work for use in a motion picture or some other audiovisual work) and the parties agree in writing that the work shall be considered a work made for hire. The rules are actually a bit more detailed, but you get the general gist.

What Are the Implications?

In a work made for hire, understand that the employer, *not the employee or independent contractor*, is considered to be the author. The employee or independent contractor receives payment for the job, and may even be listed as the creator, *but the employer gets ownership and all the generated dough* (except, perhaps, the writer's share of performance income, which you'll learn about later).

Given the significant implications of a work made for hire, just make sure to understand the conditions of any relationship in which you compose songs, and never sign any agreement you don't fully understand! Okay? Now let's move on!

Copyright and Joint Works

Joint works are another condition in copyright law that gets a bit more challenging to tackle than the preliminary issues discussed at the outset of this chapter.

A joint work is exactly what it says. When two or more people come together to create a song, and each person contributes lyrically (i.e., words) and/or musically (i.e., melody, hooky beat, or track), the resulting composition is jointly owned. Many songs written today are cowritten and co-owned—just take a look at the credits of a few of your favorite songs.

As with any partnership in life, things get a bit more tricky when it comes to dealing with business matters. Therefore, a few principles regarding joint works must be understood by all of the work's authors. The most important principles have to do with ownership and control.

Ownership of Joint Works

A primary concern regarding joint works is the division of ownership. Let's begin by taking a look at what copyright law says, then explore the exceptions to copyright law per written agreement, and finally consider its "all for one and one for all" philosophy.

Division of Ownership Under Copyright Law

There's a presumption under copyright law that the authors of a joint work are automatically considered equal contributors. This simply means that if a band comes together and contributes musically and/or lyrically in writing a song, then *each writer automatically owns an equal share of the rights—no matter how big or small their musical or lyrical contribution actually was.*

Be clear that a joint work means that each writer owns a piece of the whole song. For example, if one writer composes 100 percent of the lyrics and another writer composes 100 percent of the music, each writer owns 50 percent of the entire song. Said another way, should you ever want to separate your contribution later to create a new song, the new composition becomes a derivative of the original—and the initial coauthors own a share of the new work, too.

In his book *All You Need to Know About the Music Business*, Donald Passman uses a great metaphor to illustrate joint works: "It's like scrambling the white and the yolk of the egg together. The two parts are not separable afterward."

AFTERTHOUGHT: WHAT CONSTITUTES A CONTRIBUTION? Those who contribute lyrically (words, raps) and/or musically (melody, preexisting riff, groove, "track," or integral "beat") become joint owners/authors. Merely an arrangement idea or recorded performance does not warrant authorship in the song.

Exceptions to Copyright Law per Written Agreement

Keeping in mind what copyright law says, if the split percentage in ownership of a composition is intended in any way to be something other than equal, there must be a written agreement setting forth what that split really is. For instance, if all of the members of your band agree that the bass player's contribution in a song should only entitle him to a 10 percent share in ownership rights, this must be put in writing!

Neil Gillis, president of Round Hill Music, says that he would never walk out of a writing session without first making it clear among all the writers what percentage of each composition he owned. A simple agreement containing the titles of the songs, authors, and percentage shares (called a split sheet) will suffice. It's not a bad idea to also record writing sessions on a small digital recorder or voice memo and to keep copies of original lyric sheets. Should a dispute between writers ever materialize, you'll be more than ready to prove your participation. Unfortunately, disputes are not uncommon.

SIGNING AWAY SHARES

You may be wondering whether any musician would carelessly agree to a smaller percentage share than he or she actually deserves. It's been known to happen!

In fact, I've known several musicians who, throughout the course of performing with one legendary rock singer (who must remain anonymous), signed away 100 percent of their song shares in return for a small sum of money paid up front. Not realizing the potential value of their shares over the long term, the guys felt that it was what they needed to do at the time to keep their positions in the band.

One musician who worked for the same artist, however, held out. He was fired immediately, but he still holds ownership in the song. Twenty years later, he's still getting paid.

The "All for One and One for All" Philosophy

With all this talk of what's copyrightable and who's entitled to what, you might ask what happened to the "all for one and one for all" philosophy that most young bands and writers swear by. This is where a band has an initial agreement stating that all of its members will receive an equal split in the songs, regardless of who comes up with what.

Consider the following:

- **It Works in the Beginning:** The all-for-one, one-for-all philosophy makes perfect sense for most writing teams in the beginning stages of their careers. After all, if a group of writers stuff themselves into a practice room to spend hours of their valuable time experimenting with song ideas and recording demos, it's really unfair that the harmonica player gets zero interest in a song just because he wasn't feeling as lyrically or melodically creative as the others that day. And when all the writers make perfectly relevant suggestions for something like the chorus hook, a competitive battle over whose chorus idea gets used is really unproductive. I know this all sounds a bit immature, but it can be a very real problem in a group or some other team situation.

- **It's Less Effective When There's Success:** Once a group becomes successful and everyone in the industry begins telling the vocalist or guitarist that he or she is the real star and genius of the band—trust me, the divisions in the new songs will likely change in that person's favor. This is also when the Jimmy Pages and Robert Plants of the world begin wandering off on their own and creating demos of complete song ideas to bring back to the band. In other words, this is usually when other band members who don't proficiently write words or music get cut out altogether! It may be a harsh reality for members to face, but one or two writers in a group dynamic are usually the principal creators, and it takes a great deal of maturity on the part of the other members to recognize this.

Control of Joint Works

The next issue of importance regarding joint works involves how the control of the rights to a song is shared. Let's take a look at your licensing rights under copyright law, exceptions to copyright law per written agreement, and transfer and sale of copyright.

Rights Under Copyright Law

Under U.S. copyright law, each individual writer of a composition can issue as many "nonexclusive" licenses of a song as he or she wants (to record companies, film companies, etc.), as long as he or she accounts to, and pays, all of the other writers their respective shares. Note that a nonexclusive license means that other licenses for other uses (for films, etc.) can be issued simultaneously.

For example, if four writers each own 25 percent of a composition, one writer can license (grant permission) the use of the complete song in a film for $4,000, as long as he or she pays each of the other three writers $1,000.

At the same time, another writer can license the use of the same song in a television show for $4,000 as long as he or she pays the others their fair share of the dough. (And the person issuing the licenses had better remember to report the payout to Uncle Sam properly so he or she will pay taxes only on the $1,000 and not the $4,000. But that's entirely another issue.)

YOU CAN USE IT, BUT DON'T ABUSE IT

As Leah Furman illustrates in her book *Korn: Life in the Pit*, when the rock group Korn recorded its debut album, the group used a previously unrecorded song, "Blind," that vocalist Jonathan Davis cowrote and jointly owned with his former SexArt bandmate Ryan Shuck. Under U.S. copyright laws, this would have been perfectly legal, except that Jonathan Davis failed to mention that Shuck had ever existed.

Ryan Shuck rightfully sued Korn for copyright infringement. The case was settled out of court and Shuck still receives both writer's credit and royalties from the song to this day.

But here's the storybook ending: despite Shuck and Davis's dispute, the former bandmates buried the hatchet and remained friends. In fact, Shuck's band, Orgy, ended up signing to Korn's record label, Elementree, and selling hundreds of thousands of records.

Exceptions to Copyright Law per Written Agreement

As one might imagine, too much freedom of use of a song among the writers can eventually cause problems. One coauthor may not want to see a composition licensed in a specific film, such as a porn movie, while the other coauthors may be thrilled by the idea. Or, even worse, one leaving member/cowriter of a band may form a new group, procure a recording agreement, and want to record one of the group's original signature songs on his or her new album first, while the original remaining members had also hoped to be the first parties to break the new song. It happens.

Clearly, when two or more writers get together to write a composition, it's advisable for the coauthors to have a written agreement between them that not only confirms their individual shares in a song (as previously discussed), but also defines *how a composition can and cannot be used, and who can use it first.* Some successful artists are known for going as far as having long-form agreements granting them primary control of a song whenever they collaborate with other writers. This means that if you ever write with such an artist, it's possible you can own a 25 percent share in a composition and have absolutely no say in how the song will be used.

Restrictions to Transfer or Sale of Copyright

Finally, let's take a look at one more brief point regarding joint works and the control each writer can or cannot exercise. It deals with transferring or selling copyrights, which typically happens when you sign a publishing agreement with a publishing company.

Remember, according to the principles of copyright law you've just learned, the joint owners of a composition can issue as many nonexclusive licenses as they want, as long as they account for them to the other owners. But note one important distinction: there's a difference between licensing rights and selling rights, and *under no circumstances can the individual writers transfer or sell the rights in the entire composition unless all the writers jointly agree!*

If that isn't clear, then compare it to two friends who jointly own real estate. If one owner wants to sell his share (perhaps even to you), it's his right; however, he cannot sell the entire property to another person without your permission.

YOU CAN LICENSE IT BUT YOU CAN'T SELL IT

Suppose you've cowritten a song with a friend who is about to release an album with a major label. Since there's been a lot of hype generated around the band, your friend decides to seek the assistance of an experienced music publishing company to help issue licenses for the use of his songs, place his songs in films and television, and, as an added bonus, pay him an advance against future royalty earnings. The price for all of this, however, is that he has to transfer copyright ownership in all of his songs on his forthcoming record (as is generally the case when signing most publishing agreements).

So here's the point of the story: your friend is permitted to transfer his rights in the song that you cowrote, but he cannot transfer the entire song unless you *jointly* agree. In essence, he can sign over his shares in the song to a publishing company, while you retain your rights and sign with a publisher of your choice (or you can handle the publishing yourself). While this might all seem like common sense, sense isn't always common.

Compulsory Licensing for Records

Moving into yet another area of copyright law, there's an exception to your exclusive bundle of rights that we must now discuss. This exception allows other artists the right to record and distribute phonorecords (audio-only recordings) of your songs, including digital transmission (a.k.a. digital phonorecord delivery, DPD, or iTunes-type downloads) and ringtones.

These rights all fall into a legal category called "compulsory mechanical licensing" or "compulsory licensing" for the making and distribution of records. Musicians categorize these rights simply as "cover songs"—compositions that are conformed to the style of the performer.

What Are the Conditions?

Section 115 of the United States Copyright Act spells out the details of compulsory licensing.

In simple terms, the law states that *anyone wishing to use your song for the making and distributing of records can do so* if the following conditions are met:

1. ***Recorded:*** You have already authorized the first recording of the song on record.
2. ***Distributed:*** The recording of the song has been distributed for sale to the public.
3. ***Used for Records:*** The person wishing to use your song agrees to the use for audio-only recordings (CDs, vinyl, ringtones) and DPDs (downloads) only.
4. ***Changed Minimally:*** The person wishing to use your song refrains from changing the lyrics and melody substantially (in other words, they can only interpret a cover of your song). Note: Ringtones, though 30-second edits of a full song, are permissible and not considered to be changed substantially. And finally . . .
5. ***License Obtained and Fee Paid:*** The person covering your songs obtains a license and pays a "set fee" determined by law (more on the fee later).

According to some theories, the compulsory licensing rule grew out of a concern in Congress that the music business could become a monopoly. As a result, the members of Congress wanted to limit your rights as an author by letting others use your songs too, but only after you. Makes sense to me.

Financial Benefits

If all this compulsory stuff has got you a little perturbed, don't worry; you'll get a set fee for the reproduction of your works by others.

A panel of copyright royalty judges called the Copyright Royalty Board (CRB) sets a fee called a "statutory mechanical royalty." Disregard the specifics of mechanical royalties for right now; they are covered in "Mechanical Royalties" in subsequent chapters. You can also read more about them at the Copyright Office website (www.copyright.gov), or through an agency you'll soon become more familiar with, known as the Harry Fox Agency (www.harryfox.com).

Just be assured that mechanicals can add up to a great deal of money if another artist makes your song successful and sells a significant number of recordings. In fact, the artist covering your song may give it a whole new life and allow you to earn mechanicals for years to come (as well as other royalties from the performances of the song on radio and on the Internet).

Creative Downsides

There's perhaps one downside to all of this compulsory stuff—the artist covering your song may make it more famous than you, and the public, which generally doesn't understand album liner notes in respect to ownership, may never know that you were the author.

When I was a student at Berklee College of Music in the late '80s, I worked with Joe Cook, an R&B artist who hit the *Billboard* Top 100 in 1957 with his song "Peanuts." Frankie Valli, however, who covered the song sometime later, was associated with the song more than Cook. Cook complained regularly that he didn't get his just respect. So sad!

Did you know that Fleetwood Mac wrote and recorded "Landslide" before the Smashing Pumpkins covered it, that the Guess Who wrote and recorded "American Woman" before Lenny Kravitz covered it, and that Bob Dylan wrote and recorded "All Along the Watchtower" before Jimi Hendrix covered it? Okay, so you knew this bit of history, but you'd be surprised at the number of people who don't!

Does the Compulsory Licensing Provision Apply to You, Too?

In closing, you may be wondering now whether you're allowed to cover another person's song. Yes, of course! As long as the above-noted conditions are met, you too can cover someone else's song on your record. Recording and distributing a song, especially if it is extremely cool or it's a hit, can do a lot of good for you.

First, it can help change people's perception of you—they'll associate you in their minds with the band you covered. And it can help build awareness of your career—people searching on the web for already famous artists can easily stumble upon your act. So rejoice!

For more information on covering songs, be sure to see the boxed text below.

AFTERTHOUGHT: COVER VIDEOS ARE A DIFFERENT BEAST Don't confuse the compulsory licensing of phonorecords (audio-only recordings) with audiovisual recordings (such as DVDs or videos you see on YouTube). Videos fall under something called synchronization, and obtaining authorization for these rights requires getting permission from the publisher. Synch licenses are discussed later in this chapter.

WHEN YOU COVER SOMEONE ELSE'S SONG

So, how does someone go about licensing a song for use on an audio-only phonorecord?

At the most complex level, a "compulsory mechanical license" can be obtained by sending a "notice of intent to obtain a compulsory license" via certified mail to the writer/publisher of the song and including your name and band name, the name and address of your record company, the date of release, and the "configuration" of release (i.e., CD and/or DPD). To find the contact information for writers and publishers, you can conduct a search via the Copyright Office or performing rights organizations (ASCAP, BMI, or SESAC). You must then follow very specific accounting provisions by paying on all records made and distributed monthly and issuing certified statements via an accountant annually. Sound complicated? Get further information on compulsory mechanical licenses by visiting the Copyright Office (www.copyright.gov) and reading circular 73.

At the simplest level, a "mechanical license" can be issued directly by the publisher or his or her representatives on less onerous accounting terms and lower royalty rates, and prepayments can even be negotiated. For instance, the Harry Fox Agency (www.harryfox.com), an organization that issues mechanical licenses on behalf of its writers and publishers, makes licensing simple with its Songfile service (www.songfile.com). Britt Draska, former director of royalties at Lakeshore Entertainment Group, says Harry Fox allows you to prepay a flat fee (plus administration charges) when you're pressing and distributing a limited run from 250 to 2,500 CDs in the United States or creating 150 to 2,500 permanent downloads of a song to be distributed from a server located within the U.S. By covering a popular song, you can generate interest in your own band. As long as you take care of business properly, everyone wins!

Duration of Copyright

Getting close to the end of this chapter, I'd say you know enough about copyright to be curious about how long you get to own one of these valuable creatures. You're also ready to learn whether you can ever get these rights back should you transfer them in a contract with an established music publisher. Let's take a look at the copyright term, reversion of copyright, and right of termination.

The Copyright Term

When discussing the term of a copyright (or copyright "duration") I'm going to keep things simple and focus on the U.S. Copyright Act of 1976 (effective January 1, 1978) and the latest amendments regarding the copyright term.

Self-Written Songs: Your Life Plus 70

All compositions written on or after January 1, 1978, receive a copyright term for *the life of the author plus 70 years*. I know you can't take your prize possessions with you when you die, but your family (for instance) can enjoy the fruits of your labor for another 70 years after you pass—as long as you properly manage your affairs in a will that transfer these rights to them.

By the way, until not too long ago (1998), the duration of copyright was only life plus 50 years. But thanks to the late, great Sonny Bono (who was married to Cher) and something called the Sonny Bono Copyright Term Extension Act, the copyright term was amended to life plus 70 for all compositions written on or after January 1, 1978. So be sure to give a shout out to ol' Sonny!

Joint Works: Last Author's Life Plus 70

The copyright term for joint works is 70 years after the death of the last surviving author.

Works Made for Hire: 95, or 120

The copyright term for a work made for hire lasts for *95 years from publication or 120 years from creation*, whichever comes sooner.

Public Domain: A Long Time

After the copyright term has ended, the composition falls into something called the "public domain," which essentially means that anyone can use the composition free of licensing fees (Congress apparently feels that this is something for the betterment of society and that it furthers the arts, while not giving any one person too much control of their copyrighted works). But don't worry; by the time your works fall into the public domain, you won't mind if someone uses your work for free, because you'll be a long time gone.

Okay, enough of this morbid stuff. I suggest you get around to reading more about public domain and the copyright term in general at www.copyright.gov, but let's move on for now.

AFTERTHOUGHT: PUBLIC DOMAIN OR NOT? Should you ever want to find out whether a song is in the public domain, perhaps to rearrange it or to create a new derivative from which you can earn royalties, the Copyright Office conducts detailed searches of its databases on your behalf at a cost, and offers a number of other options, too. See www.copyright.gov and circular 22.

Reversion of Copyright

So what happens when you transfer or sell your copyrights, as in the case when you sign a publishing agreement? Are you permanently transferring ownership and other rights for the life of the copyright (LOC)? The answer is yes! Well, sort of.

A Clause Found in Publishing Agreements

In most publishing contracts there's a clause incorporated into your agreement called "reversion of copyright."

The reversion of copyright clause stipulates that your copyrights will revert to you, under certain conditions, at a predetermined time in the future (say, about 10 years after your contract expires and all advances have been recouped). This is great news, right? Yes! Well, sort of!

Up for Negotiation: Not Part of Copyright Law

Reversion of copyright is not part of actual copyright law; *it's a clause that must be negotiated by your attorney into your publishing agreement.* The good news is that when you have a little negotiating power and a good music entertainment attorney, getting reversion is not difficult.

Thirty-Five-Year Statutory Right of Termination

In the worst-case scenario, if you failed to negotiate a reversion clause in your agreement with a music publisher, or you just signed an all-out crappy deal, copyright law provides that you'll have another shot at getting your copyrights back. This is called the right of termination.

What It States

Thanks to a revision in the 1976 Copyright Act, the right of termination states that all original copyright owners (or their heirs) *will have a chance to reacquire ownership 35 years after the date of copyright transfer.*

You'll have to successfully complete a number of legal formalities—which are way too confusing to deal with given the scope of this book—but with a smart attorney helping you out, you should be fine.

Richard Berry, who wrote the song "Louie Louie," sold the rights to the song for $750 after he was convinced it had had its run. However, after the song was covered by the Kingsmen, it had a rebirth, was licensed in a variety of different media, and played all over the radio for years. According to my sources, termination rights eventually helped Berry to get the song back.

Applies to U.S. Only

Termination laws have some limitations. For one, they only apply within the United States and to new licenses issued after the termination date. Thus, the original music publisher still keeps all foreign rights and has the right to continue to collect on any licenses issued prior to the termination.

Works "Not" Made for Hire Only

Another limitation to the termination laws is that it applies only to works *not* made for hire. Once again, a work made for hire is when you're hired to compose under the scope of very specific guidelines, and the employer, not you, owns the resulting copyright. Since you never own the copyright in a work-made-for-hire condition, you can never get the song back.

Better Than Nothing, but Fight for Reversion

Finally, while 35 years is a long time, remember that right of termination can be a godsend if you wrote a hit song that's stayed active over the decades and you have no other way to get it back.

Kyle Staggs, director of music business affairs at Universal Pictures, does a great job at wrapping this section up:

> You'll never get the same results by relying on the copyright termination laws as you will with reversionary language, but it is still good to know that termination laws exist. What I'm really saying is this: termination laws can be helpful, but fight damn hard to get reversionary language negotiated into your publishing agreement. If you are ever so lucky as to write a hit, but unlucky enough to sign a bad deal, reversion will be your savior.

So that's about it, folks. Now let's move on to more advanced copyright basics in chapter 16. Good work!

16

Music Publishing, Part 2

Even More Copyright Basics

"The copyright bargain: a balance between protection for the artist and rights for the consumer." —Robin Gross, attorney

Rejoice! You've come a long way in our discussion about copyrights, and now we can talk more thoroughly about advanced issues. These include copyright registration, the copyright notice, copyright infringement, and even a few words about sound recording copyrights. Finishing off this chapter, attorney Steve Winogradsky answers a few important questions about foreign copyright, mix tapes, and the copyright challenges that face the music industry today.

Copyright Registration

When the big day comes for your songs to be commercially distributed to the public—such as when you decide to press your own CDs or vinyl and sell them at your shows, or you decide to prepare your music for digital distribution and sell and stream it from various websites—it's strongly recommended to register your compositions with the Copyright Office.

As previously mentioned, as soon as you give your original idea a tangible form, you automatically have a copyright. So, you might ask, what precisely are the benefits of copyright registration? What are the requirements? And how do I get it all done?

The Benefits of Copyright Registration

Registering your compositions with the Copyright Office in Washington, D.C., makes a public record of the basic facts of your songs. There are three other specific benefits:

Rebuttable Presumption of Ownership

First, you get the "rebuttable presumption" that you're the original author and owner of a composition. This means that as long as you register a work within five years of its first publication, the burden of proof falls on any other party that says the contrary. So just remember that if you randomly register the next Madonna single, you won't get very far in a court of law when valuable evidence indicates you're lying.

Right to File an Infringement Case

Second, you get the right to file an infringement case in a court of law should someone use one of your compositions without your permission, knowledge, and/or compensation. Another way to say this is *you "cannot" file an infringement case until you register your compositions with the Copyright Office.*

Potential to Receive Court Fees and Statutory Damages

And third, you may qualify to receive court fees as well as "statutory damages" in an infringement case.

Statutory damages are a fee set by a judge when the "actual damages" of an infringement are difficult to prove. The amount awarded for just one act of infringement (such as a shipment of your band's counterfeited recordings) can range anywhere from $500 to $150,000.

To qualify for statutory damages, you must register before someone infringes your copyright, which is pretty difficult to plan, because you never know when someone is going to screw you. Therefore, Kyle Staggs at Universal Pictures suggests that "the most prudent course of action is to register all of your copyrights either (1) as unpublished works prior to the initial release date or (2) within three months of the initial release date. Without this, you may even find it difficult to find an attorney to represent you in an infringement case. So just register."

Requirements of Registration

Now that you've got the benefits of registration down, you should know that registration with the Copyright Office requires the copyright author/claimant/agent to do three things:

- Fill out an application form.
- Pay a non-refundable fee.
- Submit a non-returnable "deposit copy" (such as a CD) of the complete work(s) being registered. (Both words and music on a phonorecord should be clear and audible.)

Methods of Registration

Be clear that there are essentially two different methods for registering your copyrights: offline and online.

Offline: Paper Registration ($85 per Song)

You can download the forms you'll need to register your songs from the Copyright Office website (www.copyright.gov) by clicking on the tab "Register a Copyright" and selecting form PA (performing arts) for your words and music. Note that if you also own the sound recording of your music, you can use form SR (sound recording).

Mail the completed application form, a check or money order (in the amount of $85 per song), and a deposit copy or copies to the following address: Library of Congress, U.S. Copyright Office, 101 Independence Avenue, SE, Washington, D.C. 20559.

Online: Electronic Registration ($35 or $55 per Song)

You can also register your songs online via the Copyright Office website (www.copyright.gov) by clicking on the tab "Register a Copyright" followed by "Log in to eCO" (the electronic copyright office).

This method is 1) cheaper (you pay $35 for each one of your songs, as long as you are the sole author of the song and master), 2) faster (you receive a certificate of registration within three to six months as opposed to potentially years), and 3) more convenient (you can upload deposit copies as electronic files and pay for everything with a credit card). Note: For a joint work with multiple authors/owners, the cost is $55 per online registration—still a better deal than paper registration.

Tips to Save Money

Okay, so now you understand how to register your songs, but you aren't very happy about the extra fees. Right? Well, if funds are tight, there are two alternative forms of registration you may want to consider: collection of works and supplementary registration.

Registering a Collection of Works

To save money, you can register all of your compositions on one registration under a "collection of works" for $55, as long as all the songs are unpublished works and written by the same author(s), or they are published works as one complete album and written by the same author(s).

For instance, you can register a batch of 10 unpublished songs under the title "John and Jane Doe's Summer Songs of Love" (sappy, but you get the point), as long as each song was written by John and Jane Doe. Or you can register a published album containing 10 songs, titled "John and Jane Doe's Debut Album" (or whatever), as long as each song was written by John and Jane Doe. If registering online and uploading files (up to 135 three-minute standard 128 kbps bitrate MP3 files permitted), the cost would only be $55, instead of $550 for 10 separate joint registrations.

However, since all of the compositions will be indexed in the copyright database under one title, this form of registration is not as effective, because individual songs will be more difficult to locate if someone is searching for them. Note that a person might request a database search when he or she is trying to determine the status of protection for one of your songs, or trying to hunt you down for licensing opportunities because they can't find you elsewhere.

Registering a Collection of Works and Supplementary Registration

To both save money and secure a more effective form of registration than what a collection of works offers, Kyle Staggs of Universal Pictures suggests that you first file a collection of works online for $55, and then follow up soon after with a supplementary registration of the individual titles for a fee of approximately $130. (That's a total of $185.)

Notes Stagg, "By filing a collection of works and supplementary registration, each title will be indexed, making it easy for any third party to find you."

AFTERTHOUGHT: NEED MORE INFO? For more detailed and up-to-the-minute registration information, call the Copyright Office at 202-707-3000 or 877-476-0778, go online to www.copyright.gov and click on electronic copyright office or forms, or download Copyright Circular 50.

The Copyright Notice

Now that you've read the section on copyright registration, it's the perfect time to talk about putting a notice of copyright on all of that wonderful art you create and distribute to your public.

Do You Really Need the Notice?

As of the United States' official entry into the Berne Convention (an international copyright treaty), which occurred with the Berne Convention Implementation Act on March 1, 1989, a copyright notice is no longer as important as it was.

However, including a notice on your works (especially those works that are "visibly perceptible") is prudent, since it clearly indicates to others that you're serious about protecting the work you so proudly publish. Furthermore, should someone rip you off, the defendant in a case can't claim that he or she didn't know your work was protected, because its status will be obvious!

What Is the Correct Way to Write the Notice?

There are a few different ways that you can write the copyright notice on visibly perceptible works (such as lyrics in liner notes). What follows is the method that I prefer to use most:

1. Write the word "copyright" followed by a circle with a C in the middle (©).
2. Include the year of first publication (the date when you distributed it to the public). And finally . . .
3. Include the author's name and/or publishing company name.

For example, if publishing their words and music in 2020, John and Jane Doe might write the following: Copyright © 2020 by John and Jane Doe Music. (Note: If you prefer, you can also abbreviate: © 2020 by John and Jane Doe Music, or Copyright 2020 by John and Jane Doe Music.)

Why Are There So Many Different Notices on Album Covers?

When examining your collection of vinyl, CDs, cassette tapes, or whatever else you have lying around your studio, you'll see that there are often a variety of notices and names included. This is because there are typically a variety of different works of authorship that are part of albums.

- ***Lyrics:*** The author/owner of the lyrics printed visibly on the inside booklet (which could be you and other cowriters) is indicating his or her copyright.
- ***Artwork:*** The author/owner of the artwork in which your music is packaged (which could be you or the record label) is indicating his or her copyright.
- ***Master:*** The author/owner of the sound recording in which your music is embodied (which could be you or the record label) is indicating his or her copyright. Note: Masters have an entirely different copyright than your songs, noted by a circle with a P in the middle (℗). We'll discuss masters more later, I promise.

So, that's about all for this section on notices. Now let's talk about what happens when people ignore your rights and infringe your copyrights anyway! Roll up your sleeves, and get ready to fight!

Copyright Infringement

You've taken all the steps we've discussed to ensure the maximum protection of your songs, so you shouldn't have anything to worry about—right? Wrong! Even after you've made a public notice of your songs by registering them with the copyright office, infringements can still occur.

What Is Infringement?

Section 501 of the Copyright Act states that copyright infringement occurs when someone uses your original works without your permission, knowledge, or compensation.

Rapper Vanilla Ice ripped off David Bowie and Queen's classic "Under Pressure" when he recorded and distributed his hit "Ice Ice Baby." And Led Zeppelin ripped off Willie Dixon's song "You Need Love" when it recorded and distributed "Whole Lotta Love." The list of infringement examples can fill this page. You probably know of a few cases yourself.

Any Substantial Damage?

When you discover that someone is infringing on your rights, you must first consider what the damage really is. Of course, in principle it's wrong (how dare someone steal your art!) and it's your right to stop them from doing it, but for any attorney or judge to take an infringement case seriously, you need to have suffered a substantial loss.

For instance, if you hear your song played in a television commercial or in a movie, or see it released by a major label and on sale on iTunes, you've probably suffered a loss of income as a result. However, if you hear that your former bandmates recorded one of the songs you cowrote with them and sold 20 copies of the CD in the past year, there's really very little damage other than your hurt feelings. You can hire an attorney for $150 to $300 (or more) to write a cease and desist letter (demanding your former band stop selling the song without your permission), but the real truth is that no one really gives a damn.

What Do You Have to Prove?

To illustrate what you may have to prove when someone infringes your rights, let's take a look at a real-life case study between a major label band and an unsigned local opening act.

In the early 1990s, a small, unsigned band hired an attorney to sue a successful major label recording artist for copyright infringement (sorry, the names must remain confidential here). In the suit, the band claimed that the artist's hit song contained a chorus that was an exact replica (both melodically and lyrically) of one of their own.

Here's how it all went down.

1. ***Registration:*** The band showed that they had registered the published song with the Copyright Office within three months of the first publication, which was long *before* the major-label act had registered it.
2. ***Access:*** The band was able to prove the likelihood that the artist could have stolen its composition. This is called "proving access"—the local band had opened for the artist on several occasions and had newspaper clippings and testimonials from the promoter to back it up.
3. ***Substantially Similar:*** The band was able to show that the artist's chorus was "substantially similar" to their own. A music expert testified and matched the notes of the two songs side-by-side on a staff.
4. ***Unique in Character:*** The band and its music experts were able to show that their chorus was so unique in character, it undoubtedly had not been copied unintentionally. In other words, the infringement was "willful."
5. ***Witnesses:*** The band brought in a witness whose life the lyrics documented—a friend who had been in a serious car accident and almost died.
6. ***Proof of Publication:*** The band exhibited newspaper clippings showing the recording for sale with mention of the song in question as the featured track.
7. ***Damage:*** The band was able to show that they had suffered substantial financial loss as a result of the infringement, by showing Soundscan reports of sales and *Billboard* charts indicating the song's charting position.

Needless to say, there was substantial evidence in the band's favor. The case was settled out of court, and the band received an undisclosed sum of money. Bam!

Sampling and Infringement

Moving into a more frequent area of copyright infringement, let's talk briefly about "samples." Samples are song snippets (either rerecorded or lifted from an existing sound recording) to enhance a musical track.

While there is a lot of confusion in this area, just be clear that samples require permission from, and compensation to, the copyright holders of the music and/or the copyright holders of the sound recording (which may be two or more separate entities).

No, you cannot use up to four bars of music (such as a significant guitar melody or riff) without it being a copyright infringement.

By not properly "clearing" a sample use before releasing a project, you are accepting the risk of having to either 1) clear the rights at a later date for a much higher fee/split, or 2) defend yourself in an infringement lawsuit. Plain and simple. So be careful!

FAIR USE DEFENSE: DON'T TRY THIS AT HOME

While on the topic of samples and infringement, you should know about a case involving 2 Live Crew versus Roy Orbison, and something called fair use in copyright law.

Fair use is a defense that alleged infringing parties often use. Fair use means that small amounts of copyrighted material can be legally reproduced for purposes of critical review, parody, news reporting, teaching, etc. without getting a license and paying a fee.

Rappers 2 Live Crew composed a song "Pretty Woman" using the intro and first line of lyrics to Roy Orbison's "Oh Pretty Woman" and released it.

A lawsuit by Orbison's camp followed and the ruling shocked many. The judge felt that although 2 Live Crew's song contained parts that were significantly similar to Orbison's original, 2 Live Crew's version contained social criticism and parody of Orbison's original, and thus 2 Live Crew's version qualified as a fair use.

Just don't try this at home, folks! It's touchy stuff that could land you in a long battle.

Best Course of Prevention

Finally, to close out this section on infringement, you may be wondering what's the best course of protection against being infringed and against infringing others.

Against Being Infringed

The best course of protection is to do the following: work with reputable people, acknowledge your contributions to coauthored songs in writing, and register your songs prior to their publication (or within three months of the date of publication). That's really all anyone can do!

Against Infringing Others

As for being careful not to infringe others' rights, be mindful when sampling other people's works—an area where infringement is most likely—and get proper clearances and permissions from the publishers (and/or master owners) prior to publication.

Further, should you create something original that sounds too familiar, know that it just might belong to someone else—ask your peers to identify the source before you run off and record and distribute it. Would you believe that John Lennon (yes, the almighty Beatle) was charged for "accidental infringement"? Yup, it's true!

More on Copyright: Sound Recordings Are Copyrights, Too

Let's finish this chapter with a discussion of sound recording copyrights.

In case you didn't just have a big "aha moment," the music and lyrics of a song are a copyright, and the series of sounds that make up a recording of that song are a separate and distinct copyright. This means that if you write and produce as a DIY artist, you may own two copyrights in one recording. Hurray!

Key Points of Distinction

While much of what we already discussed about a copyright in your words and music applies to the "sounds" fixed on recordings, here a few key points of distinction:

- ***Laws Are Newer:*** Before 1972, a sound recording copyright did not exist (strange as this sounds, being that copyright dates back to 1909)—only common laws or statutes enacted in certain states provided protection in sounds. Thanks to stricter anti-piracy laws in 1972 and amendments in the Copyright Act of 1976, master recordings created today are better protected and are recognized as a "sound recording copyright."
- ***Authors/Owners and Works Made for Hire:*** The author and owner of a sound recording is typically the performer(s) whose performance is fixed, the record producer who processes the sounds and fixes them in the final recording, or both. However, in most recording situations, the record company (which could be you) tries to maintain these rights via explicit contract language that waives the creators' rights.
- ***Registration:*** The registration of a sound recording copyright with the Copyright Office in Washington, D.C., requires a separate registration from your musical compositions. However, in certain cases (such as when the owner of the sound recording and the musical composition are the same person), the underlying work may be registered together with the sound recording. See copyright circular 56A via the Copyright Office website (www.copyright.gov) for more information.
- ***Notice:*** Notice of copyright for a sound recording is represented by a circle with a P inside (℗), rather than a circle with a C inside (©). I'm looking at the back of one of my favorite Led Zeppelin albums right now, and it says "Copyright © ℗ 1972 Atlantic Recording Corporation" on the back to indicate the label's ownership in both the artwork on the album and the sound recording.
- ***Limitations of Exclusive Rights:*** The authors and owners of sound recording copyrights are entitled to "exclusive rights" (reproduction, distribution, performance, derivative) similar to the rights of songwriters. However, there are some limitations.
  - **Soundalikes:** Others can legally create soundalikes (imitations) of your sound recordings as long as they make it clear that they are not the original. For instance, a producer may be able to get the rights from the owner of a musical composition to sample a piece of music, and then create (or replay) the sound recording to sound like the original without getting the rights from the sound recording owner.
  - **Terrestrial Broadcasts:** Transmissions of sound recording copyrights (i.e., AM and FM radio stations that go over the air) do not require payment to the authors or owners of the sound recordings. This was written into law back into 1972 and is something that sound recording owners have been battling for years.
- ***New Exclusive Rights for Digital Performances of Sound Recordings:*** The good news is that amendments in the Copyright Act specific to sound recordings provide for an exclusive right for "audio-only" performances online. More specifically, the Digital Performance Right in Sound Recordings Act of 1995 and the Digital Millennium Copyright Act of 1998 established that "non-interactive" broadcasters (that "do not allow for customization" of their service—e.g., web radio stations like Pandora, satellite radio like SiriusXM, etc.) have the right to broadcast master recordings but must pay a set fee to the owners (the record companies), *including the musicians on the sound recordings*. SoundExchange (www.soundexchange.com), a company appointed by Congress, collects these monies and splits them up—50 percent to labels, 45 percent to featured musicians on sound recordings, and 5 percent to the unions representing the non-featured musicians (the AFM for musicians and SAG-AFTRA for vocalists).

That's about all! Just be clear that the rights in your music and lyrics are a copyright, and the series of sounds that make up a recording of these songs are a separate copyright. In most cases, each requires a separate license and fee to the authors and owners.

Thanks for hanging in throughout this chapter. If you'd like, please read on just a bit further. Attorney Steve Winogradsky offers the answers to some frequently asked questions. Really good stuff! Check it out.

Q&A with Attorney Steve Winogradsky

Steve Winogradsky is a partner in Winogradsky/Sobel, a firm providing music licensing, clearance, administration, and other business and legal services to composers, songwriters, publishers, recording artists, and multimedia producers. The author of *Music Publishing: The Complete Guide* (Alfred Publishing 2013), an adjunct professor at California State University, Northridge, and an instructor at UCLA Extension, Steve decodes a few frequently asked questions, including international issues and future challenges.

Q: How is copyright protected outside of the United States?

S.W.: The Berne Convention, which is just one of many international copyright treaties, states generally that the author/owner of an original work shall enjoy protection in other countries that have signed the Berne agreement.

The author's work is governed exclusively by the laws of the country where protection is first claimed. However, if a work is published simultaneously in several countries, the signatory country that has the shortest term of protection is defined as the country of origin.

There are over 167 countries along with the U.S. that are signatories of the Berne Convention. Rather than list them all, it might be easier to list non-signatories (including Iran, Iraq, and Afghanistan). For more specific information, see www.copyright.gov/circs/circ38a.pdf.

Q: Foreign versus U.S. copyright—what's the difference?

S.W.: The copyright term, moral rights, and sound recording copyrights may provide three examples of how foreign copyright differs from U.S. copyright. I'll explain each of these:

- ***Term:*** Countries that are signatories to the Berne Convention provide for a minimum of at least 50 years after the death of the last surviving author. Japan and Taiwan provide for life plus 50. India provides for a term that's a little longer—life plus 60. But in the United States the term of copyright (for works created after January 1, 1978) is even longer—life of the last surviving author plus 70 years.
- ***Moral Rights:*** The concept of "moral rights," or *droit moral*, is recognized in certain European countries and Canada, granting the creators certain rights in how their work is used, even if they no longer own the work. This includes the right of attribution (credit) and the right to preserve the integrity of the work from alteration, distortion, and even mutilation. The United States does not fully recognize moral rights in its copyright laws.
- ***Sound Recordings:*** Finally, sound recording copyrights are protected outside the United States in a way that requires terrestrial broadcasters (i.e., radio stations that broadcast on the air) to pay licensing fees to sound recording owners. The United States is one of the only countries that does not recognize these rights. In fact, sound recordings were not even granted U.S. copyright protection until February 15, 1972.

Q: Is there a legal difference between selling and merely "distributing" an infringing work?

S.W.: Many artists feel they can borrow copyrighted material from other artists to demonstrate their talents and pay homage to the authors (as with mix tapes), as long as they don't sell the works.

However, the rights of reproduction and distribution are exclusive rights of the copyright owner and are not waived just because copies are given away and not sold. Any reproduction or distribution without proper permission and payment is an infringement of copyright.

Q: We hear some beats turning up again and again in many different songs by many different artists. How does this happen?

S.W.: Young artists these days often create works by finding (or leasing) beats from various producers or online services, such as the sample licensing platform SoundClick (www.soundclick.com).

With most sample libraries like this, the license from the company grants a user the right to include those samples in new works. The new work has its own copyright protection, both as a composition and as a sound recording. But other parties can license the same beat at the same time and include it in their new works, which receive their own distinct copyright protection.

Often, however, you may have the option to license beats "exclusively" at a higher price, which may be the way to go if you want to guard against the possibility of several artists using the same beat at the same time.

Q: What are the greatest challenges for protecting copyright today?

S.W.: The greatest challenge that copyright laws face today is keeping pace with the changes in technology. New methods of distribution and new business models are popping up all the time, and the current laws do not always take them into account.

Although there is discussion about undertaking a major revision, Congress moves slowly to modify the Copyright Act. And, when a change does go through, will it cover anything that comes up the day after a new law is passed? Hopefully, there will be some forward-thinking parties involved in the revision process.

Also, parties within the industry need to resolve their differences so that everyone is treated fairly. There are still major differences in how record companies and music publishers are compensated in various media, causing those factions to continue to argue about who gets what share of income. Add to that the desire of broadcasters and websites to pay as little for music as possible, and the whole business model could fall apart. Stay tuned as the drama unfolds.

17

Music Publishing, Part 3

Income Streams—Mechanicals, Performances, and Print

"Music is an art. Making a living from it is a serious business."
—Billy Mitchell, author, The Gigging Musician

Congratulations and welcome to part 3! You've come a long way. Now that you understand a little bit about copyrights, we can begin to talk more about the process of music publishing.

In this chapter, we'll focus on shares of the publishing pie and publishing incomes (including mechanical royalties, performance royalties, and print). There's a lot to cover and this is all important stuff, so grab that cup of coffee and that yellow highlighter pen, and let's get this party started.

Shares of the Publishing Pie

There's an interesting tradition in the publishing business for naming the different shares of income on a composition.

By virtue of creating a song (i.e., a copyright), you automatically inherit both a writer's share and a publisher's share of income for all of your time and effort. That's right! I bet you didn't know that. Let's take a closer look.

Writer's Share

The writer's share is bestowed upon you for all the wonderful artistic things you do, such as coming up with the words, melody, or hooky beat or track.

Publisher's Share

The publisher's share is bestowed upon you for all the business responsibilities you have, like owning the copyright, issuing licenses, and collecting monies.

How Is the Money Divided?

When money from deals comes in, the writer (which is you) is allocated a 50 percent share, and the publisher (which is also you) is allocated the other 50 percent share. If one dollar is collected by the publisher, who takes 50 cents, the balance of 50 cents goes to the writer.

Does This All Seem Crazy?

If this sounds crazy, it is, but it's just the way the publishing system works. It's like having dual personalities making good use of both sides of the brain; the right side, or creative side, is the writer, and the left side, or analytical side, is the music publisher—but there's still one brain!

You may ask, "Can't I transfer the publishing ownership and business responsibility to an experienced music publisher so that I can concentrate more on being a creative writer?"

Absolutely! In fact, "publisher" in the following text can mean you or an established publishing company. But before we get into the details of publishing deals, you'll want to understand a few more things about the income you might earn when your songs are released to your adoring public.

Types of Publishing Income

There are several types of income derived from music publishing:

- Mechanical royalties
- Performance royalties
- Print royalties
- Synchronization fees
- Electronic transmissions
- Foreign sub-publishing incomes

We'll discuss these here and in the next chapter, starting with mechanical royalties.

Mechanical Royalties

As defined by the United States Copyright Act and established by provisions set in law, mechanical royalties are licensing fees (paid typically by the record company) for the use of your songs on "audio-only" recordings. For simplicity, I'll focus on CDs and vinyl in this section, though note that a mechanical is also a digital download, a ringtone, and more—we'll look at those later.

Don't confuse mechanical royalties with artist record royalties (discussed in chapters 13 and 14). While both have to do with the sale of your records, artist record royalties are percentages that are usually based on the wholesale published price to dealer (or the suggested retail price), subject to the recoupment of numerous recording and other expenses—meaning you may never get paid these royalties.

Mechanical royalties, however, are mandatory payments by law and should not (unless you agree to it) be subject to recoupment of recording costs by a record label.

A Brief Backstory

Mechanical royalties have quite a long and interesting story—from why they are called a mechanical, to the evolution of the statutory rate over the years, to who decides on the rates.

Why Is It Called a "Mechanical" Royalty?

The word "mechanical" refers back to the old days when music was mechanically fixed or copied to piano rolls—the ones you see in western movies when the piano plays by itself.

The word "royalty" simply refers to the money you get from the reproduction of your work.

Put the two words together and you get "mechanical royalty." Piano rolls are no longer around, but the name has obviously stuck.

The Evolution of the Statutory (or "Stat") Rate

Before the Copyright Act of 1976 (effective January 1, 1978), the statutory mechanical licensing rate had been just 2 cents per song for over 60 years. After rising to 2.75 cents per composition in 1978, the rates rose incrementally until they came to a sudden halt in 2006.

The Current Statutory Rate

Today, the current statutory mechanical licensing rates for CDs and vinyl hold as follows:

- **Songs of Five Minutes or Less:** 9.1 cents per composition per record made and distributed (which is the rate sometimes referred to as the "minimum statutory rate"). So, if you write a song that is three minutes long, you get 9.1 cents.
- **Songs Greater Than Five Minutes in Length:** 1.75 cents per minute per composition made and distributed (which is the rate sometimes referred to as the "maximum statutory rate"). If you write a composition that's five minutes and 10 seconds long, it's rounded up to six minutes (1.75 × 6 minutes = 10.5 cents).

Who Decides on the Rates?

Presently, a panel of copyright royalty judges, often referred to as the Copyright Royalty Board (CRB), adjusts the statutory rates. There has been a lot of heat in this area lately, so keep your ears open for changes by checking the Copyright Office website (www.copyright.gov) or the Harry Fox Agency website (www.harryfox.com). In fact, a re-examination of the statutory rate is set for 2017.

Is This All Subject to Change for Signed Artists?

Finally, you should know that a great deal of what you just learned about mechanical royalties is subject to change when you're a signed recording artist, or you're writing songs for, or with, a signed recording artist. Why? Because of a provision found in recording contracts called the "controlled composition clause."

The Controlled Composition Clause (CC Clause)

No matter what copyright law might say about mechanical royalties and your rights, controlled composition clauses ask artists essentially to waive their rights and to accept less favorable terms.

These terms, which we are about to examine, apply to any song written or cowritten by you, and any song in which you have an income or other interest.

While controlled composition clauses were once the most important section of any recording deal, they are becoming somewhat less important due to the following conditions:

- They only apply to CDs and vinyl (since downloads and ringtones are explicitly exempt, thanks to the Digital Performance Right in Sound Recordings Act of 1995).
- CD sales are slowly diminishing, and streaming music (which pays different rates that we'll discuss later) is becoming the standard. And . . .
- Many artists are releasing records themselves and are not signing deals at all.

All things said, CC clauses are still extremely important to understand, so read on for a brief overview of the many deductions that your record label will take.

Key Deductions Found in CC Clauses

There are about 10 ways that the record company will chisel down your payments. Here goes:

1. **The Minimum (Five or Less) Rate:** No matter how long your songs are, the record label bases your mechanical royalty on the "minimum statutory rate" (i.e., the five-minutes-or-less rate, or 9.1 cents). I wouldn't worry about this deduction, though. Unless you're doing something really wrong, most radio-friendly songs average 3.5 minutes.
2. **The Controlled (Three-Quarter) Rate:** The record company also typically reduces the minimum statutory rate to 75 percent of the rate (i.e., $0.091 × .75 = $0.068, or 6.8 cents per song). This is called the "controlled rate" or the "three-quarter rate." Note that escalations can be negotiated on subsequent albums. For instance, on albums three and four, the label might pay you 85 percent of the minimum stat rate (i.e., $0.091 × .85 = $0.077, or 7.7 cents per song). But again, this is negotiable.
3. **The Cap (10 Songs):** The record company via the controlled composition clause also sets a limit on the amount of money it will pay per album. Whether you have 10 songs on your album or 14, the label typically pays on an equivalent of 10 songs (e.g., $0.068 × 10 songs = $0.68 or 68 cents). Thus, if there are 14 songs on an album, you will only get $0.049 per song ($0.68 ÷ 14 = $0.049). But, with all things said, if you are an artist with a strong buzz, the cap might be negotiable to a 12-song limit.
4. **Changing Rates:** Although the statutory mechanical rate is subject to change (i.e., to go up), the CC clause also locks in your rate on the day your record is delivered or released. For example, if the label released your record on December 31, 2005, when the statutory rate was $0.085, you would be paid a percentage of that rate (i.e., .75 × $0.085 per composition), even though the rate rose to $0.091 on January 1, 2006 and has stayed there.
5. **Free Goods Reduction (or Just 85 Percent of Sales):** The CC clause also reduces the number of records you're paid on. Despite what the laws say (that mechanicals are paid on all records made and distributed), the label only pays on 85 records out of every 100 records shipped. The other 15 percent is counted by the label as "standard free goods"—a so-called discount the label claims it offers to retailers to buy your record ("for every 100, 15 are free"). Because the label doesn't get paid on the 15 records, they treat them as "non-royalty-bearing records." If you have negotiating power, the record label may agree to pay mechanicals on 50 percent of the 15 percent standard free goods (i.e., 92.5 percent of all CDs and vinyl sold).
6. **Reserves:** Moving on to CC clause deduction number 6, the record company pays you only for "records that are sold and not returned by retailers." To ensure that they make no mistakes in their accounting, they'll withhold 50 to 75 percent of your mechanicals for up to four quarters (one year) after the reserves were first taken. Yikes.
7. **Midprice Records and Budget Records:** The record company further reduces your mechanical rate by 75 percent (e.g., .75 × $0.68 = $0.51, or 51 cents) for "midprice records" (i.e., records marked down to between 60 and 80 percent of the full price). And they will reduce your royalty 50 percent (e.g., .50 × $0.68 = $0.34, or 34 cents) for "budget records" (i.e., records marked down to below 60 percent of the full price).
8. **Promotional Records:** For records that are shipped by the record company to retailers during special promotions, or for free "promotional records" given to radio stations that are marked "not for sale," the labels will not pay a mechanical royalty at all. I guess, the way the label sees it, if they are not getting paid, then neither are you.
9. **Video Limitations:** The record company insists that it will not pay you mechanicals for compositions reproduced in "promotional" videos (such as YouTube-type videos) or "home videos" (like concert DVDs and "making of"–type DVDs). Mark Goldstein, former vice president of legal affairs at Warner Bros. Records, notes that the licensing fee the record company is referring to here is essentially

a synchronization fee (which you'll learn about later in chapter 18). However, the language under the video limitation clause is often kept broad enough to cover any other kind of fee that might possibly come up.

10. **Outside Songs:** Finally, since cover songs or wholly written songs are considered "non-controlled" and not privy to the CC clause (since you do not have any ownership interest in these compositions), the label makes sure that overages are on you. What I mean is this: suppose you have a three-quarter rate (6.8 cents per song) and a cap of 10 songs (68 cents per record). If you compose 8 songs and use 2 outside songs licensed at 9.1 cents for each (18.2 cents total), your per-song rate will be lowered from 6.8 cents to 6.2 cents per song (68 cents cap, less 18.2 cents for outside songs, equals 49.8 cents; divided by the 8 songs you wrote, this comes to 6.2 cents per song). More advanced artists have some negotiating power in this area, but until you move up the ranks, just keep in mind that the fee paid to the publisher to use an outside song comes out of your cap per record, which ultimately reduces the mechanical royalties paid to you.

THE HARRY FOX AGENCY (HFA)

While on the topic of mechanical royalties and mechanical licensing, you should know about a major organization called the Harry Fox Agency (HFA). You've probably heard about them already in the news, but I nonetheless introduce them in detail here.

- ***Who Is HFA?*** Founded in 1927 by the National Music Publishers Association (NMPA), the Harry Fox Agency (HFA) is the major mechanical rights society in the United States.
- ***What Does HFA Do?*** When a record company wants to use your composition on a phonorecord, a mechanical license must first be issued for this reproduction by the music publisher. HFA is more than happy to issue this license and monitor the record label to make sure the proper mechanical royalties are paid according to the number of records that are sold.
- ***Who Does Fox Represent?*** HFA represents well over 36,000 music publishers. In fact, Ed Pierson, formerly of Warner/Chappell Music, notes that most publishers, both big and small, use Harry Fox's services.
- ***What Are the Benefits of Using HFA?*** HFA is especially cost-effective for music publishers that represent a huge repertoire of songs, since they would otherwise have to employ their own staff just to keep up with the work. Another advantage of HFA's services is that the company periodically audits record companies. Audits can cost as much as $35,000. You might find it very disturbing to know that most record companies audited by HFA show an underpayment of royalties to music publishers. The truth is that record companies are known to get sloppy.
- ***What Does HFA Charge?*** HFA will issue mechanical licenses and collect royalties for a fee of approximately 8.7 percent of the gross mechanicals collected. This fee is known to change, so keep your eyes open for the latest news.
- ***How Can I Learn More About HFA?*** Visit www.harryfox.com to learn about HFA's licensing and royalty services, rights management, and new business opportunities.

Performance Royalties

Moving on from mechanical royalties, the second major type of income derived from music publishing is performance royalties.

Performance royalties are the monies that you receive for the public performance of your composition by a variety of different song users. Remember that as part of your exclusive rights assigned in the Copyright Act, anyone who wishes to perform your music publicly must obtain a license and pay you a fee.

This section briefly reveals who uses your music publicly, how performing rights licenses are issued, and which performing rights organization you should join to ensure payment.

Who Uses Your Music Publicly?

The first item concerning performance royalties that needs mentioning is precisely who uses music. While there are a variety of different entities, here are a just a few examples:

- ***Radio Stations***
- ***Television Networks***
- ***Cable TV Stations,*** such as HBO, MTV, and VH1
- ***Internet Sites***
- ***Digital Streaming Sites,*** including noninteractive webcasters like Pandora and satellite radio like SiriusXM
- ***Interactive Streaming Services,*** such as Spotify and Rhapsody
- ***Nightclubs***
- ***Bars***
- ***Concert Halls***
- ***Mobile App Providers***
- ***Businesses*** that use music "on hold"
- ***Shopping Malls***
- ***Funeral Homes***
- ***Skate Parks***
- ***In-flight Radio Stations***
- ***Hotels***
- ***Colleges and Universities*** and finally . . .
- ***Stores and Restaurants*** (note that stores under 2,000 square feet and bars and restaurants under 3,750 square feet are exempt)

AFTERTHOUGHT: WHAT ABOUT MOVIE THEATERS? Movie theaters are exempt from paying licensing fees. Why? It has to do with a 1948 lawsuit between Alden-Rochelle (a movie theater firm owned largely by film studios and producers) and ASCAP (a performing rights organization). You can learn more about the case by searching for it on the Department of Justice's website (www.justice.gov).

Who Issues Licenses to Music Users?

Now that you have a sense of the vast number of entities that use music, it is important to discuss generally how your music will be licensed. As I'm sure you can imagine, this is no simple task. Consider the following:

1. ***Determining Rates:*** Unlike a mechanical royalty (where there's an established fee for the use of your songs on phonorecord), the system in the performing rights area is much more intricate than simply saying that you get *x* amount of money for the performance of one of your compositions. The process requires substantial negotiations.
2. ***Licensing and Monitoring:*** Next, if you think about the number of radio stations that exist in the United States alone (over 10,000), it would appear impossible for smaller music publishers (or even the larger companies) to individually issue licenses to each and every one, collect royalty payments, and police the world to make sure that all other music users are paying licensing fees.

So, what are your licensing solutions if you can't handle these duties by yourself? Good question! This bring us to the next section on performing rights organizations (PROs). Read on.

Performing Rights Organizations (PROs) to the Rescue

Performing rights organizations were established to provide an efficient licensing system to the authors and owners of copyrights just like you and me.

The three major performing rights organizations in the United States are:

- ASCAP (The American Society of Composers, Authors, and Publishers)
- BMI (Broadcast Music, Inc.)
- SESAC (originally the Society of European Stage Authors and Composers)

While each organization conducts its business differently, all three have similar functions and one general principle: to protect the performing rights of songwriters and publishers. (Note: Global Rights Music, another company that deals with performing rights, has been getting a lot of attention lately. However, I'm leaving them out of our discussion for now since they are a relatively new company and rather small.)

Here's how the PROs generally operate.

Recruiting Affiliates

To follow through with their mission, PROs must first get music publishers and writers to both affiliate and register their compositions.

To help do this, PROs hire membership coordinators who speak at music business conferences, host informative workshops, and even arrange private meetings in their offices. Of course, the PROs also have detailed information on their websites.

Issuing Blanket Licenses

Next, on behalf of their affiliates, performing rights organizations issue "blanket licenses" to music users for a negotiated fee. These licenses grant music users the rights to use all of the compositions in the PRO's catalogue.

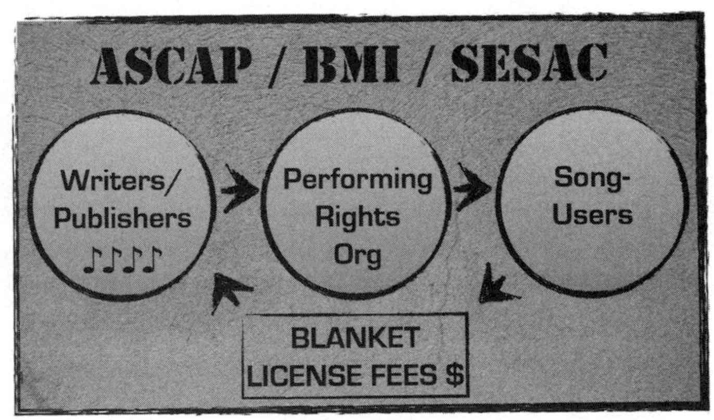

Collecting Licensing Fees

Moving on, the PROs then collect fees from music users and throw the money into a big pool to be divided up between all of the writers and publishers based, appropriately, on the number and type of performances.

Note that PROs attempt to determine fees for music users based on a number of variables. For instance, a radio station's broadcast range and/or yearly advertising revenue may determine licensing fees. If you're truly interested in detailed schedules of available licensing fees, check out each PRO's website or call a representative.

Monitoring Songs

As if all of the above were not enough, the PROs also monitor licensed song users to get a representation of the copyright titles broadcast during each royalty period; then they determine how much each publisher and writer should be paid.

Of the various media that might be monitored, PROs focus primarily on tracking radio stations, television and cable networks, digital service providers (streaming sites, satellite radio, etc.), and top-grossing concert tours, since these are still the primary sources of license proceeds and the easiest media to track.

If you want to read more about tracking methods, be sure to check out the boxed text below.

GENERAL MONITORING METHODS

While the methods of monitoring by the PROs are quite complex, what follows is an attempt to provide a basic overview. Not all organizations use the same approach. For more specific info, check each PRO's site.

- ***Radio:***
  - **Digital Monitoring Services:** PROs use monitoring technologies such as Nielsen Broadcast Data Systems, Mediabase, BlueArrowSM, and TuneSat. These work generally on the same principle: encoding songs with recognition technology, tracking, and uploading data into a centralized database where it can be retrieved.
  - **Logs:** PROs also use logs to monitor radio. Logs are a part of a sample survey whereby a diverse array of radio stations are asked to list every song they play over a two- to three-day reporting period each year. These playlists, including titles, artists, and the respective performing rights organizations, are then uploaded (or they can be sent in by e-mail) into a mainframe database, where the information is used to calculate the frequency and selection of songs being used on all other radio stations.
- ***Television:***
  - **Cue Sheets:** PROs receive and review cue sheets from television shows. A cue sheet is a producer or editor's instruction detailing what songs were used, the composer and publisher of each song, and how, when, and where each one was used. Cue sheets also include information about whether the use was for a feature, background, or theme. As attorney Steve Winogradsky puts it, a cue sheet serves as an "invoice" for the publishers and writers, advising the PROs on who needs to be paid for the music in any particular program.
  - **TV Data:** PROs review various data regarding programming for television, observe what shows actually air, and then match this with cue-sheet data to ensure payment.
  - **Digital Monitoring:** PROs also use digital monitoring methods as a supplement to cue sheets.
- ***Digital Service Providers (Spotify, etc.):***
  - **Checking Precise Data:** PROs receive detailed data from digital service providers for review.
- ***Top-Grossing Tours:***
  - **Reviewing Set Lists:** Finally, PROs also receive set lists of the top-grossing artists and tours from personal managers to determine payments due. From what I'm told, SESAC examines set lists of local bands performing in small venues as well.

Paying Royalties: Just How Accurate Are the PROs?

The last function of a PRO is to send out statements to its writers and publishers four times per year.

But just how efficient and accurate are the PROs? Consider the following:

- **Radio:** Since there are only so many hours of research performing rights organizations can conduct in a cost-effective manner, it's more likely that only songs frequently played on the radio get picked up through monitoring. Does this mean the system basically favors hit songs? I hate to say it, but generally, yes. You could end up with nothing. So much for the myth among musicians that every time your song is played on the radio, it's an automatic "cha-ching"—money in the bank. But with new developments in technology that allow more efficient tracking of radio play, this situation is likely to get better and better in the coming years.

- **Television:** As far as larger television stations are concerned, monitoring by cue sheets is relatively accurate. Therefore, if your song is performed on larger stations, even only once, it's likely you will receive payment. Hurray! However, for smaller stations that may be monitored by means other than cue sheets, note that it is still possible for your work to go unnoticed and unpaid. Sorry!
- **Digital Service Providers:** If you're wondering about the Internet and the monitoring of digital information, service providers do have the capability to maintain and report detailed data, but the PROs still have to figure out how to effectively sort through that data and report it accurately. Oh, darn! In any case, as previously stated, the licenses collected here are still only a fraction of those from the traditional media sources (radio and television) mentioned above, but things are getting better, especially with the popularity of streaming music sites.
- **Top-Grossing Tours:** Finally, the monitoring of live concerts (specifically the 200 top-grossing tours as reported in the magazine *Pollstar*) is getting more accurate and getting more attention. But again, the licensing monies generated here are hardly as substantial as those from radio and TV.

AFTERTHOUGHT: SO, HOW MUCH CAN A HIT SONG EARN? According to Jeff and Todd Brabec in their book *Music, Money, and Success*, one hit song on the radio can easily generate a total (combined writer/publisher earnings) of anywhere from $500,000 to $1 million in performance royalties a year. A theme song on a prime-time network television show can generate an average of $120,000 a year. Pretty nice, wouldn't you say?

PRO Affiliation: Making Sure You're Paid

Now that you understand a little more about what PROs do, it's a good time to discuss the process of PRO affiliation and title registration so you can ensure that you're paid.

Affiliating as the Writer and Publisher

There are two distinct methods of affiliation with the PROs: affiliation as a writer (which can be you), and affiliation as a publisher (which can also be you). Why two separate affiliations?

Note that the payment of performance royalties is quite different from the payment of other royalties derived from your songs. Rather than just collect licensing fees and send the appropriate shares to music publishers (who then pay the writers), PROs send writers their full writer's share of the earnings—*no matter if the writer is also the publisher, and no matter if the writer is signed with an established music publisher.* Supposedly this system was created to protect writers who were signed to unscrupulous companies.

In any case, as you can see, two separate affiliations are necessary.

Title Registrations Must Match

A title registration process is also required when affiliating with a PRO to ensure that you are paid. This involves providing basic information about your songs (e.g., title of song, percentages of ownership, etc.). But be clear that both the writer's registration of the song and the publisher's registration of the song must match and be at the same PRO.

To clarify, allow me to use my own PRO—ASCAP—in this example: If I compose an original song and own 100 percent of both the writer's and the publisher's share, I must affiliate 50 percent of the song (or 100 percent of the writer's share) with ASCAP, and 50 percent of the song (or 100 percent of the publisher's share) with ASCAP. And should I ever enter into a publishing agreement where I transfer the rights in my copyrights to an established music publisher, my publisher must register the publisher's share with ASCAP to match my writer's registration with ASCAP. Got it? Good!

Which PRO Should You Join?

And finally, now that you understand the affiliation process, I can wrap up this entire section with the number one issue on the minds of all you wonderful readers: which PRO should you join? Of course, a representative from each organization would argue that his or her PRO is best, but I share a few unbiased tips below that I believe will help you make your decision.

1. ***Consider the Additional Services and Benefits:*** Compare all of the different services that the PROs offer—PROs are not just about licensing, collecting, and administering. Find out about songwriting workshops, discounts to online classes, health-care benefits, credit card options, and conventions (such as the ASCAP I Create Music Expo held in Los Angeles each spring).
2. ***Visit the Reps and Go with the Right Vibe:*** Visit your local branch representative and simply get a sense of his or her vibe. Will this representative take your calls and answer your questions when you need help? Is he or she a pleasant person who makes you feel like you have a friend in the business? This is all super important, you know!
3. ***Do Your Homework:*** Finally, visit each PRO's site and read! Weigh how reasonable all of the information seems to you based on your specific needs. To help you, I've included a competitor analysis I created in the box below. Okay? Good luck!

So, that's pretty much it for performance royalties. Next up is print—the last section of this chapter. Hang in there, you're almost done.

PERFORMING RIGHTS ORGANIZATIONS AT A GLANCE

Below is a simple competitive analysis of the three major performing rights organizations in the U.S. Please keep in mind that information and rates are subject to change, but every effort was made to present the most up-to-date data. Enjoy.

- *History:*
  - **ASCAP:** ASCAP was established in 1914 and is run by writers and publishers. A nonprofit organization, it only holds on to a small amount of the money it collects for operating fees and then sends out the rest to all of its members.
  - **BMI:** BMI was established in 1939 and is run by broadcasters, but its day-to-day decisions are made by management. Like ASCAP, BMI is a nonprofit organization that keeps some of the monies it collects for operating fees and then sends out the rest.
  - **SESAC:** SESAC is a "for profit" organization founded in 1930. SESAC is a much smaller organization than ASCAP and BMI, representing only 5 percent of all the licensed music out there. As a private organization, SESAC is not monitored by the Justice Department like ASCAP and BMI, and it can conduct business as it wishes.
- *Joining:*
  - **ASCAP:** Applicants must have at least one work written and published (or soon to be published). There's a one-time charge of $50 for writers and a one-time charge of $50 for publishers to join.
  - **BMI:** Applicants must have a song written and published (or soon to be published). It's free for writers to join, and publishers pay a one-time fee of $150 (for an independently owned company) or $250 (for a partnership or corporation). But check for new terms at www.bmi.com, as this fee may soon be eliminated altogether.
  - **SESAC:** Applicants must be selected by a referral process. Since SESAC is a much smaller organization, it has precious resources that must be utilized carefully. SESAC prides itself on giving the best individual attention. Speak with a representative about eligibility.

- ***Contract Terms:***
  - **ASCAP:** ASCAP has a one-year contract for both writers and publishers. Contracts are subject to automatic renewal for the initial terms stated, unless prior written notice is received by certified mail.
  - **BMI:** BMI has a two-year contract for writers and a five-year contract for publishers. Like ASCAP, contracts are subject to automatic renewal for the initial terms stated, unless prior written notice is received by certified mail.
  - **SESAC:** SESAC has a three-year contract for both writers and publishers. Again, like ASCAP and BMI, contracts are subject to automatic renewal for the initial terms stated, unless prior written noticed is received by certified mail.
- ***Contact Information:***
  - **ASCAP:** www.ascap.com
  - **BMI:** www.bmi.com
  - **SESAC:** www.sesac.com

Print Royalties

For the final section of this chapter, let's briefly discuss one more type of income derived from music publishing: print royalties.

Print royalties are the monies you make when your compositions are sold in sheet music and music books.

While print is sure to become more significant in the digital world (with sites that sell downloadable sheet music and apps that display lyrics), print today represents only an extremely small percentage of the overall income derived from your songs. In fact, unless you have a hit song or hit album, it's not likely your songs will ever make it into print.

Nevertheless, print is worth mentioning, so here's a brief—and I mean brief—overview.

HISTORICALLY PRINT WAS KING

In what is known as the Tin Pan Alley era (1911 through the 1940s), print represented a significant income to publishers and songwriters—since it was the predominant form of distributing and selling music.

In case you're wondering, Tin Pan Alley referred to the concentrated areas in New York City and London where music publishers' offices were located and where pianos could be heard daily as writers tried to pump out the next big hit. Pedestrians in the streets and alleys would say the sound reverberating against the buildings sounded like hundreds of tin pans, hence the name Tin Pan Alley.

Will print regain any of its old significance in this digital age? Only time will tell.

Types of Print Uses

There are four primary uses of your songs in print music form:

- ***Single-Sheet Music:*** Single-sheet music, often called piano sheet music, is just what it sounds like: individual sheet music sold in music stores. Sheet music can be a big seller for currently popular or classic songs, especially ballads. Examples include "The Wind Beneath My Wings" by Larry Henley and Jeff Silbar, "What a Wonderful World" by George David Weiss and Bob Thiele, and "At Last" by Mack Gordon and Harry Warren.

- ***Folios:*** Folios are music books that contain a complete library of music by one artist. Examples include *Led Zeppelin Complete* (Alfred Publishing), *The Best of the Police* (Hal Leonard), and *The Best of KISS* (Hal Leonard).
- ***Matching Folios:*** Matching folios are music books that match a particular record by an artist. The album cover is also the cover of the folio, and there are usually pictures of the artist inside. Examples of matching folios include *Jimi Hendrix—Are You Experienced?* (Hal Leonard), *Master of Puppets* by Metallica (Hal Leonard), and *The Wall* by Pink Floyd (Hal Leonard). And finally . . .
- ***Mixed Folios:*** Mixed folios are music books that contain works by a variety of different artists. Mixed folios are probably the most popular of the three folios because they contain so much variety. Examples include *The Gigantic Guitar Songbook* (Hal Leonard), featuring songs like "Come Together" by the Beatles, "Hey Joe" by Jimi Hendrix, and "Radar Love" by Golden Earring. Another example is *The Motown Anthology* (Hal Leonard), featuring songs like "My Girl" by the Temptations, "I'll Be There" by the Jackson 5, and "Let's Get It On" by Marvin Gaye.

Division of Print Incomes: Based on RSP and Wholesale

Okay, so now that you've reviewed the different types of traditional print uses, you're ready to learn about how you're paid. Just keep in mind that things are handled quite differently than some of the other types of publishing income already discussed.

Unlike mechanicals and performances, whereby the publisher receives a sum of money and essentially splits it in some percentage between the writer and the publisher (i.e., the writer's share and the publisher's share), print music is the only domestic type of publishing income derived from a royalty system based on the suggested retail price or wholesale price. Let's take a look at how this works.

Single-Sheet Music

The music printer (the company under contract that transcribes the music and makes the books for a term of three to five years) pays the music publisher a royalty of 20 percent of the retail price. The current retail price is approximately $5 for a single sheet of music, so the publisher receives around $1.00 ($5.00 × .20 = $1.00).

Of this $1.00, the publisher then pays the writer a flat rate of around 10 to 12 cents. Why is this so low? Because that's just the way it's always been, and no one has thought to change it.

If you publish your own music, you don't have anything to worry about, because you're both the writer and the publisher. However, if you enter into a deal with an established music publisher, don't expect much from single-sheet music sales.

Here's a recap:

- **Publisher:** 20% of retail selling price
- **Writer:** 10–12 cents flat rate

AFTERTHOUGHT: DIGITAL PAYS MORE? Websites that sell single-sheet music are becoming more and more popular. The retail selling price is the same as it is in physical stores (around $5.00), but the royalty paid to the publisher by the printer is far greater (50 percent as compared to 20 percent). Thus, the writer's payment should be far greater, too (at least 23 to 25 cents).

Folios

Moving on to folios, the division of print income works a bit better for writers than it does in the case of single-sheet music.

The printer pays the publisher a royalty of 10 to 12.5 percent of the retail selling price. The current average retail price is $25, so if the publisher has a 10 percent royalty, it receives around $2.50 per folio sold.

The publisher pays the writer a royalty of about 10 percent of the *wholesale* price—the price for which the printer apparently sells the book to retailers (which is basically half of the retail price of $25: $12.50). If the writer has a 10 percent royalty, he or she receives about $1.25 per folio sold ($12.50 × .10 = $1.25—which is basically half of what the publisher gets).

Here's a summary:

- **Publisher:** 10 to 12.5% RSP
- **Writer:** 10% wholesale (about half of publisher's share)

Matching Folios

Royalties for matching folios are generally treated the same way as royalties for plain folios. (God forbid I should have to repeat that again, but I'll at least repeat the summary below.)

- **Publisher:** 10 to 12.5% RSP
- **Writer:** 10% wholesale (about half of publisher's share)

Mixed Folios

And finally, to conclude this section and this chapter, royalties for mixed folios are generally treated the same way as royalties for plain folios and matching folios, only they are prorated based on the number of royalty-bearing works in the book. Remember, a mixed folio contains the compositions of a number of artists, not just yours.

To illustrate, if there are 20 compositions in a folio and you've written 5 of them, the publisher collects the prorated amount of 5/20ths—that is, one-fourth, or 25%—of the standard 10 to 12.5 percent royalty rate, and typically pays the writer a royalty in the range of 10 percent of the wholesale price, again prorated based on the number of works in the book.

So, to plug in some real numbers, let's say the retail selling price of a mixed folio is $25 and the publisher has a 10 percent royalty rate. The publisher then collects about 62.5 cents per mixed folio sold ($25 × .025 [one-fourth, or 25 percent, of the 10 percent royalty] = 62.5 cents). Since the wholesale price of the mixed folio is about half of the retail selling price quoted above, the writer receives about 31 cents per mixed folio sold ($12.50 × .025 = 31 cents).

Here's a summary:

- **Publisher:** 10 to 12.5% RSP prorated
- **Writer:** 10% wholesale prorated (about half of publisher's share)

AFTERTHOUGHT: COULD FOLIOS, OTHER THAN MIXED, BE PRORATED? For those of you who are really sharp, you may have noticed that I assumed that all songs in folios and matching folios are written by one person or band. But actually, there could be co-authored songs with other writers and even complete outside songs by other writers. In these cases, the prorated royalty method used above for mixed folios would apply.

18

Music Publishing, Part 4

Synch, Electronic Transmissions, and Sub-publishing

"Money's a horrid thing to follow, but a charming thing to meet." —Henry James

Continuing with our discussion on types of publishing income from chapter 17, where we talked about mechanicals, performances, and print, let's jump right into three more revenue streams: synchronization, electronic transmissions, and sub-publishing monies. There is a lot to cover here, so let's get started now.

Synchronization Fees

Synchronization (or synch) refers to the art of merging your music with visual images in motion pictures, television, CD-ROMs, DVDs, the Internet, video games, and other audiovisual media.

Despite a few exceptions (mainly PBS television), synch is completely negotiable. This means that while there are certainly reasonable industry norms, a publisher has the right to set his or her fees and has the authority to grant (or deny) permission for any uses of this type.

Income for Rights Holders in the Song

There are two significant types of income to be derived from the use of your compositions:

- ***Publisher Synch Fees (Up-Front Publisher Fees):*** The actual "synch fee" (or up-front publisher's fee) for the rights in your song, which, again, is negotiable. We'll discuss various points of negotiation in a moment, I promise.
- ***Public Performance Monies (Back-End Monies):*** The public performance income paid on the "back end" via ASCAP, BMI, and SESAC as a result of the initial synch use. "Don't let the term 'back end' fool you. Performances from synch can be significant," says music attorney Steve Winogradsky.

Income for Rights Holders in the Sound Recording: Aren't They Paid, Too?

In addition to the synchronization income that is paid to the rights holders in a song, there is a distinct type of synchronization income that is paid to the rights holders in the sound recording. This income is called a master use fee.

Master use fees are traditionally negotiated on a "most favored nation" basis. This means that the master use fee is the same as what is paid for the composition, or what is paid for the composition is the same as what is paid for the master—whichever is negotiated first.

Typically, do-it-yourself artists and bands will own the rights both to their compositions and to the sound recordings, entitling them to the two initial payments combined, or what is called the "all in" fee.

On the other hand, artists or bands who are part of a signed recording act will typically not own the copyright in the sound recording. Therefore, it's the record label that negotiates and collects the master use fee for the actual sound recording, while the publisher negotiates and collects the synch fee for the music embodied on the master recordings.

For practical purposes, the following discussion in this section will focus, by example, on the rights holders in the songs, but what follows really applies to master rights holders too.

LED ZEPPELIN SAID NO, TILL JACK BLACK BEGGED THEM

Keep in mind that synchronization is 100 percent negotiable. This means that publishers (and master rights holders) can negotiate their fees and grant (or deny) permission for any synch uses.

The gods of rock 'n' roll (Led Zeppelin) eventually gave in to a request to use "The Immigrant Song" in the movie *School of Rock*, after Jack Black sent them a video plea.

In the video, Black stood on a concert stage with an audience full of extras and cast members, and started a group chant that begged Led Zeppelin to permit the use of the song. The song was used for just 15 seconds under dialogue between Black and the costar. According to chitchat among my peers, Zeppelin received a decent amount—$150,000 for the use of the song. Not bad for just 15 seconds of work in a short scene at the middle of the film.

But on what precisely are synch fees based? Is it stature of the artist, timing, and whether their song is a major star in the film? These are all good questions. So be sure to get back to the text.

Points of Negotiation: Knowing How Much You Should Get

As previously mentioned, synch fees are 100 percent negotiable. In the words of Michael Eames, president of PEN Music Group, "Synch fees are the Wild Wild West."

That being said, there are some industry standards and practices used when negotiating synch fees that you should know about. Below are nine points and questions that publishers typically take into consideration when setting their fees. Read on.

Licensee / Type of Use (Film, TV, Video Games, Commercials)

The first point of negotiation deals with the type of license that is being requested.

- **Film: Major Motion Picture Studio or Independent Film Company?** You can charge more money for a major motion picture use than you could if your song was going to be used in an independent film. In fact, deals for independent films are often structured as "step deals," in which a smaller sum of money may be negotiated up front, with additional payments made later once certain criteria are met (such as the film achieving distribution or reaching a certain level of box office receipts).
- **Television: All Rights (Free TV, Paid TV, Satellite TV) or Separate Rights?** The more TV rights you give, the more dough you get. But note that most deals these days will require you to license all rights together rather than separately.
- **Video Games: Is It a Well-Known or Lesser-Known Game?** The more popular the video game and company, such as Electronic Arts, Activision, and Sony, the higher the fee you can charge. Keep in mind, though, that there aren't hundreds of companies out there, and fees tend to cap at a high four figures for

video games. Okay? Oh, and as far as getting a royalty for sales per unit, note that unless the game is a music-centric game like Rock Band or Guitar Hero, don't expect to receive one. Sorry! And finally . . .

- **Commercials for Television: Is It a Well-Known or Lesser-Known Brand?** Obviously, the more popular the company brand (like Coke or Pepsi), the more that you may be able to negotiate.

Context: Featured, Background, Trailers, Themes

The second point of negotiations deals with the context of the license that is being requested.

- **Featured: Is There a Featured Use?** If your music is going to be "featured" in the scene of a movie or television program (meaning your music and lyrics are carrying a scene and the actors are not talking), you can generally charge more than if your song is used as a "background."
- **Background: Is There a Background Use?** If your music is in the background (meaning your music is used in a scene coming from a "source" like a car radio or jukebox, and the actors are talking), you will usually get less money than for a featured use.
- **Main and End Titles: Is There a Title Use of Your Song?** If your music is going to be used over the "main title" (opening credits) or "end title" (closing credits) of a film or a television program, you can generally charge more than if your song is used just in the main body of the work.
- **Out-of-Context Use (Trailers): Is There an Out-of-Context Use?** If your music is going to be used "out of context"—that is, in some way other than how it is used in the film (e.g., it's also used in the trailer for a film or in the promo for a television show), you may be entitled to a fee above the initial film or TV payment. And finally . . .
- **Theme Use: Will Your Music Be Used as the Theme?** If your music is going to be used as the theme song of a television show, rather than just in the context of one scene, the fees will also be higher.

AFTERTHOUGHT: SONGS, SCENES, AND VIOLENCE If your composition is requested for use in a scene with potentially negative implications, such as during a murder or rape scene in a movie, you should be able to negotiate for more money, or you may not even want your song to be used at all.

Other Media (Limited or All Known and Hereafter Devised)

Moving on, the third point of negotiation deals with "limited media" and "all media" requests.

- **Limited Media: Just Film and/or TV?** If the use of your music in the program is limited (e.g., to television only, or Internet only), the amount you can negotiate for will be less than a request for all media.
- **All Media: Home Video and Wireless Distribution?** If your music is requested for use in a film and/or television program for eventual release on home video, wireless services, iPods, the Internet, and all other media "now known and hereafter devised," the fee should also be higher.

The Term (Years or Forever)

The fourth point of negotiation that can affect your synch fee deals with the term.

- **Year(s): One, Three, or More?** Your song may be requested for as short a period as one year and as long as 10 years. Shorter uses will get less money.
- **In Perpetuity: Will It Be Used Forever?** Licenses that last in perpetuity will command a higher fee.

Exclusivity (Exclusive or Nonexclusive)

Now at number 5 of 9 negotiation points (yes, we're more than halfway home), let's consider exclusivity.

- **Exclusive: No One Else Can Use It.** If someone wants exclusive use of your music (which often occurs in the case of TV commercials), there's a premium that must be paid. Since you will not be able to use your composition in whatever areas the exclusivity covers, you are potentially losing income and must be compensated.
- **Nonexclusive Rights: Will Others Be Able to Use It?** Since you can still license your music to other users in nonexclusive deals, you will obviously get less money than you would in exclusive deals. Note: Many synch uses these days are nonexclusive.

Territory (United States or the World)

Moving on to the sixth point of negotiation, territory is yet another factor to consider.

- **The World: Will the Use Be Everywhere?** Though most film and TV licenses these days are drafted for "rights to the entire world," keep in mind that the license should also reflect a higher fee than U.S.-only deals.
- **The United States: U.S. Only?** U.S.-only deals command less than deals for the world.

Credits

The seventh point of negotiation deals with the credits you receive in film and TV.

- **Film: Credit over End Titles?** Remember that exposure in a prominent film can lead to other uses of your compositions, which leads to more money. Thus, if you're receiving credits in a film, you might consider backing down a bit on the price.
- **TV and Web Series: Credit Listed?** Just like with film, exposure in a prominent TV show can lead to other uses of your compositions, which leads to more money. Keep this potential benefit in mind during the negotiation process.

Timing (Short or Significant)

Getting close to the end of this section on negotiating synch fees, the eighth factor to consider when determining your price is the length of time during which your composition is used.

- **Significant Uses: Minutes?** Music, especially in films, is often extended for several minutes (sometimes for the entirety of the song). The longer the use, the more you can charge.
- **Short Uses: Seconds?** Music is also used in very brief portions, especially in the transitions of scenes. The shorter the use, the less you can charge.

Stature of the Artist/Song (Successful or Not)

The ninth, and last, point of negotiation I'll discuss deals with the stature of both the song and the artist.

- **Successful: Don't You Know I'm a Star?** The more popular the song is, the more you can charge. You can be sure that Bob Seger received hundreds of thousands of dollars (if not millions) for the use of his hit song "Like a Rock" in the Chevrolet commercials that aired for years.
- **Unknown: Don't You Respect DIY Artists?** DIY artists will often have a tough time with negotiating synch licenses, simply because many music users making the request know that DIY artists are looking for a break and will do it for free. But keep in mind that while you may make nothing on the front-end synch, the back-end monies from performances can be extremely advantageous (not to mention the benefits you'll receive from the exposure). Just make sure to understand everything you sign and to seek out an experienced and knowledgeable business professional to help you.

EXAMPLES OF PUBLISHING FEES FOR ACTUAL SYNCH USES

Ever wonder what well-known and unknown songs make in various uses? Let's find out.

- *Well-Known or Current Hits (Major Artists):*
  - **Television:** $40,000 and more (per use per song) for use over the main or end title credits, or $120,000 and more (per use per song) as the theme of a television program.
  - **Film:** $100,000 and more (per use per song) for use of your compositions over the main or end title credits of a film. Can you believe the techno band The Prodigy was offered $500,000 for the use of just one of their songs in a film and they turned it down? Note that if a director really wants your music, the money here is big.
  - **Video Games:** $1,000 to $5,000 as a flat buyout for the song (remember that there are no per-unit royalties typically offered unless the game is a music-centric game like Rock Band).
- *Unknown or Noncharting (DIY Artists):*
  - **Television:** $250 to $2,500 per use per song.
  - **Film:** $500 to $5,000 per use per song.
  - **Video Games:** Free to $2,500 per use per song.

Note: Remember that the above rates are for the song only. There is an additional "master fee" (that typically matches the publisher's fee) paid to the master owner (which is typically the record company, including majors, indies, or DIY recording artists).

Additional Incomes: More Than You Bargained For

Now that you know a little bit more about how to negotiate synch fees, you'll be happy to know that more money could become available beyond the initial synch use. In fact, the use of your song in a film can snowball into a number of potential revenue streams. Let's take a look at four examples:

- *Mechanicals:* If the record label that holds the rights to release the film's soundtrack album wants to include your song, you will earn a mechanical royalty per record or download of your song sold.
- *Radio Performances:* If your song then gets played on the radio to promote the film or soundtrack, you earn a performance royalty as well.
- *Video Advertising:* If clips from the movie are played on video channels (such as YouTube) and ads are generated, you may receive advertising monies. And finally . . .
- *Foreign Theatre Performances:* If the film ever makes it into theaters outside of the United States—you guessed it—you earn a performance royalty for the public performance of your composition (remember that theater performances in the U.S. are not payable due to a 1948 lawsuit between ASCAP and a movie theater firm).

As you can see, the use of your song in just one film can often generate monies that are more than you ever bargained for. Not bad at all for a day of songwriting!

SYNCH LICENSES AND YOUTUBE VIDEOS: SO WHAT'S REALLY THE DEAL?

Does a music video (such as the one where the young kid sits on his bed playing a cover song) require a synch license? Yes! Does a young kid sitting on his bed playing a cover song get a synch license from the publisher? Usually not! So then, what's the deal?

YouTube and other digital service providers (DSPs) know that they are potentially hosting hundreds of thousands of infringing music videos. At the request of the music publisher, YouTube issues "takedown notices" to music users (like the young kid sitting on his bed playing a cover song) and even shuts the user's channel down. If you've seen a YouTube channel with the language "This site has been closed down due to copyright infringement," then you know what I'm talking about. Says attorney Steve Winogradsky, "You don't want this to happen to you."

As an alternative to takedown notices, YouTube places ads (that its customers purchase) on infringing videos and then pays out a share of the ad revenue to music publishers and other rights holders. According to my good buddy Michael Eames of PEN Music Group, rights holders are supposed to submit the titles of all the songs that they own/represent/administer so that YouTube knows how to divide up all the dough from what they call "user-generated content."

Another way that this may be handled is via multi-channel networks like Fullscreen (www.fullscreen.com), Maker Studios (www.makerstudios.com), and Machinima (www.machinima.com)—large (often well-funded) video organizations that offer individual YouTube channel owners partnership agreements and assistance in a variety of areas (audience development, cross-promotions, programming, and more). Fullscreen, in particular, clears music licenses with rights holders on behalf of its members, which could include—you guessed it—the young kid sitting on his bed playing a cover song.

So you see, folks, while you may see a significant number of videos online and wonder why everyone is getting away with posting them, now you know that there is a lot more going on than what meets the general public's eye.

Electronic Transmissions: Downloads, Streams, and More

Moving away from synch, I will now take on the fifth type of publishing income, known as electronic transmissions. This is not a totally new "type" of income in itself, but rather a "source" that encompasses the various incomes previously discussed.

Electronic transmissions include:

- Album or single-song downloads
- Ringtones
- Interactive and noninteractive audio streaming
- Video streaming
- Downloadable sheet music
- Lyric websites and lyric apps
- Planet Uranus Stream and other new stuff

Electronic transmissions are a new, exciting, unsettled, and volatile area that's subject to change due to evolving laws and practices. They've sent the music industry into a state of flux and made it a total pain in the ass for an author like me to nail down precise facts and figures. I'll provide the basics and a few thoughts, but stay connected to the web for the latest news.

Permanent Digital Downloads (i.e., iTunes-Type Royalties)

The first of the electronic transmissions I'd like to tackle is the digital download from online sites like iTunes (www.itunes.com) and eMusic (www.emusic.com).

Permanent downloads are "permanent" because consumers can copy, burn, upload, own, and essentially "do as they please" with them.

- ***Type of License:*** Permanent digital downloads require a mechanical license and a statutory mechanical fee paid to the music publisher.
- ***Payment:*** Music publishers receive the full statutory mechanical rate of $0.091, then pay the writers.

AFTERTHOUGHT: DOWNLOADS AND RINGTONES EXEMPT Remember that in the Digital Performance Right in Sound Recordings Act of 1995, permanent downloads became exempt from the controlled composition clause found in recording agreements (a clause that limits the amount in mechanicals that the label has to pay). So, yes, this means that mechanical income from these sources is not limited. Good news for publishers and writers.

Ringtones

Another type of electronic transmission and permanent download is the ringtone.

Ringtones are snippets of your recorded songs that are downloaded via mobile carriers like Verizon and used on cell phones—a song alerts you that someone is calling, and a song (or ringback) alerts the caller that the phone is ringing or busy.

- ***Type of License:*** Ringtones also require a mechanical license and a statutory mechanical fee (different from downloads) paid to the music publisher.
- ***Payment:*** Music publishers receive a statutory rate of $0.24, then pay the writers.

AFTERTHOUGHT: RINGBACKS PAID DIFFERENTLY? Jeff and Todd Brabec in *Music, Money, and Success* state that ringbacks are treated differently from ringtones. Ringbacks have no set compulsory fee and are negotiable. Publishers usually get 10 percent of the retail selling price (which equates to about 20 cents) with a minimum floor of about 10 cents.

Noninteractive Audio-Only Streaming (i.e., Webcasting and Satellite Radio)

For the third electronic transmission, I'll briefly discuss noninteractive webcasters like Pandora (www.pandora.com) and satellite radio providers like SiriusXM (www.siriusxm.com).

Noninteractive services do not allow consumers to interact (pick songs as they wish, make set lists, etc.), but only to listen. These services may be free or subscription-based.

- ***Type of License:*** Noninteractive streaming requires a blanket performing rights license issued by the PROs and a performance royalty paid directly to publishers and writers.
- ***Payment:*** Determining the amount per payment is extremely difficult to do and out of this book's scope, but please feel free to call the PROs and speak with a representative if you are so inclined or visit www.ASCAP.com, www.BMI.com, or www.SESAC.com.

AFTERTHOUGHT: SOUND RECORDING PERFORMANCES AND SOUNDEXCHANGE MONIES Remember that if you own the master recordings, or if your performance is embodied on a master recording (either as a featured or side musician), you are entitled to additional monies for noninteractive audio-only Internet streaming performances. Labels receive 50 percent of the monies collected by SoundExchange, featured musicians receive 45 percent, and non-featured musicians/vocalists receive 5 percent (via music unions). Be sure to go to www.soundexchange.com for more information.

Interactive Streaming-On-Demand Audio

The next electronic transmission, interactive streaming, is where all the action is. This includes music on sites like Spotify (www.spotify.com), Rdio (www.rdio.com), and Rhapsody (www.rhapsody.com).

Interactive streaming means that consumers can play songs on demand, create personalized playlists, and "interact" in other ways, but that the use is still a "conditional download." A conditional download is one that the consumer can "use" (not own).

- ***Type of License:*** Interactive streams require both a mechanical license and a mechanical fee paid to the music publisher, as well as a blanket public performance license issued by the PROs and a performance royalty paid directly to the publisher and writer (review how PRO payments are made if needed).
- ***Payment:*** The amounts received for these licenses vary by 1) considering the "service offering" (non-portable streaming subscriptions, non-portable subscriptions mixed use, portable subscriptions mixed use, bundled subscription services, and free non-subscription ad-supported), 2) subtracting the greater of an applicable percentage of service revenue and an applicable service minimum, 3) subtracting PRO-licensed activities, 4) taking the result of step 3 or a penny rate per "subscriber month," 5) finding a per-play allocation, and 6) multiplying the per-play allocation times the number of plays of each musical work. The result is fractions of pennies per stream. Don't spend it all in one place.

AFTERTHOUGHT: WHAT DOES THE [HARRY] FOX KNOW? For more detailed information on interactive streaming, be sure to check out the rate charts on the Harry Fox Agency website (www.harryfox.com). Streams ultimately amount to fractions of pennies. To generate substantial dollars, you'll need thousands of streams. As the industry evolves to streaming, streaming royalties are sure to get much better.

Interactive Streaming Video (Audio-Visual Streams)

At just past the halfway point of this section, I'd like to introduce interactive streaming video (e.g., YouTube videos).

This includes videos that are produced and uploaded by record labels (like your official promotional music videos) and "user-generated content" uploaded by users and multi-channel networks (like cover videos and lifestyle videos of kids skateboarding to the Ramones).

- ***Type of License:*** Interactive streams require a synch license paid to the publisher (and record label, when the master recording of the song is used), as well as a blanket public performance license issued by the PROs, and a performance royalty paid to the publisher and the writer.
- ***Payment:*** Publishers are doing a lot of negotiating, haggling, and foot stomping to make sure that they get paid. Right now, publishers are paid a percentage of net advertising revenue that is generated from ads placed on the videos ranging anywhere from 15 percent to 50 percent.

Downloadable Sheet Music

Moving on to number six of the nine electronic transmissions, downloadable sheet music is slowing gaining ground.

You should know that digital sheet music distributors like Musicnotes.com (www.musicnotes.com) and Sheet Music Direct (www.sheetmusicdirect.com) provide consumers the luxury of finding a variety of their favorite sheet music 24/7 to download immediately.

- ***Type of License:*** Digital downloads of printed music require a print fee paid to the publisher.
- ***Payment:*** For single-sheet downloads, publishers will get about 50 percent of the retail selling price (currently $5.00) and then pay the writer a flat rate of about 23–25 cents.

Lyric Websites

While on the topic of print royalties, my seventh electronic transmission introduces websites like LyricFind (www.lyricfind.com) and Rap Genius (www.rapgenius.com). These sites display the lyrics to popular (and niche) songs, and then charge companies to advertise their products and services on their sites.

- ***Type of License:*** Lyric websites require a print license and a print fee paid to the music publisher, who then pays the writer.
- ***Payment:*** Publishers receive a percentage (50 percent) of the advertising revenue generated. While many sites are illegal and are subject to lawsuits, more and more sites operate legitimately.

Lyric Cell Phone Apps

Moving on to number eight and another electronic transmission in the print realm, lyric cell phone apps allow users to speak a few words of their favorite songs, find the complete lyric to the composition, and display the words.

- ***Type of License:*** Lyric displays of this nature require a print license and a print royalty to the publisher, who then pays the writer.
- ***Payment:*** Rates are still being worked out but will likely be in the 20 percent range of the app's selling price for publishers, who then pay writers.

Planet Uranus Streams and Other Stuff

And finally, our last electronic transmission deals with those from planet Uranus. Okay, so the planet Uranus part is a joke, but rest assured you'll eventually receive a royalty of some kind for anything new that has been developed since the release of this book. That is, you'll eventually get a royalty once everyone is done scrambling to figure out how to deal with it. Technology has a way of getting ahead of all of us at times.

Here's what Neil Gillis, president of Round Hill Music, had to say on the matter of new technologies:

> Every time a new technology is created, the industry scrambles to figure out how to deal with it, and things can get so complicated. But, as I see it, things can be simplified if traditional laws and practices are used by all parties involved when considering in what way a new technology allows a piece of music to be utilized.

Gillis suggests we all ask the following questions:

- ***Performance:*** Is there a performance of the song, based on what we believe the law and business practice states is performance, where a license must be granted?
- ***Mechanical:*** Is there a mechanical reproduction of the song (i.e., is the song being copied) such that a mechanical license is needed?
- ***Synch:*** Is there a visual media relationship whereby a synchronization license must be obtained?
- ***Print:*** Is there an embedded lyric somewhere in the song whereby a lyric reprint of some kind needs to be involved?

Gillis chimes in again:

> Surely there are going to be new technologies invented that take into consideration other factors than the list provided above, but for the moment, the aforementioned takes the mystery out of the

"Oh my God, what is this new technology and what is it capable of doing?" dilemma, and it brings everything back to simpler terms. If everyone can only see technology as this, then maybe we can more easily begin to formulate pricing around that technology.

AFTERTHOUGHT: GOT NEWS! For the latest news on electronic transmissions, please see sites like National Music Publishers' Association (www.nmpa.org), the Copyright Office (www.copyright.gov), and the Future of Music Coalition (www.futureofmusic.org). Also, after reading this book, be sure to check out *Music, Money, and Success* by Jeff and Todd Brabec.

Foreign Sub-publishing Income

Congratulations, ladies and gentlemen. You have made it to the last income stream derived from music publishing: foreign sub-publishing income. Hang in there: this chapter is almost over.

Foreign sub-publishing income deals with the money earned when your music is published overseas. It's not really a type of income itself (it encompasses the incomes discussed previously), but it is handled differently than U.S income. In fact, U.S. publishers must seek the assistance of "sub-publishers" (publishers in foreign territories) to help with collections and other matters.

Let's first take a close look at how two primary types of income (mechanical and performance royalties) are handled differently. Next, I'll discuss something called "black box monies," and finally talk briefly about sub-publishers and "at-source" collections.

Foreign Mechanicals

If you've been paying close attention since earlier in this chapter, then you know that you're entitled to a royalty for the use of your songs based on a penny rate. The penny system only applies to the United States and Canada for the most part.

Payable on RSP or PPD of Album

In foreign territories (those outside of the U.S. and Canada), mechanicals are payable on a percentage of either the retail selling price (RSP) of the record or the price per dealer (PPD)—which is basically an equivalent to wholesale prices. Percentages differ from territory to territory but are generally in the range of 6 to 10 percent, covering all the compositions on a record.

For instance, mechanicals in Japan are currently based on 6 percent (RSP), in Germany 9.03 percent (PPD), and in the United Kingdom 8.5 percent (PPD). These rates are unaffected by either the length of the compositions or the number of songs per album.

In other words, unlike the United States and Canada, writers and publishers cannot be asked to waive their rights to mechanical payments under a system similar to the controlled composition clause. I bet that makes you happy!

Licensed/Collected by Mandatory Societies

Also much different than in the United States and Canada is the method by which foreign mechanical royalties are collected and paid to publishers.

In the United States and Canada, publishers can choose to have the record companies send mechanical royalties directly to them, or they can have an agency such as Harry Fox Agency (for the U.S.) and CMRRA (for Canada) collect on their behalf.

However, in foreign territories, mechanical royalties are licensed and collected by "mandatory mechanical rights collection societies." For instance, in Japan, mechanical royalties are licensed and collected by a society called JASRAC, in Germany it's GEMA, and in Great Britain it's MCPS.

Sub-publishers Needed

So, with all this talk of mandatory stuff, one might ask, "How the heck do I get my money?" That's a very good question.

Essentially, the Harry Fox Agency can collect foreign mechanicals through reciprocal representation agreements with affiliated foreign collecting societies and the territories they represent, but I'm told the Fox Agency overall is not the most effective means by which to handle your foreign business affairs.

Instead, U.S. publishers typically seek the help of what are known as local sub-publishers in foreign territories who will submit a claim and collect mechanicals on your behalf for a fee (more in a moment).

If you don't have a sub-publisher representing you, then your monies may go uncollected and often end up in what's known as the "black box." Sounds ominous, doesn't it? Hold that thought. I'll discuss sub-publishers and the black box in detail in a minute.

Foreign Performance Royalties

Foreign performance royalties aren't as complex as mechanical royalties, but there are a few things you need to know.

U.S. PROs Have Reciprocal Agreements

Your performing rights organization in the U.S. (ASCAP, BMI, or SESAC) has reciprocal agreements with all of the performing rights societies around the world for licensing and royalty collections.

For instance, the performing rights society in Japan is JASRAC, in Germany it's GEMA, and in Great Britain it's PRS. (Yes, if you have a great memory, then you've just realized that JASRAC and GEMA collect both mechanicals and performance royalties.)

Writer's Share: U.S. Collects

The foreign performing rights societies send the writer's share of performance royalties to the U.S. organizations (remember the "writer's share" of performances always gets paid to the writer, even for foreign performances), and then the U.S. society pays the writer directly. That's pretty straightforward, right? But it's the publisher's share of income that's more difficult.

Publisher's Share: Sub-publisher Needed

If you don't get a foreign sub-publisher to represent you, the publisher's share of performance royalties will theoretically make its way back to you via your U.S. performing rights society, but this is not an effective means of ensuring that all your performance income is collected.

So again, the U.S. publisher will want to contract with a sub-publisher to collect the publisher's share of performance monies. Without a sub-publisher, these monies, like mechanicals, are also subject to falling into the "black box."

Black Box Monies

When the foreign rights societies collect royalties earned by a song, they hold onto them and identify to whom the monies belong by checking registrations made by local sub-publishers.

If the societies are unable to identify where the money should be sent, they forward it to an escrow account known as the black box. Every society has one of these infamous black boxes holding unclaimed monies.

After a certain period of time (usually about three to six years), if no claimant has come forth, the monies are deemed unclaimed or unidentified and are then divided among all of the local publishers in the territory pro rata based on their income.

Successful writers who are contracted with a sub-publisher, and who also have negotiating power, sometimes share in a percentage of the black box fund. This means that if you do not have a sub-publisher in a foreign territory representing you, other artists will gladly take your hard-earned money instead. But this can be prevented by getting a sub-publisher.

Foreign Sub-publishers

To wrap up this entire chapter, it's probably a good time to tackle sub-publishers. We're almost done, I promise.

As briefly mentioned before, a sub-publisher is a company in a foreign territory who works with U.S. publishers to ensure your songs are registered and your money is collected.

Contracts with U.S. Publishers

A sub-publisher's decision to work with a U.S. publisher depends on several factors. After all, it's not as if they have time to work with everyone. These factors may include:

- Does the U.S. publisher have a record released by a foreign label (or have a song in a TV show or film, etc.)?
- How long has the record been out?
- How well is the record doing?

Offers an Advance or Just Collects

Depending on the above-noted circumstances, a sub-publisher may then offer an advance against "future earnings" (future earnings is what they think they'll make based on their cut).

When they think what they'll earn is minimal and offering an advance is a high risk, they may simply collect on your behalf and take a fee (this is known as a collection deal).

Registers Songs/Collects

Sub-publishers then make sure that all of the works they're representing for the U.S. publisher are properly registered with the foreign collection agencies mentioned above.

When the foreign society collects royalties earned from your songs, they acknowledge the sub-publisher's registration and forward the monies on to them.

Handles All Incomes (Synch, Print, Covers and Translations, and More)

Sub-publishers handle all uses of your songs, whether they be monies derived from recordings (physical sales, digital downloads, streams, "cover songs," and "translations"), films and television shows, and printed manuscripts and books).

Note that foreign "covers" may involve a language "translation," and thus a royalty is traditionally paid to the local lyricist. This fee will come off the top of the monies collected.

Takes a Fee (10–25) and Remits Balance

Sub-publishers take a share of the monies collected ranging from 10 to 25 percent. I once did a deal in Japan with a company for 85/15. This means I got 85 percent and they took 15 percent.

Sometimes certain income streams are divided differently. For performance income (i.e., the publisher's part of it), the sub-publisher often wants as much as 25 to 35 percent. For cover recordings, it often wants as much as 40 percent.

Once the publisher takes its cut, the remaining income is then sent to the U.S. publisher.

At-Source Royalty Collections

There's one more important thing that you should know about sub-publishers, and it concerns something called "at-source royalty collections" and the amount of money you ultimately get.

Base Your Cut at the Source

When you enter into an agreement with a sub-publisher and one dollar is collected (or whatever the currency is called in that territory), theoretically the sub-publisher takes $0.15 (on a 15 percent deal), and credits the other $0.85 to the U.S. publisher.

I use the word "theoretically" because you must negotiate that your cut is based "at source"—*that is, based on the amount collected in that country*. Otherwise, your monies can be dramatically reduced should your sub-publisher hire other sub-publishers (who also take a cut of the dough) before you get your cut.

An at-source deal also means that when you have a more established publishing company representing you in the U.S. for "the world," on say a 75/25 deal, the U.S. publisher absorbs the cost of the sub-publisher out of its 25 percent. Simply put, you always get 75 percent of foreign income collected, regardless of sub-publishing matters.

So, that's about it for sub-publishing and types of publishing income. Happy spending!

DART MONIES AND RECORD RENTAL REMUNERATION

Wait! For yet one final type of income, you should know about DART monies and record rental remuneration.

Pursuant to the U.S. Audio Home Recording Act of 1992, publishers and songwriters (as well as record companies, featured recording artists, and non-featured musicians) are due a percentage of the taxes collected from the manufacturers of digital audio recorders and digital audio tapes. These "private copy royalties," often called DART monies (for Digital Audio Recording Technologies), make up for the monies lost when people copy our precious art at home. In addition to DART monies, "record rental remuneration" royalties or "foreign royalties" from Japan (where CDs are rented and then often copied at home) may also be due to you.

Publishers and songwriters who are entitled to these monies (a.k.a. "interested copyright parties") may file a claim during January and February with the Copyright Office Musical Works Fund. The performing rights organizations (ASCAP, BMI, and SESAC) can act as an authorized agent on your behalf (albeit these monies really have nothing to do with performances), but a separate authorization agreement must be entered into with your affiliated PRO.

Sound recording copyright owners and featured musicians on sound recordings can collect royalties via membership with AARC (Alliance of Artists and Recording Companies). Non-featured musicians (i.e., session players on sound recordings) can collect these monies through the Sound Recording Intellectual Property Rights Distribution Fund via the American Federation of Musicians (AFM) and/or SAG-AFTRA.

DART monies and record rental remuneration monies may not amount to much for you (especially if you are relatively unknown), but you should know about every little bit of money that you may be entitled to. It's your right!

19

Music Publishing, Part 5

Publishing Companies and Types of Deals

"Those who say 'don't give up your publishing' may not understand totally how publishing deals work."—*Neil Gillis, president, Round Hill Music*

Welcome to the next-to-last chapter on music publishing! Now that you understand a little bit about the types of income you can earn by owning a copyright, we can begin discussing why you'd want to give up any of that dough to an outside established music publishing company.

In this chapter, I'll focus on publishing deals: from what publishers do to the types of deals that they offer. Neil Gillis, president of Round Hill Music, finishes up the chapter by answering some frequently asked questions. Let's get right to this.

What Established Music Publishers Can Do for Your Career

You already know that by virtue of creating a copyright, you inherit the rights to that work as music publisher. You also know that music publishing produces many sources of income, including mechanical royalties, performance royalties, synch fees, and more.

So, you might ask, "Why should I sign over my copyright ownership and a percentage of these wonderful future earnings to an established music publisher?" Good question.

Let's take a look at song plugging, securing recording agreements, paying advances, distributing marketing funds, and handling administrative duties.

Song Plugging (TV, Film, and More)

Music publishers find uses for your songs in a number of different areas—from placing them with other artists to using them in video games, film, and TV. The latter is perhaps the most significant. You can hear major artists like Sting publicizing Jaguar cars, Led Zeppelin promoting GM, and Oasis endorsing AT&T.

Even lesser-known artists are "in synch" (pardon the pun). The right exposure on a television show can be an alternative method for breaking new artists into the mainstream.

Brendan Benson of the Raconteurs received significant attention when his music was used in an iPod ad. Ingrid Michaelson's career picked up momentum after her music got placed in an Old Navy commercial.

Securing Recording Agreements (Cowriters and Credibility)

Publishing companies are also known to help their talented artists/writers procure recording contracts with record labels.

The publisher may team you up with seasoned writers to help you compose a collection of well-crafted songs and then strive to place your songs in television shows and other media to create as much excitement about your career as possible.

An artist's affiliation with a reputable publishing company can be an attractive feature in and of itself to a record label. It sends a message throughout the music industry that a credible establishment stands behind your career.

TEAMING YOU UP WITH SONGWRITERS/PRODUCERS

Singer/songwriter Alanis Morissette was signed to MCA Music Publishing when a company representative introduced her to the successful producer/writer Glen Ballard, who was also signed to MCA.

Together, Morissette and Ballard crafted songs that helped land the singer a major recording deal and subsequently a Grammy for best album of the year. By the way, that album (*Jagged Little Pill*) went on to sell over 30 million copies worldwide. Damn!

With a little help from her friends at MCA, Morissette was able to put all the right pieces of her career together. This exemplifies just one of the many things publishers can do.

Paying Advances

As if the above were not enough, music publishing companies also offer their writers advance monies. Unlike recording funds, these monies are not used for numerous recording and other expenses. Rather, you can use the advance as you'd like (a nice enticement, wouldn't you say?).

While advances have gotten smaller over the years for newer artists, they can still range anywhere from a few thousand dollars to as much as few hundred thousand.

Factors that determine advances (and potential signatories, for that matter) include:

- ***Songs:*** Is there hit song potential?
- ***Live Performance:*** Do you have an energetic live performance, and does the audience seem to respond well to your music?
- ***Placement Resources:*** Are you a writer/producer with resources to place your songs with top artists, in movies and television, or video games?
- ***Signed/Unsigned:*** Are you a writer/artist who has already signed a recording agreement?
- ***What Record Label:*** If you're already a signed artist, then which record company holds your contract?
- ***Clout of A&R:*** What's your A&R representative's success rate at the label?
- ***Enthusiasm of the Label:*** How enthusiastic and supportive is the record company about your future?
- ***How Much Radio Play:*** If the record company has already released your first single, is it getting played on the radio?
- ***How Much Streaming:*** How many audio and audiovisual streams are you generating?
- ***Sales Figure:*** Is your record selling well?
- ***Tour Plans:*** Are you booked on any upcoming major tours?
- ***Professional Team:*** Do you have a reputable manager, agent, and/or attorney representing you?

Simply put, the more value the publisher sees in your compositions, the more money they may be willing to pay you up front. For some artists, the advance can be just a small taste of all the money yet to come. And for others, the advance might be the only income that they ever will see.

WHEN THE ADVANCE REALLY COUNTS

In the early 1990s, the band D-A-D (an abbreviation for Disneyland After Dark) entered into a publishing agreement with Warner/Chappell Music and received a $1 million advance. The buzz in the industry was that D-A-D was sure to be the next big band.

But, as it turns out (according to one source at Warner/Chappell Music who wishes to remain anonymous), D-A-D's album was DOA, "dead on arrival." Sales figures reached a whopping 606 units—perhaps an exaggeration, but you get the point.

If you feel badly for the band, imagine how much worse off they would have been if they hadn't had the publishing agreement at all. This doesn't suggest that you should bet against yourself, but it definitely provides one example of how unpredictable this business can be, even with a publisher.

Distributing Marketing Funds

Getting close to finishing up this discussion on what publishers can do for your career, you'll be happy to know that some companies are known to earmark advance dollars toward marketing.

Warner/Chappell Music continued to offer support to the band Remy Zero even after they were dropped from Capitol Records. Warner/Chappell's support provided the band the security they needed to write and find a new deal. And it paid off! The band signed with another label and enjoyed success with their single "Save Me," which was used regularly on a popular television show.

The moral of the story here is clear: the record business is based on a one-shot, do-or-die philosophy. Since enormous odds are stacked against you, the question then becomes whether or not you want the major muscle of an established music publisher helping to promote your band. Remember, the more people you can get in your court, the better off you'll probably be!

Handling Administrative Duties

Last but definitely not least, beyond the creative and financial components previously mentioned, a music publisher can provide important administrative services, such as:

- ***Registering Copyrights:*** Registering your compositions with the Copyright Office in Washington, D.C.
- ***Registering Song Titles with PROs:*** Making sure your songs are properly registered with one of the three performing rights organizations (ASCAP, BMI, or SESAC).
- ***Generating Income:*** Issuing all types of licenses for the use of your songs, including mechanical, synch, and print licenses, and negotiating the proper compensation.
- ***Collecting Monies:*** Making sure all generated income is collected worldwide (enlisting foreign sub-publishers to collect on your behalf).
- ***Policing Infringements:*** Keeping a watchful eye out for unauthorized uses of your songs and filing infringement claims. And finally . . .
- ***Conducting Audits:*** Filing the occasional audit to be sure you're getting every last dime from the use of your songs.

As you can see, administrative duties would be a handful for an artist on his or her own. Because established publishers don't have to be artists like you, they can concentrate on tasks like this all day long. It also just so happens that established music publishers are pretty good at it.

Types of Publishing Deals

Now that you know what music publishers can do for your career, we can take a close look at the various types of publishing deals that exist.

These include exclusive songwriter agreements, co-publishing agreements, and administration deals. Then we'll finish up with self-publishing.

Exclusive Songwriter Agreements

For years, music publishers served as the mighty middlemen between writers who needed their songs placed and artists who needed songs to record.

Even as more artists began writing their own material, music publishers retained a tremendous amount of leverage in the industry. Publishing was simply a mysterious concept to everyone, and you can bet that music publishers liked it that way.

The Beatles and Bob Dylan are two examples of artists who signed exclusive publishing agreements early in their careers. Exclusive deals were once the standard.

Ownership Splits (50/50)

In exclusive songwriter agreements, publishing companies acquire 100 percent of the copyright in a composition for the full duration of the copyright term (unless a reversion clause is negotiated) to both pitch and administer the entire song, typically for the world. This is a big piece of the pie, and arguably a bigger piece than some publishers really deserve.

In the words of Ed Pierson, formerly of Warner/Chappell Music, "These types of one-sided deals made publishing companies huge cash cows." (Just take a look at the pie diagram.)

Incomes (Credited Toward Advance)

Finally, for every $1.00 the publishing company collects in earnings, the company keeps $0.50 and the writer is credited the remaining $0.50. (Just add a few zeroes onto these numbers for the full effect.)

These monies, with the exception of your writer's share of performance royalties (which is always paid to you directly by your performing rights organization), are charged against the initial advance. Once the advance is recouped, you start collecting your allotted share for subsequent earnings.

That's pretty much it for exclusive songwriter's agreements.

Co-publishing Agreements

Moving on to the next deal offered by publishing companies, let's discuss co-publishing.

Rumor has it that after Brian Lane (the manager of the classic rock band Yes) balked at the idea of relinquishing 100 percent of the band's copyright to its songs and 50 percent of its earnings, the concept of co-publishing was born.

Co-publishing deals (also called co-pub deals) have become the most common arrangements today for the writer/artist. In fact, the co-pub deal has become the norm for many individual songwriters as well.

Ownership Splits (75/25)

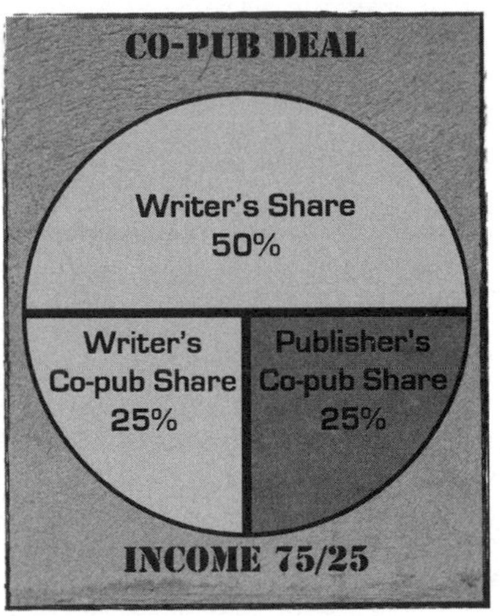

In co-publishing agreements, the publishing company acquires only 50 percent of the copyright in a composition for the full duration of the copyright term (unless a reversion clause is negotiated) to both pitch and administer the entire song, typically for the world. This is a far more favorable deal than the exclusive songwriter deal mentioned above.

Just don't be misled by the word "co-publish." While you may retain 50 percent of the publishing, the publishing company still administers 100 percent of the copyright. (Please see the pie diagram.)

Incomes (Credited Toward Advance)

Finally, for every $1.00 the publishing company collects in earnings, the publishing company gets $0.25 and the writer is credited the remaining $0.75. (That's 50 percent [the full writer's share] plus 25 percent [half of the publisher's share]). Once the publisher recoups the advance, the writer gets paid.

Administration Deals

Finally, let's take a look at the last type of deal arranged with an established music publisher: administration deals (also called admin deals).

Though co-publishing made publishing deals more favorable to the writers, many artists still questioned precisely how much new revenue the publishing company was generating for them.

In other words, for artists with the means to self-publish their music via record deals and other offers that roll directly in, and they don't need up-front resources in the form of a publishing advance, why give up half of the copyright and 25 percent of the earnings? Rather, why not keep the publishing rights and let the publisher handle only the boring admin stuff for (typically) the world? Makes you think, doesn't it?

Ownership Splits (100/0 with a 10 to 20 Percent Fee)

In an admin deal with an established publisher, the music publishing company acquires no ownership in the copyright of a composition, but rather receives a 10 to 20 percent fee (with 15 percent being the norm) for a term of one to seven years to just administer the entire song.

This arrangement has become increasingly popular these days for artists who write and perform their own music and/or have the means and experience to place their songs. (Please see the pie diagram I've provided.)

Incomes (Typically No Advances)

Wrapping up admin deals, for every $1.00 the publishing company collects in earnings, the publishing company gets a fee of $0.15 (when it's a 15 percent deal) and the writer receives $0.85. Remember that in admin deals there's usually no advance to recoup, so the $0.85 essentially goes into the writer's pocket.

Note that if an artist ends up being successful, his or her willingness not to receive an advance or assistance with placements in exchange for retaining ownership and a greater share of the profits really pays off. It worked for classic artists like R.E.M. and Prince, who signed administration deals early in their careers. They bet on themselves and, as some have put it, "hit the jackpot."

AFTERTHOUGHT: ADVANCES ARE POSSIBLE While advances for admin deals are typically lower than, say, a co-pub deal, Kyle Staggs of Universal Pictures says, "Substantial advances are sometimes offered for admin deals. When this is done, the advance is based on (1) so-called pipeline income (i.e., income that is verifiable as collectable by the administrator immediately upon execution of the deal) and (2) the songwriter's/publisher's proven past income. The advance may be $35,000 on the high range, but I saw one for $500,000, which admittedly was an extremely rare case."

Self-Publishing/Self-Administrating (Doing It All Yourself)

And finally, to take the concept of ownership, control, and profits to the extreme, many writer/publishers choose not to do a deal and instead to "hang on to their music publishing" and handle all of the administration duties through various DIY resources.

This often occurs when: 1) no deal is offered, 2) a deal is offered but you want to hold out for a better advance, or 3) you have adequate resources to publish and handle administrative duties independently.

Ownership Splits (100/0 with Various Fees)

In the self-publishing/self-administrating scenario, the writer/self-publisher maintains 100 percent of the copyright in the composition and plugs and administers in whatever ways, and for whatever fees and percentages, he or she can arrange with various services. (Please see the pie diagram and compare it with the other deals above.)

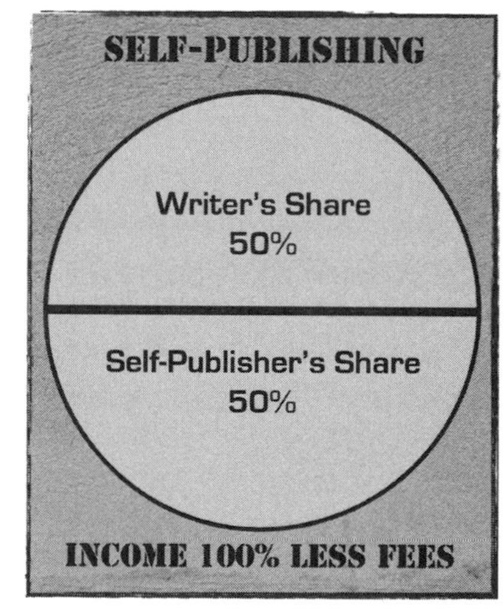

Incomes (No Advances)

Finally, for every $1.00 the writer/self-publisher collects in earnings, the self-publisher keeps $1.00 (less any fees paid to certain services that are hired to help handle some business).

While the prospect of retaining full control of the copyright and the greatest share of the income is tempting, keep in mind that it also means that there is a whole hell of a lot more work to do as well. Also, because there is no publishing company, there is no advance to use as a resource. One must always weigh the pros and cons of every situation.

So that's it for this chapter. Be sure to check out the interview with Neil Gillis, president of Round Hill Music, on the more specific details and terms of music publishing deals.

DO-IT-YOURSELF-FRIENDLY ADMINISTRATORS/DISTRIBUTORS

Do-it-yourselfers, who act as both the record company and the self-publisher, can easily affiliate with a number of online companies to both distribute their music and collect royalties. One such service, CD Baby, distributes physical CDs via its site and retail connections, downloads and streams via iTunes and Spotify, and songs via its connections in the film, TV, and game industry. As if that weren't enough, CD Baby also collects all generated incomes resulting from the publication of your music, including advertising monies from live videos, art videos, and user-generated content posted online (e.g., YouTube videos), foreign publishing monies, and more.

Here are a few breakdowns of the money you may make, again using CD Baby as an example:

- ***CDs*** (Using CD Baby's Store)

  $10.00 (your price)
  – $4.00 (CD Baby's flat rate)
  = $6.00 (your share per CD)

- ***Digital Downloads*** (Via CD Baby)

  $0.99 (standard per-single download price)
  – $0.09 (CD Baby's cut)
  = $0.90

- ***Digital Downloads*** (Via iTunes)

  $0.99 (standard per-single download price)
  – $0.30 (iTunes' cut)
  = $0.69
  – $0.062 (CD Baby's cut: 0.09 × 0.70)
  = $0.63 (your share per single download)

- ***Streaming (Via Spotify and Other Services):*** CD Baby receives reports monthly from each streaming service based on geography. These reports indicate an allocation per stream (fractions of pennies). CD Baby takes 9 percent and remits that to the artist when the artist's "pay point" (i.e., $10.00 minimum) is met.
- ***YouTube Royalties:*** CD Baby collects monies generated from ad revenues (and subscriptions) on art videos, live videos, and user-generated content. Of the monies collected, CD Baby takes 30 percent.
- ***Other Royalties:*** CD Baby assists in collecting other publishing monies (e.g., mechanicals, performances in cooperation with the PROs, and other incomes) that may be due in foreign territories, as well as in the U.S. CD Baby's service (called CD Baby Pro) takes 15 percent for this.

Q&A with Music Publisher Neil Gillis

Neil Gillis is the president of Round Hill Music, based in New York City. In the following interview, Gillis discusses the terms of contracts with song pluggers and music libraries, offers the finer points of publishing deals with established music publishers, and comments briefly on record companies that demand your music publishing rights.

Q: What kinds of deals should a DIY artist expect to be offered by a music exploitation company (i.e., a song plugger, music library, or some other company that places music)?

N.G.: The deals are really all over the place, but I'll give you two examples. The first one is the nonexclusive exploitation deal, and the second one is the exclusive exploitation deal. Both contain something called re-titling.

Q: What is a non-exclusive DIY exploitation deal?

N.G.: The DIY artist negotiates with a music exploitation company on a "nonexclusive" basis, giving it the right to pitch a song (or group of songs, such as an album) in film and television for a period of one to three years. When the exploitation company gets a placement, it takes a fee ranging from 25 to 50 percent of the generated incomes, which could include both synchronization and performance monies.

The DIY artist is still free to do whatever he or she wants with the songs: sell records at shows, get music on the radio, and get placements in film and TV via his or her own efforts (or through the efforts of another exploitation company).

To help differentiate between the performance incomes that are generated by the exploitation company and the performance incomes generated by the artist, there is a common practice of re-titling (or renaming) a song. In other words, the exploitation company will register a work with its appropriate performing rights organization under a completely different title. And at the same time, the DIY artist will register (or will have already registered) the very same song under the title he or she gave the song upon creation.

Note that re-titling is not something that all exploitation companies practice—and in fact, it's actually frowned upon by the Copyright Office, many supervisors, and even studios like Disney.

Nonetheless, re-titling does happen in the real world. Note, though, that the artist, in allowing the exploitation company to re-title the song and create a so-called new work or "derivative work," does not transfer copyright ownership in the original song. The DIY artist continues to own the song.

Q: And what is an exclusive DIY exploitation deal?

N.G.: The DIY artist would negotiate with the music exploitation company on an "exclusive" basis (meaning that no one else can pitch the songs in film and television at the same time), but he or she is still free to do whatever he or she wants with the songs in other areas, like selling CDs at shows, getting music on the radio, etc.

To help differentiate incomes generated by the different parties, the song may be re-titled, but the exploitation company does take ownership in 100 percent of the so-called new or derivative work. This essentially means that the exploitation company has the right to collect the incomes it generates from the re-titled work for the full life of copyright.

But again, deals are really all over the place and subject to individual terms. I strongly advise your readers to consult with the proper business professional before signing anything.

Q: What about exploitation deals that share in the masters?

N.G.: These days it is typical for the music exploitation company to get a share of the master on synch deals, especially since many DIY artists are all-in (meaning they own the copyright in both the song and the master). The exploitation company usually takes 25 to 50 percent.

SAMPLE DIY DEAL WITH A MUSIC EXPLOITATION COMPANY

Outlined below is a typical nonexclusive deal memo offered to an independent artist by a reputable music exploitation company:

- The writer retains 100 percent of the writer's share.
- The exploitation company receives 100 percent of the publishing for perpetuity, but only on licenses that they acquire.
- The writer and the exploitation company will share 50/50 of the master monies on synch deals that the company acquires.

- The writer shall enter onto an initial term of 3 years with two successive (2) year periods which will automatically renew for (2) years until written notice is given (90) days prior to the commencement of any renewal term.
- The exploitation company has the right to re-title all musical compositions.

[Note: The above deal was reviewed by several industry professionals and confirmed as being fairly normal, except the "term," which they thought should be as short as one year.]

Q: Moving on, what are the important terms in standard music publishing contracts?

N.G.: First let me say that "publishing deals" (i.e., where a writer is on contract for all the songs he or she writes over several years and an advance is offered, etc.) do not grow on trees—especially at the bigger companies. A writer has to have a lot going on—hit songs, a great manager, and more.

While the publishing advance (the amount the writer gets up front) is often treated as being the most important term in the contract, there are other deal points that can be equally, if not more, important. The two that come to mind are "reversion of copyright" and "prior approvals." Following this I'll touch on the advance.

Q: Deal point 1: reversion?

N.G.: Reversion of copyright, as your readers must already know after reading chapter 15, deals with the point in time after the expiration of the deal when your rights return to you. This can be very important in terms of how your career moves forward.

Upon getting your copyrights back, assuming you had any success, you can shoot for a new deal and renegotiate for a larger advance, or you can just self-publish and benefit from earning a greater share of monies by virtue of owning the songs outright.

Q: Deal point 2: prior approvals?

N.G.: Prior approvals are vital in that they are your control factor in terms of how a publisher can and cannot utilize your works. For writers, this is a huge issue, since their songs are their babies. Prior approvals could include who can cover your songs, the types of products your music can be associated with, whether your songs can be used in political campaigns, and more.

Q: Deal point 3: the advance?

N.G.: Finally, the advance is important because it may say something about how much the company believes it can generate for you. It can also be important because artists often need money up front to take care of their bills so they can concentrate on their writing.

However, one must not overestimate the importance of the advance at the expense of the factors mentioned above. If your attorney can get reversionary language, prior approvals, and a large advance, then more power to you. But note that these deal points do not automatically go hand in hand and all deserve equal attention in contract negotiations.

Q: Can you explain the "term of agreement" versus "term of copyright"?

N.G.: Many people get these two phrases confused. Let me define each term:

The "agreement term" in a publishing agreement refers to how long the publishing deal will last. (It has nothing to do with copyright duration, as you'll see in a moment.) Agreement terms are usually based on a certain number of years, or, in many cases, a certain number of records.

"Copyright duration" is different from the agreement term. It refers to the length of time the publisher will continue to own your songs—that were created during the term—after your agreement term has expired.

For instance, the publisher may continue to hold on to your songs after the agreement term for the full life of copyright (LOC); or, if you've negotiated a reversion of copyright clause into your agreement, the publisher may have to revert the rights back to you at a specified time (say, 10 years after the agreement term expires). It all depends on the finer points of your agreement and what you're able to negotiate.

Q: What are "option periods"?

N.G.: "Option periods" describe the publisher's choice or "option" to extend the term of your deal upon it expiring.

For instance, if your publishing agreement is time-based, your publisher may exercise its option (or multiple options) to continue the agreement for another year(s).

If your agreement is record-delivery based, your publisher may exercise its option (or multiple options) to continue your agreement for another record(s).

Q: What is the "delivery commitment" found in publishing contracts?

N.G.: Your "delivery commitments" define what you're responsible for delivering to your publisher during the term of your agreement.

For instance, your agreement may require you to write a certain number of "commercially acceptable" songs, or it may require you to write a certain number of songs that get recorded and released by you or by other artists who want to use your songs.

Delivery commitment language is extremely important for artists to consider when negotiating their deals, since they can end up getting stuck in a deal that theoretically never ends.

Q: How do 360 record deals affect publishing?

N.G.: Many independent record labels have historically been known to ask their artists to sign over their publishing rights. With current deal structures [like 360 deals], a number of majors are doing the same. It is not a new concept by any means. It is an old practice that meets a need in the current climate. That need is for a label to diversify and generate income from more than just record sales—as most people know, record sales have been declining for most labels due to unauthorized digital downloading for several years.

If you choose to consider signing over your publishing rights to a record label under a 360 deal, then you have to ask yourself two basic questions.

First, is this label really going to bring anything to the table and add value to your songs? Does this label truly understand publishing and have a legitimate business in that regard, or are they just going to pass this off to a third party to do the business for them while they gain the benefit of this revenue share?

Second, does this label and its publishing entity want to cross your income from either deal against the other? Note that if your income is crossed (for instance, if your publishing monies are used to pay back unrecouped recording expenses), it could be a long time before you get paid. Needless to say, this is not a good thing.

In closing, if a young band should feel that they have to sign with a record company that wants publishing, they need their attorney and their management team around them to make sure that the deal is fair from both an economic and creative standpoint. Never jump at any deal without thinking it through. Good luck!

20

Music Publishing, Part 6

Starting Your Own Publishing Company

"I don't need anyone to hold me, I can hold my own." –Ani DiFranco

And finally, welcome to the last chapter on music publishing and starting your own publishing company! I like to think of this as a bonus chapter—it's short, sweet, and refers back to all of the things you learned in the last couple of chapters.

In any case, with no further ado, here are six steps to starting your own publishing company, followed by a number of tips for pitching your own music in film, TV, and games. Please enjoy.

Six Steps to Starting Your Own Publishing Company

Here's a brief overview of the bare minimum you must do to get set up your own publishing company.

Step 1: Affiliate with ASCAP or BMI

The first step in starting your own publishing company is to contact one of the two performing rights organizations (ASCAP or BMI), affiliate yourself as a writer and a publisher, and register your songs (a process often called title registration). As you know, PROs will make sure that you are paid for the public performances of your compositions.

Note: I purposely left SESAC and Global Rights Music (the newest performing rights company) out of this discussion since their members must typically be selected by a referral process. Please speak with a representative to find out about eligibility.

Publisher Affiliation

As a self-publisher, you're required to pick a name for your publishing company. You're also required to include two alternate titles (three names total) in case your first name is already taken by another publisher. The more unique the name, the better your chances of securing that name. ASCAP charges a one-time fee of $50 and BMI charges a one-time fee of $150 (for an independently owned company) or $250 (for a partnership or corporation).

Writer Affiliation

Writers are required to have a separate writer affiliation with the performing rights organizations. Remember that the performing rights organizations always send the "writer's share" of earnings directly to the writer, regardless of who the music publisher is—even if it's you.

ASCAP charges a one-time fee of $50 for writers; BMI charges nothing.

Title Registration

Finally, as both writer and publisher of your songs, it's absolutely essential that you provide your performing rights organization with detailed information (name, title, shares in a song, etc.) for every composition you publish so that you can be entered into their system and paid.

If you're the sole writer of a composition, you own 100 percent of the writer's share and 100 percent of the publisher's share. If you write a composition with your four-member band and you're dividing the credit equally, then each member owns both 25 percent of the writer's share (4 × 25 = 100) and 25 percent of the publisher's share (4 × 25 = 100).

AFTERTHOUGHT: BANDS FORM ONE COMPANY Bands commonly form one publishing company under a partnership agreement (or corporation). Under these circumstances, all of the songs are registered to that company as the sole publisher. Incomes are then divided under the terms of the agreement.

Step 2: Register with SoundExchange

Moving on to the second step in self-publishing, let's talk about registering your sound recording copyrights with SoundExchange.

If you own your master recordings (and/or if you perform on your masters as a featured or non-featured musician), SoundExchange pays out monies when sound recordings are broadcast digitally by webcasters (SiriusXM satellite radio, Pandora, etc.).

Of the monies collected, 50 percent is paid to the record label, 45 percent to featured performers, and 5 percent to non-featured performers (via the unions, AFM and SAG-AFTRA). SoundExchange is like ASCAP and BMI for sound recordings. Registration is free, easy, and fast. Check out their site today at www.soundexchange.com.

Step 3: File a DBA (Doing Business As)

The third thing you must do to become a self-publisher is to file for a DBA statement with your county clerk's office. A DBA, or "doing business as" statement, is sometimes called a "fictitious business name."

A DBA will enable you to cash checks made out to your publishing company name. Can you imagine the headaches you'd have trying to cash a check made out to John Doe Songs without any identification proving the connection? That's what a DBA is for.

Getting a DBA

Getting a DBA is easy. Search online for your local county clerk's office. You'll need to fill out specific forms that the clerk will provide, pay a fee ranging from around $45 to $60, and submit the contents of the form to a local newspaper for printing (a procedure for which your county clerk will provide assistance); then you'll receive your certificate soon after.

Opening a Bank Account and Getting a Tax ID Number

Finally, you also need to set up a bank account under the name of your publishing company. When opening the account, you may need to provide a Social Security number or a federal tax identification number (which, for a business, is basically the equivalent of an individual Social Security number).

A tax identification number can be obtained through applications filed with the IRS. (Contact the Internal Revenue Service at 800-829-1040 or www.irs.gov.)

AFTERTHOUGHT: GOT BUSINESS ENTITIES? Sole proprietor, partnership, corporation, S corporation, or LLC? Another important aspect of starting your own publishing company may be the formation of a business entity to provide certain tax benefits and shield you from certain liabilities. It's not absolutely necessary when you're starting out, but you should discuss this with your accountant. You can also see the interview with attorney Jeff Cohen in chapter 3 for more information.

Step 4: Registering Your Songs with the Copyright Office

Moving right along to the fourth step of starting your own publishing company, let me briefly remind you to register your copyrights with the Copyright Office in Washington, D.C. (something I already discussed in detail in chapters 15 and 16).

But don't confuse title registration with ASCAP and BMI and copyright registration with the Copyright Office—be clear that the two are not the same. Okay? Cool!

If you have any questions regarding how to fill out a copyright form, the Copyright Office will be more than happy to assist you.

The fee to register your copyrights using paper forms is $85 per song. The fee to register your copyrights electronically is $35 per song (as long as you are the sole author of the song and master) or $55 per work with multiple authors/owners. You can also register a group of songs as a collection of works on one registration for $55 (see chapter 16 for details). Call the Copyright Public Information Office at 202-707-3000 or visit www.copyright.gov.

Step 5: Handling Other Administrative Duties

Once you've established your own publishing company, how do you collect your publishing income?

You're already set up to receive public performance royalties of your songs through ASCAP or BMI, and digital performance royalties of your masters through SoundExchange.

But what about other incomes like mechanicals and synch? Read on, my friends.

Mechanical Royalties

As previously discussed in the "Mechanical Royalties" section of Chapter 17, when a record company wants to use one of your songs on phonorecord (CDs, digital downloads, etc.), they'll ask you to sign a mechanical license. (If you're an unsigned artist releasing your own music, then obviously you are the record company and probably won't issue yourself a license.)

Record companies can then send you your mechanical royalty statements directly, or if you choose you can have a major mechanical rights collection society such as the Harry Fox Agency (HFA) issue mechanical licenses and collect royalties for you.

HFA charges a percentage of your gross earnings, which is currently 8.7 percent, but this is subject to change, so check their website frequently for updates.

Synchronization Fees

When someone wants to use one of your songs in a film, television commercial, television show, video game, etc., they'll contact you and ask you to agree to a synch license.

Monies can be sent directly to you from the various organizations with whom you contract. Friends of mine receive checks in the mail regularly.

However, unless you're banging on advertising agencies' doors, schmoozing with directors at parties, and generally being a salesperson, it's not likely your phone is going to be ringing off the hook—unless, of course, you have a hit song and/or your label's film and TV department is on the hunt for you.

Be sure to check out the boxed text at the end of this chapter on pitching your own music in film and TV.

Print Royalties

A print license is required when someone wants to use your songs in sheet music, folios, lyric websites, and more. Publishers can directly issue licenses and collect royalties.

However, unless your music is in high demand, it's unlikely that established printers will want to produce and sell your books, or that popular websites will want to reprint your lyrics.

Certainly, you can always print up your own books and post lyrics on your own websites, but you're probably not going to issue yourself a license.

Sub-publishing Income

Finally, remember that to collect sub-publishing income, you must find a sub-publisher in the territory in which your music is to be published. You have essentially three options:

1. You can ask the record or film company releasing your music overseas to recommend a sub-publisher.
2. You can also contact one of the performing rights or mechanical rights agencies (such as GEMA in Germany or JASRAC in Japan) and ask them for a list of their registered local publishers.
3. Finally, if your music is generating significant income overseas, you may be able to arrange a deal with a U.S. publishing company that has worldwide offices. Warner/Chappell Music, Universal Music Publishing Group, BMG, and Sony/ATV Publishing, and smaller publishers like PEN Music Group and Round Hill Music all have worldwide affiliates.

Remember that sub-publishers usually take from 10 to 25 percent of what they collect.

Step 6: Leave It All Up to a DIY-Friendly Administrator (CD Baby, TuneCore)

To end our discussion on starting your own publishing company, let me touch briefly on a new breed of administrator I like to call "DIY-friendly administrators" or administrator/distributors. These are the folks who, unlike the well-established music publishing companies, will work essentially with anyone to ensure that all your money is collected and you're paid. Let's face it, this stuff is not easy or fun.

DIY-friendly companies can do the following and more:

- ***Physical Distribution/Collection:*** Make your physical recordings (CDs, vinyl, etc.) available for order in stores, collect monies, and send you payments.
- ***Digital Distribution/Collection:*** Distribute your digital recordings (downloads and streaming music), collect incomes, and make payments.
- ***Public Performances:*** Help you register with the performing rights organizations to ensure the proper collection of all public performances of your compositions.
- ***Synch:*** Place your music in synchronization (films, TV, and adverts).
- ***Video Ad Monies:*** Collect advertising monies you may be entitled to from live videos, art videos, and user-generated video content (like the videos you see on YouTube).
- ***Foreign Monies:*** Collect monies you may be due in foreign territories.

While each service offers something different, and fees vary, be sure to check out services offered by CD Baby (www.cdbaby.com) as well as TuneCore (www.tunecore.com).

So that's about it for now—your publishing company should be all set up and ready to roll. Be sure to check out a few more tips on pitching in the box below. Peace and much success.

HOW TO PITCH YOUR OWN MUSIC IN FILM, TV, AND GAMES

Collecting incomes correctly is no easy task when you choose to self-publish. Generating monies through pitching is no walk in the park, either. Here are a few basic tips to help you place your music in film, TV, and games:

- ***Have Great Songs:*** Write music with memorable hooks and clear lyric subjects. Your music must also evoke strong feelings and be applicable to specific moods and scenes.
- ***Have Broadcast-Quality Recordings:*** Create recordings with strong vocal and instrumental performances, current instrumentation and mixes, and cleared samples. Have both "clean" (no-profanity) versions of your music and instrumental (no-vocal) versions of your music available.
- ***Get Your Split Sheets Together:*** Be sure that all cowriters (if any) are in complete agreement about what portion of the song (or masters) they all own, and have all of their publishing names and PRO affiliations available.
- ***Know Your Music:*** Be ready to describe the vibe and mood of your music in as few words as possible, and understand what television shows or films—as well as what types of scenes (car chases, love scenes, etc.)—are best suited for your songs.
- ***Conduct Research:*** Utilize the *Hollywood Reporter* (www.hollywoodreporter.com) to find films and TV shows in production. Utilize the *Film & Television Music Guide* (www.musicregistry.com) and/or the Internet Movie Database Pro to find contact information for music supervisors, producers, production companies, and music publishers.
- ***Seek Placements in Student Films:*** Research institutions with film, video, and/or game art and design departments and get in touch. Today's film students are tomorrow's festival winners and successful directors.
- ***Network at Film Festivals:*** Meet and mingle with film directors and TV/film music supervisors by attending festivals. This can lead you to future work!
- ***Utilize Placement Services:*** Join Taxi (www.taxi.com), Pump Audio (www.pumpaudio.com), or Smashtrax Music (www.smashtrax.com). These services provide licensing opportunities in television shows, films, and video games. Taxi will even critique your songs and offer helpful tips to improve your writing.
- ***Approach Music Libraries:*** Check out Opus 1 Music Library (www.opus1musiclibrary.com), Riptide Music (www.riptidemusic.com), and FirstCom Music (www.firstcom.com). Ad agencies, film directors, and game companies look to music libraries for music, and you just might get a placement.
- ***Be Professional:*** Remember, this is a business of relationships. If you're able to get in contact with Joe Placement, be professional, be concise, and be nice.
- ***Represent with Authority:*** Introduce yourself as the representative/owner of your own company. The people you call don't always need to know you are the artist/writer.
- ***Be Ready to Audition:*** Send a recording of your music and/or e-mail a link where supervisors can preview your music online. SoundCloud (www.soundcloud.com) is a popular site for this.
- ***Be Patient:*** Remember that other independent musicians have been trying to place their music in film, TV, and games for years before you. Hang in there.
- ***Know What to Negotiate For:*** Never sign anything you don't understand! Further, have some understanding of the standard rates your music can generate. While at the beginning of your career, all offers may be "take it or leave it," you'll know what's fair.
- ***Become an Intern:*** Volunteer to work at a music publishing company for free. Form relationships first, and when someone asks you more about what you do, have your music ready to play. How sneaky of you!

21

Live Performing and Touring, Part 1

Purpose and Opportunity

"Without a specific objective in mind, life on the road is the road to nowhere."
—Chris Arnstein, tour manager

Live performing and touring is one of the most primal ways for artists to introduce their music to the marketplace, increase their fan base, and eventually make money. By playing before target audiences night after night, interviewing with radio stations and the press, and asking new fans to spread the word of mouth on their social networks, a new group can build a grassroots following of music lovers that will support them loyally for years to come.

For many young artists, live performing and touring may appear to be a nonstop party and the ultimate money-making machine. It's true that live performing and touring can be fun and eventually become a significant portion of an artist's revenue pie—but there's also more to them than meets the eye.

In this chapter I'll provide a behind-the-scenes look at when and why to perform live and tour, and how and where to get gigs. In the next chapter, I'll talk about the money: how you're paid for live performance deals, how live performance deals are negotiated, and live performance contracts and riders. Sound good? Then let's do this.

When and Why to Perform Live and Tour

There are a variety of different levels of live performing and touring—each with its own purpose.

Level 1: The Development Phase—Testing the Waters

The first level of live performing and touring is built right at home as you develop your craft. It consists of the following:

- ***Playing Locally, Frequently:*** A band must play everywhere and anywhere that it can early on—from block parties, to house parties, to high school talent shows, to local clubs. The band might even hop into a rented van for a one-night road trip into the next town just to experience the thrill of hitting the road. Overall, this is how each member becomes more proficient on his or her axe and how the band gets tight as a unit. At this stage, a band plays for free. The focus is what the group learns, not what it earns.
- ***Finding Your True Artist:*** A band must experiment with its sound, look, and style. It must figure out what it stands for in the marketplace and it must hone its songwriting skills. The objective at this stage is discovery—figuring out just who the hell they are, what they have to say, and why anyone should care about them. The band observes its audience and finds out what fans respond to, and do not respond to.

- ***Learning the Stage:*** Finally, a band should master the art of live performing—including transitioning from one song to the next, engaging the crowd with interesting commentary, and figuring out how to handle disasters (i.e., knowing what to do when the mic goes out, the bass drum head breaks, or the amp blows). Learning how to cope in these instances separates the pros from the novices.

Level 2: The Business-Minded Phase—Going In for the Local Kill

After a band pays it dues at the first level, it must start thinking more about business and becoming more focused in its efforts. This phase usually involves the following:

- ***Playing Locally, Sparingly:*** A band must now become more focused by playing venues that appeal to its target audience and limiting its performances to once or twice monthly. At this level, the idea is to go for quality and not quantity. Each show should be an amazing night to remember—with visual and audio effects, courtesy of hired sound and light techs; highly energetic performances; an after-party that gets people talking for weeks; a shuttle service to and from the gig; and a packed house as a result of insane marketing efforts. No gig should be a lame gig. This is where the real work starts.
- ***Building Awareness Among Fans and Industry:*** A band must also work diligently at connecting with its audience. This can be done by meeting with fans after every show, collecting e-mail addresses, updating social media content, forming street teams to get the fans involved in handling promotional tasks, and showing appreciation to the super fans that go the extra mile. Further, a band must try to connect with industry people. This can be done by interviewing at local college radio stations, inviting local journalists to its shows, attending local charity events, posting quality YouTube videos, attending the best conferences, and just networking and being part of the local scene.
- ***Securing Deals, Dollars, and Team Players:*** Finally, a band must act like its own professional entertainment company by recording its own music and making plentiful sales, finding song placements and collecting generated incomes, getting the best local gigs and drawing healthy crowds, and creating merchandise and making sales at shows. After accomplishing this and more, a band might then start using the momentum to attract personal managers, music libraries, song pluggers, and even record labels to help get them to that next level of their careers. There is no whining or impatience at this level, just a realistic understanding that it may take a long time to get to the top.

Level 3: The Traveling Salesperson Phase—Supporting Your Record

After attracting the attention of those who can help by first helping themselves (which, by the way, could take months if not years), a band may now be ready to graduate into the third phase of live performing and touring. This phase usually consists of the following:

- ***Hitting the Road for Extended Periods:*** A band hits the road for several weeks at a time in support of its new record. This is done with the financial assistance of fans (via crowdfunding techniques), personal investors and sponsors, or a record label that can help cover the incredible expenses involved. Make no mistake, gas, tolls, hotels, transportation, crew, sound, lights, food, insurance, taxes, and commissions to your pro team (attorney, manager, and business manager) can all add up.
- ***Maximizing Your Efforts:*** A band realizes that its time out on the road (night after night and city after city) is invaluable. It knows that the objective is to stimulate sales and increase awareness—not to fuck around and get drunk. The band meets with every college radio DJ, every venue booker, every retail shop, every blogger and local press agent, every fan, and every group on the tour. Additionally, the band strives for continual improvement each night, trying to outdo itself from one performance to the next. As if this weren't enough, a band uses its precious spare time to continue writing and demoing songs for its next record while still on the road. The band knows all too well that time on the

road does not stand still, and that if it is going to maintain a long-term successful career, it must keep the quality product coming.

- ***Figuring Out How to Tour Efficiently and Effectively:*** Finally, a band realizes that touring is akin to a long business trip, and coming home from the road with a profit or breaking even is its primary objective. A band works collaboratively while out on the road to minimize expenses without any whining and rock star drama. While never sacrificing the quality of its shows, a band makes practical decisions regarding transportation, hotels, salaries, number of crew members, rider requests for food and liquor backstage, staging, and so much more. The band also finds ways to increase revenue through creative merchandising, including shirts, hats, autographed sticks, painted bass drum heads, and artwork (String Cheese Incident even sold live recordings of its shows every night for $10 a pop). Essentially, the band figures out how to tour efficiently and effectively so that it can continue to stay out on the road and generate income for years to come.

Level 4: The Making-the-Money Phase—Getting It While the Getting Is Good

Finally, after working long and hard over the course of several years, overcoming incredible odds, and maybe even scoring a couple of hit singles, you've made it to level four of touring. This phase consists of the following:

- ***Reaping the Benefits on the High Road:*** A band plays the largest venues and festivals and receives the highest fees and percentages for weeks and months at a time. Lady Gaga grossed $181 million on her "Born This Way Ball" tour and U2 grossed $730 million on their 360° tour. Surely, a band pays numerous expenses, but it still comes home with substantial profits. In fact, at this level of touring, a band's touring expenses may even be underwritten by corporate sponsors, making the profits that much higher (e.g., Budweiser has sponsored Rihanna and Pepsi Cola has sponsored Beyoncé). To generate additional monies, the band sells meet-and-greet packages and VIP packages to its fans. Britney Spears offered a hefty $2,525 opportunity to meet her and snap a picture before her Las Vegas shows. Miley Cyrus, known as the "queen of the meet and greet," charged $959. Justin Bieber charged $250.
- ***Keeping Fans Happy and Paying the Price:*** A band goes out of its way to deliver the ultimate tour experience for the fans. U2 played under a 115-foot-tall, 200-ton structure resembling a large spider set up in the middle of each stadium. Lady Gaga played in front of a 400-square-foot, five-story castle complete with LED lighting in each room. No expense is spared at this level of touring, but this also means that millions are spent (it costs Lady Gaga $1 million per show to set up and break down her staging). Expenses may include special effects, pyrotechnics, costumes, dancers, wardrobe personnel, riggers, lighting directors, and all of the extra trucks and busses needed to haul all of the extra gear. But the fans really appreciate it, and expect it.
- ***Making That Money and Saving It:*** Finally, the smart members of a band are wise enough to save their money and invest it while the getting is good. Smart artists know that life in the big leagues and touring out on the high roads can easily come to a crashing halt—as it does for many artists. And when it does come crashing down, some groups are never heard from again. Others resurface down the road on their nostalgia tours. While these groups may go back to playing smaller venues, they continue making really decent money for many more years to come.

THE HARDEST-WORKING MAN IN SHOW BUSINESS

Guitarist Joe Bonamassa is a great example of someone who climbed the ranks of the live performing and touring world, who learned how to tour and make money, and who is still going strong.

Opening for B.B. King when he was only 12 years old, Bonamassa played relentlessly around upstate New York for the next 10 years while honing his craft and creating a buzz.

After building up a great deal of credibility as a rising blues star, Bonamassa eventually recorded an album with the band Bloodline (featuring the sons of famous artists like the Doors, Miles Davis, and the Allman Brothers) and hit the road. Eventually, Bonamassa moved on to releasing his own solo debut album on his own label, J&R Adventures.

Since his first solo album release, Bonamassa has recorded 11 studio albums, 11 live audio albums, and 7 live DVDs. He tours relentlessly in support of all of his releases (an average of 200 shows annually), sells an impressive line of merchandise at his shows, and performs guitar clinics at schools around the country. Pretty impressive!

Needless to say, Bonamassa is truly one of the hardest-working men in show business and evidence of what you can accomplish when you are willing to stick at it for the long haul and pay some serious dues. Look for Bonamassa to be touring in a city near you.

How and Where to Get Gigs: 9 Tips to Consider

Now that we've discussed the various stages and realities of touring, it's time to talk about getting gigs. Here are 9 tips to consider—from do-it-yourself methods to getting an agent.

Tip #1: Get Local Club Referrals from Similar Local Bands

The quickest way to get gigs is to seek contacts and recommendations from experienced local bands on your circuit. With these referrals, call or e-mail the club promoter, tell him or her that so-and-so sent you, and then direct him or her to your website, where MP3s, video clips, and bios can be reviewed.

Craft an effective sales pitch by focusing on the customer benefits: tell the promoter what he or she will gain by presenting your group and what positive impact your performance will bring to the bottom line of the bar or club. If you can't initially get in touch, be sure to follow up daily and always be pleasantly patient.

Getting gigs really isn't rocket science at this stage of the game. Says talent agent John Pantle of APA, "You just have to be a businessperson and sell yourself."

Tip #2: Form Band Alliances and Gig Swap

Another method for getting gigs is to form alliances with other like bands. Surf the Web and contact cool artists in your hometown and surrounding cities, help them promote by posting their website links on your social networks, and attend their live shows. Treat these relationships with the same intensity as the relationships with promoters and clubs.

If one group has a weekend date, they may be able to pull you in as the opener, and vice versa. Better yet, if one group gets signed, they just may tell their label about you and even ask you to go out on tour. For instance, Papa Roach took a friend's band, Alien Ant Farm, on tour not too long ago. Never underestimate the value of forming band alliances. This is important!

Tip #3: Consider Contacting Colleges

Colleges provide yet another opportunity to perform live, make new fans, expand your territory, and even make a few bucks in the process. Colleges usually have budgets ranging from $150 to $750 for new music every week. Sounds like the right gig to me.

Get an updated phone list for colleges in your area by either conducting an online search or asking another local band to share its list with you. Contact the student activities department and tell them that you would like to be considered as part of their weekly entertainment concerts or "nooners" (colleges often have regular "noontime" concerts). Also try contacting NACA (National Association for Campus Activities—www.naca.org), which is perfect for getting you connected with college bookers nationwide.

Tip #4: Keep Your Eyes on Corporate Sponsors

Companies like Jägermeister (www.jagermeister.com), Zippo lighters (www.zippohottour.com), Jim Beam (www.jimbeam.com), and Ernie Ball (www.ernieball.com) have long reputations for providing up-and-coming bands with opportunities to perform—from "battle of the bands" competitions to opening slots on sponsored tours. Would you believe that indie artist Eric Hutchinson was asked and paid by Jeep to tour in one of its vehicles, blog about the experience, and then appear on *The Tonight Show*? This is just one of many opportunities.

To pursue gigs with corporate sponsors, create a list of corporations whose products are associated with your target fans. Use the Internet to gather each of these companies' names, marketing directors, addresses, phone numbers, and submission policies. Get in touch and tell them that you share a similar demographic audience and would be excited to promote their products. You can also try referring to *IEG's Complete Guide to Sponsorships* and the *IEG Sponsorship Sourcebook* (www.sponsorship.com) for further ideas about working with sponsors. Getting these gigs is not easy, but as with anything else, you just have to be persistent.

Tip #5: Watch for Unsigned Artist Openings on Festival Tours

Festivals like Bonnaroo (www.bonnaroo.com), Vans Warped Tour (www.vanswarpedtour.com), and the Voodoo Music + Arts Experience (www.worshipthemusic.com) are great places to play since they already draw thousands of like-minded music lovers.

Promoters of these events are usually more than willing to give deserving local bands a shot at an opening slot. If you truly feel that you're ready, look for submission policies on the websites of these festival events and make your move.

Or, in the words of Ozzy Osbourne bassist and Mercenary Management owner Blasko, "Why not jump in the van anyway and play the parking lots of these festival tours as fans go in and out of the venue?" Good idea, Blasko. Now that's what I call taking charge of your career and making things happen. Be sure to check out the movie *No Room for Rockstars*, which documents a number of bands that actually utilized this technique.

Tip #6: Play Industry Conventions

Industry conventions, like the SXSW music convention in Austin, Texas (www.sxsw.com), and NAMM in Anaheim, California (www.namm.org), may provide additional gigging opportunities. These events attract large numbers of industry people and enthusiasts from around the world. And the best part is that you can maximize your promotional dollar at these events by killing a few birds with one stone—performing, networking, and even picking up some other work.

As told in *Music Marketing for the DIY Musician* by yours truly, Mayfield, a Los Angeles independent band, drove from Los Angeles to the popular Sundance Film Festival in Park City, Utah, to perform at an industry showcase. While at the festival, it also played at a number of hotel parties for various film directors and music supervisors, and it picked up a few more last-minute gigs for entertainment-based companies in attendance as well. This eventually landed the band a placement in an internationally released film with a major star. Pretty cool!

Tip #7: Play Where Fans Go: Consider All Alternative Venues and Events

Winding down to the last few tips, another method for getting gigs is to consider all the other places not yet mentioned where your target fans may hang out. Depending on your audience, these could include bookstores, independent record shops, art galleries, skateboard parks, military bases, tattoo conventions, coffee shops, wineries, and house parties. All of these places are typically less competitive than your average club, and they can provide a faster route to building awareness in your local marketplace. Just play the role of private investigator, conduct an online search, and start getting in touch with the various folks in charge. You'll be surprised at the number of opportunities you'll uncover.

Tip #8: Hire a Personal Manager

If a group is able to generate a buzz and advance its career on its own, a personal manager may now be enticed to come aboard to assist the group in getting gigs. First and foremost, managers will try to secure a licensed talent agent to procure employment for their artists and negotiate live performance deals. A manager will also try to pull favors from friends in the business (managers, agents, promoters, etc.) to hook you up with more successful bands with whom you can tour. Finally, a manager may even find ways to arrange money to buy you into certain festival tours. In other words, it's possible to convince a record label, publisher, or some other investor that getting you on a specific tour and in front of a certain number of people is a valid marketing expense. Buy-ins do exist. I've seen them. And still do!

Tip #9: Get a Talent Agent

The last method for getting the right gigs and getting paid is to hire an experienced talent agent. Once your group is generating substantial live performance fees, drawing large local crowds, or getting attention from labels and publishers, a talent agent with national clout may become interested.

A talent agent will work with your manager to formulate your tour strategies, package you with other bands, determine whether you should open or headline, route a tour, price your tickets, determine when to put your tickets on sale, negotiate live performance deals, collect deposits, and monitor show publicity. Bottom line: your talent agent's business is live performing and touring, and when an agent gets behind you, you're probably farther along the way to getting on the right gigs and tours and getting paid than you ever were before. (Be sure to read chapter 11 for more on talent agents.)

Q&A with Tour Manager Chris Arnstein

Chris Arnstein is a personal manager, international tour manager, and booking agent who has provided services for the Eagles, Madonna, Journey, Stevie Nicks, Joe Walsh, Julio Iglesias, and Earth, Wind & Fire.

In this informative interview conducted before he passed away, Mr. Arnstein speaks candidly and offers practical advice about the realities of hitting the road, and talks about the financial, moral, and ethical responsibilities involved in pursuing one's dreams. You won't want to miss this.

Q: What does live performing and touring mean to you from a business perspective?

C.A.: Live performing and touring is the business of brands—the unique experience, sound, style, and live show that makes the public want to turn off the TV, get in the car, and drive out to the venue every time you perform.

Whether it's Beyoncé or just the hottest local act, the buying public needs to have a realm of expectancy. They want to know what they're getting for their money, and they expect you to deliver on that brand promise or they'll gladly pay their allegiance elsewhere.

Develop a great band and a great brand. Until you've truly got a live show that's brilliant, unique, and consistent, you've got nothing!

Q: What is the biggest misconception young artists have about hitting the road?

C.A.: Most bands think that hitting the road is like going to summer camp. They're totally unclear on its purpose. But one must always try to determine the return on the investment of time, money, and resources before hopping in the van. Unless there is a well-thought-out marketing plan, a band's time on the road is the road to nowhere. It's just a vacation from reality.

Q: How do bands get the opportunity to go out on the road?

C.A.: Bands and artists get the opportunity to go out on the road because someone feels that their presence is worth more than the cost of having them perform.

A promoter considers every expense before deciding to present you before an audience.

A record label analyzes its return on investment, or "ROI," before agreeing to offer you deficit tour support.

And a headlining act considers the cool cachet (or hipness) you'll bring—and the extra tickets you'll sell—before bringing you out on the road.

Make no mistake: bands get the chance to go out on the road because of business first. No business, then no show.

Q: What are some of the biggest problems that musicians experience while touring?

C.A.: Many artists fall into the trap of living their lives in a bubble when out on the road. They're up on stage every night and do not know how to turn themselves off. They believe their own hype and pretend that being an artist absolves them of all hard work and pushing their careers forward. Their nightly mission becomes getting laid rather than shaking fans' hands, meeting radio station personnel, and schmoozing with venue promoters. This is a big mistake. One's time on the road (and on the earth) is extremely valuable and must be maximized for success.

The second most common problem that musicians incur while touring is failing to remember that the tour will one day come to an end, and that it might be some time before they go back out again. This means that you'd better save as much money as you can on the road (assuming that you're making any money at all) and learn to set up business opportunities at home that you can immediately dive back into (and back out of). This is especially a challenge for young artists. Should they quit their job at Home Depot or Starbucks just for the chance to do a two-week leg of a tour, they'd better pray that they can get their gig back, or they'll wind up living on someone's couch.

Q: What other words of wisdom do you have that can help musicians and bands for the years ahead?

C.A.: Just remember that every day that you're chasing your dream, you have one day less to be doing something more practical. This is a tough business and the odds are stacked against you. So be sure to make every move count. Work hard. Think business first. Create an amazing brand. Have some fun, too. And don't forget to put me on your guest list when you're a big star. Good luck.

22

Live Performing and Touring, Part 2

Deals, Negotiations, and Contracts

"It's not that promoters are lying, cheating scumbags, but there's a good chance that they are, and you have to assume the worst." —*Mark Goldstein, former vice president of business affairs at Warner Bros. Music*

Now that you've read chapter 21, you should have a better understanding of when and why to tour, as well as how and where to get gigs.

Now it's time to continue our discussion on live performing and touring with a chapter about the deals and dollars involved (if any).

Let's get right on the road and talk about how you're paid for live performance deals, how live performance deals are negotiated, and what goes into live performance contracts and riders.

How You're Paid for Live Performance Deals

There are a variety of ways that you get paid for a live performance. The most common are as follows:

- Nothing (i.e., you're playing for free)
- Pay-to-play
- A straight percentage
- A flat guaranteed fee
- A guaranteed fee versus a percentage

A number of factors determine which of these payment methods is used, including the stature of the artist, the size of the production, the size of the venue, whether the band is an opening act or a headliner, and the reputation of the talent agency (if there is one) negotiating on the band's behalf. The concert promoter wants to pay as little as possible, and the band wants to make as much as it can. This makes the deals, as well as the sums of money negotiated, difficult to nail down. The truth is, anything goes. Let's take a look.

Nothing (a.k.a. Free)

In the "nothing" or free deal, a situation that exists at the beginning stages of your career when you're playing in small clubs and bars, the booker offers zero monetary compensation. But don't despair. Money isn't everything. You can always put out the tip jar, sell merch, and think of all the other benefits you get. The "nothing deal" helps you to . . .

- Get tighter performing before large audiences.
- Hone your songs and figure out what people respond to.

- Build a "community" buzz (with press, college radio, and local stores). And finally . . .
- Prove yourself to promoters so as to get better gigs.

You see, the free deal doesn't sound so bad after all, does it? And the best part is, if you can hang in there long enough and maintain a great attitude, you just might move along to the other methods of payment discussed next. Let's take a look.

Pay-to-Play

The pay-to-play arrangement is yet another situation you'll encounter when playing local clubs at the beginning of your career. This is an arrangement in which a club promoter essentially contracts you to buy tickets in advance to help cover his or her costs, leaving any profit you make to go in your pocket.

The promoter prints up *x* number of tickets with your name, date, and time under a written contract that says you will return, for example, $100 to him or her on the date of the show. If you sell 20 tickets at $5 each (20 × $5 = $100), you break even. If you sell 40 tickets at $5 each (40 × $5 = $200), you make $100.

The pay-to-play arrangement doesn't sound too difficult, right? The punk rock band Pennywise did it for years when they were just starting out, as did tons of other bands that went on to become super successful. The challenge, however, is when you're booked to play the most popular clubs in your hometown and the promoters ask you to pay $900 or more on the night of the show. Should you experience this, my advice is as follows: stick to smaller bars or alternative venues (like house parties and cellars) until you've built up some fans.

PAYING TO PLAY: UNDERSTANDING WHY THE SYSTEM EXISTS

To understand how the pay-to-play system evolved, you have to see it from the club promoter's and owner's side of it: they're providing you a place to showcase your talent and to throw a pretty happening party. In their minds, they're doing you a favor by letting you perform.

Understand that running a club costs a crapload of money. First you have to scout out a location, renovate and remodel, get a liquor license, put in a stage with lights and a sound system, hire and pay personnel (bartenders, security guards, and waitresses), pay for insurance, and cover rent and electricity. This adds up, and promoters need to cover their "basic nut" (general expenses).

Since there are so many bands out there that talk up a big game about how great they are and then draw no more than four people (Mom, Dad, Grandma, and Granddad), and because there are so many other venues competing for customers on a given night, promoters ask for a guaranteed payment until your band can prove they can pack the place.

You see, that's all promoters care about: putting asses in seats—whether that means you fart the alphabet or shred the Star-Spangled Banner. This is just business. They want you to take an equitable share of the risk, and only you know if this cost is worth it. So until you buy your own club, get used to the pay-to-play system. And just remember: if you're an entrepreneur and know how to sell, you will prevail.

Straight Percentage

Moving on to yet another method of payment, let's look at the straight percentage deal, another feature of the early stages of your career at the club level.

In a straight percentage deal, a promoter pays you a percentage of the total money taken in at the door. Percentages can range from 100 percent of the door money down to 50 percent, and may be arranged to kick in after a certain number of people walk up and pay.

A common arrangement for a young band in L.A. might be 50 percent of the door after 20 people pay entrance. Obviously, the harder you promote your show and the more people you can bring in, the more money you make. "But just make sure to have your own people counting heads at the door so that you always get the fair end of the deal," cautions tour professional Chris Arnstein, who has worked with the Eagles, Madonna, and Julio Iglesias. "Promoters are not always to be trusted."

John Pantle of APA (www.apa-agency.com) tells me that percentage deals aren't only reserved for local bands just starting out, but for the big acts, too. If a group knows that it has a big draw with the potential of selling out a club, a straight percentage can work out quite nicely. Reverend Horton Heat, a popular band on the national club circuit, often plays the House of Blues in Los Angeles and asks for a straight percentage deal. The band usually sells the venue out and makes good money, while the venue profits from selling liquor inside and parking spaces outside. Everyone's happy.

But percentage deals can turn a tour into a nightmare if shows are poorly attended, since a band on the road depends on earning a certain amount of dollars to pay its expenses and get from one city to the next. For this reason, the following forms of payment are typically used.

Flat Guarantee

A flat guarantee deal—an arrangement that usually exists once a band can draw a large crowd in clubs, and/or after they've latched onto a reputable talent agency or record label—is one in which a promoter pays you a guaranteed sum of money for your performance. For newer bands, this amount can range anywhere from $100 to $600, and for more successful bands, the amount is substantially more. So it really depends on the artist's stature and the venue capacity.

For a new band touring in unfamiliar territory where its fan base is questionable, a guarantee (even a small one) can help ensure that you'll at least be able to cover your estimated costs. For the more established artist, a flat guarantee (if it's high enough) can also be advantageous since the promoter is taking all of the risk. If the promoter pays a high fee and ticket sales are low, he or she could potentially lose a lot of money. Therefore, in order to split the risks between the promoter and the artist, the two parties might agree upon deals like the "versus" deal discussed below.

Guarantee Versus Percentage

A "guarantee versus percentage" deal—an arrangement that is usually reserved for more established artists playing at larger venues (theaters, amphitheaters, sheds, arenas, stadiums, festival events)—is one in which a promoter pays you either a negotiated guaranteed fee or a negotiated split of 80 to 90 percent of the adjusted gross receipts (whichever is higher).

Adjusted Gross Receipts

Adjusted gross receipts are the sum of all tickets sold, minus all expenses. Some expenses may include the following:

- ***Hall Rentals:*** Hall rentals for the venue in which you perform.
- ***Opening Act:*** Opening-act fees for the bands that play before you.
- ***Insurance:*** Insurance for theft and damage to your equipment and for personal injury.
- ***Police:*** Police to make sure fans behave and to control traffic outside the venue.
- ***Security:*** Security guards to keep fans from getting out of control and for watching buses and trucks parked around the venue.
- ***Barricades:*** Barricades to keep fans from climbing onstage and entering unauthorized areas within the venue.

- ***Medical Personnel:*** Medical personnel and supplies, in case of injuries at the venue.
- ***Advertising:*** Advertising (including radio, TV, Internet, and print) to ensure that people show up for the event.
- ***Telephone:*** Telephone usage backstage for the road manager and production crew.
- ***Power, Sound, and Lights:*** Power, sound, and lights to ensure top-quality sound and visuals.
- ***Electricians:*** Electricians to make sure the wiring for the lights and sound is functioning properly.
- ***Stagehands:*** Stagehands to set up and break down equipment.
- ***Box Office Personnel:*** Box office personnel to sell tickets and take tickets from fans as they pass through the venue gates.
- ***Clean-up Crews:*** Clean-up crews to remove garbage from the night's performance.
- ***Dressing Rooms:*** Dressing room facilities (which includes everything from the furniture and phone to towels and couches).
- ***Catering:*** Everything from snacks, beer, and pizza to fully cooked nutritious meals. And finally . . .
- ***Runners:*** Runners (people on call to run around taking care of last-minute business matters, such as making sure all of the band's catering requests are met).

Determining Your Pay

After the promoter deducts all of his or her expenses from the gross receipts, what's left over is multiplied by a negotiated percentage ranging from 80 to 90 percent. This determines how the band is paid: the guarantee fee or the percentage.

To illustrate, if a successful band's negotiated guarantee was $250,000, the gross receipts from a sold-out concert were $750,000, and the promoter's total expenses were $400,000, the balance of $350,000 would be multiplied by, say, 90 percent to get $315,000. Since $315,000 is more than $250,000, the band's pay for the night is $315,000.

Here's a breakdown of how the band's pay might look:

$750,000 (gross ticket sales)
– $400,000 (promoter's expenses)
= $350,000
× 0.90 (90%: the band's negotiated percentage split)
= $315,000 > $250,000 (adjusted gross receipts > the band's guarantee)
= $315,000 (the band's pay for the night, which is $65,000 above the guarantee)

AFTERTHOUGHT: PROMOTER'S PROFITS John Pantle, talent agent at APA, says that many promoters will also add a 15 percent "promoters' profit" between the expenses and the point of releasing monies. In the example above, the promoter would take 15 percent of the $315,000 (or $47,250), lowering the artists' pay to $267,750 instead of the $315,000.

Closing Out the Show

As you can see above, expenses have a great deal to do with how you get paid in versus deals. Therefore, you should know that promoters often drum up false receipts, exaggerate expenses, and lie by underestimating the number of people who actually paid to attend a concert, all with the intention of inflating expenses and reducing the split. For these reasons, a tour manager must be scrupulous in reviewing all expenses when "closing out" a show with a promoter.

Mark Goldstein, former vice president of business affairs at Warner Bros. Music, puts it strongly, but fairly: "It's not that promoters are lying, cheating scumbags, but there's a good chance that they are, and you have to assume the worst."

Chris Arnstein adds these final words of wisdom:

> In general, settlement is a game of hide-and-seek. The promoter's job is to inflate expenses and thus reduce the amount he or she has to pay. Hence, the job of the person settling the show for the act is to figure out how the promoter will try to work the system, demand the contractually agreed-upon expenditures, and destroy any inflated or created expenses on behalf of the promoter. Seasoned settlers know the tricks of the trade and recognize the game. They enter into the negotiations with some level of respect between them, like poker players, so that compromises can be reached in a businesslike manner and not based on ego. Closing out the job is where thousands of dollars on a tour can be lost for the artist. This is serious business.

How Live Performance Deals Are Negotiated

Now that you understand how you are paid for live performance deals, let's talk about live performance deals are negotiated.

Early in an artist's career, when he or she is performing for free or even paying to play, live performance deals are often dictated by the set terms of the venue promoter.

However, as an artist's career begins to grow in stature and his or her audience size increases, the venue capacities get larger and the methods by which deals are negotiated can be more sophisticated.

Let's take a look at the gross potential, mega-promoter negotiations, co-headlining negotiations, and multi-band festival negotiations.

The Gross Potential

As mentioned in chapter 11, it's the job of the talent agent to negotiate performance agreements on behalf of the artist.

One way they do this is to first consider the seating capacity of the venue in which the artist will be performing, as well to consider the ticket price that is most acceptable to charge. Keep in mind that there are usually several ticket prices within a venue depending on the proximity of the seats to the stage.

The capacity of the venue is then multiplied by these ticket prices to result in a figure called the "gross potential," which is the total amount of admissions that could be earned for the night.

For simplicity, say the seating capacity of a venue is 15,000 and the average ticket price is \$50. Fifteen thousand seats multiplied by \$50 results in a gross potential of \$750,000.

Another factor that must now be considered is the promoter's estimated basic expenses. If those expenses are, for instance, \$400,000 (and considered "reasonable" by all parties), they are subtracted from the gross potential. That's a difference of \$350,000 (\$750,000 – 400,000 = \$350,000).

Negotiations are then worked downward from the \$350,000 to a point at which both sides believe it is a reasonable risk to put on a show.

Now let's take a look at the equation.

15,000 (capacity of the venue)
× \$50 (average ticket price)
= \$750,000 (gross potential)
– \$400,000 (promoter's estimated expenses)
= \$350,000 (amount at which negotiations work backward, to perhaps \$250,000)

Note that if the promoter is also the owner of the venue, he or she will count on the money taken in from food, alcohol sales, parking, etc., for a reasonable profit. Also, many promoters get a kickback from ticketing companies, and many venues sell advertising (on LED and plasma screens) throughout the building or complex. But, if a promoter is simply renting the venue and does not share in these ancillary revenues, he or she must always consider the possibility of the venue selling under capacity (below the gross potential) in calculating what he or she can afford to pay the artist.

Per-Show Versus Per-Tour Mega-Promoter Negotiations

Another factor that may affect what an artist earns from a live performance is whether deals are negotiated on a per-show or a per-tour basis.

When booking U.S. tours, talent agents individually negotiate performance deals with a variety of promoters across the country. However, there are also mega-promoters (such as Live Nation or AEG) that own a variety of large venues across the United States and Europe. In essence, the talent agent negotiating on behalf of the band is negotiating for an entire tour or a package deal.

Business manager Jeff Hinkle of Gudvi, Sussman & Oppenheim explains:

> These per-tour package deals basically work the same as the single-show "guarantee versus percentage" deals. But rather than receiving the greater of a negotiated fee or a percentage of the net profits (or losses) for just one night, the artist earns the greater of his or her negotiated guarantees for the entire tour or a percentage of a "pool," which is the net profits (or losses) from all of the shows added together. For instance, let's say the artist's guarantee is $150,000 per show for a total of 20 shows on a tour. That's a total of $3 million in guarantees for the entire tour (20 × $150,000 = $3 million). And now let's say that the pool or net profits from all of the shows added together is $5 million. Being that the artist receives the greater of the total negotiated guarantee or a percentage—typically 90 percent—of the pool, the artist would receive a percentage of the pool totaling $4.5 million (0.90 × $5 million = $4.5 million in net profits > $3 million in guarantees).

Co-Headlining Negotiations

Now that you understand how negotiations are handled for one band, let's take a look at what happens in co-headlining situations.

Jeff Hinkle explains:

> In a co-headlining tour, the guarantees and overage percentages for each artist are always the same. So basically a settlement with co-headliners works the same as it does with just one. However, sometimes, to make it easier, the promoter will pay the closing artist 100 percent of any overage that is due, and that artist will then settle up with the other artist for his or her share of the overage.

Multi-Band Festival Tour Negotiations

Finally, Jeff Hinkle explains what happens in festival situations when there are many bands on a bill.

> In a festival situation, where several bands are performing, usually each group negotiates its own guarantee, without an overage percentage. Overage percentages are not as common in festival tour negotiations because the accounting is too difficult.

JUST A HANDFUL OF THE COOLEST FESTIVALS

As Bill Silva (manager, publisher, promoter) once said, "No matter what state the record business is in, fans will always pay to be part of communal events such as live concerts and festivals." I couldn't agree more. Here is a brief list of some of the coolest festivals today. Been to any of them?

- ***Coachella Valley Music and Arts Festival***
  - **Location:** Indio, CA
  - **Past Lineups:** Outkast, Muse, Arcade Fire, The Knife, Queens of the Stone Age, Beck, the Replacements, Skrillex, Calvin Harris, and more
- ***Lollapalooza***
  - **Location:** Revolving cities
  - **Past Lineups:** Eminem, Arctic Monkeys, Zedd, Lorde, Outkast, Calvin Harris, Foster the People, and more
- ***Wakarusa***
  - **Location:** Ozark, AK
  - **Past Lineups:** The String Cheese Incident, Bassnectar, The Flaming Lips, STS9, Umphrey's McGee, Edward Sharpe & the Magnetic Zeros, Michael Franti & Spearhead, John Butler Trio, and more
- ***Electric Daisy Carnival***
  - **Location:** New York, NY
  - **Past Lineups:** Adam F, Afrojack, La Roux, Calvin Harris, R3hab, Zeds Dead, Foreign Beggars, Empire of the Sun, and more
- ***Sasquatch***
  - **Location:** George, WA
  - **Past Lineups:** Outkast, The National, Queens of the Stone Age, M.I.A., Foster the People, Kid Cudi, Haim, Neko Case, Foals, Major Lazer, Cut Copy, Die Antwoord, Elbow, Violent Femmes, and more

Live Performance Contracts and Riders

Congratulations! You made it to the last section of my chapter on live performing and touring. To close out, I'd like to discuss live performance contracts and riders.

The first pages of a contract between an artist and concert promoter include basic terms such as payment, percentage splits, dates, times, and load-in of equipment. Attached to this contract, however, is a separate document called a "rider."

A rider outlines the specifics of what a band needs for a performance. It can run to more than 20 pages, depending on whether a group is at the beginning stages of its career and playing locally or at more established venues. Let's investigate this further.

In the Beginning: Local Gigs to the Early Stages of Touring

For groups that are just starting out and playing locally, your rider is probably not going to be any more than one page that says you'll get "a warm glass of shut the hell up" (a phrase from the movie *Happy Gilmore*). In other words, you can make several requests for beer backstage, warm towels, and other stuff, but you're probably not going to get many of these requests fulfilled until you start generating some real money for promoters.

At the Mid-Level to Big Leagues of Touring

For more established artists, which can mean the mid-level to big leagues of touring, a group's rider might include personal requests for dressing rooms and catering, sound and lighting, and legal stipulations like cancellation policies and anti-bootlegging provisions.

In percentage-based deals, where the artist gets either a guarantee or a split of the profits (i.e., the total ticket sales minus all the promoter's expenses), remember that every expense listed on the band's rider potentially reduces the money the group will take in at the end of the night. The more items you need, the farther away you are from your back end. Therefore, to ensure maximum profits per performance, close attention must be paid by the group's talent agent and personal manager when establishing an agreement with the promoter.

Below are just a few of the items that may be listed on a group's rider:

- ***Dressing Room Accommodations:*** Some groups may have more elaborate dressing room needs, beyond the basic requests for a clean room, ample chairs, a mirror, a toilet, and a sink with running water. A group may want a specific room or even multiple rooms. The Black Crowes, for example, are known to request specific carpeting, black lights, lava lamps, incense, and throw pillows in their dressing room.
- ***Catering:*** Most bands make specific requests for the food and drink they want backstage. In addition, there are requirements for breakfast, lunch, dinner, and tour bus supplies. Some groups may have simple requests, while other artists require lavish spreads. Pretzels, candies, gum, pizza, soda, bottled water, beer, hard alcohol, potato chips, cheese and crackers, deli meats, roast beef dinners, vegetarian pasta, baked or broiled fish, and even lobster can be found on a group's catering rider. Most bands leave a lot of the food uneaten backstage (usually to be devoured by the guests), so a group can actually limit its expenses by making prudent catering requests.
- ***Free Tickets:*** Most bands also include a guest list with free tickets to be distributed to family and friends. Just remember, though, that when a group is working to collect a percentage basis of the net profits, each ticket given away potentially reduces the total gross income and thus the total income that the band will have earned at the end of the night. By the way, Elvis Presley is said to have given away no free tickets to his performances. On the other hand, Katy Perry gives away "free tickets," but she tells the folks at Will Call to charge her guests $20 when they arrive to pick them up. Wow! Nice move, Katy!
- ***Security:*** Although we've all heard the lead singer of a band cuss out security guards for not letting the fans start a mosh pit or get closer to the stage, the band essentially hires and pays security to be there as indicated in the rider. Security ensures the safety of the band and the band's staff and also protects the equipment and touring vehicles. Security costs are yet another expense deducted from the gross receipts before the artist receives a split of the profits.
- ***Internal Transportation:*** Moving right along, a group may also request that a passenger van and a responsible driver be available on the day of the performance. Some groups may even request that multiple vehicles or limousines be available to them at all times of the day.
- ***Sound and Lights:*** A band may also make specific requests on the rider for sound and lighting, along with the requirements for power or generators. This list may include specific needs for certain types of microphones or soundboards.
- ***Insurance:*** The rider may also include provisions that require a venue to have general liability insurance. This will protect the band in case of personal injury or damage to the group's equipment.
- ***Cancellation Provisions:*** A group, upon cancellation of a performance by the promoter, may ask for 100 percent of the agreed payment with two weeks' notice, or for 50 percent with one month's notice. By the way, should a group miss a show due to sickness, death, or an act of God (e.g., a hurricane or earthquake), it cannot be held responsible for loss or damages the promoter may incur as the result of a cancellation. This clause in live performance agreements is called "force majeure."

- ***Video and Audiotaping:*** And finally, the last-but-not-least rider request deals with video and audiotaping. Many groups prohibit the recording or filming of their live performances to prevent the unauthorized reproduction and sale of their music. The Grateful Dead, however, allowed its fans to both tape and film their live performances. The venues in which the group performed often looked like a sea of telephone poles, with thousands of microphones affixed to boom stands pointing toward the stage. Quite impressive!

THE TOP 20 RIDER REQUEST COUNTDOWN

Most bands treat rider requests very seriously; specific items can bring peace of mind to certain artists while out on the road for several weeks. These requests may also reflect the promoters' attention to detail. However, other requests are just downright silly and perhaps frivolous, made to prove that, after being mistreated for so many years, one can now make other people jump through hoops. In any case, here is the Top 20 Rider Request Countdown:

20. ***Justin Bieber:*** Requested one Vicks Personal Steam Inhaler, Purell antibacterial soap, and an assortment of plain white T-shirts and "lo-rise" socks.
19. ***Eminem:*** Requested that his dressing room be stocked with large jumbo shrimp, "fresh meat," Gundelsheim pickles, and 25 lb. dumbbells.
18. ***Rihanna:*** Requested a large throw rug (plush, with an animal print) in her dressing room with a six-foot couch that needs to be "White, Cloth, Plush (No leather)" and "wide enough for her to stretch out on and take a nap."
17. ***Katy Perry:*** Requested two cream-colored egg chairs, one of which should have a footstool; a coffee table in a "perspex modern style"; a pair of floor lamps in "French ornate style"; and a refrigerator with a glass door.
16. ***M.I.A.:*** Requested a "European" cheese and cracker tray, a "small tray of hummus and pita bread," Italian chocolates, rum, vodka, tequila, white wine, red wine, and a six-pack of Heineken.
15. ***Kanye West:*** Requested moisturizing products (including Neutrogena, Nivea, and L'Occitane brands), as well as toothpaste and deodorant manufactured by Arm & Hammer.
14. ***Akon:*** Requested one pound of "fresh Bing cherries," fresh-baked oatmeal and sugar cookies, three containers of "tangerine or mango Altoids," and a $300 bottle of Ace of Spades champagne. Additionally, Akon "requires a juicer and blender for juicing and making smoothies."
13. ***Drake:*** Requested E-Z Wider rolling papers, one pack of Dutch Master President cigars, four dozen "natural scented incense sticks" and "Dr. Bronner's peppermint soap."
12. ***Adele:*** Requested a pack of Marlboro Lights and a disposable lighter, an assortment of chewing gum, and a small plate of "freshly made, individually wrapped sandwiches" that "must NOT contain tomatoes, vinegar, chili or citrus fruit."
11. ***Taylor Swift:*** Requested one bag of frozen edamame backstage and that her tour bus be loaded with Starbucks grandes, Ben & Jerry's pints, and a jar of Ragú spaghetti sauce.
10. ***Christina Aguilera:*** Requested police escorts that had the authority to route the vehicles in which she was traveling through any potential traffic delays to and from the venues.
9. ***Cher:*** Requested one "wig room" backstage to store her wigs.
8. ***Marilyn Manson:*** Requested Cristal champagne and beef jerky.
7. ***Mariah Carey:*** Requested Cristal champagne with bendable straws.

6. ***The Killers:*** Requested Maker's Mark and Absolut vodka on Mondays, Wednesdays, and Fridays; Jack Daniel's and gin on Tuesdays, Thursdays, and Saturdays; Jameson Irish whisky and tequila on Sundays; and Coors Light, Corona, and red wine every day.
5. ***Axl Rose:*** Requested Dom Perignon, Wonder Bread, cigarettes, and pornography.
4. ***Prince and Willie Nelson:*** Each requested one physician to administer vitamin B-12 shots before their performance.
3. ***Iggy Pop:*** Requested a Bob Hope impersonator backstage.
2. ***Diddy:*** Requested that all food and ice be inspected for hair and insisted that catering personnel wear nets on their heads.

And the drum roll, please. The number one rider request of all time . . .

1. ***Van Halen:*** Requested M&M candies be provided backstage with all of the brown ones taken out.

Note: For more wacky rider demands, check out the Smoking Gun (www.thesmokinggun.com).

23

Merchandising, Part 1

Rights, Types, and Companies

"No matter what state the music industry is in, people always seem willing to pay for authentic, high-quality souvenirs of a show." —Brad Andersen, Global Merchandising Company

Merchandising refers to the process of selling T-shirts, hats, lunch boxes, and other goods that bear an artist's name and/or likeness. When these products are sold in conjunction with a concert tour, new bands can cover their road expenses, and established artists can make fortunes.

Even with new technologies disrupting the way music is "sold" (or, rather, streamed for "free"), merch will continue being a strong revenue source for unique and creative brands!

Says Dave Kusek, former CEO of Berkleemusic, "Just think of the merchandising empires built by Jimmy Buffett, Jay-Z, and KISS. This is revenue that comes from something other than music. The merch is the 'tail wagging the dog' and it has made these artists wealthy."

In this chapter, I'll discuss your merchandising rights, companies, and types of deals. In the next chapter, I'll dive deeper into the finer points of tour merchandising contracts. Finally, in part 3, I'll tackle retail deals and close with an interview on doing all of this stuff yourself. Enjoy.

Merchandising Rights

The first step in understanding merchandising is to understand your merchandising rights. Let's take a brief look at publicity rights and trademarks.

Publicity Rights

Publicity rights refer to an individual's entitlement to grant or not grant the use of his or her name and/or likeness for commercial purposes.

In other words, you have the right to decide who, if anyone, can use your personal name and likeness on T-shirts, hats, posters, or other products for commercial sale.

Trademarks

Trademarks (often used interchangeably with "service marks") refer generally to a band's authority to grant or not grant the use of its name, symbol, and/or slogan for commercial sales.

In other words, as long as your band's name is an original one, you've exploited it in commerce, and/or you've registered it with the United States Patent and Trademark Office (www.uspto.gov), you have the right to decide who, if anyone, can use it (I'm simplifying trademarks, of course, but you get the point).

For more information on trademarks, see the interview with attorney Jeff Cohen in chapter 3. Now let's discuss a few of the things you can do with your merchandising rights.

Grants of Rights

Now that you understand your merchandising rights, we can talk about what you can do with them. There are essentially three possibilities:

1. ***Retain Your Rights and Handle the Merchandising Independently:*** Many young and unsigned artists retain their merchandising rights, pay an experienced printer to supply them with products, and then handle their merchandising independently. In this scenario you are acting as a self-merchandiser, which means the profit margins can be high, but you also do all of the work—from the investing to the designing to the selling.
2. ***Grant Your Rights to a Record Company (360 Deals):*** Many developed artists sign with a record company under a 360 deal structure, grant their merchandising rights to the label's merchandising arm (or a third-party company), and let the label handle all of the manufacturing and sales in return for a royalty. In this scenario, you are really leaving it all in the hands of the record company. But the truth is, if you want to get signed these days, many artists who lack negotiating power may really have no choice at all.
3. ***Grant Your Rights to a Merchandiser:*** Finally, many elite artists with a strong buzz and a great attorney retain their rights upon signing a record deal, and enter directly into an agreement with a merchandising company who manufactures products, pays a royalty, and offers an advance against future earnings. In this scenario you can find a merchandising company of your preference, negotiate a merchandising deal you want (which can include a rather large advance), and receive the support of a professional merchandiser (which becomes important as your career blossoms).

So that's pretty much it in regard to what you can do with your rights. Now let's take a look at some of the players in the merchandising business by examining merchandising companies.

Merchandising Companies

There are essentially three levels of merchandising companies in the business today. These are:

- ***Major 500-Pound Gorillas:*** Large companies that offer merchandising deals with royalties and significant advances. These companies are typically part of larger corporations.
- ***Independent Mid-Sized Companies:*** Mid-sized companies that may offer deals with royalties and advances (though the advances are usually smaller than the majors'). These companies are typically independent of larger corporate entities. And finally . . .
- ***Smaller Internet-Based Companies:*** Smaller companies that do not typically offer merchandising deals with royalties and advances, and act simply as printers and suppliers. These companies are usually independent of larger corporate entities.

Bob Fierro of Zebra Marketing says it's important to note the distinctions between these companies before entering into an agreement with a merchandiser:

> You shouldn't be attracted to a company primarily because of its size, its roster, or its ability to offer a large advance. Rather, you should pick a company based on how excited it is about working with your band; the ideas, designs, and products they're interested in manufacturing for you; and the

quality of services they provide. It's also about relationships—do you like them and do they like you? These are equally important factors to consider before entering into a merchandising agreement with a merchandiser.

A FEW EXAMPLES OF MERCHANDISING COMPANIES

To give you a better sense of the players in the merchandising business today, here are some actual names:

- ***Level 1: 500-Pound Gorillas (Deals with Royalties and Larger Advances)***
  - Bravado (www.bravado.com)
  - Band Merch (www.bandmerch.com)
  - Global Merchandising Services (www.globalmerchservices.com)
  - Epic Rights (www.epicrights.com)
  - The Araca Group (www.araca.com)
  - Live Nation (www.fanfire.com)
- ***Level 2: Mid-Sized Companies (Deals, but with Smaller or No Advances)***
  - Richards & Southern Merchandise and Apparel (www.richardsandsouthern.com)
  - Music City Merchandise (www.musiccitymerchandise.com)
  - Tinman Merchandising (www.tinmanmerchandising.com)
  - Sandbag (www.sandbagheadquarters.com)
  - Impact Merchandising (www.impactmerch.com)
  - Revolve Merchandise (www.revolvemerchandise.com)
- ***Level 3: Smaller Companies (Custom Printing [Supply Deals], or Fulfillment Online)***
  - Merch Direct (www.next.merchdirect.com)
  - Contagious Graphics (www.contagiousgraphics.com)
  - Jakprints (www.jakprints.com)
  - MerchNow (www.merchnow.com)
  - Red Rocket Merchandising Corp (www.redrocketcorp.com)
  - The Print Lab (www.theprintlab.com)

Types of Merchandising Deals

And finally, now that you've been introduced to merchandising companies, let's wrap up this chapter by talking about the types of deals the larger merchandisers offer. There are generally two types: tour merchandising and retail merchandising.

Tour Merchandising

Tour merchandising refers to the sale of merchandise at your live performances. This is where a great portion of the money is made in the merchandising industry.

Read on to learn more about the philosophy behind tour merchandising, how it works, and what kind of money it could generate for you.

The Philosophy/Approach

Merchandisers know that concertgoers are pumped up at live events and want a souvenir to prove to their friends that "they were there." So they create items like T-shirts and hoodies, with tour dates and cities on the back, and bands' names and logos on the front. Breakable items like coffee mugs, lunch boxes, and dolls do not sell well at live events, and thus these items are usually reserved for retail.

The Function (Set-up, Meeting VIP Coordinators, and More)

Merchandisers hire their own personnel to deliver merchandise to each venue, "check in" the product, set up in the booths, return to count the number of items sold by venue staff at the end of the night, count the merchandising, and then move on to the next city to do it all over again.

Should there be any fans who purchased "VIP packages" (tickets and special merchandising items, "swag bag" packages, or redemption cards), the merchandiser meets up with the artist's VIP coordinator to hand off the goods.

The Money

Finally, if tour merchandising seems like a lot of effort just for the sake of selling "a few measly T-shirts, hoodies, and hats," note that major stars gross hundreds of thousands in merchandising sales alone in a single night. Ozzy Osbourne grossed half a million in just one night. Needless to say, that's not small potatoes!

Retail Merchandising

Moving on to the second type of merchandising deal, retail merchandising refers to selling products through department stores, T-shirt shops, record stores, Internet sites, and mail-order operations. When compared to tour merchandising, retail merchandising is an entirely different beast. Let's see how it compares.

The Philosophy/Approach

Merchandisers know that fans will want to buy T-shirts unique to the live performances, so they work at designing additional shirts exclusively for sale at retail outlets. For instance, you can get KISS T-shirts at retail stores that use designs that are unavailable at the live shows and don't include tour dates and cities printed on the back. Novelty items (such as dolls, lunch boxes, and stationery products) are also more available at retail stores than they are at live events since they are more likely to sell.

The Function (Distribution, Sublicenses, and More)

Merchandisers manufacture product and sell it to retail outlets (including mom-and-pop, mid-level, and mass-market stores) at wholesale prices. Sublicenses are established with third-party companies to manufacture specialty items (lunch boxes, etc.) and to oversee distribution and sales.

The Money

Finally, while retail merchandising is far less profitable and popular then tour merchandising, successful artists like Michael Jackson, My Chemical Romance, and Guns N' Roses have all made substantial cash from it.

"Even newer, visually compelling bands like Black Veil Brides can make a killing at Hot Topic stores and smaller-market stores," says Brad Andersen of Global Merchandising. "Who knows, perhaps you'll be the next success story in the merchandising business. I'm rooting for you!"

So that's about it. Now that you have a general understanding of merchandising, we can dive into the deals and dollars with the larger companies in the next chapter. There's tons to learn. So turn the page and let's rock!

24

Merchandising, Part 2

Contract Terms for Tour Merchandising

"Merchandising sales often exceed all other income for an artist and are the number one opportunity to monetize a fan base." —Ben Brannen, cofounder and president of atVenu

In chapter 23 you learned about merchandising rights, merchandising companies, and the types of merchandising deals.

Now, in this chapter, let's get into the finer points of merchandising deals with the larger merchandising companies. I'll start with tour merchandising.

Key Touring Terms in Merchandising Contracts

Key touring terms in merchandising contracts include royalties, advances, performance guarantees, the agreement term, creative issues, territory, exclusivity, and the sell-off period. I'll tackle each of these, beginning with royalty rates.

Royalty Rates

There are two royalty structures for touring: U.S. tour royalties and foreign tour royalties.

U.S. Tour Merchandising Royalties

U.S. tour merchandising royalties are structured typically as follows:

- **Net Split (75/25–85/15):** Merchandising royalties today are usually based on a net split ranging from 75/25 to 85/15 (artist/merchandiser). However, your royalty for higher-cost items like tour jackets is sometimes less. In any case, net is defined as all monies from sales on the tour, less credit card fees and taxes, the costs of manufacturing and design, and all other verifiable expenses associated with creating and selling product. Brad Andersen at Global Merchandising tells me that merchandisers provide detailed accountings (often called "transparency reports") to all managers, lawyers, and artists who need to verify expenses after the tour. There's generally an "open book" policy.
- **100 Percent Recoupable:** Keep in mind that any royalties due from sales must first go back toward paying off any monies you've received in the form of a merchandising advance (note that advances will be discussed in the next section).

Foreign Tour Merchandising Royalties

Foreign tour merchandising royalties are usually handled in the following way:

- **Net Split (70/30–80/20):** Merchandising royalties in foreign territories are treated similarly to those in the U.S., but the splits are a little lower—typically 70/30 to 80/20 (artist/merchandiser). This is because there are higher costs associated with touring abroad, including gas, shipping, tariffs, and more. Once again, net is defined as all monies from sales, less all verifiable expenses associated with creating and selling product. Detailed accountings are always available to managers and lawyers of bands who wish to see them.
- **100 Percent Recoupable:** Finally, as with royalties earned in the U.S., keep in mind that any royalties due must first go back toward paying off your merchandising advance.

HALL FEES AND VERIFIABLE EXPENSES

You already know that merchandising royalties today are usually based on a net split (the net being defined as all monies from sales on the tour, less credit card fees and taxes, the costs of manufacturing and design, and all other "verifiable expenses" associated with creating and selling product). But one of these "verifiable expenses" that deserves the spotlight for a moment is something called a hall fee.

Hall fees are percentages (usually 25 to 30 percent) of the gross merchandising sales (less taxes) that the venue takes on the night of your performance. Since the venue staff assist merchandisers with selling your merch (or hire concession companies to do it for them), provide space in their building, and hire security to chase off bootleggers, the venue feels they deserve to get paid. But remember that the higher the hall fee, the lower the net, and the lower your cut.

So who negotiates the hall fee? Your agent does when negotiating your live performance fee, and they'll keep it as low as they can—sometimes as low as 15 to 20 percent for bigger stars. So, now that you know about hall fees, just be sure to hug your talent agent today and tell him or her that I sent you!

Merchandising Advances

Moving away from merchandising royalties, now let's get into the merchandising advance, another key issue found in merchandising agreements.

What's an Advance?

Merchandising advances are essentially merchandising royalties paid up front. It is not uncommon for a successful band to get a merchandising advance of $1 million to $2 million, a mid-level band to get $300,000 to $500,000, and a younger band to get $0 to $50,000. These figures may appear arbitrary, but they're usually determined by forecasting the potential gross sales and considering your net royalty split.

Forecasting Gross Sales

Forecasting your potential gross sales involves looking at the following seven factors:

- **Stature:** The level of demand for the artist
- **Number of Dates:** The number of performances on the tour
- **Venue Capacity:** The number of people the venues hold
- **Paid Attendees:** The number of people who will pay to see the show
- **Price:** A fair price at which the merch can be sold

- **Target Audience:** The demographic makeup of the fan
- **Competition:** What other like bands have historically grossed on tour

Bob Fierro says merchandisers have actually gotten really good over the years at forecasting your potential gross sales down to the very last person who pays to see your show (known as a per-head figure). The per-head figure is the projected amount spent on merchandising by each fan who pays to see you perform over the course of the entire concert tour. To me, the per-head figure seems more "merchandiser speak" than anything else, but nonetheless, please be sure to check out the boxed text below.

WHAT THE HELL IS A "PER-HEAD" FIGURE?

The per-head figure is the projected amount spent on merchandising by each fan who sees you perform over the course of a concert tour. Though my calculations are a bit backward from how the real merch folks do it, the following example should help you to better understand per-head counts.

Say a metal band like Slayer is scheduled to play for 30 nights in 2,000-seat-capacity theaters (putting the projected total audience at 60,000). With this number in mind, and with sheer wizardry and vast experience, merchandisers can project that the band will gross an average $10 in merchandising sales per head. But I use the following calculation . . .

If you know the band is playing before 2,000 screaming metal dudes per night, you can estimate that at least 1/3 of them (or 666 people, no joke intended) will pay $30 for a T-shirt. This brings the projected gross sales to $20,000 per night (666 × $30 ≈ $20,000), and the total gross for the tour to $600,000 ($20,000 × 30 dates = $600,000). By dividing the $600,000 by 60,000 paid attendees, you're left with $10 per head. After considering expenses and your royalty rate, an advance can be determined.

By the way, if you're wondering how merchandisers estimate per-head counts on festival tours when it's hard to determine who the fans really paid to see, they adjust their calculations by reducing the count of the paid attendees for the night, for example, by half.

So now you should know a little bit more about per-head figures. Rejoice!

Paid in Increments (or Rolling Amounts) Throughout the Tour

You should also know that your merchandising advance is paid in increments throughout the tour—so if you were planning on taking the lump sum and skipping town, you'd better change your plans.

All jokes aside, Brad Andersen tells me that you might receive a significant portion of the advance up front as an incentive to sign the deal, another advance after reaching certain sales plateaus, and then the balance of the advance toward the end of the actual tour.

100 Percent Returnable and Recoupable

The last point I'd like to make about advances is that they are fully recoupable against future royalties as well as 100 percent returnable (meaning you may have to give it all back if you don't meet certain "performance guarantees"). Yup, you heard right. In fact, you may have to include interest on the payback as well. So be sure to pay close attention to our next section below.

Performance Guarantees

Now that you understand merchandising advances, we can discuss performance guarantees.

A performance guarantee is a contractual promise that you will perform a specific number of live shows in front of a specific number of people, or you will repay the total unrecovered balance of your advance with accrued interest. Oh, my!

When It Really Matters

Before freaking out, you should know that this really only matters when your band breaks up in the middle of a tour or someone suffers an untimely injury or death, and the merchandiser is afraid it will never be able to recoup its advance from sales. By the way, if the advance you received has already been spent, merchandisers are known to sue if necessary to get it back.

What Usually Happens (It Rolls Over to the Next Tour)

Says Bob Fierro, if you fall short of meeting your performance guarantee, the merchandiser will—usually—let the advance repayment "ride" and wait to recoup the advance on your next tour. However, as you'll see when I discuss agreement terms below, be clear that this means that you are essentially trapped in your merchandising agreement and the merchandiser is not required to pay you another advance until he or she makes back every last dime with interest!

BANKRUPT! A REAL-LIFE DRAMA!

In merchandising contracts there are "performance guarantees" that stipulate that a band must play before a certain number of people over the course of the tour, and that the merchandiser must recoup its total advance paid to the band, or else the band must repay the unrecouped balance—even if the group breaks up.

One very successful group that had received a substantial advance for merchandising on its forthcoming tour was sued when the lead singer quit and the band subsequently fell apart. No tour, no merchandising sales, no return on the merchandiser's investment.

Each band member had to file for bankruptcy because they didn't have the funds to pay back the advance. Their wives had all bought cars and put down payments on houses. Now, that definitely sucks! Even worse, this broke up a few marriages, too.

The Agreement Term in Merchandising Deals

Dovetailing nicely from the performance guarantee, now you're ready to learn about the agreement term, yet another key deal point found in merchandising agreements. The term is usually based on "album/tour cycles," recoupment of the advance, or "buyout" of the advance.

Album/Tour Cycles

An album/tour cycle begins with the release of one album and continues through your concert tour (or tours), ending 60 days prior to the release of your next album.

One reason the agreement term is structured this way is that all of the images, designs, and logos used in promoting an album may be used when creating merchandising products.

Your album title, cover artwork, or special logo may all be replicated in T-shirt designs, baseball caps, and/or bumper stickers. Since each album release exudes a new vibe and image, an album/tour cycle is a logical milestone at which to evaluate the relationship between parties.

Till Recoupment of the Advance, or Else!

The term of merchandising agreements and album/tour cycles may seem like a simple concept, but it can actually get quite complicated—since it is also based on recoupment of the advance. You see, if your advance is unrecovered at the end of your cycle, your merchandiser automatically gets the rights to your next tour without having to renegotiate anything at all or pay you another advance. If you recouped all but $10,000 of a $100,000 advance, you could still be locked into your original agreement—even if you're unhappy with your merchandiser's services and you want to get out of the agreement.

Buyout Rights

Finally, taking the above matter into serious consideration, if you have a great attorney, he or she may be able to negotiate for a "buyout clause," which would permit you to authorize a competing merchandising company to pay the unrecouped portion of your merchandising advance and buy you out of your existing deal.

To illustrate, Rob Zombie wanted to get out of his contract with his merchandiser (Bravado) but had a large unrecouped balance on his advance. So Global Merchandising Services, who really wanted to work with Zombie (and vice versa for Rob), bought Zombie out.

While it is not impossible for newer bands with a little leverage to get this clause written into their agreement, attorney Don Passman says that you'll probably have to fight hard for it.

Creative Issues in Merchandising Contracts

Getting close to the end of our discussion on key terms in merchandising deals, now it's time to tackle creative issues. Creative issues are a really big deal for most artists, so I'm sure you'll be happy to hear that most merchandisers are flexible when it comes to these contract matters.

Rights of Approval

Most artists are given the right to approve all merchandising designs on products to be sold, and to approve the quality of the work once it is complete. In fact, the merchandiser sometimes asks the artist to supply them with a series of photographs and designs.

Deciding on the Designs

Your name and likeness, album artwork, and the dates and cities of your upcoming tour are typical elements incorporated into product designs for T-shirts, hats, and posters. When artists are unsure of what they want, merchandisers will offer their expertise.

Says Bob Fierro, "There's a science behind designing that catchphrase, logo, and design, and then putting it all together in just the right way so that a product sells like hotcakes, and merchandisers know this all too well."

Getting Permissions and Paying Fees

Moving on to the legal side of creative issues, you should know that all artists are responsible for getting permission from, and paying fees to, the owners of any outside designs used in connection with the merchandising.

There are two major issues:

1. **Preexisting Designs and Photographs:** To get the rights to use a special design or a unique photograph from a book, you may be asked to pay a fee or a royalty from the sale of merchandise that features that artwork, and the cost will come out of your pocket.
2. **Album Cover Artwork:** Finally, to use the artwork from your forthcoming album in connection with merchandising sales, you may be asked by your record label to cover the costs of producing the applicable artwork. "But in most cases," notes Bob Fierro, "the record company will let this one slide."

That's about it for creative issues, ladies and gents. Be sure to check out the boxed text below for a few examples of the most iconic/creative merch designs to this day. Enjoy!

THE MOST ICONIC/CREATIVE MERCH DESIGNS

The coolest and best-selling merch designs often start with the coolest logos and/or album cover designs. What follows are a few of the most iconic and best-selling band T-shirts of all time. Look them up on the Web if you haven't seen these already.

- Black Sabbath purple logo T-shirt
- The Grateful Dead's electric skull logo
- Rush's *2112* album T-shirt
- Iron Maiden's Eddie the Head mascot T-shirt
- Pink Floyd's *Dark Side of the Moon* album T-shirt
- Nirvana's smiley face logo T-shirt
- Guns N' Roses' *Appetite for Destruction* album T-shirt
- Run-DMC's logo T-shirt
- WuTang Clan's logo T-shirt
- KISS's logo T-shirt
- The Red Hot Chili Peppers' logo T-shirt
- The Ramones' presidential logo T-shirt
- AC/DC's *Back in Black* album T-shirt
- Deadmau5's mouse head logo T-shirt
- The Misfits' skull logo T-shirt
- The Rolling Stones' tongue logo T-shirt

Territory (The World, North America, or X-Japan)

Moving right along, the next thing you need to know about key terms in merchandising agreements is territory. You should know that merch deals are designated in geographic regions, as follows:

- **The World:** Your merchandiser will typically want your merchandising rights for the world. This is especially true for newer artists who do not have negotiating power.
- **North America Only:** Once you're an established artist and have some negotiating power, you may be able to talk your merchandiser into limiting your agreement to certain territories, such as North America. This way you can negotiate with companies in foreign territories for an additional merchandising advance.
- **The World, Except (X) Japan:** And finally, promoters in Japan are especially eager to acquire merchandising rights when you venture into their country on tour, and are sometimes willing to pay large advances. Therefore, even if you're a new artist, you may be able to get your merchandiser to designate your territory as being "the world, except Japan" (or some other territory you want to eliminate). Whether you are successful at doing this depends largely on your attorney.

AFTERTHOUGHT: X–NORTH AMERICA Things in this world always work in reverse. The London-based boy band One Direction signed a merch deal for the world, X–North America, because it figured it could cut a better deal for its U.S. tour with a U.S.-based merchandiser.

Exclusive Rights in Merchandising Deals

Near the end of our list of key terms in merchandising deals is exclusivity. Remember that when signing a merchandising deal, the merchandiser will typically have the exclusive right to handle your merchandising under a number of specific circumstances.

To the Designated Territory

When you're a new group entering into an agreement with a merchandiser, remember that you're signing over the exclusive rights to utilize your name, likeness, and logo in connection with the manufacture, advertisement, distribution, and sale of products. In plain English, this means that you cannot enter into an agreement with another merchandiser during your contract term unless it is for a deal in an "undesignated territory," as pointed out in the previous section.

To the Band, and/or Individual Members

It's also important to note that merchandising companies want to secure the rights to your band as a unit, as well as the rights to each individual band member. This means that if you leave the group and start your own solo project, you may still be obligated to pay any unrecouped balances.

To Promotion and Sponsor Giveaways

Finally, the exclusivity clause may restrict radio stations and sponsors from giving away promotional materials (such as the stickers and hats specifically created by your record label for promotional purposes) within a 20-mile radius of your live performance, and within a 48-hour period before the event. Since radio sponsors are a means to help sell tickets and promote the show, you may be able to negotiate for a limited number of giveaways.

The Sell-Off Period

And finally, for the last-but-not-least key term found in merchandising agreements, allow me to talk about the "sell-off period."

This defines what happens to excess product at the end of your merchandising agreement. It's a common clause in merchandising contracts, as well as in book contracts. In fact, here's how it all went down at the end of the term for one of my book deals, which, if you have a good attorney, is exactly how your merch deal will play out.

- ***Offer to Buy at Cost:*** The company offered to sell me the books at cost. I bought hundreds and continued to sell the product online and at live events while signing a deal with a new company and revising the layouts and designs for a new release.
- ***Nonexclusive Right to Sell Remaining Stock:*** They sold the remaining stock at reduced prices nonexclusively to various outlets (online and off) for a period of six months, and paid me a reduced royalty as set forth in my agreement.
- ***No Stockpiling 120 Days Prior:*** They were prohibited from manufacturing large quantities (called stockpiling) 120 days before the term ended, which prevented them from having tons of stock to continue selling over the six-month period. And finally . . .
- ***Unsold Product Gets Destroyed:*** All unsold product typically gets destroyed after six months. But to be honest, there wasn't any. They sold it all online at reduced prices.

That's pretty much it for tour merchandising. Now, in the next chapter, you'll learn what happens on the retail merchandising side of merchandising agreements, as well what happens when you're handling the merchandising independently. This is some good stuff. So why not turn the page now and get started?

25

Merchandising, Part 3

Retail Deals and Independent Merchandising

"Leave it to KISS to do everything! We appear in comic books, puzzles, condoms, and anything else we damn well please!" —*Gene Simmons*

In chapter 24 you learned about the finer points of merchandising as it relates to touring. Now let's examine retail merchandising issues as well as handling merch independently.

Key Retail Terms in Merchandising Contracts

As previously stated, the parts of your merchandising agreement that deal with touring are more complex than retail issues, and touring is where most bands make the majority of money. However, it's a good idea to briefly discuss the royalties you'll get for retail merchandising sales.

Royalty Rates: Retail Merchandising

Royalty rates for stores and websites, sublicenses, and foreign sales are structured as follows.

Retail Stores and Websites (10 to 20 Percent of Wholesale)

Merchandising royalties for sales in retail stores and for resellers of merch on the Internet are lower and computed differently than they are for live performance sales.

- **Rate (10–20 Percent of Wholesale Depending on Store):** Your merchandiser pays you a royalty rate ranging from 10 to 20 percent in the United States, depending on the type of store where the merchandising is being sold (mom-and-pop, mid-level, and mass-market), as well as on the stature of your band. Just be clear that royalties for retail sales are based on the wholesale price, which is the price at which your merchandiser sells products in bulk to distributors and retailers. So if your merchandiser sells a shirt for $10 wholesale to a top-line retail store (who, of course, may mark it up to $25 or more), the artist earns a royalty of $1.50, assuming his or her rate is 15 percent (the wholesale price of $10, multiplied by 15 percent = $1.50). That's it!
- **Recoupable Against "All" Advances:** Note that any monies due in merchandising royalties must first be used to pay off any unrecouped advances, including those on the touring side of your agreement. That's right. This is called "cross collateralization."

Sublicenses (75 to 85 Percent of What Merchandisers Receive from Sublicensors)

Moving on, sublicenses (i.e., for products like lunch boxes, dolls, and other items that bear your name, logo, and/or likeness) are handled as follows:

- **Royalty Rates:** Your merchandiser enters into agreements with third-party companies to manufacture specialty products. The sublicensor ships these products into retail stores, monitors sales, and pays your primary merchandiser an advance and a royalty. Your merchandiser keeps a 15 to 25 percent share of these monies and remits the balance of 75 to 85 percent to you. Essentially, your merchandiser does nothing more than act as the middleman.
- **Windfall or Not (Just Look at KISS)?** Don't expect to earn much from sublicenses early in your career, since the sales are really only minimal. However, should you get to the level of a group like KISS, you could very easily earn several millions in sublicenses alone for products like lunch boxes, coffins, and other offerings (assuming, of course, that this "stuff" fits your desired brand image).
- **Recoupable:** Remember that these monies are recoupable against all advances.

Foreign Retail Royalties

The last retail category I'd like to discuss is foreign royalties. Foreign royalties are treated as follows:

- **Rates:** 80 percent of your U.S. royalty rates
- **Recoupable:** Royalties due to you must first go back toward paying off all advances

So that concludes retail merchandising, ladies and gentlemen. See, that wasn't so bad. We got through that rather quickly.

Now be sure to check out the next section, featuring an interview with Bob Fierro on independent merchandising (a.k.a. doing it all yourself).

BEYOND YOUR TYPICAL T-SHIRTS

Here are some examples of branded products outside the typical line of T-shirts, stickers, and hats.

• Friendship bracelets • Key chains • Refrigerator magnets • Condoms • Branded license plates • Bottle openers • Matchbooks • Lighters • Rolling papers • Mouse pads • Beer koozies • Shot glasses • Dog tags • Temporary tattoos • Jewelry • Hotel-style door hangers • Guitar picks • Calendars • Personal paintings (artwork) • Playing cards • Laminated lanyards • Comic books • Tour books with photographs • Water bottles • Autographed 8 × 10 pictures • Coffee mugs • Necklaces • Bookmarks • Bandannas • Computer bags • Stuffed animals and toys • Foam fingers • Christmas stockings • Cell phone and iPod skins (covers) • Autographed drum sticks and drum heads • Belts • Flip-flops • Shorts • Backpacks • Lunch boxes • Cinch bags • Dolls

Q&A with Independent Merchandiser Bob Fierro

Zebra Marketing is an entertainment merchandising company that handles custom screen-printing and production, licensing, concessions, and wholesale distribution.

Its clients past and present include Henry Rollins, the Red Hot Chili Peppers, Crystal Method, Motörhead, The Prodigy, Paul Oakenfold, and Brian McKnight (to name a few), as well a number of local do-it-yourself artists in Southern California. Zebra Marketing has been in business for over 25 years.

In the following Q&A, Zebra's president, Bob Fierro, discusses the process of independent merchandising, from artwork and printing to selling merchandise on the road.

Q: Are "merch deals," in the traditional sense, reserved for the most successful artists and bands?

B.F.: Well, first let's take a look at the three basic levels of merchandisers with whom a "merchandising deal" might be contracted: major merchandisers, mid-level to small merchandisers, and smaller Internet-based companies.

Major merchandisers, just like the major record companies, have to report a profit; and despite their substantial cash flow, the net profit margin from merchandising sales can often be too small to keep them in business. Therefore, they must focus on artists most likely to turn substantial profits, like Eminem, 50 Cent, and Madonna. You get the idea.

Mid-level to small merchandisers are those more than able to work with bands that are perhaps just signed and have a good buzz happening, etc., but can't compete with the large advances of the majors—that is, if they even offer advances at all. But, as I always say, while the advance is the first thing a band and its manager will look for, it shouldn't always be the most important consideration.

Finally, smaller Internet-based companies are those that are seemingly everywhere on the Web, ready and eager to work with young bands. Some of these companies are even signing young bands, offering merchandise up front for them to take out on the road—and nothing more, but tying them into long-term agreements. The problem with these deals is that, if all of a sudden the band starts to take off, it's stuck in an agreement with some small company that quite possibly offered a one-sided deal.

The truth is that a band at the beginning stages of its career can easily handle the merchandising on its own, by following a few simple steps.

Q: I'll say a few words, you tell us what we need to know: do-it-yourself merchandising?

B.F.: There are generally four preliminary steps to getting started: 1) selecting the company, 2) submitting artwork and design, 3) selecting the T-shirts and other products, and 4) deciding on the quantity.

Q: Selecting the company?

B.F.: Selecting the company can be as simple as getting on Google and finding a printer like Zebra Marketing (www.zebramarketing.com) or the Print Lab (www.theprintlab.com) using the key words "screen printing" and "promotional items." Or you can simply ask other indie bands in your area for local recommendations.

Most shops are experienced and ready to arrange "supply deals." They supply you with the merch, and you pay them a fee upon picking the merchandise up from their shop.

If you're hitting the road for any significant period of time, just make sure the company has some actual tour experience. A company must understand the necessity of getting merchandise to the band on time and into the specific city should you run out and need it. This requires much more planning and experience on the part of the company than you may expect. If the merchandise arrives one day late, the band will have already moved on to the next city.

Q: Submitting artwork and designs?

B.F.: Most indie bands are pretty creative about designing their own logos and coming up with T-shirt designs. I'm often blown away by the stuff I see—designs down the sleeves, logos front and back and on the shoulders, lyrics or catchy slogans—it is often more specialized than the majors would do.

Bands can always get their art school or graphic design buddies to set up their artwork using Adobe Photoshop (www.adobe.com), which is the standard at Zebra for submitting artwork.

When artists really have no clue about designing shirts, they can work together with the print company to help them get the artwork designed and formatted for printing.

Q: Picking the products? T-shirts, stickers, or patches?

B.F.: T-shirts and tour programs are the number-one sellers. Other products I've seen work well for bands include laminated lanyards (the tour passes that artists wear around their necks), stickers, patches, hats, bandannas, hoodies, and rock art silk-screen posters.

Just be creative and take note of which products and styles are selling the best. Like anything else, the more experience you get, the better at merchandising you will become.

Q: Quantity?

B.F.: Price breaks begin after 12 dozen shirts with increased savings per shirt at 24 dozen. Despite these savings, it's usually better to order a smaller line of items at a smaller quantity first. Once you've determined what products are selling the best, you can have a larger quantity printed up.

Q: Cost per shirt?

B.F.: The cost depends on the quality of the shirt (Hanes, Gildan, or Anvil cotton shirts will cost about $1.75 blank), how elaborate the artwork is, the number of colors used, and the quantity of shirts to be printed.

On average, colored shirts printed on both the front and back usually run between $4 and $4.50.

Q: Price?

B.F.: Keeping things simple, most merchandisers set their prices based on an analysis of what certain target demographic audiences want to pay, and can afford to pay, for a specific item.

Q: Profit margin per shirt?

B.F.: There are about five different things to consider:

1. ***Price:*** You must consider the price of the shirts to the fans. Fans of indie bands are known to buy T-shirts at a price of $5 to as high as $20.
2. ***Sales Tax:*** You must consider sales tax. Check your local state and city taxes. In Los Angeles, sales tax is 9.1 percent.
3. ***Hall Fees:*** You must remember that venues typically require around 25 to 30 percent.
4. ***Costs of Goods:*** You have to factor in the cost for the shirts (known as the "cost of goods") at an average of about 20 percent.
5. ***Miscellaneous Expenses:*** You must consider miscellaneous expenses for freight and shipping charges and/or for the staff you pay for selling the shirts at around four percent.

Once you deduct all these expenses, the average profit margin per shirt for the artist who is handling his or her merchandising is around $10.54 for a $20 T-shirt.

Remember that this figure can vary depending on what you charge per shirt, whether you're responsible enough to deal with tax, whether the venue in which you are performing enforces a hall fee, and whether you pay someone to help you sell merch.

Now let's take a look at a basic DIY merch equation:

$20.00 (price of the shirt to consumer)
– $1.82 (9.1% Los Angeles sales tax: $20 × .091)
= $18.18
– $3.60 (20% hall fee: $18.18 × 0.20)
= $14.54
– $4.00 (20% cost of goods: $20 × 0.20)
= $10.54

Q: Methods for selling merch at live shows?

B.F.: There are a number of important things artists can do that I'll attempt to briefly list.

1. ***Have an Attractive Booth:*** Make sure to set up an attractive merch booth that is going to get people to come over and check out the products.
2. ***Announce That You're Selling Merch:*** Announce that your products are on sale during your band set. This is in no way selling out; rather, it is buying in.
3. ***Accept Different Payment Methods:*** Be able to accept various forms of payment: cash, check, and credit cards. You can use the PayPal (www.paypal.com) or Square (www.squareup.com) swiper app that attaches to your smartphone, or you can look into opening your own merchant account. Speak with your CPA or local bank.
4. ***Hire a Pro Salesperson:*** Get someone who knows how to sell. On the local level, you can probably use someone who's just attractive, personable, and fairly responsible. However, when you hit the road, you should really think about getting someone who has experience selling merch on tour.

Q: Selling merch on the road?

B.F.: Sometimes your road manager may even be willing to do the merchandising in addition to his regular duties, or he'll phone ahead to each of the venues, making sure that a local experienced merchandiser will sell for you.

An experienced merchandiser knows that selling merch night after night is a lot like science. The sizes, styles, colors and quantities are serious considerations. On the latter note, you don't want to unload too much and risk it getting stolen or damaged. Further, you have to respect the wishes of the headlining act (when there is one), who will limit the number of items you can sell.

Q: Dealing with sales tax?

B.F.: In smaller clubs and ballrooms, the club will ask for its hall fee and then ask you to fill out a receipt saying that you will pay the state and local taxes yourself.

Larger venues usually have inside concession companies that take out the local and state sales tax and pay it for you.

Q: Let's finish with selling merch online.

B.F.: A band that is responsible in fulfilling orders and drawing hits on its website can use e-commerce solutions like PayPal (www.paypal.com) to sell items, like mugs, that do not sell that well at live shows.

Some companies like CafePress (www.cafepress.com) even allow you to set up an on-demand homepage where you don't have to manufacture any merch up front. Check them all out for yourself.

Other DIY services to check out for your more general needs are Spreadshirt (www.spreadshirt.com), Zazzle (www.zazzle.com), Fat Rat Press (www.fatratpress.com), Vistaprint (www.vistaprint.com), StickerJunkie.com (www.stickerjunkie.com), and Branders.com (www.branders.com).

That's pretty much it. Happy merchandising and good luck.

WAIT, LET'S TALK MORE ABOUT MERCH AND DIY ARTISTS

To ensure that you truly comprehend the power of independent merchandising, allow me to close this chapter and interview with a few more brief points.

First, when a young band is out on the road and earning little or nothing for its live performances, merch is an immediate cash transaction that can mean the difference between eating and starving. Just ask the independent band Clepto, who practically lived in their van for years while touring many parts of the world. As they put it, "Merch was good food."

Second, merch is a strong brand builder for young bands—it's a way for artists to connect emotionally with their fans, but, more importantly, it's a way for the fans to identify with something important and special about themselves—and that connection is priceless.

Third, merch is an exceptional promotional tool. Think about it—every one of your fans who purchases your cleverly designed T-shirts online or at your show becomes an immediate walking and talking billboard. Now that's what I call a great way to start spreading the word of mouth.

And finally, merch can be conveniently created using handy DIY tools, ordered via affordable local printers, or handled via a "merch on demand" service with no up-front costs.

So, no matter how you slice it, merch packs a powerful DIY punch! Plain and simple! Now get out there and get some merch manufactured today. Happy sales!

Part 5

Future Predictions

26

The Music Business 2020

Future Forecasts by the Pros

"It's difficult to understand the future unless you participate in it."
—Jim Griffin, Cherry Lane Digital

No one can know for sure what awaits the music industry in the near future—especially after witnessing how quickly new technology has changed the traditional music business in just the past five years.

But with that being said, I believe that you'll still find the following predictions by various leading music industry professionals interesting.

What can we expect in the year 2020? Let's see what a group of attorneys, music publishers, managers, producers, and music business educators had to say about this. Enjoy.

Copyright Laws: Making Way for New Trends in Music

Several trends have emerged and will continue to emerge as the music business evolves into a service-based business. More and more people are tuning in to all-you-can-listen streaming programs like Spotify (www.spotify.com) and Rdio (www.rdio.com).

In this same vein, younger fans want all of their content to be accessible on all of their devices, but do not care whether they own the content or not. They also want the opportunity to interact with the music they listen to, be it through remixes, mash-ups, or fan videos on YouTube. Unfortunately, our copyright laws are antiquated and do not allow these trends to develop.

Over the next 5 to 10 years, I think we will see an overhaul of the United States' copyright system. I also expect to see artists further expanding their brands into nontraditional revenue streams. Soon, fans will be able to surround themselves almost entirely with their favorite artists through branded products, multimedia projects, and other avenues we have not even begun to explore yet.

—Dina LaPolt, LaPolt Law, P.C.

Fair Compensation for Creators

In 2008, I predicted that by 2013 music would have become a service, not a product, and that consumers would have greater access to music through wireless technology. Much of that has come true for the benefit of the consumer due to services like Pandora (www.pandora.com) and Spotify (www.spotify.com), but the new issue is how to get musicians paid fairly for their work.

Over time, perhaps by the year 2020, I believe that consumer participation in these (and similar) services will increase and revenue models will develop that compensate creators for their work in ways that will dwarf the micro-pennies being paid at the time of this writing. Keeping creators fed is the only way to keep them creating, and it is essential that those payments increase in order for musicians and the music industry to survive.

—Steve Winogradsky, attorney and author of *Music Publishing: The Complete Guide*

Success That's Earned on Your Own: DIY Style

By the year 2020, the world will likely be saturated with music. There will still be superstars whose music has reached the masses through the efforts of a support team, but the vast majority of musicians will have to achieve success on their own.

The good news is that technology is making that possible. Successful DIY musicians will be skilled in using social media and analytics to connect with their fans and fund their projects; partnering with products-and-services companies for branding and advertising campaigns; licensing their music for film, television, games, ads, etc.; leveraging relationships with electronic media as part of their marketing strategy; and booking and promoting their tours and concerts, all with an ultimate goal of getting their music into the ears of the curators of the outlets for consumption, which will exist in business models that are still emerging.

Cutting through the clutter will be a challenge, but great music combined with an entrepreneurial spirit and a lot of hard work will be the winning formula.

—Don Gorder, chair and founder, Music Business / Management Department, Berklee College of Music

Affordable DIY Services That Capture New Revenue Streams

Many recent music industry trends have not been favorable toward artists and songwriters: we've gone from selling CDs for $10 to downloads for 99 cents to streams for under half a penny. This has made it more difficult for artists to monetize their music.

As a consequence, independent artists and songwriters will become more conscious of how to leverage their intellectual property into alternate revenue streams. You will see many more companies offering affordable services to DIY artists to capture performance royalties, Internet royalties, mechanical royalties, YouTube royalties, and synch licensing for film, TV, games, and commercials. Each of these incremental revenue streams will be small, but in the aggregate they will become a needle-moving part of the artist's revenue mix.

—Tony van Veen, CEO, AVL Digital Group / CD Baby / Disc Makers

Success Will Be Driven by Touring and Merch

As the record business is further eroded by "free music," it will reach its decline and the postmodern record industry will be cut to its knees.

In 2020, instead of record sales determining the success of an artist, live performance will dictate the value of an act. Merchandising will also become a high art form. Only those with a great live act and a memorable and distinct brand will survive.

—John Hartmann, former manager of Peter, Paul & Mary; Crosby, Stills & Nash; America; Poco; the Eagles; and others

The Concert Business Will Be Shaped, but Never Replaced

While technology is developing at rapid speeds and disrupting many businesses, especially the record business and recorded music, it's only helping the concert business and how people are brought together.

People have always strived to congregate together—whether it be for religious ceremonies, theater productions, sporting events, or musical concerts—and technology only facilitates this behavior. Social networks help fans engage new bands, digital cameras allow fans to shoot live clips and post them on websites in real time, and websites and ticket vendors allow fans to view tour dates and purchase advance tickets. By 2020, all this will have already evolved.

Through advancements in technology and pure human need, the concert business will become stronger than ever. Sure, the way concerts are marketed or sold will be somewhat shaped, but the concert business will never be replaced. Develop a great live show and thrive!

—John Pantle, agent at APA Talent and Literary Agency

Business Skills Are Paramount in a Fast-Paced and High-Tech World

Long gone are the days when labels signed bands and developed them for years till they became successful. It's a freelance world, and everybody's hustling for work all the time. For musicians, this will be just as true in 2020 as it will in 2030 and beyond. Therefore, you need to think of yourself as a business, and continue to sell that "business" for as long as you want to keep working.

It's critical that you, with your right-brain *creative* mind, learn the left-brain *analytical* skills you'll need to navigate the business world. This includes understanding finances, as well as developing "soft (communication) skills" like critical thinking, business writing, and oral presentation—skills that are all especially important in a fast-paced and high-tech world.

Make no mistake, in 2020 you'll need to know more than ever how to hustle for work and take care of business. Remember, this is show business. If you want to play, you're going to need to do a lot of work.

—Chaz Austin, Ed.D., former career development director, Musicians Institute;
author of *How to Find Work and Keep Finding Work for the Rest of Your Life*

Shifting Demographics Mainstreamed

In making predictions about the music industry in 2020, I envision that the topography of the music landscape will be much more inclusive of artists who are representative of the shifting population demographics.

I believe that Latin artists, communicating in English, Spanish, and "Spanglish," will be mainstreamed, and that Asian-American singers, bands, and producers will become major creative forces. Songwriters will continue to bond together into "writing camps," and will exert an ever-greater influence as shapers of talent, and as arbiters and producers of content. Mixers and remixers will become more dominant, as Electronic Dance Music (EDM) unites the globe through worldwide anthems.

What will never change is the power of motivated, forward-thinking creators to configure music to challenge, change, and inspire the lives of listeners.

—Dan Kimpel, coauthor of *It All Begins with the Music: Developing Successful Artists and Careers for the New Music Business*

More Automated and Sophisticated Marketing Everywhere

While my crystal ball broke last week, I predict that marketing music in 2020 will become more sophisticated and automated.

People will have bots (or avatars) that are digital representations of them. These bot agents will know their music preferences and travel around the Internet buying songs, concert tickets, and related merchandise for their human bosses. It might even get to the point where musicians and record companies will have bots that market their services directly to customer bots (an updated take on "have your agent contact my agent").

In addition to going to concerts, fans will have the option to download performances 24/7 and watch them on smart screens and mobile devices. If mobile devices have a small screen, they will have the capability of projecting a holographic image of the performance.

—Ira S. Kalb, professor of marketing at the Marshall School of Business at University of Southern California; president, Kalb & Associates

Extended Product Lines and Stronger Brands

In 2020, music will be consumed everywhere—on platforms that are seen today and others that have not yet been envisioned.

To survive, musicians will have to embrace this technology, but they must also realize that music and the distribution and sale of it will be only one part of their revenue pie (and perhaps even the smallest piece).

Artists will have to extend far beyond just selling recordings (streams, downloads, vinyl, or whatever new format is discovered), hitting the road, and selling merchandise. Artists will need to grow their product offerings into licensing, sponsorships, production, cowriting, acting, modeling, restaurant franchising, investing, directing, educating, and so much more in order to survive and thrive in the new music business.

Thus, in 2020, protecting the artist's true vision, values, integrity, authenticity, and overall brand image is paramount. Those who understand marketing will grow brands that are stronger than ever—relating to target markets and engaging fans on a far more personal level.

Long gone are the days of the "mass" broad-stroke mentality and narrow-mindedness in marketing artists. It's a new world in 2020. The industry will evolve and the marketing-savvy artist will evolve and thrive with it.

—Fred Croshal, Croshal Entertainment Group, LLC

"Captured" Musical Performances, Not "Manufactured"

In 2020, I believe that music lovers will no longer accept the mediocre quality of the music they listen to. Recorded music of great sonic excellence and dynamic emotional artistic substance will now be an attribute worth discovering and paying for. More artists will rediscover the fundamental joy of performing live, together, in the recording studio, as they would on stage, and the ensuing musical collaboration will result in an explosion of emotion that will weave its way into the core fabric of the listener. In 2020, we will capture the performance, not manufacture it. Real music, played by real musicians, in real time.

—Jeffrey Weber, Grammy Award–winning record producer, music industry professional, and author

A Focus on Exciting Music—Not the Latest Technical Trends

Good music will always be the future, whether it be 2015, 2020, or 2025.

When jazz arrived on the scene, it was controversial, exciting, and real—as were rock, rap, and EDM. They propelled the business forward and gave it life. But what's next?

The year 2020 must be marked by a new direction in music that shakes up the world and puts the focus back on the art and the creators—not on the latest technical trend.

Who cares about downloads, streaming, or whatever new technology is invented? In 2020, music will shine again! Those who create something unique will thrive.

—Mike Gormley, LA Personal Management; former manager of the Bangles, Oingo Boingo, and Danny Elfman

Opportunity for Smart Entrepreneurs, Not for Artists

In 2020, an ever-increasing number of digital aggregators, social networks, and streaming services will provide tools and services allowing artists to bypass the record companies and release music independently—and we'll see more and more artists releasing music into the already competitive marketplace with hopes of success.

But this doesn't mean that success will come any easier for young artists. None of these service companies will provide any of the help that the "evil" record companies provide. They won't cover recording costs, hire a talented producer, make a great-looking video, hire a radio promoter, book you to appear on TV, offer an advance so you can quit your day gig, or take any of the other countless risks associated with a building a successful music career for an artist. Yet these services will take a percentage of the artists' sales and/or ask for up-front fees.

Make no mistake, in 2020, the music business will be ripe with new opportunities, but it will be mostly for the services and smart business entrepreneurs, not so much for artists.

—Steve Gordon, attorney at law, author of *The Future of the Music Business* (4th Edition), and future of music blogger at www.futureofthemusicbusiness.com

The Industry's Salvation: Memorable Song Melodies

Melody is the salvation of the recording industry. I am reminded of this every time I hear Paul McCartney (who clearly knew the "melody secret"), and I see 10-year-old girls giddy with delight singing "She Loves You," "Yesterday," and "Hey Jude" right along with their moms and grandmothers. The Beatles' songs are timeless because of their melodies and their hooks.

When the music industry collectively decides to get off this "it has to be edgy" jag and returns to moving millions of people with strong songs comprised of hummable melodies with great lyrics, rhythms, and beats, millions of their dollars will once again flow back into the coffers of the music industry. Technology won't be the forefront of the discussion, it will once again be the music. Will this happen in 2020? We'll have to wait and see.

—Samm Brown III, film composer (scores4cinema.com), RIAA Award–winning hit record producer, songwriter, arranger, orchestrator, conductor, and host of a talk show on the entertainment business (sbrownkpfk.com) on KPFK 90.7 FM radio in Los Angeles

Chapter Review and Discussion Questions

Chapter 1. Pursuing a Career in the New Music Industry: 15 Tips for Career Success

1. What is the "clique of the future"?
2. What is the "decision-making tree"?
3. What is the "mental-movie method" and who created it?
4. In regard to paying your dues, it is not always what you ______, but what you ______.
5. Explain the "Three Magic O's" and who created them.

Chapter 2. Band Membership, Part 1: Formation and Self-Management

1. Name at least five places that one might find musicians.
2. What is one thing you'd include on your "criteria for forming" list and why?
3. What are the five standards necessary to run an effective team? Explain each.
4. What is one thing that you think is most helpful in running a successful meeting?
5. What is "noodling" and how can it be bad?

Chapter 3. Band Membership, Part 2: Partnerships, Trademarks, and Business Entities

1. How are partnerships formed?
2. State partnership laws vary, but if a group does not have a written band agreement that stipulates anything to the contrary, all members may be presumed to have what?
3. Is it necessary for a band to hire an attorney to draft a band membership agreement? Why or why not?
4. What is a majority vote? What is a unanimous vote? What is one time you would not use a unanimous vote?
5. How might a band handle the rights to its name when it concerns leaving members?

Chapter 4. Contract Employment or Self-Employment, Part 1: Gigs and Unions

1. A freelance musician can generally be described as being what?
2. A contract employee can generally be described as being what?
3. In what two areas is the distinction between a freelance musician and a contract employee really important?
4. What does the AFM stand for and what does it do? What does SAG-AFTRA stand for and what does it do?
5. True or false: Instrumentalists who are also vocalists sign up for both AFM and SAG-AFTRA.

Chapter 5. Contract Employment or Self-Employment, Part 2: Employment Agreements and Negotiations

1. What is a buyout?
2. What is a per diem?
3. What is an incidental?
4. What is a retainer?
5. Name a few steps one might follow to get an equipment endorsement.

Chapter 6. Contract Employment or Self-Employment, Part 3: Taxes and Insurance

1. What is a 1099 form?
2. What is a W-2 form?
3. What is a W-4 form?
4. Might your accountant's services for preparing your taxes be something that you can use to reduce your tax liability?
5. In the states where it applies, what benefit does "state unemployment" provide?

Chapter 7. Solo Artist and Employer: Pros, Cons, and Responsibilities

1. What is one advantage and one disadvantage of going solo? Explain?
2. What is a "solo artist in disguise"?
3. What is a "leaving member clause" and how does it apply to solo artists?
4. Explain a "work made for hire" as it relates to the business responsibilities of a solo artist.
5. If all you pay is ___________, all you'll get is ___________.

Chapter 8. Entertainment Attorneys: What They Do and What They Cost You

1. An attorney typically receives what percentage of the deals he or she negotiates?
2. What are label-shopping agreements? What is the commission an attorney receives under this arrangement? Explain.
3. What is a conflict waiver and when is one used?
4. Explain the concept of a retainer.
5. Explain the process of changing legal representation.

Chapter 9. Personal Managers: Roles, Options, and Agreements

1. The ethical manager typically gets what commission? Are there instances in which the commission may be less or more? Explain.
2. What is the name of the clause inserted into management agreements that is intended to limit the royalties a manager gets *after* the term of your agreement for the deals he or she negotiates, or substantially negotiates, *during* the term of the agreement?
3. In the early stages of your career, what is your most prudent management option?
4. The laws in California (and many other states) say that anyone who procures employment must be what? Explain.
5. What are some of the roles a personal manager may play in your career?

Chapter 10. Business Managers: Bills and Investments

1. When paid on a percentage of the deal, the business manager typically gets what commission?
2. List and explain at least three roles that a business manager plays in your career.
3. Thoroughly explain how the business manager provides touring services.
4. Explain the concept of power of attorney. Is it good or bad?
5. Must business managers in the state of California be licensed? How about in your state?

Chapter 11. Talent Agents: Work, Scope, and Contracts

1. An agent receives what commission for the deals he or she negotiates?
2. What are some of the roles a talent agent may play in your career?
3. Do agents collect deposits? If so, how much?
4. What is the difference between a personal manager and a talent agent?
5. What does the term "full-service agency" typically mean? Explain.

Chapter 12. Record Producers: Creativity, Budgets, and Fee Structures

1. Record producers working for signed recording artists (at a major label or larger indie label) typically get both an advance and a royalty for their services. Is this true or false? Explain.
2. Explain the concept of "record one royalties" as it applies to producers.
3. List and explain at least three of the administrative responsibilities a producer might have on a recording project.
4. Explain the concept of "all-in" royalties as it applies to the producer.
5. "Mutual consent" may be applied to what situation involving the record producer?

Chapter 13. Making and Selling Records, Part 1: Types of Record Deals and Companies

1. List several methods that an artist can use to fund his or her record.
2. What is bartering?
3. What is a net profit deal, and when are you must likely to see this deal?
4. What is a 360 deal, and when are you must likely to see this deal?
5. Contrast and compare DIY, indie, and major label deals.

Chapter 14. Making and Selling Records, Part 2: Key Deal Issues in Recording Contracts

1. What is the difference between consulting and approval rights?
2. Does a guaranteed release clause guarantee a release?
3. Explain the difference between "active" and "passive" income in 360 deals.
4. Fully explain the term "recoupable" and how it applies to artist record royalties.
5. Explain the difference between "firm records" and "option periods."

Chapter 15. Music Publishing, Part 1: Copyright Basics

1. How is a copyright formed?
2. What is the exclusive bundle of rights you get?
3. Why might a "split sheet" be useful when discussing joint works?
4. The compulsory licensing provision allows an artist to cover a song on his or her record and then license or use that cover version in a film or video. True or false? Why or why not?
5. What is reversion of copyright and why is it important?

Chapter 16. Music Publishing, Part 2: Even More Copyright Basics

1. What are the three benefits of registering with the Copyright Office?
2. What is a "deposit copy"?
3. What is a "collection of works"? Explain in detail.
4. What does a circle with a P in it represent?
5. Is the copyright notice necessary? Why or why not?

Chapter 17. Music Publishing, Part 3: Income Streams—Mechanicals, Performances, and Print

1. What is a mechanical royalty? What is a CC clause?
2. Explain the concept of a "blanket license."

3. What are the three major PROs in the United States? What factors might influence you to choose one over the others?
4. The writer's and publisher's share of all public performance money goes to the publisher. The publisher then pays the writer. True or false? Explain.
5. What is the difference between a folio, a matching folio, and a mixed folio?

Chapter 18. Music Publishing, Part 4: Synch, Electronic Transmissions, and Sub-publishing

1. What is an "all-in" fee?
2. What does the term "most favored nation" mean, and when might it be applied?
3. Are "title registration" and "copyright registration" the same thing? Explain.
4. Explain what Neil Gillis has to say about electronic transmissions, traditional laws, and determining in what way a new technology allows a piece of music to be utilized.
5. What are "black box monies"?

Chapter 19. Music Publishing, Part 5: Publishing Companies and Types of Deals

1. What can established music publishers do for your career?
2. What percentage of the copyright does one give up in an exclusive singer/songwriter deal?
3. What percentage of the copyright does one give up in an co-pub deal?
4. What percentage of the copyright does one give up in an admin deal?
5. How is the income divided in a co-pub deal?

Chapter 20. Music Publishing, Part 6: Starting Your Own Publishing Company

1. What is SoundExchange?
2. Of the monies SoundExchange collects, _____ percent is paid to the record label, _____ percent is paid to featured performers, and _____ percent is paid to non-featured performers (via the unions AFM and SAG-AFTRA).
3. What is a DBA and why is it important? Explain.
4. What is a sub-publisher and why are they important?
5. What are DIY-friendly administrators and what do they do?

Chapter 21. Live Performing and Touring, Part 1: Purpose and Opportunity

1. Summarize the "four levels" of touring discussed in this chapter.
2. What are alternative venues? Name at least five that may be practical for your band and explain why.
3. What is NACA? Explain how it might be useful to your career.
4. What is gig swapping?
5. Does a personal manager book gigs? Explain.

Chapter 22. Live Performing and Touring, Part 2: Deals, Negotiations, and Contracts

1. Explain the concept of pay-to-play from the club owner's perspective.
2. What is the equation for the gross potential?
3. Explain a "versus deal."
4. Are "percentage deals" practical when an artist hits the road? Why or why not?
5. What is a rider and what are three different matters that might be addressed on one?

Chapter 23. Merchandising, Part 1: Rights, Types, and Companies

1. What are publicity rights?
2. What are trademarks?
3. What are the two major types of merchandising? Which one is typically more profitable, and why?
4. What are some of the things you can do with your merchandising rights?
5. How might merchandising be useful to a new band when out on the road?

Chapter 24. Merchandising, Part 2: Contract Terms for Tour Merchandising

1. How are royalties split in tour merchandising deals?
2. How are royalties split in tour merchandising deals in foreign territories?
3. What is a hall fee?
4. What are some of the factors that might determine the amount of a tour merchandising advance?
5. Are merchandising deals recoupable? How about returnable? How might the advance and the "agreement term" relate to each other in merchandising deals?

Chapter 25. Merchandising, Part 3: Retail Deals and Independent Merchandising

1. How are royalties split in retail merchandising deals?
2. What are sublicenses? Provide at least 5 examples.
3. When handling the merchandising independently, what are some of the methods for selling it live? What are some of your own ideas?
4. Why is getting a merchandiser with tour experience important?
5. Is it always best to buy the largest quantity of merch items to get better price breaks? Why or why not?

Chapter 26. The Music Business 2020: Future Forecasts by the Pros

1. Of all the forecasts for the music business in 2020, which do you support the most and why?
2. What major body of law is likely to be revised? What are some of the issues?
3. Do you feel that the touring industry will remain strong in 2020? Why or why not?
4. What is one thing in the music business that you believe that people will always respond to—no matter what the current technology is in 2020 or beyond?
5. Where do you personally see the music business heading in 2020 and why?

Chapter Activity Assignments

Chapter 1. Pursuing a Career in the New Music Industry: 15 Tips for Career Success

Find one book in the business, entrepreneur, or self-help category and write a brief review of how it can help artists pursuing a music career? Use specific examples or concepts from the book.

Chapter 2. Band Membership, Part 1: Formation and Self-Management

Set goals, break down the work, and estimate the schedule/costs for your own band. If you do not have a group, use a friend in a band or use your studio project for this assignment.

Chapter 3. Band Membership, Part 2: Partnerships, Trademarks, and Business Entities

Put together your own band membership agreement utilizing the concepts that are important to your band, arranged in a way that you think is most fair to the members considering the circumstances. Keep it simple and do not try to write like an attorney if you are not an attorney. If you do not have a band, then interview one of your friends' bands or create a hypothetical.

Chapter 4. Contract Employment or Self-Employment, Part 1: Gigs and Unions

A topic that was not discussed in this book but is great to know about (to ensure a fair resolution of your employment problems) is the small claims courts. Find the name, address, and website for the small claims court in your county and find out what they do, who may file a case, and the process of filing a case. Include any other important information you can find. Hotlines are usually provided. Speak with a representative, visit the small claims courthouse, and then write about the experiences you have.

Chapter 5. Contract Employment or Self-Employment, Part 2: Employment Agreements and Negotiations

Visit your local branch of the American Federation of Musicians and SAG-AFTRA, pick up any brochures they may have, and view the various wage scales that are indicated. What important information did you discover? Given your personal experience and sense of self-worth as a musician, what do you think you should be paid per week to go out on the road? How about to do a recording session? What are some of the other issues that you think are important to put in an agreement with an employer? Explain in detail.

Chapter 6. Contract Employment or Self-Employment, Part 3: Taxes and Insurance

As a freelance musician, explain how you might get insurance coverage. Please provide the carrier's name, the policy's name, and the contact information. How much does it cost each month? What does it cover? What is the co-payment? If you are on your spouse's or parents' insurance policy, please include that information as well.

Chapter 7. Solo Artist and Employer: Pros, Cons, and Responsibilities

Find one solo artist you admire who was once part of a band. What caused the artist to move on and go solo? Did the group part on good or bad terms? What are some of the business and legal issues that you discovered? Are the other members of the group doing well, or did they break up never to be heard from again?

Chapter 8. Entertainment Attorneys: What They Do and What They Cost You

Contact a lawyer referral service in your area (or the closest area to your hometown). What is the name and contact information of the referral service? What services do they provide? Call the hotline and speak with a representative. Tell him or her what your legal concerns are and that you are seeking representation. What did the representative tell you? What does the service cost? What did you learn? What are some of the other ways you can find an attorney? If you already have an attorney you work with, who is it and what do you like about him or her?

Chapter 9. Personal Managers: Roles, Options, and Agreements

Create a list of the reasons why a manager would want to work with you. Consider your age, accomplishments, talents, and experience. Just think objectively and realistically. Remember that a manager earns a commission on the monies that you are making and that his or her incentive to work with you may be minimal if you are just starting out. Who are some of the managers on your local scene and how have they helped the groups they manage?

Chapter 10. Business Managers: Bills and Investments

Find a CPA in your territory who has experience working with musicians. What is that person's name? How long has he or she been in business? What are some of the helpful tips he or she can offer you about lowering your tax liability? Speak with the CPA on the phone and ask about his or her fees. Is this affordable for you? What are some of your other options for filing taxes?

Chapter 11. Talent Agents: Work, Scope, and Contracts

Create a list of the reasons why a talent agent would want to work with you. Consider your accomplishments, talents, experience, and money that you are currently making. Just think objectively and realistically. Remember that an agent earns a commission on the deals he or she negotiates and that his or her incentive to work with you may be minimal if you are just starting out. Who are some of the agents in your area? Who are the bands that they work with?

Chapter 12. Record Producers: Creativity, Budgets, and Fee Structures

Create a list of three producers whom you would want to work with if the opportunity presented itself. Be specific. Refer to the technical and creative reasons for your choice, such as the sound they get on the snare drum, the approach they take to beat making, or the innovative methods that they create before anyone else. List their names and the artists they have worked with. If possible, research what the artists have to say about the producers and why they enjoyed, or did not enjoy, working with them.

Chapter 13. Making and Selling Records, Part 1: Types of Record Deals and Companies

Of the various recording deals stated in this chapter, what scenario would you like to find yourself in: DIY, indie, major, production, or other? Be honest and be realistic. If applicable, list the precise company you would like to be with and say why you chose that company. Who are some of the other people on their roster? How successful are these artists? Who handles the company's distribution?

Chapter 14. Making and Selling Records, Part 2: Key Deal Issues in Recording Contracts

Find a sample recording agreement online (surely there is one floating around in cyber space that you can download). Now, using the terms that you have learned in this chapter, take a crack at reading the contract and underlining important terms and issues. Does the contract seem standard or fair to artists? Why or why not? What would you want changed? What are the issues that most concern you?

Chapter 15. Music Publishing, Part 1: Copyright Basics

Create your own "split sheet" that you might use on your next writing sessions with joint writers. Keep in mind that you want to create something that other musicians will understand and be willing to sign. Research split sheets online to examine the key issues that are addressed.

Chapter 16. Music Publishing, Part 2: Even More Copyright Basics

Visit the Copyright Office website (www.copyright.gov) and attempt to register one of your compositions. If you do not have a composition you wish to register at this time, then visit the site and go through the process until the final step of paying. Write about the experience. Was the site difficult to navigate? What did you learn? Explain the process. Did you call an operator for help?

Chapter 17. Music Publishing, Part 3: Income Streams—Mechanicals, Performances, and Print

Visit all three of the performing rights organizations' websites and read about their membership policies. What are their current fees (if any) for signing up? Which website seemed the easiest to navigate? Is there a membership department that you can call for information? What did they say? Did they appear helpful? If you are already a member, than tell me about some of the current events that they have scheduled for its members. Are there any songwriting camps, conventions, or other benefits that can further your career? Will you be attending? Explain in detail.

Chapter 18. Music Publishing, Part 4: Synch, Electronic Transmissions, and Sub-publishing

Find three television shows that you think would be perfect for your music. Explain why. What are the characteristics of your music that would work so well with the vibe of the show? Are there any games where your music would be a good fit? If so, why? How about branded products? Would your music work well in a beer commercial or with some other product? Now, how does your music match up to the music that is currently being used in the aforementioned media? Is your music broadcast quality (of the highest sound quality and performance level)? Please explain in detail.

Chapter 19. Music Publishing, Part 5: Publishing Companies and Types of Deals

Write a complete summary of at least one music publishing company that exists in the United States. What is the company? Who are the executives who work there? What are their submission policies (if any) for new artists? Who are some of the other clients they represent?

Chapter 20. Music Publishing, Part 6: Starting Your Own Publishing Company

Write about the process of self-publishing. How do you plan on getting your music out to your audience? How will you collect the income generated? If using outsourced companies for administration purposes, which companies will you use and why? What are the rates that they charge? Please explain in detail.

Chapter 21. Live Performing and Touring, Part 1: Purpose and Opportunity

Contact the activities director or booker at a local college and find out how you might submit your music for a future event. What are some of the events that the college will be presenting in the future? (Do not report that you could not get ahold of anyone—with thousands of colleges across the United States, that is not an acceptable answer.) How about other alternative venues that you can play? Are there any conventions coming through town that might provide an opportunity for you to perform? If so, what are they? Who is the promoter? Explain.

Chapter 22. Live Performing and Touring, Part 2: Deals, Negotiations, and Contracts

Create your very own tour itinerary and budget. Define a territory, find a few clubs within that territory, and find out what they might be willing to pay you for your band to perform (you do not have to actually book the gigs, but you should be able to get an amount that they would be willing to pay a band of your caliber). Now factor in gas, tolls, hotels, food, crew, transportation, and money for unknown risks (like car trouble, someone getting ill, etc.). Also factor in the cost of merchandising and what you hope to sell each night (based on past history or research you conduct with other bands in your area). Is the tour profitable?

Chapter 23. Merchandising, Part 1: Rights, Types, and Companies

Research one of the major players in the merchandising business. How long has the company been around? Who are their clients? What types of products are being sold? Are you impressed by the quality of the merchandising you see? How much do they charge for each product?

Chapter 24. Merchandising, Part 2: Contract Terms for Tour Merchandising

While this was not discussed in detail in the book, research the issue of counterfeiting. How bad is it in the United States? What are some of the things that are being done to stop it? Is the music business the only industry that is being harmed, or is the sports industry also suffering lost sales?

Chapter 25. Merchandising, Part 3: Retail Deals and Independent Merchandising

Find a merch company that you might like to work with. What is the name of the company? What do they charge to create and ship T-shirts? What types of designs will you use? Do you have any cool slogans that you have created? Be sure to use actual price quotes. Do not make up these numbers. Be ready to submit an actual quote from the company.

Chapter 26. The Music Business 2020: Future Forecasts by the Pros

Read a few excerpts from the book *The Future of the Music Business: How to Succeed with the New Digital Technologies* (Music Pro Guides). Do this by either purchasing the book, looking inside the book on Amazon, or finding the author's blog and reading a few excerpts. What are some of the interesting issues that you uncovered? You can also research important websites like the RIAA (www.riaa.com), NMPA (www.nmpa.org), or Future of Music Coalition (www.futureofmusic.org). What did you find out about the future of music from the business and legal side? Is it hopeful? Please be detailed yet concise.

Index

To Timothy O'Sullivan and the photographers who work in his footsteps